Susan Sirkis

Database Design

Applications of Library Cataloging Techniques

Database Design

Applications of Library Cataloging Techniques

David L. Clark

McGraw Hill

FIRST EDITION
FIRST PRINTING

Library of Congress Cataloging-in-Publication Data

Clark, David L., 1945-
Database design : applications of library cataloging techniques / David L. Clark.
p. cm.
Includes bibliographical references and index.
ISBN 0-8306-3443-6
1. Data base design. 2. Cataloging—Data processing. I. Title.
QA76.9.D26C53 1991
025′.00285′574—dc20 91-19894
CIP

For information about other McGraw-Hill materials, call 1-800-2-MCGRAW in the U.S. In other countries call your nearest McGraw-Hill office.

Vice President & Editorial Director: Larry Hager
Book Editor: Sally Anne Glover
Production: Katherine G. Brown
Book Design: Jaclyn J. Boone EL2

To Suzanne,
a healer of both body and spirit.

Contents

Part II
Data entry fields

Part III
For more information

Acknowledgments

I would like to thank the following individuals and organizations for the help that they have provided.

The Los Angeles City Historical Society, especially Joe and Marie Northrop, Christie and Louis Bourdet, Hynda Rudd, Don Ray, Rob Freeman, Teena Stern, and Bill Mason, for their support and encouragement over the years.

The users of the History Database program, especially Carolyn Kozo, Carol Baldwin, Larry Booth, Rick Hayes, and Teresa Strottman, for their many excellent suggestions.

David Bearman, of Archives and Museum Informatics, for single-handedly attempting to introduce a tradition of vigorous criticism into the archival profession. David is the person whose opinions I would most wish to hear in private, and least wish to hear in public.

Brian Stone, President of Alcyona Computer Consultants, and the other staff members of Alcyona, including Jeff Hunt, Jeff Jakus, and Rob Camerda, whose support could serve as a model for other computer dealers.

Jonathan Sisk, President of the Pick educational firm JES and Associates, for the writing and teaching that he has done on the use of the Pick system.

The UCLA History Department, particularly Eugen Weber and Albert Hoxie, for all that I learned.

Notices

ACCESS®, PICK®, and PICK/BASIC®	Pick Systems
dBase™	Ashton-Tate
Everex®	Everex Corp.
IBM®, IBM PC®, PC-XT® PC-AT®, PS/2® IBM PC BASIC®, and IBM PC DOS®	International Business Machines Corp.
Microsoft BASIC® Microsoft Word® and MOS-DOS®	Microsoft Corp.
Norton Utilities™	Peter Norton
QuickBASIC® Radio Shack, and Radio Shack Model 100®	Tandy Corp.
R:BASE®	Microrim, Inc.
Revelation®	Cosmos Inc.
WordPerfect™	WordPerfect Corp.
WordStar®	MicroPro International Corp.

Introduction

In the great Hindu epic *The Bhagavad-Gita,* the Lord Krishna tells the warrior Arjuna that a virtuous act is one that is done for the sake of the act itself, rather than to accomplish any purpose. From this description I believe that most research and cataloging activities would qualify as acts of exceeding virtue.

Researchers, writers, academics, librarians, archivists, museum curators, collectors, historical societies and other voluntary organizations, business executives, and professionals seeking to advance in their fields through publication, all spend great amounts of time and effort collecting information. Yet it seems that the more information we collect, the more overwhelmed we become with it. We drown in a sea of our own paper.

The subject of this guide is how to stem the tide of information overload, and how to control your information rather than letting it control you. The book will show you how to organize your information by combining the concepts and facilities of computer database management with the cataloging methods developed by librarians and archivists.

This book is a how-to guide for people who have information to manage, but who have no previous experience with database management or with library or archival procedures. Each of the sections includes step-by-step instructions demonstrating how to manage an inventory, a photo collection, a collection of objects, or a body of textual information such as research notes or the records of an organization.

With this book, you'll learn how to use standardized cataloging methods as a natural complement to database management. Catalogers in libraries and archives have found solutions for the problems of inconsistency that plague most databases. Rather than inventing new solutions, the sensible course is to learn and use methods that have already been developed from an enormous body of experience.

For researchers and writers

When writing a chapter or article, the researcher usually starts with a stack of three-by-five note cards, spreading them across the desk like a blackjack dealer would do in Las Vegas. The researcher then works his or her way through the cards, translating the notes into a first-draft text. The cards in many cases are difficult to decipher, either because they are handwritten or because they include abbreviations whose exact meanings are difficult to recall weeks or months after the notes were written.

Computer database management can make the writing process much easier and more efficient. If the information is stored in a computer database, you can begin writing the chapter or article as a first draft. Your draft can include footnotes, an index, a table of contents, section headings, and a bibliography.

What happened to the stage of moving from note cards to text? There are no note cards. You can eliminate the step of rewriting and retyping note cards!

During research, you can enter information directly into a computer database. You can also gather data in the field with a portable computer. After collecting information at libraries, archives, and other locations on a portable computer, you can transfer the data directly into a database on a desktop machine. In less than a minute, a day's work travels by cable from the smaller to the larger computer, and is immediately integrated into the database.

You type the information into a data-entry form. The last field on the data-entry form is a long DESCRIPTION field. Here you enter the material that you want to use in your text. Type this in as a first-draft manuscript, with complete sentences, rather than in cryptic, note-taking style. When you're ready to write the chapter or article, tell the database program to send the information to your word processor.

Writing footnotes is one of the most tedious tasks in scholarly writing. You won't have to write footnotes anymore! The database program will write them for you, from the bibliographic information in your database.

With a well-managed database, you can eliminate the drudgery of writing. Rather than wasting your time retyping the same information from notes to text, you can devote your time to the more productive task of editing the material into a final, polished form.

Recycle previous research

The researcher spends most of his or her time reading through primary source materials and recording notes and excerpts. The majority of the information gathered will not be used in the published work. The unpublished material still has value, however, particularly in the case of historical materials, because the information doesn't lose its value over time. Research on the French Revolution doesn't become out of date five years later.

Even one lone researcher, over the course of years, will develop a large inventory of information. But can you find a particular quote or fact that you recorded five years ago? Would you welcome the opportunity to write about a topic that you researched several years past? How much work would be involved in getting to those materials again? Your note cards are probably in storage, where they could be damaged or lost. If you can find the notes and they are still legible, they might be full of abbreviations that you made up at the time and whose meanings have long been forgotten.

Combining computer database management with cataloging procedures will allow you to use information that you collected in the past in the same way that a business uses its inventory. The data is there for you to immediately recall from the database whenever you have a question. You can take advantage of each new project by deepening your understanding of the previously collected information, and you'll be able to treat the total body of information as a coherent whole.

Retrieve and combine bits of information

Having information available in a database greatly facilitates the research process. During research, information is most often collected in small, isolated bits and pieces. Computer database management allows you to explore the links between many scattered pieces of information, and to recognize patterns that you might not otherwise detect.

A typical example of the need for integrating isolated pieces of information occurred while I was doing research on the beginnings of the political career of Pierre Mendès France. In 1932, he spoke at nearly 400 local meetings in the course of his successful parliamentary campaign to represent the district of Louviers in Normandy. The local press reported at length on the meetings, and on the activities of local organizations and their officers. In addition, the files of Mendès France's local office have been preserved. These include detailed reports from the French Radical party's committee meetings in almost every village and town of the Louviers district. When viewed individually, the items of information hold little interest, but by pulling together similar information unfolding over the course of the election, I discovered that the distinguishing mark of the campaign, and the primary cause of its victory, was the network of personal connections and associations that the Radical Party had woven like a web across the district.[1]

Access information in machine-readable form

The use of a computer database allows you to access important sources of information in machine-readable form. Such information can be loaded directly into your database, without typing. One example of machine-readable information would be an interview transcript typed on a word processor. As business offices adopt automated procedures, an increasing volume of information is available electronically. The researcher can cut up the information into the appropriate pieces and send them over to the database.

Publications such as the *Harvard Business Review* are available electronically, in full-text form, via online databases that are accessible over telephone lines. The online services also offer bibliographic information, that researchers can store for further investigation.

New employment opportunities

New research and cataloging methods hold promise for researchers and subject specialists not only in the improvement of traditional scholarly work, but also for additional work in the areas of consulting, cataloging, and public history. A computer is unable to judge the significance of a piece of data. Information transferred from file cabinets to computers will become more useful and accessible only when the information is cataloged by people with knowledge of the material.

In the past, when each individual historical repository used its own home-grown, idiosyncratic methods of description, cataloging could be performed only by those with long tenure at the institution. Such cataloging suffered greatly because many catalogers could not recognize what they were asked to describe, much less appraise its significance.

---

[1] David L. Clark, *"La naissance du mouvement Mendès France à Louviers dans les années trente,"* in *Pouvoirs: Revue française d'études constitutionnelles et politiques*, Vol. 27 (1983), pages 49–58.

Adopting uniform descriptive standards creates the potential of hiring people with special knowledge to provide subject access and other forms of intellectual control over historical research collections. An individual specializing in a given subject, who has also learned to use computer database management and standardized cataloging tools will be able to apply this special knowledge and understanding of the cataloging process to the holdings of any institution.

For reports and institutional histories

Computer database management is an essential tool for keeping track of the progress of a research project. The normal method of research has been to write down the information on index cards. Handwritten notes are not easily read, even by their author, and they are useless to anyone else. As a result, no one really knows how well the work is going.

Using a computer database program is a far better method. The researcher and project supervisor can review the research at any time in clear, legible, first-draft manuscript form. The researcher can easily print out reports containing the information gathered each month, or information on particular topics of interest to the organization. In addition, portions of the material can easily be used by the organization before the entire project is finished. Information could be pulled out for use in an organizational newsletter or for celebrations surrounding an anniversary year.

Deliver a report and a database

If you're performing research for a client, computer database management can make the product you deliver far more valuable. In addition to handing over a written document such as a report or an institutional history, you can also deliver a database. The organization will have access to all of the information gathered during the project, including those items that did not find their way into the final book or report. The information is easily understood, because it has been written in draft manuscript style.

Information on any researched subject can be retrieved by searching the database. The data can also be made available in printed form, with printed indexes for names, subjects, and sources. With the database immediately at hand in either printed or electronic form, the organization could easily look up the history of its policy positions on a certain issue.

For professionals in any field

Many professionals outside of academia spend considerable time reading, writing, and gathering information. Computer database management and library cataloging methods will help a professional in any field gain better control over a body of textual information. Database management and cataloging techniques would help a public relations office keep track of its press releases and information appearing in the media about its clients. Database methods would also help a business with an inventory manage items that require more than a brief description. For example, a computer equipment retailer might maintain a database of descriptive information about the potential uses for the various items of equipment.

Database and cataloging procedures warrant scrutiny by anyone engaged in information exchange, such as vendors and distributors who communicate inventory information electronically. The library exchange networks and MARC (Machine-Readable Cataloging) format provide a model for creating standardized descriptions that can be transferred among all the members of a network, even though they use many different types of equipment.

Become known through publication

In most professions today, writing articles or books for publication is a prime means of becoming well-known and for advancing in the field. However, few people can afford the many hours needed to collect and organize data with manual methods. The database management facilities described earlier for researchers and writers apply equally to anyone who gathers information and writes. For a clinical nurse specialist as much as for an historian, previous work should serve as a permanent inventory, ready for immediate use as opportunities arise.

Collect your data in the course of your daily work

The need to use time efficiently puts a greater importance on streamlined methods. It is very difficult for a person holding a full-time job to find the time to research and write. Rather than collecting data as a totally separate enterprise, the best procedure is to gather relevant information in the course of going about your daily work. The information will be collected in bits and pieces by entering it into a data-entry form on a notebook-sized computer, as described previously for researchers and writers. After it is placed in a database, the information can be organized into useful patterns. Later, the data can be transferred to a word processor for final writing.

For librarians, archivists, and museum curators

Database management offers much-needed assistance to the thousands of historical societies, archives, museums, and other repositories that are struggling to gain control over their primary source materials. The National Information Systems Task Force discovered that among the more than 20,000 historical archives in the United States, the great majority invested "most of their personnel resources in collecting and organizing data for manual information systems which are heavily redundant and labor intensive."[1] Only one to two percent of the materials under archival control were described in computerized form.

---

[1] David Bearman, *Towards National Information Systems for Archives and Manuscript Repositories: The National Information Systems Task Force (NISTF) Papers*, (Chicago, Illinois: Society of American Archivists, 1987), page 56, 87-88. According to the American Association for State and Local History, the 10,000 historical organizations are served by approximately 50,000 professionals, 100,000 board members, and more than a million volunteers. Larry E. Tise, "1988 Annual Report of the American Association for State and Local History." *History News*, Volume 44, Number 1 (January 1989), page 17. The *Humanities in America Report* of the National Endowment for the Humanities found there to be over 10,000 historical associations in the United States. The number of historical groups has doubled in the past 20 years, and is growing rapidly. The report went on to declare that "Museums, libraries ... and historical organizations now provide such extensive education in the humanities that they form a kind of parallel school." National Endowment for the Humanities. Humanities in America: A Report to the President, the Congress, and the American People. Washington, DC: National Endowment for the Humanities, 1988.

The methods and equipment described here in this book been carefully chosen so that they can be used by either a small repository or even an individual researcher with limited experience and funds, or by an institution with a large collection. The result of using methods that can be applied on either a small or large scale is to extend the exchange of machine-readable information down to levels where it has not penetrated before.

Reduce your labor

While researching historic photographs of Los Angeles, I found that the only way to make thorough use of a library photo collection was to find the person who originally organized the system. Each collection did not really have a system, but rather a set of idiosyncrasies. The system at each repository was, of course, completely different.

Today, there is hope of avoiding the great amounts of time and effort that have been wasted in the past, while making historical research materials much more easily available. The hope comes from combining computer database management with standardized procedures such as use of the Library of Congress Subject Headings, and the MARC (Machine-Readable Cataloging) format.

Even those who have used a computer system for years might not have learned the database fundamentals, and so they might not understand the differences between a word-processing program, a free-text program, a filing program, and a true relational database management program. Understanding and using good database management procedures makes using the other two elements of the cataloging process, the MARC format and Library of Congress Subject Headings, much easier. The lack of understanding of database concepts can be the greatest single handicap to cataloging efforts today.

Database management methods greatly improve the efficiency and cost-effectiveness of cataloging. The use of Default Choices can reduce the amount of typing required for data-entry by a factor of 50 to 90 percent, depending on the degree of similarity between the items cataloged. Relational database management, relating together information from different files, avoids redundancy and inconsistency.

The facilities of Data Validation, Data Normalization, and cross-checking through Authority Files improves the consistency of the material entered into the database. Methods such as Global Search and Replace make it much easier to clean up or change a database. If a name has been misspelled 10,000 times, a database program can perform the correction across the entire database, rather than requiring that the user edit each individual record. A database program can also restructure the information when such changes are necessary, perhaps in preparation for transfer to another system or machine.

For collections

Libraries, archives, museums, and other organizations can use computer database management to improve information access for researchers, gain additional revenues for repositories, and provide patrons with copies of database records in printed or electronic form. If both the repository and the patron use a MARC-compatible format and Library of Congress Subject Headings, the information can be loaded directly into the patron's own personal database for immediate use. The ability to provide such services will give a repository an edge over other institutions equal in the quality of their materials but unequal in database or MARC-format literacy.

For those repositories that house photographic collections, photo sales offer the best opportunity for generating outside revenue. Photographs commonly sell for more than 500 percent of the cost of duplication. Computer database methods will increase the speed, thoroughness, and cost-effectiveness of the search and retrieval operations that support photo sales. If a repository misses a photo that a patron wanted, the institution has lost a sale. But for a staff person to spend three days looking for the photo would cost far more than the sale is worth. The combination of computer database management and cataloging methods will allow a repository to make the best use of its materials.

Add photographic images to a database

From the standpoint of preservation, image processing systems have much to offer to collections of photographs and documents. The availability of the image in a computer database will greatly reduce the need to access and handle the physical object. The actual photograph or document can then be stored in a less convenient but more controlled location, and pulled out only when extra copies need to be made.

In a digital image processing system, a picture or document is captured in the form of dots. The dots are called *pixels* for "picture elements." For each pixel the computer will store information about darkness and perhaps also color. The density of pixels determines the resolution of the image, and the amount of storage capacity needed.

Digital images provide great flexibility. You can capture the images yourself with a scanner. Thus you can add new images to the database as they arrive.

Once captured, a digital image is pure information, a series of computer bytes holding values for the individual pixels of the image. In the form of pure information, the image is not subject to deterioration.

As pure information, a digital image can used and transmitted in many ways. It can be sent over the telephone lines, combined with text in a desktop publishing program to produce a newsletter, or projected onto a large screen for a public presentation. Images and text can be displayed simultaneously on the same screen. The image's features can be altered to improve its clarity or to emphasize certain aspects.

Images are of little use without a solid database. The mechanics of image capture and storage are not sufficient to produce a useful system. It will accomplish little to store 40,000 or more images on a disk if users can't find the images that they need. The imaging system must be linked to a powerful database program. The database program should provide user-friendly searching strategies and the facilities to maintain database integrity. A dirty database is no better than a filing cabinet, and can be worse.

An image processing system should function as simply one component of a database application. The database program would make use of different image-processing facilities just as the same program would be used with different printers, monitors, and other peripheral devices.

Catalog now, capture the images when you can afford the hardware. Do not rule out image-processing simply because you can't afford it now. The broad usefulness of image capturing for business and government will create a large demand, which in turn will lead to the creation of progressively better and more economical systems. Within a decade, facilities for image capture, storage, and retrieval might be as common on personal computers as word processing on spreadsheets is today.

If you have a need for image-processing, the best course of action would be to catalog your information now into a well-constructed database. The cataloging process will take more time than image capture. Make the leap into image storage and retrieval when the price of the hardware comes down to a level that you can afford.

For organizations

Every organization needs a membership roster. The organization must know who is a member, whether each person has paid his or her dues on time, and how to contact the membership.

Computer database management methods allow the organization to maintain a complete roster with utmost efficiency. The combination of database management methods and the accumulated cataloging experience of librarians and archivists will help the organization to avoid the major pitfalls of redundant and inconsistent data.

Search out volunteer workers, potential donors

Every organization needs hard workers and generous donors. Through computer database management, the organization can use its membership roster as a creative tool rather than merely as a list. The entry of appropriate information will allow the organization to search out volunteers for many different tasks. The use of a database will help to avoid the common pattern of depending on a few people to do all of the work. Instead, you can search through the hobbies, abilities, and interests of the entire membership to match members to tasks.

A database will allow a financial officer to perform detailed statistical analyses of the monetary contributions from members and individuals. The analyses can be done entirely via database functions, without requiring any but the simplest data entries from those typing the roster.

For managers

Managers can take advantage of database reporting functions to keep track of system usage and to construct well-documented progress reports.

The manager can keep track of who is on the system, and what they are doing, through a display such as that shown in FIG. I-1. In this case, the display showing what is happening on the system is part of the menu that appears automatically for the History Database program, running on the Pick operating system, which allows many users to have access to the database at the same time through terminals or extra computers acting as terminals. The main computer holding the database can be an IBM PC, and it can hold the DOS and Pick systems at the same time.

The top portion of the menu shows which computers or terminals are in use, and who is using them. In those cases where the account name appears as PATRON or RESEARCHER, the user can search the database, but cannot change the data or use the printer. Terminals are connected to the main computer through serial ports; the main computer itself is therefore

```
HISTORY DATABASE 24851 Piuma Road Malibu, California 90265 Phone: (818) 888-9371

                    USERS CURRENTLY ONLINE   (Your port is shown first)

Port Account, Name                    Location                   Start Date Time
0    HISTORY.DATABASE, Kozo           Main computer, Photo staff 10/20/1990 09:00AM
1    HISTORY.DATABASE, Baldwin        Terminal, Photo staff      10/20/1990 09:30AM
2    PATRON, Smith                    Terminal, Photo reception  10/20/1990 11:30AM
3    RESEARCHER, Hayes                IBM PC, Public Affairs     10/20/1990 10:45AM
4    PATRON, Jones                    Terminal, Public Affairs   10/20/1990 10:20AM

                                MAIN MENU FOR PICK
Type:        To:

HISTORY      Enter the History Database program

END          Always END before turning off your terminal or computer.
             On a terminal, turn off the terminal after giving the END command.
             On a computer, END will take you back to DOS or to power-off.
             The main computer holding the data should END after all other ports

MENU         Return to this menu, the Main Menu for Pick
```

Fig. I-1. Menu showing current system usage

considered port zero. The date and time when each user came online are shown in the right-hand columns.

Past system usage can be shown in a manner similar to current usage, as demonstrated in FIG. I-2. In alphabetical order by account and user name, the display gives an accounting of each separate start-up date and time, showing how long the user stayed online, and how many pages were printed.

```
                              PAST SYSTEM USAGE

Account, Name                  Port  Start Date Time     Time       Pages
                                                         Hrs Mins   printed

HISTORY.DATABASE, Baldwin      1     10/18/1990 09:15AM  8   14     17
                                     10/19/1990 09:25AM  7   45
HISTORY.DATABASE, Kozo         0     10/18/1990 08:45AM  8   30     23
                                     10/20/1990 09:00AM  8    5      6
PATRON, Jones                  4     10/20/1990 10:20AM  1   15
PATRON, Smith                  2     10/20/1990 11:30AM      35
RESEARCHER, Hayes              3     10/20/1990 10:45AM  6   10
```

Fig. I-2. Screen display of past system usage

Similar screen displays can show a review of previous searches conducted on the database. The manager can quickly see which staff members have become most proficient in their search techniques, and who needs help. More skillful searchers can use this information to help those with less skill.

Construct progress reports

Database reporting functions can quickly tell a manager how many new cataloging records have been added to the database in a given time period, and provide a variety of statistical breakdowns on the progress of the cataloging effort. When similar photographs or a number of documents are included in a single record, the report can include the total number of records, the total number of photos or documents brought under control, and the average number of photos or documents per record.

Figure I-3 provides a quick summary of the results achieved by a cataloging project. The report shows that 61,124 units—in this case photographs—have been cataloged in 7,010 records, for an average of 8.71 photos per record.

```
                  CATALOGING RESULTS

TOTAL number of units cataloged          =  61,124
COUNT of cataloging records created      =  7,010
AVERAGE number of units per record       =  8.71
```

Fig. I-3. Cataloging results, overall summary

Further statistical breakdowns could show the number of photos or documents and the number of records added to the database on a yearly, quarterly, monthly, or daily basis. Figure I-4 shows a portion of the daily summaries of the results achieved by the same cataloging project. The grand total appears at the end.

CATALOGING RESULTS PER DAY

ENTRY-DATE	TOTAL RECORD COUNT	TOTAL RECORD SIZE	AVG RECORD SIZE	TOTAL UNITS	AVG UNITS PER RECORD
08/27/1989	115	36,849	320	115	1.00
02/06/1990	82	31,571	385	1,551	18.91
12/14/1989	65	30,387	467	2,718	41.81
05/25/1990	98	43,248	441	330	3.36
06/22/1990	228	88,077	386	297	1.30
06/28/1990	361	147,175	407	366	1.01
07/13/1990	160	57,305	358	165	1.03
07/18/1990	197	67,135	340	202	1.02
07/27/1990	87	36,629	421	542	6.22
08/17/1990	104	36,027	346	152	1.46
08/20/1990	117	37,585	321	119	1.01
08/24/1990	131	44,120	336	192	1.46
08/31/1990	434	169,359	390	434	1.00
09/11/1990	246	78,647	319	272	1.10
09/12/1990	144	52,101	361	245	1.70
09/13/1990	275	84,683	307	287	1.04
09/14/1990	349	97,624	279	476	1.36
09/17/1990	112	37,795	337	121	1.08
09/19/1990	87	27,490	315	104	1.19
GRAND TOTAL	7,010	2,629,244	375	61,124	8.71

Fig. I-4. Cataloging results, daily summary

The column "Total Record Count" shows how many records were cataloged each day. "Total Record Size" shows the total number of characters added to the database, while "Avg Record Size" shows the average size in characters of each record. "Total Units" shows the total number of photographs cataloged, while "Avg Units per Record" presents a daily average of the number of photographs grouped together into a single cataloging record.

With these statistics, a manager could quickly trace the factors boosting or depressing productivity. A manager could also call up individual statistics for each cataloger. For financial reporting purposes, the report could distinguish between different projects or funding sources. Any of the search criteria used in database searching can also be employed for statistical reporting.

Part I

Combining Database Management with Cataloging Procedures

1

The practical value of database management and cataloging

While doing research in France on the subject of the early political career of Pierre Mendés France, I came to know the chief archivist of the department of the Eure, Marcel Baudot. Baudot was also a respected historian who wrote a fine work on life in France during the World War II German occupation. He had considerable material to use for his work because he had served as head of the Resistance for his department.

The unique manner in which Baudot set about to organize local forces was to convert the department's existing information network of archives and libraries into an information network for the Resistance. The German army never guessed that interspersed among the book orders and manuscripts were communications on anti-aircraft emplacements and the movement of trains bearing troops and ammunition. The messages were then relayed by radio to Allied Bomber Command.[1]

You wouldn't usually think of the skills of an archivist as relevant to a situation like that faced by the Resistance. Yet the primary skill of an archivist or librarian is the ability to manage information. That ability is relevant wherever there is information to be managed. The collective experience of archivists and librarians is even more relevant when there are large amounts of information, its sources are diverse, and the information is complex.

Researchers and writers today need to develop their information management skills to engage in a different sort of resistance, a resistance to the modern flood of information that threatens to engulf our work and to drown our primary tasks, which are interpretation and analysis. The most effective basis for organizing our own resistance is to combine the skills

---

[1]Marcel Baudot, interview by the author, July 23, 1973. Baudot was chief archivist of the department during the period 1925–1947 and then served as an *Inspecteur des Archives*. During the Occupation he was chief of the Forces *Françaises de l'Intérieur* in the Eure. He is the author of *L'opinion publique sous l'occupation: L'exemple d'un département française* (Paris, 1960).

developed in the course of research with techniques borrowed from those fields most directly concerned with information management.

My specific recommendations are the following:

1. Individual researchers should learn and use the descriptive cataloging methods devised by archivists and librarians.
2. The techniques of library and archival cataloging should be incorporated into computer database management systems that will remove the large amounts of repetitive drudgery normally associated with cataloging work.

Using standardized procedures

Cataloging and database management are means to an end. The purpose in both cases is to gain better control over source materials. Standardized cataloging methods form a natural complement to computer database management. Catalogers in libraries and archives have addressed and provided solutions for the problems of inconsistency that plague most databases. Rather than inventing new solutions, the sensible course is to learn and adopt methods that have been derived from an enormous body of experience. The most effective procedure will be to combine the latest technology with what librarians and archivists know about information.

It is a superstition of our time that computers possess magical powers capable of overcoming the dilemma of information overload. Discussions held today on the subject of computer information retrieval remind me of the conversation in Shakespeare's Henry IV (act 3, scene 1) between Glendower and Hotspur. Glendower, in the manner of a proud computer owner bragging of his equipment's ability to retrieve data, declares, "I can call spirits from the vasty deep." The more pragmatic Hotspur retorts, "Why, so can I, or so can any man. But will they come when you do call for them?"[2] Or in today's terms, "Your computer may hold the information, but can you find it when you need it?" Anyone can cram information into a computer, but to call up that information later is another matter.

If you refer to motor vehicles as "Automobiles" in one database record and as "Cars" in another, you will not be able to search your database in a useful manner. If you change the way that you write the name of a person or an organization from one record to the next, you will not be able to easily find all of the records for that person or agency. The need to establish consistent standards for naming subjects, people, and organizations is a typical cataloging problem, for which solutions have been devised and documented in detail over the past two centuries. Computer database management, which started only yesterday, will be most effective when combined with the longer range experience of the cataloging tradition.

No database, not even a personal one, is intelligible without documentation that explains how the database is to be used. The application of standardized procedures relieves you of most of the burden of documenting your database. You can simply use this guide and other manuals that explain how to employ the procedures you choose.

In the last twenty years the library and archival communities have adopted a standard format for storing textual data. The MARC (Machine-Readable Cataloging) format provides a

[2]William Shakespeare, *Henry IV*, Act 3, Scene 1.

framework in which to hold the data, and defines how each data element should be used. Use of the MARC format provides you with a stable data structure and set of definitions, and even allows you to exchange information through the national bibliographic utilities. Facilities provided by a computer database management program can make the MARC format accessible to novices. The Library of Congress Subject Headings list provides a controlled set of terms for describing subject content, and the Anglo-American Cataloguing Rules furnish guidance for achieving consistency when entering information such as personal names and the names of organizations.

A database will allow you to reach your information in many different ways

The concepts and practices of computer database management and of library and archival cataloging procedures bear directly on the tasks that you face. For example, imagine a very simple database used to keep track of books. You give the name BOOKS to your database. For each book, you record the author, title, year of publication, publisher, and the publisher's address. A data entry form for the BOOKS database appears in FIG. 1-1.

```
AUTHOR:

TITLE:


YEAR:

PUBLISHER:

PUBLISHER-ADDRESS:
```

Fig. 1-1. BOOKS database data entry form

In database parlance, a file is composed of separate records. Figure 1-1 shows a single record, which will hold information about a single book. A record is composed of fields. Each field holds a different piece of information, such as the name of the author or the title of the book. The information in the database thus has a clear structure, with each separate element of information in a separate field.

Because the information has structure, we can search and retrieve individual pieces much more easily than if the pieces were simply thrown in together. For example, to find all of the books by mystery writer Raymond Chandler, rather than hunting through a long list on paper we can just tell the database:

SELECT BOOKS WITH AUTHOR = "Chandler, Raymond"

You may be thinking, "I could simply keep my paper list in alphabetical order by author." Yes, you could. But how then would you find the book by title? You would have to write a duplicate list in order of title.

The computer can look up the information in many different ways. To find Chandler's novel *The Big Sleep*, you could tell the database:

SELECT BOOKS WITH TITLE = "The Big Sleep"

Or you could search by year of publication:

SELECT BOOKS WITH YEAR BEFORE "1950"

Or you could ask for a particular publisher:

SELECT BOOKS WITH PUBLISHER = "Random House"

The ability to find information via many different paths makes that information more useful to you. Database management also increases the value of your time and the value of your materials. Here's an example. I wrote a history of Los Angeles before I had begun to use a computer. In the course of writing that history I gathered many marvelous Raymond Chandler quotes such as, "Cops never say good-bye. They're always hoping to meet you again in the line-up."

Several years later I presented a paper to the Modern Language Association on "Raymond Chandler's Los Angeles." But since I had organized my note cards by subject rather than by author, I had to sift through six long drawers of cards to comb out the Chandler quotes. Had the information been stored in a computer database, I could have searched at will by subject, author, or many other criteria.

When you record a piece of information, you cannot anticipate all the ways that you may eventually want to use it. A database program will allow you to use your information in ways that you had never imagined.

Save time and space

Our BOOKS database of author, title, year, and publisher seems pretty simple. Is there really anything important to learn about it? Yes. Consider an example of an esoteric database management rule that has a practical application. Figure 1-2 shows examples from our BOOKS database. The database records describe books in the series edited by Jonathan Sisk for TAB Professional and Reference Books. This series covers using the Pick operating system for database management. PUBLISHER-ADDRESS has been added to the fields to show how to contact the publisher to order a book.

What is wrong with our database structure? Take a look at the field PUBLISHER-ADDRESS.

Our PUBLISHER-ADDRESS field violates the rule of database management that no field should depend solely on another field. PUBLISHER-ADDRESS depends solely on the field PUBLISHER. The other fields, AUTHOR, TITLE, YEAR, and PUBLISHER, all tell something about the book. PUBLISHER-ADDRESS tells only about the publisher. The entry for PUBLISHER-ADDRESS is the same in every record. As long as PUBLISHER remains the same, so does PUBLISHER-ADDRESS.

Why care that a database management rule has been violated? The most obvious reason for caring is that information has been repeated unnecessarily. If the database includes a thousand books from TAB, you would have to write and store the same address a thousand times. In the fourth grade, having to write your name on the blackboard a hundred times was

```
AUTHOR:Clark, David

TITLE:Programming with IBM PC Basic and the Pick Database System

YEAR:1989

PUBLISHER:TAB Professional and Reference Books

PUBLISHER-ADDRESS:P.O. Box 40, Blue Ridge Summit, PA 17294-0850
```

```
AUTHOR:Sandler, Ian

TITLE:The Pick Perspective

YEAR:1989

PUBLISHER:TAB Professional and Reference Books

PUBLISHER-ADDRESS:P.O. Box 40, Blue Ridge Summit, PA 17294-0850
```

```
AUTHOR:Sisk, Jonathan

TITLE:Programmer's Guide to Pick Basic

YEAR:1987

PUBLISHER:TAB Professional and Reference Books

PUBLISHER-ADDRESS:P.O. Box 40, Blue Ridge Summit, PA 17294-0850
```

Fig. 1-2. BOOKS database examples

considered a punishment. It seems silly to waste your time and your computer disk space with the same kind of repetition today.

A less obvious but more important consideration is the following. What will you do when the publisher changes his or her address? You will have to go back and change the information a thousand times. In all likelihood, you will not change the old records. New records will be entered with the changed address, while the old records still carry the former location. When information is stored redundantly, inconsistency and error are the usual results.

What should you do instead? Create a separate file for PUBLISHERS. You will have two files, BOOKS and PUBLISHERS. (See FIG. 1-3).

Store the address of the publisher only once, in the PUBLISHERS file, rather than many times in the BOOKS file. If an address changes, you will need to change only one record, not many records.

```
AUTHOR:Clark, David

TITLE:Programming with IBM PC Basic and the Pick Database System

YEAR:1989

PUBLISHER:TAB Professional and Reference Books
```

```
PUBLISHER:TAB Professional and Reference Books

PUBLISHER-ADDRESS:P.O. Box 40, Blue Ridge Summit, PA 17294-0850
```

Fig. 1-3. BOOKS and PUBLISHERS database records

In the language of database management we have discovered the rule of Third Normal Form, which states that fields must be mutually independent. Each field should describe the entity that is the main object of the record, rather than merely describing another field.

For the sake of convenience, you might want the address of the publisher to appear with the other information about the book when you display or print a record. A computer database system can go from one file to another to combine an address from the PUBLISHERS file with the name of the publisher in the BOOKS file. You may have seen the term "relational" applied to database systems. A relational database management system allows you to put together information from different files.

By applying the principles of database management found in the BOOKS database example, you save time and computer storage. You also avoid future problems that you might not have anticipated when you started.

Prevent a dirty database

The rules of library and archival cataloging will also help you. For example, the most common and aggravating problem that you will encounter with a computer database occurs when you are unable to find information that you entered. You are sure that you entered descriptions of automobiles into the database. So where are the records? What happened to them? Perhaps you described the subject of the records as "Cars". And now you are looking for them as "Autos". Computers are extremely literal. If you enter the data as "Cars" and then ask for it under the heading "Autos", the system will not work as you expect.

The same problem will occur if you entered the name of the publisher of a book in different forms. Consider again our example of the BOOKS database. When entering data, you might carelessly record the publisher's name, not only as "TAB Professional and Reference Books", but also under such variations as "TAB Publishing", "TAB Reference Books Company", and "TAB Computer Books." The result will be inconsistency in your database.

Library and archival cataloging experience offers a solution. Store a single form of the heading in an Authority File. The name appearing there will be an authorized heading. When entering the name of the publisher, the authorized headings is the only form that you will use.

Since you have already created a PUBLISHERS file to store the addresses of publishers, use that same file as your Authority File.

In a manual system, you would have to look up the name in the Authority File each time by hand. Using a computer database system, the computer will warn you if it has not seen a heading before, and it will make a guess at the heading that you might have intended. Thus, if you typed "TAB Publishing", the system would ask, "Did you mean to enter: TAB Professional and Reference Books?"

The concept of an Authority File comes from library and archival cataloging. The tools that make the Authority File easy to use come from computer database management. By combining database and cataloging methods, you can assure consistency in your entries and prevent the heartbreak of a dirty database.

It is very discouraging to spend great amounts of time, effort, and expense entering data, only to discover that, because of unseen structural flaws introduced at the beginning, the database will not do for you what you had hoped to achieve with it. You and the other people who need the information eventually turn back to the old methods of rummaging through paper files. The lesson to take from others who have undertaken similar tasks is that if you are organizing a sizable amount of data, it pays to do it correctly from the beginning.

2

Standardization

Standardization is a necessary corollary to using computers to store and exchange information. The computer cannot understand what you intended to say when you cataloged a particular record; the machine understands only the exact words and numbers that you entered, so your entries must be consistent.

If the information is not for your own personal use alone, or if you plan to access information entered by others, then it is important to agree on common standards for description and communication. When exchanging information, two computers must adhere to a standard method of representing the data.

ASCII: American Standard Code for Information Interchange

How can two completely different machines, such as the Radio Shack portable Model 100 and the IBM desktop PC-XT, exchange data? They both speak ASCII. ASCII is an acronym for the American Standard Code for Information Interchange, and is pronounced "as-key". The ASCII standard provides a common designation for each character on the computer, and thus allows computers of different types from different manufacturers to exchange information.

One of the most-used and least-understood adjectives applied to computers today is "compatible." When explaining how information can be exchanged between the portable Model 100 and a desktop machine, I have often found a reaction of disbelief and the response, "But, they're not compatible." Through the ASCII standard, computers that are not compatible in the sense of using the same type of equipment can still be "information compatible."

The computer does not actually store characters, such as the letter "a". Instead, the machine stores numbers that the ASCII standard defines as representing certain characters. The numbers 65-90 inside the computer are interpreted as upper case letters A-Z and the numbers 97-122 are interpreted as lower case letters a-z. Because all letters are really numbers to the computer, the difference between lower and upper case letters is significant. Observe that in a list of terms sorted by computer, the computer will often place an upper case

"Z" before a lower case "a". To the computer, all of the upper case letters come before any of the lower case letters. If a computer appears not to care whether a character is upper or lower case, it is only because a programmer has inserted a special routine to conceal the distinction.

When entering data into a computer, the distinction between upper and lower case should always be observed, particularly in the case of subject terms and names that are likely to be searched, and that may also be sorted for a printed index. The upper and lower case distinctions of the Library of Congress Subject Headings are consistent and should be adhered to.

Controlled Vocabulary

To fully appreciate the importance of standardization, you must understand the concept of Controlled Vocabulary. As you place materials in a file cabinet, the easiest way to organize the information is to assign file headings, and to group like materials together behind the various headings. Before long, however, you find inconsistencies and contradictions in your file heading assignments. You discover that you have created a heading named "Citrus" and another named "Oranges." Photos of orange groves have ended up sometimes in one folder, sometimes in the other. You need a Controlled Vocabulary.

When entering terms into a database that will later be searched, it is imperative that the vocabulary of terms be controlled. Even when multiple subject terms can be included, you cannot describe automobiles as "autos" sometimes and "cars" at other times and expect to conduct an intelligent search.

As you begin the process of attempting to control the terms you use, you soon discover that maintaining a consistent list of terms is far more trouble than you expected. You might find that on your home-grown list of subject headings, you have three different terms that really carry the same meaning, while in other cases you have described three different types of objects with the same term. If you try to maintain this list for several years, you will also run into problems of new terms entering common usage and old terms changing in meaning. But you will probably give up long before that happens.

Library of Congress Subject Headings

Your task of cataloging would be much simpler if you could somehow sub-contract the work of maintaining a Controlled Vocabulary to someone else. As you begin to think of using a vocabulary created and maintained by another person or institution rather than constructing your own, it might occur to you that if many people used the same vocabulary, they could describe like items in the same manner. The database would be accessible to someone other than the person who created it. This hypothetical, third-party dictionary would greatly improve the ease with which information could be exchanged. You have now stumbled across the Library of Congress Subject Headings.

History and development of the Library of Congress Subject Headings The Library of Congress Subject Headings (LCSH) have become the *de facto* standard for subject cataloging and indexing. The present classification system for the headings dates back to 1898. The Library of Congress has published its list of subject headings for use by other libraries since 1914. The thirteenth edition appeared in 1990. New editions now appear annually.

The new annual editions reflect the growing volume of usage by a variety of institutions and bibliographers and the greater need for changes and additions. The 1986 edition was printed in two volumes; the 1988 edition required three. The 1986 list contained 145,000 headings, and the 1988 tomes held 162,750.

The current cost of the big red books is $150. Smaller historical societies and individual researchers unable to afford an annual tariff of this amount should cultivate friendships among the staff of larger libraries that update annually. The old editions could be passed down, like the clothes that an older brother has outgrown. The subject headings are also available on CD-ROM disk. Within the next few years, it will probably become common to have the headings available in convenient electronic form, eliminating the need to make annual purchases.

The Library of Congress Subject Headings cover the terms that you could expect an educated person to understand. For specialized materials, alternative lists are available. Examples include subject headings from the National Library of Medicine and the National Agricultural Library.

(The primary use of the headings is for topical subjects. Of the 162,750 headings contained in the 1988 list, topical subjects accounted for 131,000. The next most populous category was that of geographic places, such as "France" or "Los Angeles (Calif.)". Personal names occupied 9,000 entries in the list, of these, 8,000 were family names. Corporate headings accounted for 2,000 listings. Specific products also appear as headings; for example, "Douglas airplanes" and "Douglas DC-3 (Transport plane)." In a computer database, you should also place the company name in the field for names of organizations (MARC 610: Subject Added Entry—Corporate Name.

The official guide to the use of the headings is the *Subject Cataloging Manual* of the Library of Congress. The manual is nearly as long as the headings list.)

The Names Authority File

The concept of a Controlled Vocabulary may be extended beyond the assignment of topical subject headings to many other kinds of information. After the use of Library of Congress Subject Headings, the most common use of a Controlled Vocabulary is for the names of persons, organizations, and places. The list of terms for each type of name is kept in a Names Authority File. When the name of a company, for example, is to be included in a cataloging record, the cataloger will refer to the Names Authority File for Corporate Names for the proper form.

The Library of Congress also provides Names Authority Files, but they tend to include only names of national importance. In most cases, an organization will create and maintain its own lists. If the list of possibilities is limited to an easily-managed number, the process will be much easier. For example, there are eighty-five separate incorporated municipalities in Los Angeles County. If the cataloging entry for County is Los Angeles, then the entry for City should come from the approved list. A database program will warn you if your entry does not match your list of possibilities. You will not have to refer manually to a paper list.

A list of names of persons would not be as limited as a list of cities. In the case of persons, you may often add new names to your Names Authority File. A database program will also make the process of adding new terms much easier.

Fields that are most important for searching

The fundamental question to ask in deciding upon the descriptive conventions for a field is "How important is this field for searching?" For fields of primary searching importance, such as subjects which are topical terms, personal names, or the names of organizations, the exact form of the entry must be specified, and entry in that form must be controlled through Authority Files. In contrast, the various note fields would rarely be searched. Entries in these seldom-searched fields can therefore take the form of expository writing.

The MARC (Machine-Readable Cataloging) format

The need for a Controlled Vocabulary soon leads us to the need for a controlled format or structure in which to place our controlled list of terms. A useful, standard method for the description of source materials has emerged in the last decade with the adoption of the MARC (Machine-Readable Cataloging) format by library and archival professions on both the national and international scale.

The use of a common format developed when the Library of Congress began supplying catalog cards to other libraries. Rather than each library separately cataloging *Gone with the Wind,* it was clearly much easier and more efficient for each library to obtain the Library of Congress catalog card. From common catalog cards grew the idea of a common cataloging format. Libraries wishing to use a common format began to follow the cataloging practices of the Library of Congress. The MARC format developed from Library of Congress practice. A family of MARC formats emerged for different types of materials, including books, serials, maps, music, and archives. At present, the various formats are merging into one single, common format. MARC is the leading force in the growth of library automation today.

MARC is not tied to any particular brand of computer hardware or software. MARC only specifies what the cataloging records shall contain, not how the computer program will handle them. Through MARC you can specify what information you will record, where you will place that information within your cataloging record, and what headings you will assign to distinguish one type of information from the rest.

Although MARC is intended as a medium for communication, like a trade language, the MARC format field definitions have a definite utility of their own, which you would want to apply even for use by an individual repository or researcher. In a standardized manner, the MARC field definitions help to pin down and document the correct usage for each field. Otherwise, each repository and researcher would have to write separate documentation defining usage conventions for every field. In most cases the documentation would never be completed, with the result that the same field would be used in different ways.

It is far easier to rely upon the existing MARC documentation than to write your own. In addition, a librarian or archivist who reads the records will already know the MARC field designations, rather than having to learn an entirely different, home-grown system. For these reasons I strongly recommend the MARC format, even for an individual researcher or a business archive that does not intend to exchange data with anyone.

You may also use additional guides, such as the *Anglo-American Cataloguing Rules,* to specify the form in which a piece of data such as a personal name will be written. You can thus achieve standardization not only for your file headings or subject terms, but also for all of the information you record.

You can now look forward to that blissful day when the historian interested in equipment used by oil producers will be able to go to any repository and ask to see materials for which MARC Field 650 (SUBJECT ADDED ENTRY—TOPICAL HEADING) contains the Library of Congress Subject Heading "Petroleum industry and trade—Equipment and supplies." Of course, this development will take time to accomplish. The process will be much easier if you can leave the management of the details to a computer database program.

Data compatibility

In the midst of the current widespread concern about future hardware compatibilities, it should be understood that data compatibility matters far more than hardware compatibility. If two different institutions define a data field in the same manner, problems of exchanging the data can probably be handled by technicians. If the two institutions use a field in completely different fashions, the data is probably not transferable, even if the hardware is identical.[1]

The MARC format does not specify hardware or software; it lays out a structure of data fields. The format must then be filled in according to standard descriptive conventions and controlled vocabularies. The result is data compatibility and successful information exchange.

Sharing data, files and costs

An information exchange network produces an important result beyond the exchange of cataloging records about specific photos, documents, and collections. A logical by-product should be the sharing of the Authority Files created and maintained in the course of cataloging those photos and documents. Each participating researcher and repository will have available for use far more extensive Authority Files than any single individual or institution could afford to create alone.

The sharing of Authority Files will be particularly valuable for those with an interest in the same subject area. Researchers and catalogers will find the files useful not only for ensuring the use of uniform terms in the cataloging process, but also for identifying items about which the authority files provide at least partial information. The process is similar to that of triangulation employed by surveyors, who use the length of two sides of a triangle and the angle between them to determine the length of the third side.

One example of an Authority File that could be used to identify photos and documents is the list that the Los Angeles City Historical Society is preparing of all those who have held elected office in Los Angeles, with the dates of their tenure. The list could be incorporated into an Authority File for Personal Names. When a cataloger found a photograph of an office-holder acting in an official capacity, and had the name of the person but not the date, the cataloger could use the Authority File to establish the range of possible dates. The reverse process would also be possible, if the cataloger had the date and the title of office, but not the name of the person. The cataloger could "triangulate" from two known elements to identify the third.

---

[1]For further discussion of this point, see: Blackaby, James R., "Creating Common Databases" in *A Common Agenda for History Museums: Conference Proceedings*, February 19-20, 1987, edited by Lonn W. Taylor, Nashville, Tennessee: American Association for State and Local History, 1987, page 47.

Anyone charged with identifying time periods, building names, and locations for photographs of city skylines and street scenes would love to have an on-line Authority File for buildings with the name of each building, the location, and the dates when the building was constructed and torn down. Such a file could be used to identify dates by buildings and buildings by dates. The dates, locations, and building names for the most prominent and architecturally significant structures in a city might already be available in the published guides to architecture. The information need only be entered into the computerized Authority File. Organizations active in lobbying for architectural preservation might be willing to create a file of this type for use by others. Associations with a strong interest in a specific locality, such as home owner groups in historic districts, might be willing to compile the information for their own areas.

There are many limited, specific fields of information, such as the history of the electric railroads in a particular community, for which Authority Files could be created by local individuals and organizations who already possess the information and expertise. The information could be used by catalogers to pinpoint the identities of other features. For example, if the cataloger had a photo of Long Beach with an early model Pacific Electric car, an Authority File with dates of construction and routes would indicate the time period and street location.

Authority Files are extremely useful as cataloging tools, but their creation and maintenance requires great amounts of time and effort. It is clearly not cost effective for organizations trying to identify photos for the same geographical area to go it alone in creating and maintaining such files. The availability of common Authority Files, which would aid each institution's own internal cataloging efforts, might become the greatest single incentive for the individual repository to participate in projects for information exchange. Creating and maintaining Authority Files is made easier with the use of database management methods.

3

Do you need a database?

Database management methods reduce the time required to catalog, while also improving the completeness and readability of the information. But such considerations normally apply only to a sizeable body of material. Before going farther, you should ask yourself whether or not you need a database. To answer that question, apply the kitchen table test. If you can lay all of your materials out on the kitchen table so that you can see everything at the same time and easily find any individual item, then you don't need a database program to store that information.

When the materials begin to pile up and fall off the edges of the table, the next stage traditionally is to place the items in a file cabinet. Since the materials can no longer be seen all at the same time, they must now be organized and identified in some way. In short, they must be cataloged.

As you move farther and farther away from the kitchen table stage, you will be dealing progressively less with physical objects and more with ideas. A quantitative difference has caused a qualitative change. The failure to recognize this change results in collections of several million photographs managed as if all the photos could be spread out on a kitchen table. There are many such collections. Access to them is subject to the vagaries of memory and the personal interests of the curators.

The physical change in the disposition of your materials should bring with it a change in your thinking. You must stop rummaging through your materials to find a particular item that you remember, and you must start thinking abstractly. You then apply terminology that fits not only one specific item, but many items that share common characteristics that you deem to be the most important for your purposes. You might group together photos that show orange groves. From this point on, you must deal with your materials in terms of general models and categories, because you have too many items to depend on specific memories of individual pieces. A database program will help you manage your isolated bits of information as parts of broad conceptual categories.

Computers are stupid

Computers can handle only what they have been told to expect, and only in the way that they have been instructed to perform. My cat is a genius compared to any computer in the world because he can improvise. He can respond to a situation that he has never seen before. Even if his response is to hide under the bed, he is still far ahead of a computer that simply freezes, locking your data into cold storage.

You have to realize how stupid computers are in order to understand what they are good at. Their talent is for mindless repetition. They are best at removing those tasks that human beings find most aggravating. But to tap that ability, you need a conceptual understanding of the process.

Learn concepts rather than technical details

Often the greatest confusion about computers is a misunderstanding about what you need to learn in order to use one. Many people believe that in order to use a computer they will have to learn a great volume of technical details, and they avoid beginning a learning process that they believe will be long and difficult. People are also afraid that they will fail. Computer technicians do not help the situation when they offer explanations full of technical jargon and details that seem to fit into no larger pattern.

What is most important to learn is not the details, but the concepts. In this regard, the use of computers is no different than using any of the other mechanical or electrical devices that we employ everyday. For example, we all use electric lights, although we probably do not know what voltage our system is using. We understand the concept of an electric light switch, and we can cope with a great variety of switches that are slightly different from each other.

You do not have to be a mechanic to drive an automobile

The best analogy for computers is probably the automobile. Many computer users make the mistake of learning the various procedures by rote memorization, without learning the underlying rationale. This might be compared to learning how a particular parking brake works, without understanding why you need to set the parking brake.

On occasion, the driver might forget to set the parking brake, find that nothing disastrous happens, and conclude that setting the brake is not really necessary. Then one day the person parks on a steep hill, doesn't set the brake, and the car crashes down the hill.

In a similar situation with a computer, it is the computer that will be blamed. But the fault is with the person who did not learn the underlying concept. The auto, the computer, or any other machine will do only what you tell it to do. You must understand what you are trying to accomplish.

4

To begin using a computer

Let's begin by taking some of the mystery out of computers and establishing what you must be able to do to use a computer. You might be afraid that you can't learn to use one, but you can. Figure 4-1 shows a typical computer prompt requesting that you enter the date. If you are using a computer running the DOS operating system, call up this display with the command DATE.

```
Current date is Tue 1-01-1980
Enter new date (mm-dd-yy):_
```

Fig. 4-1. Date prompt #1

Today's date is November 10, 1990. I am now going to enter the date in the following form by typing the information and pressing the ENTER key. (See FIG. 4-2).

```
Current date is Tue 1-01-1980
Enter new date (mm-dd-yy):11-10-1990
```

Fig. 4-2. Date prompt #2

The date looks fine. But the computer rejects my input. (See FIG. 4-3.)

```
Current date is Tue 1-01-1980
Enter new date (mm-dd-yy):11-10-1990
Invalid date
Enter new date (mm-dd-yy):_
```

Fig. 4-3. Date prompt #3

What did I do wrong? Look closely at the date that I entered and think about it before reading further. Still haven't figured it out? Don't feel bad. The first time I used a computer, I fought with it for an hour over this issue. Look closely at the year "l990". Look closely at the number "l".

When you write at a typewriter, what key do you use for the number one? Do you use the lowercase version of the letter "L" because that key is easier to reach than the number one key? The letter appears as "l", the number as "1". A human being will not even notice the difference. But a computer will. Now look at our date again. The date is invalid because I entered the letter "l" where the number "1" belonged.

Follow instructions exactly

The first lesson that you must learn from the story of the invalid date is to follow instructions exactly. If you are told to enter a certain number, you must enter that number and not something else that looks similar.

Learn the general concept

The idea in the case of the bogus number is that the computer is extremely literal. It does not understand "almost". It only understands explicit instructions.

At first glance, the computer's intolerant attitude toward human inexactitude may seem unreasonable. But the computer is no different in this respect than any other machine. If you pressed the gas pedal on your car when you meant to hit the brake, you would not blame the car for failing to understand that you wanted to stop. Computers do not do what you want them to do. Computers do what you tell them to do.

Apply the general concept to other cases

Now let's try to enter the date again. (See FIG. 4-4.)

```
Current date is Tue 1-01-1980
Enter new date (mm-dd-yy):11-10-199O
```

Fig. 4-4. Date prompt #4

The date looks terrific. "1" is a number, not a letter. But no! The computer still rejects my input. (See FIG. 4-5.)

```
Current date is Tue 1-01-1980
Enter new date (mm-dd-yy):11-1O-199O
Invalid date
Enter new date (mm-dd-yy):_
```

Fig. 4-5. Date prompt #5

What did I do wrong? Think about it. The problem occurred the first time because the number "1" closely resembles the letter "l". I treated the two as equivalent. But the computer will not accept a letter as a number. Are there any other numbers that closely resemble letters? Look closely at the day of the month "1O" and the year "9O". Look closely at the number "O". The date is invalid because I entered the letter "O" (as in "Oh, glory be") where the number "0" (zero) belonged.

No book or teacher could ever show you every case that could possibly occur. Nor could you remember the minute details of each case. Just remember that when you are given an instruction, you must try to carry it out as precisely as you can. In the beginning, proceed as slowly and as carefully as necessary. The more important task is to understand the general concepts that determine what works and what does not. Then apply those concepts to the individual cases that arise.

A guided tour of the computer keyboard

To find out where you are on the computer screen, look for the blinking cursor. If you type a character, that is where the character will appear. When you are entering textual information into a database or a word processing document, use the arrow keys to move the cursor around the screen. The arrow keys, also called the cursor keys, appear on the right hand side of the keyboard.

To move the cursor

Do not use the BACKSPACE key and the SPACEBAR just to move the cursor around. The BACKSPACE key deletes the character to the left of the cursor position. Pressing the SPACEBAR enters a character, just like typing the letter "a". A space is a character. If you are in Insert mode (as explained next) put the cursor to the left of any visible character and press the SPACEBAR. The visible character will be shoved over to the right.

Over-type or Insert?

If you are using a computer at this moment, are you in Over-type mode or Insert mode? How would you know the difference? In Over-type mode, when you type a character, the new character will replace any character already at that spot. The new character is "typed over" the old one. In Insert mode, when you type a character, the new character will push over to the right any character already at that spot, rather than replacing it. The new character is "inserted" at the location of the old one.

If you are entering data into a field in a database program, the length of each field on the screen display might be fixed. If the field is already full, and you try to insert another character, the computer will beep. You must delete an old character before you can insert a new one, or switch back to Over-type mode.

The difference between Over-type and Insert is shown in FIG. 4-6. The word "cost" appears on the screen. The cursor is on the letter "s". The cursor is represented by an underline mark. If you type the letter "a" in Over-type mode, "cost" will become "coat" as "a" is typed over "s". In Insert mode, "cost" will become "coast" as "a" is inserted in front of "s", pushing over the remainder of the word.

```
Original word, cursor on "s":        cost

Type "a" in Over-Type mode:          coat

Type "a" in Insert mode:             coast
```

Fig. 4-6. Over-type or Insert mode

The ENTER key

The key may be designated as ENTER, RETURN, CR, or CRLF, or marked by an arrow pointing down and to the left, as shown in FIG. 4-7.

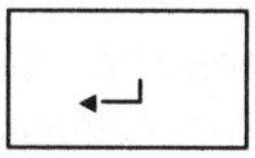

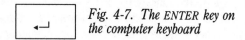

Fig. 4-7. The ENTER key on the computer keyboard

When responding to a prompt, pressing the ENTER key signifies that you want what you have typed to be entered into the computer. You have finished typing, and you want the computer to take action on the command. You may see an instruction such as "Enter the DIR command to see a Directory listing of your files". The instruction to "enter a command" means that you should type the command, and then press the ENTER key.

If you are entering text into a word processing document, pressing the ENTER key ends a paragraph and starts a new paragraph. If you are entering data into a database program, pressing the ENTER key generally means that you are finished entering information into the current field and you are ready to start on the next field.

Do not use the ENTER *key as a carriage return.* A computer is not a typewriter. The ENTER key is not the same as a typewriter's Carriage Return key. If you are entering text into a word processing document, you do not need to press ENTER at the end of every line. The program will "wrap" around to the next line automatically when you have reached the edge of the screen.

CONTROL and ALT keys

Be careful that you hit the keys you intend to hit. Go slowly at first. Many programs use shortcuts employing the CONTROL and ALT keys to issue commands or to reset options for screen display. If the computer seems suddenly to have taken off on its own, you probably pressed a CONTROL or ALT key combination, and the program is executing the commands that you have hit by mistake.

When the keyboard freezes

If you are using a computer program and the computer does not appear to be responding, wait for a couple of minutes. The program may be searching a file or loading in information such as the a copy of the data that you previously entered. On any computer that uses a disk drive, look to see if the disk drive light is flashing. If it is, then the computer is doing something.

If there is no response after several minutes, the computer may be "frozen," in the sense of doing nothing. This may occur because of a mechanical error with a peripheral device, such as a printer or tape recorder, or because you inadvertently typed a key that caused the computer to stop. The possible actions to take should be used in the following sequence, beginning with the least drastic.

CONTROL-S *means stop or pause.* CONTROL-Q *means resume.* Certain keys will cause the computer to stop or pause. On an IBM PC, a key labeled "Pause" appears on the upper right of the keyboard. The combination CONTROL-S may also be used as a PAUSE command.

Problems with PAUSE and CONTROL-S are most likely to occur at the operating system level, rather than in an application program such as a word processor or database. When you first turn on a computer running the DOS operating system, you are at the operating system level. The prompt "C>" or "C\|" appears at the bottom of the screen. If you issue the DIR command to see a Directory listing or the command TYPE with a filename to display a file, and the material to display goes by too quickly to see, you can cause the display to pause by pressing PAUSE or CONTROL-S. To resume the display, press PAUSE again, or CONTROL-Q.

If you are in the process of communicating between one computer and another, pressing CONTROL-S is the standard method of causing communication to pause. CONTROL-Q is the standard method of restarting. If you are working at a terminal connected to a multi-user system, pressing CONTROL-S may cause your terminal to freeze. Pressing CONTROL-Q will resume communication. If there is a possibility that you might have typed PAUSE or CONTROL-S, press PAUSE again, or type CONTROL-Q, or type ESCAPE.

Press the ESCAPE key to bail out

A well-behaved program should always allow you bail out of difficulty by pressing the ESCAPE key. In the hope that your program is well-behaved, press the ESCAPE key, labeled as "Esc" on the upper left or right side of the keyboard. Wait for a response. If nothing happens, try SHIFT-ESCAPE, CONTROL-ESCAPE, and SHIFT-CONTROL-ESCAPE. (If you are using Microsoft Word, and you have inadvertently wandered off into Outline View or Print Preview, SHIFT-CONTROL-ESCAPE will always take you back to the menu on the regular screen.)

Press CONTROL-BREAK or CONTROL-C to break out

If there is no response from ESCAPE, then try the BREAK key. The method of using the Break function, and the results of using it, will differ among programs and machines. For most programs, pressing BREAK is considered a fairly drastic measure. You may lose the data that you have entered since last saving a file. Therefore, make sure that you have explored the other possibilities before taking this step.

How to cause a BREAK On the IBM AT keyboard and PS/2 keyboard, BREAK appears at the upper right. To use the Break function, press CONTROL-BREAK. For many programs and computers, CONTROL-C is the equivalent of CONTROL-BREAK. On the original IBM PC keyboard, the BREAK key is marked "Scroll Lock" on top and "Break" on the front. To use the Break function, hold down the CONTROL key and press BREAK.

What to do after a BREAK After pressing BREAK, you may be dumped into a different environment. On the IBM PC, AT, or PS/2, if you see a prompt such as "C>" or "C\|", you have returned to the DOS operating system level. Type commands as you would normally do when first turning on the computer. If a menu is normally provided when you start the computer, and no menu appears after using the BREAK key, try typing the word "MENU" and pressing the ENTER key.

On the Pick operating system on an IBM PC or larger machine, if an asterisk or exclamation mark appears after you have pressed the BREAK key, you have been dumped into the System Debugger or the Pick Basic Debugger. Type the word "END" and press the ENTER key. You should now return to the operating system level.

Press CONTROL-ALT-DEL *to restart.* If the BREAK key does not do anything for you, then the next step is even more drastic. To restart the computer, hold down both the CONTROL and the ALT keys, and press the DELETE key. The computer should now restart, taking you back to the operating system level. Some computers provide a RESET key or button to use in place of CONTROL-ALT-DEL.

As a last resort, shut off the machine. On any computer, the last resort is to turn the computer off, and then back on again. On a computer with a disk drive, wait 10 seconds to turn the machine back on, to be sure that the disk drive has stopped turning. The memory should be completely cleared by restarting the computer.

5

Computer operating systems

An operating system runs the computer hardware. At the request of a program, the operating system fetches data from the disk and places new or changed data onto the disk. You might think of the operating system as the staff in a library that goes into the stacks to retrieve a book or to put a book back on the shelf.

The program acts as a reference librarian

The individual program, such as a word processor or a database program, can be compared to the reference librarian who mediates between the patron and the stacks. The patron wants information on a particular subject. The reference librarian translates that request into call numbers, which are handed to the staff who work in the stacks.

The more powerful the operating system, the more it will allow a program to do. If the staff in the stacks are quick and efficient, the reference librarian does not have to be concerned with whether the collected works of Aimee Semple McPherson are stored on Level Three or Level Seven. (Nearer to Heaven, presumably.) The reference librarian can concentrate on information, not mechanics.

The DOS operating system

The operating system most often used on the IBM PC is generally referred to as MS-DOS, for Microsoft Disk Operating System, or it is often referred to just as DOS. Microsoft is the company that supplies the system to IBM and to the manufacturers of computers compatible with the IBM PC. Programs that run under DOS include word processors, graphics programs, spreadsheet programs for financial applications, database programs, and many other types.

DOS provides a lowest common denominator of functions. The system was not created with any one particular kind of program in mind. Because of the limitations of DOS, software design is presently moving toward a multi-operating system environment, in which different systems will be used for different purposes.

The Pick operating system

In contrast to DOS, the Pick operating system was developed for a specific purpose: database management. Pick is a stable, reliable system that has been in existence for twenty-five years and is used by more than three million people. Pick provides an industrial-strength, multi-user, database management environment. Pick Systems, Inc., the producer of the system, is located in Irvine, California.

Throughout its twenty-five year history, Pick has maintained a record of 100 percent data compatibility with all previous releases. No one using Pick has ever had a problem using data originally created on an earlier version of the system. In comparison, the users of a DOS program are never sure whether the latest release will accept their old data without the need for special conversion procedures. The user of a program might be willing to accept such limitations, if the program were employed only to write letters or for other purposes that were fairly short-term in nature. Historical information, in principle, should last forever. The information never grows out-of-date.

More than 80 percent of the firms included in the Fortune 500 listing of America's largest companies use the Pick system for database management tasks. Currently more than 4,000 different programs run on the Pick operating system. The great majority of the programs perform database management functions such as distribution, accounting, or inventory control within a specific industry, such as agriculture, banking, or manufacturing.

Pick is used by Scotland Yard, the London Stock Exchange, the University of California, the U.S. Military Academy, Citicorp, McDonalds, CBS Records, and even by Apple Computers. 60 members of the United States Congress use Pick to keep track of their office records and contacts with constituents. The Scottish Health Authority maintains a Pick database of 55 billion bytes of information to keep track of the health of five million Scots. The Ford Modeling Agency maintains a visual database using the Pick operating system, which displays on the computer screen photographs of the agency's fashion models.

Pick programs have been created specifically for university, library, archival, and museum management. Pick is used by the new presidential libraries, the Holocaust library, the British national library, the New Zealand library system, the San Jose city library, for some purposes by the National Archives and the Smithsonian, and by many other libraries and archival centers. Pick is used for record-keeping by the Society of American Archivists and the Chicago Historical Society. The University of Southern California has developed a Pick program for the administration of student records, and many university bookstores employ Pick to keep track of their inventories.

Pick provides extensive facilities for use by a database management program. Under Pick, a program can read a cataloging record from the database or write a new record into the database simply by telling Pick to do it. The program does not need to have any more knowledge of the actual physical location of the data on the disk than our reference librarian had of the writings of Sister Aimee.

No single program can ever meet all the possible needs that you might have for it. If you are using a DOS program and the program will not perform the task that you require, you are out of luck. DOS does not have database management facilities available at the operating system level. Once you have exited from your program, there is little that the average DOS user can do other than copy files from one disk to another.

Under Pick, if an individual program does not handle a given database function, you could probably accomplish your purpose by employing Pick directly at the operating system level, without program intervention or the services of a programmer. You can search a file, add new information, modify old data, print or display a report, and even print mailing labels directly in the Pick operating system.

To print labels, you would enter the command "LIST-LABELS" followed by a search statement such as "WITH CITIES = Glendale" for all the pictures of Glendale. Pick will then prompt you for the dimensions of the labels to be printed. Pick's built-in database facilities make it much easier for the programmer to change or add features and for the individual user to meet special needs that may arise.

A multi-user system gives everyone access to the data

For a repository to place its database on a single-user system is to misuse the institution's most valuable and expensive resource, its information. Only one person at a time can use the database. Staff members will not become comfortable with the computer or knowledgeable about the database with the constant pressure of knowing that other people are waiting for their turns on the system. A single cataloger will tie up the system all day, blocking access by the other staff. As a result, at many sites professional librarians have worked for years within twenty feet of a computer without ever learning how to search the institution's database effectively. Imagine creating a card catalog so that only one person at a time could use it. That is what repositories are doing today with single-user computer systems.

Attempting to avoid the disadvantages of a single-user system by placing copies of the database on different computers brings a cure worse than the disease. The different versions of the database must constantly be reconciled as new information is added and older information is changed.

The multi-user Pick operating system allows a repository to make the best use of its information and of its staff by giving everyone access to the database all of the time. Staff members can reach the database to search or enter data through terminals, through extra desktop or portable computers used as terminals, or over telephone lines through modems.

Pick offers the most economical and efficient use of system resources available for database management. At a cost per user far below that of DOS networks or other multi-user systems such as Unix, Pick will allow a repository of limited means to put a terminal or computer acting as a terminal on the desk of every person on the staff who would have a reason to consult the database. If staff members can use the computer and the database freely, they will become comfortable with the computer and knowledgeable about the database, providing the repository with the best use of both its information and its people.

The use of staff time will also be improved by allowing patrons, knowledgeable researchers in particular, to examine the database directly through terminals located in public access areas. Passwords, privilege levels, and separate accounts can be used to provide whatever degree of security is considered necessary. The History Database program, for example, allows patrons to designate the photos and records that they want without allowing them to change the database.

Other advantages of multi-user terminals for patron access are that a terminal costs a fraction of the price of a computer, terminals have no moving parts, making them easy to maintain and difficult to damage, and terminals connected to a Pick system will not run DOS games. Even the cheapest and most obsolete of terminals can be employed for searching-only usage when the full-screen editor used for data entry and editing is not required. If an organization does not already have these terminals on hand, they can be obtained second-hand for less than $200 or as a tax-deductible donation.

Meeting the needs of both institutions and individuals

In the past, it would have been impossible for the same database program to meet the needs of both the institution requiring a multi-user system and the individual researcher. The individual researcher, or the small repository with a tight budget, would chose a low-cost, single-user system. The medium-sized or large institution would select a multi-user system many times more expensive. The same programs would not run on both systems. Data could not be exchanged between the systems without custom programming and perhaps also special hardware.

Pick has closed the gap between personal and institutional computing. Pick provides the same multi-user database management features and allows the same programs to run on a wide variety of machines, from IBM PC-compatible desktop computers up to minicomputers and mainframes. Because the same system will operate on large-capacity computers as well as on small and inexpensive devices, the same system can be used by historians and historical repositories at all levels, from the lone researcher to the small archives, up to the large library or museum, allowing them to share information quickly and easily.

For low-cost, multi-user operation, a small historical repository can attach two extra terminals to a standard IBM PC-compatible computer, giving three users access to the database at a cost of only $500 per terminal for each extra user. The faster and more recently introduced PC-compatible desktop computers can accommodate 10, 17, or 33 operators, still at a cost of $500 per additional terminal. PC-compatible systems will soon handle 66 users. The IBM RS/6000 can handle hundreds of operators at high levels of performance. Pick will run on mainframe-based systems with over 1,000 terminals attached.

Although a repository's needs may seem modest at first, it is important to establish at the beginning that the system chosen will continue to handle the database effectively as the volume of information grows in size and the number of online users increases. It should not be necessary to convert the database to another system. Pick is a system that a database will grow into, not out of.

Coexisting with other systems

The limitations of DOS are that it was originally designed as a single-user system with the ability to address only a limited amount of memory. As the restrictions of DOS become more apparent, software design is increasingly moving into a multi-operating system environment. A variety of operating systems will run on the same machine, with each system doing what it does best. Pick will co-exist with the DOS and Unix operating systems.

Pick and DOS can reside on the same IBM PC-compatible computer without conflict. It is easy to pass information back and forth between the two systems. For example, you might send excerpts from oral history interview transcripts from your DOS word processor to your Pick database. Later you might send text, footnotes, and a bibliography from your Pick database to your DOS word processor for final editing and polishing.

Unix is a multi-user operating system originally developed for scientific applications by the Bell Laboratories of AT&T. Combining Unix and Pick gives you all of the graphics, communications, scientific calculations, and equipment control features of Unix, along with

Pick's database management capabilities. Many DOS programs such as Microsoft Word and WordPerfect also have versions that run on Unix.

The IBM RS/6000 computer will support more than 100 users running Pick and AIX (IBM's version of Unix) concurrently. IBM has established a division to market Pick on the RS 6000, expecting the Pick-Unix combination to become standard on mid-range systems for business. Pick will also run concurrently with AT&T's Unix System V and with SCO Unix.

The bibliography of this book includes a listing of the many publications available on Pick, as well as directories of specific Pick application programs. The journals *PickWorld* and *Relational Data Base Management Computing* regularly publish updated lists of Pick publications, educational programs, user groups, tutorial programs, and dealers.

6

Database management

The most distinctive feature of database management, in comparison with other computer applications, is that a database holds information in a structured manner. Both database programs and word processors store information in files, but that is where the similarity ends. To a word processor, a file is all one document. But to a database program, a file is divided into individual units. Thus, within a database you can distinguish one unit from another and retrieve only a particular piece of information or make specific changes.

A word processor stores information in the way that a soup pot holds the ingredients that went into the soup. It would not be easy to pull the individual elements back out. A database keeps the elements separate, like an Indonesian meal with many separate bowls. A single database file will normally be assigned to hold information of a particular type. An example would be an ITEMS file to hold descriptions of individual items such as photographs or manuscripts.

A database file is divided into records. Each individual record will generally describe a whole entity of some sort. For the purpose of cataloging historical materials, an item-level record would be used to catalog a single item, such as a single photograph or manuscript, or a group of closely related items. A collection-level record would be used to record information that pertained to an entire collection.

The record in turn is divided into fields. Each holds a specific piece of information about a photograph or manuscript, such as the name of the author or photographer, the date when the document was written or the photo was shot, the names of the people and organizations depicted, and a list of subject terms assigned by the cataloger.

Each record in a given file will have exactly the same structure, in the sense that each record in that file will hold exactly the same fields. The fields may be thought of as boxes, with labels like "PHOTOGRAPHERS" and "SUBJECTS". Each record in the same file has the same series of boxes. The boxes may be empty or full. A particular field in an individual record may be left empty, if for example the name of the photographer is not known. But the record will still contain its PHOTOGRAPHERS box, ready to receive data if the cataloger should later discover the photographer's name.

Your driver's license provides a good example of a database record. The information on the license is divided into distinct fields. The license number is the Record-ID. Each record (license) must have a unique ID. Although the information on each driver's license is different, the structure of the information is always the same. We each have different names, but all of us have a NAME field on our licenses. The illustration "Driver's License, Formatted as a Database Record" illustrates database record structure. (See FIG. 6-1.)

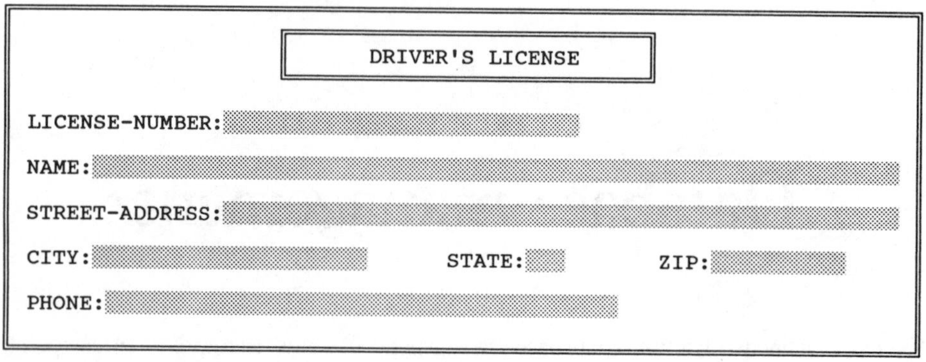

Fig. 6-1. Driver's license, formatted as a database record

Because a database holds information in a structured manner, a database program gives you far more control over that information than you would have if you held the information in a word-processing file. For example, you can find all of the photos taken by a given photographer by telling the database program to search only the PHOTOGRAPHERS field. A word processor would not distinguish the name of the photographer from any other words in the file.

A database program can be simple to use

Descriptions of the power and versatility of database management functions might leave the impression that programs incorporating such functions would be difficult to learn and use. That is not necessarily the case, at least not if the program has been developed with a particular use similar to one that you have in mind.

Figure 6-2 is taken from the History Database program, which runs on the Pick operating system and is now in use by the History Computerization Project of the Los Angeles City Historical Society. The examples should give you a picture of how database functions that were originally developed for business inventory management can be used for cataloging and research.

The History Database program provides easy-to-use methods for data entry, editing, and searching by researchers, archivists, museum curators, librarians, and others whose entries include textual descriptions. The program presents on the screen all of the information that a novice will need. Additional help messages are always available. The program helps a novice or occasional operator use the database in the same way that a reference librarian helps a novice or occasional library visitor use a library.

Data entry and editing is accomplished by filling out and changing information on a data entry form, with all of the standard word processing editing features available. Default choices

```
F1: Help     |                MAIN MENU                    | ENTER: Next
Over-Type    | Choose an action to take, then press ENTER  | Page  1 of  1

                    HISTORY DATABASE
            Computer Database Management for
            Research, Writing, and Cataloging
              Copyright David L. Clark 1986
                    24851 Piuma Road
                 Malibu, California 90265
                     (818) 888-9371

                    1. Add New Data
                    2. Edit Old Data
                    3. Display Report
                    4. Print Report
                    5. Utilities
                    6. Transfer File
                    7. Save Database
                    8. Quit

                      Pick a Number:1
```

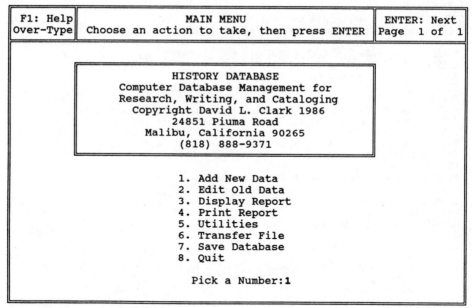

Fig. 6-2. History Database main menu

eliminate much of the typing, as the program picks the most likely entry and offers it as an initial choice to accept or change. The amount of typing saved will vary from half to over 90 percent, depending on the degree of similarity between the current entry and entries made previously.

The History Database program facilitates the use of Library of Congress Subject Headings and the Library of Congress MARC format. The program employs the standardized methods of library and archival cataloging to provide for a smooth transfer of information between different databases, and to protect the long-term value of information that may later be transferred to different systems and different machines. The numbers in brackets follow the field names in the data entry forms shown in FIG. 6-4. These are MARC field designations, indicating that the definition for each field is tied to MARC standards. Novice catalogers can enter data into a simplified data entry form without having to learn the MARC format codes. The program converts the records into the complete MARC format for information exchange.

Data entry form

Data entry and editing is performed by filling out and changing information on a data entry form, similar to filling out a form on paper. Figure 6-3 shows a database record for a photograph of the 1913 opening of the Los Angeles Aqueduct. The top rows on the form tell the novice cataloger what to do. Pressing CONTROL-O will switch the editor between Insert and Over-Type modes, just like a word processor. A new character typed will be inserted in front of the existing characters, or it will be typed over an existing character. For a help message explaining what to enter into the current field, press F1. When you are done with the form, press ESCAPE. To go to the next field, press ENTER. To go back to the previous field, press

```
CTRL-O:Ins/OT  F1: Help   ENTER:Next Field            ITEMS             Record 5 of 9
 Over-Type     ESC:Done   TAB:  Prev Field      Item-level Records      Page  1 of 1

DATABASE[001]:LADWP     COLLECTION[001]:1          PART[001]:1      SUB-PART[001]:1
ENTRY#[001]:261        ACCESSION[099]:
TITLE[245]:Los Angeles Aqueduct Opening
AUTHORS[100,700]:
PHOTOGRAPHERS[100,700]:Bledsoe, James W.
AGENCIES-OF-ORIGIN[110,710]:Los Angeles Department of Water and Power
SUBJECTS[650]:Water-supply; Aqueducts; Rites and ceremonies
PERSONS-SUBJECTS[600]:
ORGANIZATIONS-SUBJECTS[610]:Los Angeles Department of Water and Power
CAPTURE-DATES[033]:11/04/1913
ERA[045B]:1908-1913
PLACE-NAMES[651]:Los Angeles Aqueduct Cascades
STREET-ADDRESSES[651]:Balboa Boulevard at Foothill Boulevard
COMMUNITIES[651]:Sylmar
CITIES[651]:Los Angeles
COUNTIES[651]:Los Angeles
STATES[651]:California
COUNTRIES[651]:United States
DATE-PLACE-NOTE[518]:
NUMBER-UNITS[300A]:1           FORMATS[300C]:8 x 10 in.
COLORS[300B]:b&w         RECORD-TYPE[L06]:Graphic
GENRES[655]:Photographs
PHYSICAL-FORMS[655]:Glass photonegatives; Photoprints
PROJECTS[692]:LADWP Museum
FILE-HEADINGS[693]:Los Angeles Aqueduct--Construction
ENTRY-DATE[008/00-05]:10/13/1989          EDIT-DATE[005]:01/03/1990
ACTIONS[583]:Preservation needed
CATALOGERS[593]:Clark, David L.
OTHER-IDS[035]:
NOTE[500]:
DESCRIPTION[545]:Opening of the Los Angeles Aqueduct on November 4, 1913. The
photo is a broad panorama, and includes the hills behind as well as the crowd in
the foreground. The water is shown flowing down the Cascades, at the northern
end of the San Fernando  Valley.
```

Fig. 6-3. Data entry form, photograph

TAB. The data-type of the form is "ITEMS", intended for item-level records. The cataloger is currently on the fifth of a group of nine records added or edited at the same time, and on the first page of a three-page form. For the illustration, the form has been squeezed onto a single page.

A different type of data, stored with the same form, appears in FIG. 6-4. The French parliamentary election campaign was that of Pierre Mendès France in 1932. The record illustrates the French Radical Party's typical appeal to local material interests. The Radicals found that small favors were more effective than great principles. Mendès France's platform had the best of both when it offered voters "a program which combines your interests and your ideals."

Data with more textual content, resembling the notes that a researcher would take, is shown in FIG. 6-5. The same item-level form is used for notes and photographs. The notes were taken in the course of research for a history of UCLA, using the papers of Edward A. Dickson, the principal founder of the institution. In the passage cited, he declares that all of Southern California is up in arms at the latest outrage perpetrated by the Berkeley-dominated

Board of Regents of the University of California. PART and SUB-PART refer to the archival box and folder number of the collection.

A different form, for a different type of material, appears in FIG. 6-6. This form provides an historic site description for the same Los Angeles Aqueduct site whose opening was recorded in the photo cataloging record in FIG. 6-3.

To make it easy to exchange information between different files, the historic site form closely parallels the form used for cataloging photographs and documents. An organization keeping track of historic sites can thereby have quick access to photographic and documentary information about those sites, including information obtained from other organizations also using the History Database program.

The History Database program includes ready-made data entry forms for collection-level and item-level cataloging, for brief bibliographic citations, for recording information about historic sites, and for maintaining a list of names and addresses or a membership roster. You

```
CTRL-O:Ins/OT | F1: Help | ENTER:Next Field |        ITEMS           | Record 2 of 9
  Over-Type   | ESC:Done | TAB:  Prev Field | Item-level Records     | Page  1 of  1

DATABASE[001]:DLC        COLLECTION[001]:16     PART[001]:5     SUB-PART[001]:3
ENTRY#[001]:261        ACCESSION[099]:
ENTRY#[001]:1310       ACCESSION[099]:
TITLE[245]:1932 Mendès France Campaign Poster
AUTHORS[100,700]:Mendès France, Pierre
PHOTOGRAPHERS[100,700]:
AGENCIES-OF-ORIGIN[110,710]:Radical party (France)
SUBJECTS[650]:Politics, practical; Political slogans
PERSONS-SUBJECTS[600]:Mendès France, Pierre
ORGANIZATIONS-SUBJECTS[610]:Radical party (France)
CAPTURE-DATES[033]:04/01/1932
ERA[045B]:1930-1940
PLACE-NAMES[651]:
STREET-ADDRESSES[651]:
COMMUNITIES[651]:
CITIES[651]:Louviers
COUNTIES[651]:
STATES[651]:Eure
COUNTRIES[651]:France
DATE-PLACE-NOTE[518]:
NUMBER-UNITS[300A]:1           FORMATS[300C]:24 x 36 in.
COLORS[300B]:b&w          RECORD-TYPE[L06]:Archival
GENRES[655]:Campaign literature
PHYSICAL-FORMS[655]:Posters
PROJECTS[692]:Mendès France research
FILE-HEADINGS[693]:1932 Elections
ENTRY-DATE[008/00-05]:10/13/1989          EDIT-DATE[005]:01/03/1990
ACTIONS[583]:
CATALOGERS[593]:Clark, David L.
OTHER-IDS[035]:
NOTE[500]:
DESCRIPTION[545]:The Mendès France campaign posters for the 1932 election as
deputy offered voters "a program which combines your interests and your ideals"
("... un programme qui résume vos intérêts et votre idéal"). The slogan was
typical of the appeal to local material interests, particularly in rural areas,
of the Radical Party under the Third and Fourth Republics.
```

Fig. 6-4. Data entry form, election poster

```
CTRL-O:Ins/OT | F1: Help | ENTER:Next Field |          ITEMS          | Record 5 of 9
  Over-Type   | ESC:Done | TAB:  Prev Field |   Item-level Records    | Page  1 of  1

DATABASE[001]:DLC     COLLECTION[001]:6     PART[001]:20   SUB-PART[001]:10
ENTRY#[001]:126      ACCESSION[099]:
TITLE[245]:Dickson letter to Guy Earl on refusal of graduate work to UCLA
AUTHORS[100,700]:Dickson, Edward A.
PHOTOGRAPHERS[100,700]:
AGENCIES-OF-ORIGIN[110,710]:
SUBJECTS[650]:State universities and colleges; Universities and colleges--
Graduate work; College trustees; Politics and education; Regionalism
PERSONS-SUBJECTS[600]:Dickson, Edward A.; Earl, Guy F.
ORGANIZATIONS-SUBJECTS[610]:University of California.  Board of Regents;
UCLA.  Graduate School
CAPTURE-DATES[033]:06/12/1933
ERA[045B]:1930-1940
PLACE-NAMES[651]:UCLA
STREET-ADDRESSES[651]:
COMMUNITIES[651]:Westwood
CITIES[651]:Los Angeles
COUNTIES[651]:Los Angeles
STATES[651]:California
COUNTRIES[651]:United States
DATE-PLACE-NOTE[518]:
NUMBER-UNITS[300A]:1          FORMATS[300C]:
COLORS[300B]:           RECORD-TYPE[L06]:Archival
GENRES[655]:Letters
PHYSICAL-FORMS[655]:
PROJECTS[692]:UCLA History
FILE-HEADINGS[693]:Graduate School Founding
ENTRY-DATE[008/00-05]:05/22/1986          EDIT-DATE[005]:10/25/1988
ACTIONS[583]:
CATALOGERS[593]:Clark, David L.
OTHER-IDS[035]:
NOTE[500]:Letter in Dickson's handwriting.
DESCRIPTION[545]:As the Board of Regents of the University of California
continued to refuse to allow graduate work to begin at UCLA, Edward Dickson, the
regent most active in promoting UCLA, expressed his reaction to his friend and
fellow regent Guy Earl. Dickson portrayed all of Southern California as up in
arms over the "outrage" perpetrated on the Southland by the Berkeley-dominated
board: "The people here are indignant. There is growing resentment. They were
led to believe that at last the stigma that attached to the University here as
not being able to undertake graduate work was to be removed.... Now we may look
forward to years of warfare."
```

Fig. 6-5. Data entry form, research notes on archival papers

can edit, display, or print a limited set out of the total fields, or change the order in which the fields appear. You can also choose to use entirely different fields.

The data entry forms shown in FIG. 6-3 through FIG. 6-6 would actually extend over three or more computer screens. You can have as much room as you like to enter data in each field. In the last DESCRIPTION field, for example, you could enter twenty pages or more of information. The form will adjust dynamically to give you as much space as you want.

For every field a help message is available to provide guidance in filling in the field. Pressing the F1 function key causes the help message to appear at the top of the screen. Figure 6-7 provides an example of the help messages.

```
CTRL-O:Ins/OT | F1: Help | ENTER:Next Field |              SITES              | Record 1 of 7
  Over-Type   | ESC:Done | TAB:  Prev Field | Historic Sites, Landmarks       | Page  1 of  1

DATABASE[001]:HLRCLA   COLLECTION[001]:1    PART[001]:1    SUB-PART[001]:1
ENTRY#[001]:1       ACCESSION[099]:
SITE-NAME[245]:Los Angeles Aqueduct Cascades
PLACE-NAMES[651]:Los Angeles Aqueduct Cascades
STREET-ADDRESSES[651]:Balboa Boulevard at Foothill Boulevard
COMMUNITIES[651]:Sylmar
CITIES[651]:Los Angeles
COUNTIES[651]:Los Angeles
STATES[651]:California
COUNTRIES[651]:United States
SUBJECTS[650]:Water-supply; Aqueducts; Rites and ceremonies
PERSONS-SUBJECTS[600]:
ORGANIZATIONS-SUBJECTS[610]: Los Angeles Department of Water and Power
PROJECTS[692]:HLRCLA
FILE-HEADINGS[693]:
ENTRY-DATE[008/00-05]:04/30/1990           EDIT-DATE[005]:10/23/1990
ACTIONS[583]:Information needed: Landmark status, registration.
CATALOGERS[593]:Clark, David L.
CITY-IDS[035]:
COUNTY-IDS[035]:
STATE-IDS[035]:
NATIONAL-IDS[035]:
OTHER-IDS[035]:
NOMINATED-BY:
NOMINATION-DATES:
APPROVAL-DATES:
NOTE[500]:
DESCRIPTION[545]:The Los Angeles Aqueduct Cascades marks the entry-point into
Los Angeles of the Los Angeles Aqueduct from Owens Valley. The aqueduct was
built in 1908-1913 by the Los Angeles Department of Water and Power. The
official opening ceremonies took place at the Cascades on November 5, 1913. The
aqueduct made possible the growth of Los Angeles into the largest city of the
southwestern United States.
```

Fig. 6-6. Data entry form for historic sites

```
   Enter subject terms from Library of Congress Subject Headings.
   Include the main topics which the photos, documents, or objects
                     could be used to illustrate.
```

Fig. 6-7. Help message for SUBJECTS field

When you are finished entering data into the record, press ESCAPE. The "Prompt to Add Record to Database" shown in FIG. 6-8 will appear. You could choose to jump back to the previous record, to continue editing the current record, not to add the current record, and then to quit.

```
 1. Add     2. Previous Record        3. Edit      4. Do not add
                          Pick a Number:1
```

Fig. 6-8. Prompt to add record to database

Default choices: let the computer do the work for you

The use of computers in general and of database programs in particular poses a very basic trade-off. A certain amount of new thinking and learning is necessary. In return, the computer removes the need for humans to perform large amounts of repetitive drudgery. A good example of replacing drudgery with conceptual learning is the use of a default choice.

As demonstrated previously, data entry and editing is performed by filling out and changing information on the data entry form, similar to filling out a form on paper. In contrast to a paper form, however, when adding new data, the History Database program will fill in much of the information for you, based on other information held in the computer or information that you entered earlier. The amount of typing saved varies from half to over 90 percent, depending on the degree of similarity between the current entry and entries made previously.

When the program anticipates your answer, you will be presented with a default choice. A default choice is one that you accept by default. If you do nothing to change it, that is the choice you get. You would accept the default choice for a field simply by skipping on to the next field. If you do not want to accept the default choice, you would edit the field, changing the information in the field or adding new information.

Two examples of fields filled in automatically with default choices are the fields ENTRY-DATE, for the date when the record was first entered, and EDIT-DATE, for the date when the record was last changed. The program will fill in these fields automatically from the current date held in the computer's internal clock.

The field ENTRY# will also be filled in by the program to give each record a unique identifier. The program will automatically assign an ENTRY# that is one number larger than the highest ENTRY# used before.

When you start the History Database program, it will ask you to identify your name and the project that you are working on. You will choose from lists of previous users and projects. The program will later use the name and project that you identified to fill in the fields CATALOGERS and PROJECTS.

Most data entry tasks involve a great deal of repetition. If you are looking at one photo of an airplane, there is a good chance that the next photo will also show an airplane. The next plane may be from the same manufacturer, or the photo may have been taken by the same photographer. To repeat such information manually is to use the computer only as a glorified typewriter. With database management, the computer automatically duplicates those elements that do not change.

When you finish one record and start a new one, the program will present all of the data from the fields of the previous record as your default choices. For example, if you have a hundred photographs by Ansel Adams stacked together, you would type the name "Adams, Ansel" in the PHOTOGRAPHERS field only for the first record. For the records that followed, the program would automatically display the name typed previously into the field for PHOTOGRAPHERS. To accept the name as the default choice, you need only skip on to the next field. You do not have to type "Adams, Ansel" one hundred times.

When you interrupt your use of the program to do something else, the program will make note of the last record entered for each separate project that you were working on. When you return and restart the program, Ansel Adams will still be there waiting for you.

Facilities beyond the use of simple repetition from one record to the next can also be employed. If the immediately preceding record was not relevant to the task at hand, you could ask the program to find an earlier record on the subject and to use that record for the default choices.

Selected information can be cut-and-pasted from previous records and fields, in the same manner that you would use the cut-and-paste facilities of a word processor. If a long name or phrase occurred repeatedly, you could copy it into a glossary and call it up later with a single keystroke.

Names often repeat from one field to the next. Thus, the city of Los Angeles is located within the county of Los Angeles. If a record includes fields for both city and county, the name "Los Angeles" will appear twice, as shown below:

CITIES[651]:Los Angeles
COUNTIES[651]:Los Angeles

You would not have to type "Los Angeles" twice. One keystroke will allow you to reuse the information from the preceding field.

In other cases an entry can be taken from a list of the preceding entries for the same field. For example, the program can display all of the subject terms used previously and allow the user to pick the appropriate terms from the list. The same procedure would apply to previous entries for the names of persons, organizations, or places.

The most important benefit of using automatic facilities to supply information and reduce repetitive drudgery may not come from the time saved, but from the encouragement of better cataloging and research practices. The temptation to use short-cuts to avoid extra typing will be avoided. Database entries will include full names and explanations, rather than obscure abbreviations whose meanings are quickly forgotten.

Combining information from different levels

Information regarding the collection from which a photograph or manuscript came is held in a collection-level record, rather than repeated in each item-level record. An example of collection-level information would be the name of the donor of the collection. Since this information pertains to the entire collection, there is no reason to repeat it for each of the thousands of individual items held within the collection.

Figure 6-9 shows a data entry form for collection-level records. It describes the collection taken from the item-level record shown in FIG. 6-3. The record contains information that pertains either to the entire collection or to a significant portion of the collection. The amount of detail that you would include would depend on whether you were also doing item-level cataloging of the individual items within the collection.

The item-level records are linked to the appropriate collection-level data. The fields DATABASE, COLLECTION, PART, and SUB-PART in the item-level record provide a key to the collection-level record from which the item came, and to any subdivision within the collection. When information about a photo or manuscript is printed or displayed on the screen, the item-level data for the individual object can be combined with collection-level data that describes the collection from which the object came. The result is a more complete explanation than the item-level data alone would provide.

An example of combining collection-level with item-level data appears in FIG. 6-10. Selected fields from the collection-level data have been added to the item-level record to provide a complete description of the photograph and its source. The printout also contains a

```
CTRL-O:Ins/OT | F1: Help | ENTER:Next Field |      HISTORY.COLLECTIONS      | Record 1 of 8
  Over-Type   | ESC:Done | TAB:  Prev Field | Collection-level Records      | Page  1 of  2

DATABASE[001]:LADWP     COLLECTION[001]:1     PART[001]:1     SUB-PART[001]:1
TITLE[245]:Bledsoe, James W., Photographic Collection
AUTHORS[100,700]:
PHOTOGRAPHERS[100,700]:Bledsoe, James W.
AGENCIES-OF-ORIGIN[110,710]:Los Angeles Department of Water and Power
SUBJECTS[650]:Water-supply; Aqueducts--Design and construction
PERSONS-SUBJECTS[600]:
ORGANIZATIONS-SUBJECTS[610]: Los Angeles Department of Water and Power
CAPTURE-DATES[033]:01/01/1908; 12/31/1913
ERA[045B]:1908-1913
PLACE-NAMES[651]:Los Angeles Aqueduct; Owens Valley; Jawbone Siphon; Deadman
Siphon; Elizabeth Tunnel; Haiwee Reservoir
STREET-ADDRESSES[651]:
COMMUNITIES[651]:
CITIES[651]:
COUNTIES[651]:Los Angeles; Inyo; Mono
STATES[651]:California
COUNTRIES[651]:United States
DATE-PLACE-NOTE[518]:
NUMBER-UNITS[300A]:700        FORMATS[300C]:8 x 10 in.; 6 x 8 in.
COLORS[300B]:b&w        RECORD-TYPE[L06]:Graphic
LANGUAGES[008/35-37,041]:
GENRES[655]:Photographs
PHYSICAL-FORMS[655]:Glass photonegatives; Cellulose nitrate photonegatives;
Photoprints
PROJECTS[692]:LADWP Museum
FILE-HEADINGS[693]:Los Angeles Aqueduct--Construction
ENTRY-DATE[008/00-05]:01/11/1989          EDIT-DATE[005]:01/03/1990
ACTIONS[583]:Preservation needed
CATALOGERS[593]:Clark, David L.
ARRANGEMENT[351]:The collection was grouped by subject and then numbered
sequentially.
CATALOGING-AGENCY[040]:Los Angeles Department of Water and Power Museum
CUSTODIAN[851A]:Los Angeles Department of Water and Power Museum
CREDIT[524]:Los Angeles Department of Water and Power Museum
RESTRICTIONS-ON-ACCESS[506]:
```

Fig. 6-9. Data entry form, for collection-level records, page 1

heading with the name of the repository, the name of the person who printed the information, and the date and time that the information was printed.

The printed information for the photograph, combining collection-level and item-level data, appears as though it took a great deal of cataloging work to create. Yet, the data typed by the cataloger for this particular item constituted only a small portion of the total information shown. The greater part of the data was supplied by the History Database program from information entered previously or from information kept at the collections level.

Figure 6-12 demonstrates how small a part of the total data was unique to the one photograph whose cataloging records appear in FIG. 6-11. The new and unique information consisted mostly of the free-form DESCRIPTION field at the end of the item-level record.

Variable-length fields

Because structure is the most distinctive feature of a database, different database programs offer varying degrees of power and flexibility according to the manner in which they structure the information that they contain. For a database program to divide a file into records and a record into fields, the program must have some way of determining the boundary line where one record or field ends and the next begins.

Database programs such as dBASE and R:BASE, which run under the DOS operating system, divide database units according to fixed lengths. When using the dBASE or R:BASE programs, you must stipulate in advance a length for each field. The program will take up exactly that amount of disk storage space for the field, regardless of the amount of actual data entered.

The Pick operating system does not require fixed lengths. It divides one field from another not by length, but by a special character called a *delimiter* that marks the boundary point between two fields. Because the program runs under Pick, the information stored by the History Database program is completely variable in length. The program will take up only the amount of space that the data requires, plus one character as a boundary line for each field. If you leave a field empty, only one space for the boundary character will be taken for that field.

Variable-length fields give you the flexibility to include all of the fields that you need, even if some of those fields will be used on only an occasional basis. Thus, the data entry form shown in FIG. 6-9 could be used for both documents and photographs, since the form includes fields for both AUTHORS and PHOTOGRAPHERS. The field that is not relevant is simply left blank, with only one space taken for the field delimiter.

Note the connection here between the need to adopt a powerful and flexible database program and the ability to implement the MARC format. It is practically impossible to use the MARC format with a database program that uses fixed-length fields. The MARC format includes as many as 77 fields with up to 20 sub-fields, most of which will be left empty for any individual record.

When using a fixed-length field program, you would have to allocate the maximum length that might be needed for each MARC field and subfield. The program would take up that

CTRL-O:Ins/OT Over-Type	F1: Help ESC:Done	ENTER:Next Field TAB: Prev Field	COLLECTIONS Collection-level Records	Record 1 of 8 Page 2 of 2

```
TERMS-FOR-USE[540A]:
OTHER-IDS[035]:
PREVIOUS-OWNER[541]:
HISTORY-OF-OWNERSHIP[561]:The photos were taken by professional photographer
James W. Bledsoe for the department.
PUBLISHER[260B]:
PUBLICATION-PLACE[260A]:
PUBLICATION-DATE[260C]:
NOTE[500]:Bledsoe's original numbers appear on the photographs.
FINDING-AIDS[555]:Short descriptions of the individual photos appear in binder
notebooks as "Los Angeles City Aqueduct in Pictures with Notes". Information
about Bledsoe appears in the Photographers File.
CITATIONS[510]:
SCOPE[520]:Construction of the Los Angeles Aqueduct, 1908-1913.
DESCRIPTION[545]:A collection of photographs taken of the construction of the
Los Angeles Aqueduct to Owens Valley by professional photographer James W.
Bledsoe for the Los Angeles Department of Water and Power. The collection
represents an outstanding documentation of an important event. The photos show
 every phase of the construction process in detail.
```

Fig. 6-10. Data entry form, for collection-level records, page 2

```
                    David L. Clark  Date:10/25/1990  Time:10:00  Page 1

         MUSEUM OF THE LOS ANGELES DEPARTMENT OF WATER AND POWER
RECORD-ID[001]:LADWP-1-1-1-261
DATABASE[001]:LADWP
COLLECTION[001]:1            PART[001]:1            SUB-PART[001]:1
ENTRY#[001]:261     ACCESSION[099]:
TITLE[245]:Los Angeles Aqueduct Opening
COLLECTION-TITLE[245]:Bledsoe, James W., Photographic Collection
AUTHORS[100,700]:
PHOTOGRAPHERS[100,700]:Bledsoe, James W.
AGENCIES-OF-ORIGIN[110,710]:Los Angeles Department of Water and Power
SUBJECTS[650]:Water-supply; Aqueducts; Rites and ceremonies
PERSONS-SUBJECTS[600]:
ORGANIZATIONS-SUBJECTS[610]:Los Angeles Department of Water and Power
CAPTURE-DATES[033]:11/04/1913
ERA[045B]:1908-1913
PLACE-NAMES[651]:Los Angeles Aqueduct Cascades
STREET-ADDRESSES[651]:Balboa Boulevard at Foothill Boulevard
COMMUNITIES[651]:Sylmar
CITIES[651]:Los Angeles
COUNTIES[651]:Los Angeles
STATES[651]:California
COUNTRIES[651]:United States
DATE-PLACE-NOTE[518]:
NUMBER-UNITS[300A]:1           FORMATS[300C]:8 x 10 in.
COLORS[300B]:b&w               RECORD-TYPE[L06]:Graphic
GENRES[655]:Photographs
PHYSICAL-FORMS[755]:Glass photonegatives; Photoprints
PROJECTS[692]:LADWP Museum
FILE-HEADING[693]:Los Angeles Aqueduct--Construction
ENTRY-DATE[008/00-05]:10/13/1989       EDIT-DATE[005]:01/03/1990
ACTIONS[583]:Preservation needed
CATALOGERS[593]:Clark, David L.
CATALOGING-AGENCY[040]:Los Angeles Department of Water and Power
  Museum
CUSTODIAN[851A]:Los Angeles Department of Water and Power Museum
CREDIT[524]:Los Angeles Department of Water and Power Museum
RESTRICTIONS-ON-ACCESS[506]:
TERMS-FOR-USE[540A]:
OTHER-IDS[035]:
NOTE[500]:
DESCRIPTION[545]:Opening of the Los Angeles Aqueduct on November 4,
  1913. The photo is a broad panorama, and includes the hills behind
  as well as the crowd in the foreground. The water is shown flowing
  down the Cascades, at the northern end of the San Fernando Valley.
```

Fig. 6-11. Printed information for a photograph, combining collection-level and item-level data

```
Los Angeles Aqueduct Opening
Rites and ceremonies
11/04/1913
Los Angeles Aqueduct Cascades
Sylmar
Opening of the Los Angeles Aqueduct on November 4, 1913. The photo is
  a broad panorama, and includes the hills behind as well as the crowd
  in the foreground. The water is shown flowing down the Cascades, at
  the northern end of the San Fernando Valley.
```

Fig. 6-12. Actual typing required for item printed in Fig. 6-11.

amount of space even if nothing was entered. You would soon waste most of your disk space. In any case, since such programs also limit the maximum length allowed for a record, the field definitions that you would need would probably exceed the length allowed.

Under Pick, you can have as many fields as you want, and they can be as long as you want. On older versions of Pick, the maximum length of a record or field was 32 Kilobytes, or more than 32,000 characters. Under the new version of Pick, record and field length are unlimited.

Searching

Simplified searching methods help to avoid silent errors, which take place when an operator fails to retrieve relevant data because the search statement contained a subtle flaw. Easier methods allow the novice or occasional user to make searches without having to memorize field names or the exact syntax of search commands.

The "Search Methods Menu" shown in FIG. 6-13 first gives the searcher a choice of methods to use for searching. If you are unsure of what you what to do, experiment. As the menu explains at the bottom of the screen, you will have another chance to quit before anything happens. You can look at each of the methods available and then quit until you find a method that you like. After you conduct a search, you will have a chance to narrow the search further, to start a new search, or to quit before the records are displayed.

```
 F1: Help                     SEARCH METHODS                         ENTER: Next
Over-Type  Choose a method for searching the data, then press ENTER  Page  1 of  1

                          1. Simple Search
                          2. Search by Example
                          3. Search by RECORD-ID
                          4. Enter Search with a Form
                          5. Enter Search Directly
                          6. Repeat Last Successful Search
                          7. Use a Stored List (of flagged Records)
                          8. Use a Stored Command
                          9. Create a Stored List
                         10. Create a Stored Command
                         11. All (take entire file)
                         12. Review Previous Searches
                         13. Quit

                                 Pick a Number:1

 Pick a method for searching the data or take "Quit" to return to the Main Menu.
 The program will give you another chance to Quit before conducting the search.
 After each search the program will show the number of Records selected and ask
 if you wish to act on the results, to narrow the search, or to start over again.
```

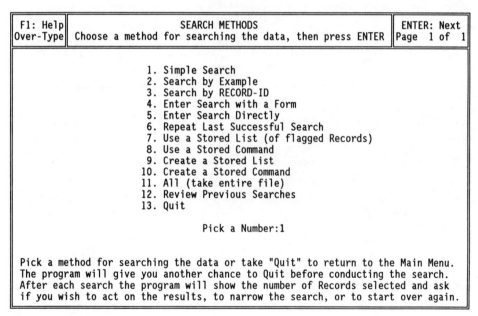

Fig. 6-13. Search methods

Simple Search The Simple Search method employs a menu. The menu lists the fields in the database and the types of search conditions that can be applied. The searcher picks the field that he or she wants to search and the test to be applied, and then lists the objects to search for, such as subject headings or the names of individuals appearing in photographs.

In the example shown in FIG. 6-14, the field to be searched is PERSONS-SUBJECTS, which would include individuals who are the subjects of the material. The individuals to search for are William Mulholland and E. F. Scattergood, the principal builders of the Los Angeles Department of Water and Power.

```
F1: Help           SIMPLE SEARCH                               ENTER: Next
Over-Type  Choose a field, a test to apply, objects to search for  Page  1 of  1

                                 FIELDS

1.RECORD-ID  9.AUTHORS            17.PLACE-NAMES     25.NUMBR-UNITS 33.ENTRY-DATE
2.DATABASE   10.PHOTOGRAPHERS     18.STREET-ADDRESS  26.FORMATS     34.EDIT-DATE
3.COLLECTION 11.AGENCIES          19.COMMUNITIES     27.COLORS      35.ACTIONS
4.PART       12.SUBJECTS          20.CITIES          28.RECORD-TYPE 36.CATALOGERS
5.SUB-PART   13.PERSONS-SUBJECTS  21.COUNTIES        29.GENRES      37.OTHER-IDS
6.ENTRY#     14.ORGS-SUBJECTS     22.STATES          30.PHYS-FORM   38.NOTE
7.ACCESSION  15.CAPTURE-DATES     23.COUNTRIES       31.PROJECTS    39.DESCRIPTION
8.TITLE      16.ERA               24.DATE-PLAC-NOTE  32.FILE-HEADINGS

                              Pick a Number:13

                               FIELD TESTS

1.Equals     3.Sounds like 5.Contains    7.Begins with 9.Before 10.After 12.Empty
2.Not Equal  4.Not like    6.Not Contain 8.Ends with   11.Between       13.Not Empty

                              Pick a Number:3

                               SEARCH FOR

Enter Objects for search separated by semicolons and spaces, such as: 1; 2; 3

OBJECTS:Mulholland, William; Scattergood, E. F.
```

Fig. 6-14. Simple Search

The type of search to be conducted is "Sounds like". A sound search will ignore differences in spelling, spacing, punctuation and capitalization among words sounding similar. The search would retrieve "Johnson", "Jonson", and "Jansen" or "Mendes-France", "Mendes France", and "Mendès France". For sound searching, the Pick operating system implements a method known as Soundex. The Soundex process reduces a word to its phonetic components.

The Simple Search menu will help to avoid many minor mistakes. If you have helped others to use a database program, how many times have you seen them type the field name for the Accession Number with one "s" too many or too few? The computer would have beeped at them, and then they might have come to tell you that "the computer isn't working."

Among the tests or conditions to use is one for an empty field. For example, if the cataloger does not know what FILE-HEADING to apply, he or she could leave the field blank, and someone else would later search for the records where FILE-HEADING was empty. If you are already using a computer program, how many of the operators at your installation know the command syntax for such a null field search?

Narrow a search in stages After each search, the program shows you how many records have been retrieved. The program gives you the choice of acting on the results obtained, narrowing the search further, starting a new search, or quitting. In the example shown in FIG. 6-15, the searcher has used the Simple Search method to retrieve materials on the subjects of "Aqueducts" or "Dams". The program has retrieved one hundred records, and displayed the result at the top of the screen. The searcher has decided that he or she wants to narrow the searcher further.

```
                         100 Records selected
1.Act on search results   2.Narrow search further   3.Start a new search  4.Quit
                         Pick a Number:2

                               FIELDS

1.RECORD-ID  9.AUTHORS            17.PLACE-NAMES     25.NUMBR-UNITS 33.ENTRY-DATE
2.DATABASE   10.PHOTOGRAPHERS     18.STREET-ADDRESS  26.FORMATS     34.EDIT-DATE
3.COLLECTION 11.AGENCIES          19.COMMUNITIES     27.COLORS      35.ACTIONS
4.PART       12.SUBJECTS          20.CITIES          28.RECORD-TYPE 36.CATALOGERS
5.SUB-PART   13.PERSONS-SUBJECTS  21.COUNTIES        29.GENRES      37.OTHER-IDS
6.ENTRY#     14.ORGS-SUBJECTS     22.STATES          30.PHYS-FORM   38.NOTE
7.ACCESSION  15.CAPTURE-DATES     23.COUNTRIES       31.PROJECTS    39.DESCRIPTION
8.TITLE      16.ERA               24.DATE-PLAC-NOTE  32.FILE-HEADINGS

                         Pick a Number:12

                            FIELD TESTS

1.Equals     3.Sounds like 5.Contains    7.Begins with 9.Before 10.After 12.Empty
2.Not Equal  4.Not sound   6.Not Contain 8.Ends with   11.Between    13.Not Empty

                         Pick a Number:1

                            SEARCH FOR

Enter Objects for search separated by semicolons and spaces, such as: 1; 2; 3

OBJECTS:Aqueducts; Dams
```

Fig. 6-15. Choice to act on search results or narrow search

After retrieving one hundred records on the subjects of "Aqueducts" and "Dams", the searcher wishes to narrow the search down to aqueducts outside of Los Angeles County. Using the Simple Search method again, the searcher has picked the field COUNTIES and applied the test "Not equal" to "Los Angeles".

After the search conditions are narrowed to aqueducts or dams outside of Los Angeles County, only eight records are retrieved. The searcher is again presented with the results and given the choice of acting on the results or narrowing down the search even further. In addition, the searcher is given the choice of going back to the previous search results, 100 records for "Aqueducts" and "Dams", in case the results of the second search are narrower than desired. The example is shown in FIG. 6-16.

```
                              8 Records selected
1.Act on results 2.Narrow again 3.New search 4.Go back to previous search 5.Quit
                              Pick a Number:1

                                   FIELDS

1.RECORD-ID   9.AUTHORS            17.PLACE-NAMES      25.NUMBR-UNITS  33.ENTRY-DATE
2.DATABASE    10.PHOTOGRAPHERS     18.STREET-ADDRESS   26.FORMATS      34.EDIT-DATE
3.COLLECTION  11.AGENCIES          19.COMMUNITIES      27.COLORS       35.ACTIONS
4.PART        12.SUBJECTS          20.CITIES           28.RECORD-TYPE  36.CATALOGERS
5.SUB-PART    13.PERSONS-SUBJECTS  21.COUNTIES         29.GENRES       37.OTHER-IDS
6.ENTRY#      14.ORGS-SUBJECTS     22.STATES           30.PHYS-FORM    38.NOTE
7.ACCESSION   15.CAPTURE-DATES     23.COUNTRIES        31.PROJECTS     39.DESCRIPTION
8.TITLE       16.ERA               24.DATE-PLAC-NOTE   32.FILE-HEADINGS

                              Pick a Number:21

                                FIELD TESTS

1.Equals      3.Sounds like 5.Contains     7.Begins with 9.Before 10.After 12.Empty
2.Not Equal   4.Not sound   6.Not Contain  8.Ends with   11.Between        13.Not Empty

                              Pick a Number:2

                                 SEARCH FOR

Enter Objects for search separated by semicolons and spaces, such as: 1; 2; 3

OBJECTS:Los Angeles
```

Fig. 6-16. Choice to act on search results, narrow search, or return to previous search

If the result of the second search had been that no records were selected because there were no materials on aqueducts or dams outside of Los Angeles County, the searcher would have been given the choice to quit, to start a new search, or to return to the previous successful search. The choices that would appear at the top of the screen are shown in FIG. 6-17. After returning to the previous search, all records relating to aqueducts or dams, the searcher could act on that search or choose to narrow the search in a different way.

```
                          No Records selected
1. Start a new search    2. Go back to previous search    3. Quit
                           Pick a Number:1
```

Fig. 6-17. If no records selected, choice to start again or return to previous search

The same prompts to narrow down a search will appear with the following search methods. After a search, you will always have the opportunity to act on the results, to narrow the search further, or to quit.

Search by Example A searching method that many find to be the most natural to use is Search by Example. The program presents a data entry form similar to the form used for cataloging, except that the form is completely blank. The searcher fills in the form with the desired values. For example, if you were looking for records on aqueducts or dams you would go to the SUBJECTS field on the form and type in the terms "Aqueducts" and "Dams" separated by a semicolon.

If you wanted to narrow the search to aqueducts and dams outside of Los Angeles County, you could narrow a search by stages as previously explained. After each search, the program will give you the opportunity to apply more narrow criteria.

Rather than proceeding one stage at a time, you could combine the criteria in one pass with Search by Example. To limit the selection to aqueducts and dams outside of Los Angeles County, go to the Field for COUNTIES and type "# Los Angeles". The hash symbol "#" is used for "NOT". When you are finished filling out the Search by Example form, press ESCAPE, just as you would when you were done with a data entry form. (See FIG. 6-18.)

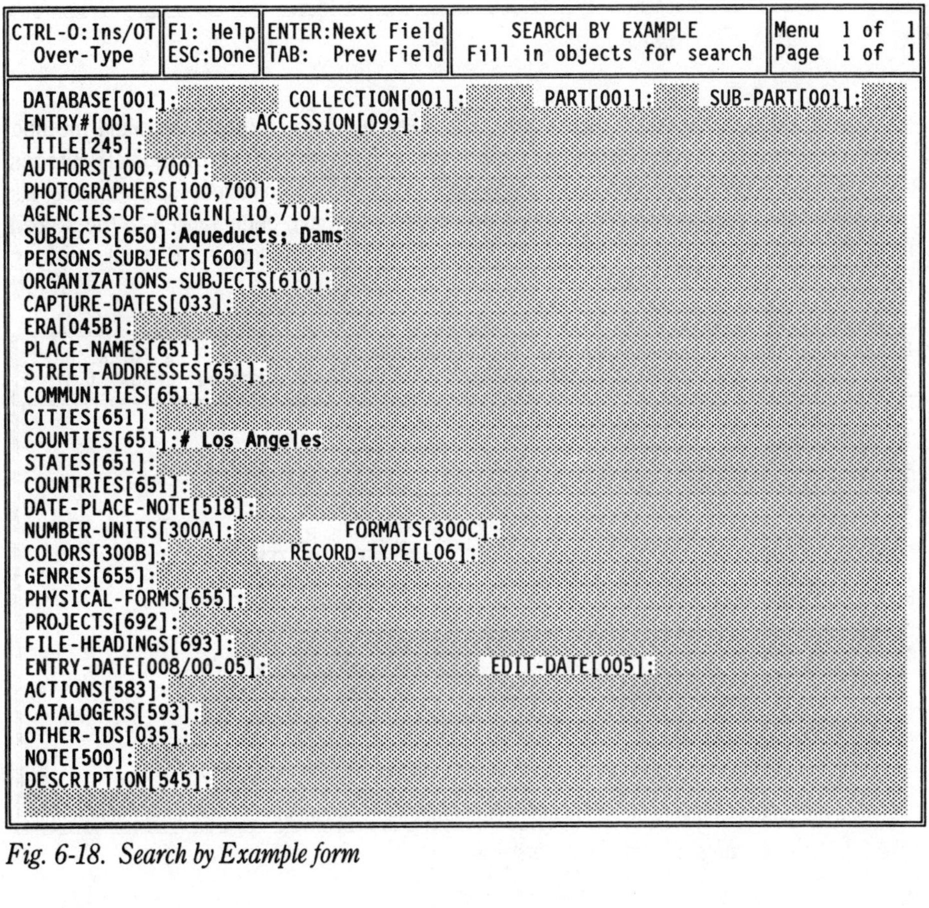

```
CTRL-O:Ins/OT  F1: Help  ENTER:Next Field        SEARCH BY EXAMPLE         Menu  1 of  1
  Over-Type    ESC:Done  TAB:  Prev Field   Fill in objects for search     Page  1 of  1

DATABASE[001]:          COLLECTION[001]:          PART[001]:        SUB-PART[001]:
ENTRY#[001]:          ACCESSION[099]:
TITLE[245]:
AUTHORS[100,700]:
PHOTOGRAPHERS[100,700]:
AGENCIES-OF-ORIGIN[110,710]:
SUBJECTS[650]:Aqueducts; Dams
PERSONS-SUBJECTS[600]:
ORGANIZATIONS-SUBJECTS[610]:
CAPTURE-DATES[033]:
ERA[045B]:
PLACE-NAMES[651]:
STREET-ADDRESSES[651]:
COMMUNITIES[651]:
CITIES[651]:
COUNTIES[651]:# Los Angeles
STATES[651]:
COUNTRIES[651]:
DATE-PLACE-NOTE[518]:
NUMBER-UNITS[300A]:          FORMATS[300C]:
COLORS[300B]:          RECORD-TYPE[L06]:
GENRES[655]:
PHYSICAL-FORMS[655]:
PROJECTS[692]:
FILE-HEADINGS[693]:
ENTRY-DATE[008/00-05]:                    EDIT-DATE[005]:
ACTIONS[583]:
CATALOGERS[593]:
OTHER-IDS[035]:
NOTE[500]:
DESCRIPTION[545]:
```

Fig. 6-18. Search by Example form

Search with a Stored List The method of Search with a Stored List will retrieve all of the records previously flagged by you or by another user of the system. While entering, editing, or reviewing data, you can flag records for inclusion on a Stored List for retrieval as a group later.

Stored Lists are used for temporary purposes. For example, you might flag the photographs that you wanted to use for an exhibit, the photos that a patron wishes to purchase, or the records that you want to retrieve and review before conducting an interview. You could also flag records for which the information was uncertain, and which required further investigation. (See FIG. 6-19.)

```
F1: Help        USE A STORED LIST OF FLAGGED RECORDS           ENTER: Next
Over-Type  Choose a list of previously-flagged Records to use  Page  1 of  1

                        1. Aqueducts-Not-LA
                        2. Exhibit
                        3. Smith-Purchase
                        4. Library-Lookup
                        5. Quit

                          Pick a Number:1
```

Fig. 6-19. Search with a Stored List

Search with a Stored Command The Search with a Stored Command method employs pre-stored commands to simplify often repeated functions. This method encourages more experienced users to set up automatic searches for those who have less experience. As shown in FIG. 6-20 the program will display the names that have been applied to the stored commands. Each name indicates what sort of records will be retrieved. For example, picking

```
F1: Help              USE A STORED SEARCH COMMAND                 ENTER: Next
Over-Type  Choose a command stored previously to use for searching Page  1 of  1

 1. ACTION-NEEDED                      16. ENTERED-LAST-YEAR
 2. EDITED-LAST-30-DAYS                17. ENTERED-THIS-MONTH
 3. EDITED-LAST-7-DAYS                 18. ENTERED-THIS-WEEK
 4. EDITED-LAST-MONTH                  19. ENTERED-THIS-YEAR
 5. EDITED-LAST-WEEK                   20. ENTERED-TODAY
 6. EDITED-LAST-YEAR                   21. ENTERED-YESTERDAY
 7. EDITED-THIS-MONTH                  22. INFORMATION-NEEDED
 8. EDITED-THIS-WEEK                   23. LAST-SEARCH*PORT-0
 9. EDITED-THIS-YEAR                   24. LAST-SEARCH*PORT-1
10. EDITED-TODAY                       25. LAST-SEARCH*PORT-2
11. EDITED-YESTERDAY                   26. PRESERVATION-NEEDED
12. ENTERED-LAST-30-DAYS               27. RETURN-TO-CATALOGER
13. ENTERED-LAST-7-DAYS                28. RETURN-TO-SUBMITTER
14. ENTERED-LAST-MONTH                 29. Quit
15. ENTERED-LAST-WEEK

                          Pick a Number:1
```

Fig. 6-20. Search with a Stored Command

"EDITED-LAST-WEEK" or "EDITED-LAST-MONTH" will retrieve all of the records entered or last edited during the last week or the last month.

The stored command "ACTION-NEEDED" will retrieve all of the records in which the ACTIONS field has been used to indicate that some additional action is needed, such as looking up additional information about the materials. The choice "RETURN-TO-CATALOGER" will retrieve the records that should be returned to the cataloger for changes. The stored commands named "LAST-SEARCH" followed by the port number allow a user to repeat the last search of any port on the system. (The IBM PC that is used to hold the database is considered port zero. The other ports are terminals or additional IBM PCs attached to the main computer.)

Review previous searches The program keeps a file of every search command entered, and the results obtained. A more experienced user can review the past searches conducted to determine how best to help or instruct less experienced users. The reviews can also be printed to use for teaching purposes.

In the case shown in FIG. 6-21, a novice searcher has complained of not finding any data on the subject of "Water-supply". A review of the search shows that when filling in the Simple Search menu, the searcher mistyped "Water-supply" as "Water-spply". The review also shows how the program has taken the selections made on the Simple Search menu and used them to construct a search statement.

```
                 1. Next          2. Print          3. Quit
                             Pick a Number:1

Searcher: Novice, John J.      File: ITEMS     Date: 10/26/1990    Time: 10:20AM
Search Method: Simple Search
Field: SUBJECTS[650]          Field Test: Equals         Objects: Water-spply
Command: SSELECT ITEMS WITH SUBJECTS[650] = "Water-spply"
Result: No Records Selected
```

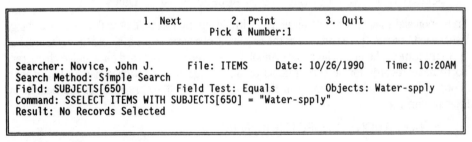

Fig. 6-21. Review of a previous search

Sophisticated searching methods The usefulness of a database is multiplied by combining simplified searching methods with Stored Lists of flagged records, Stored Commands for specific purposes, and a Review of Previous Searches to find mistakes made by novices. The information is then more easily accessible to the individual researcher or to the staff of an archives or library.

As users gain experience, they might want to use more direct searching methods. The Search with a Form method prompts the operator to fill out a form that may include multiple search conditions. The method of Search Directly allows the user to type his own command, without program intervention. The names of the fields, however, appear at the top of the screen, and the last search command created appears as the default choice, to be edited as desired. Even the more direct procedures still avoid the need to memorize field names or command syntax.

Those users who graduate beyond simple searching methods can use either the direct methods or Search by Example in sophisticated ways. Besides "#" for NOT, other symbols to use with a Search by Example form include the less than symbol "<" for LESS THAN or BEFORE and the greater than symbol ">" for GREATER THAN or AFTER. To limit the selection to photos taken since 1920, place that condition in the CAPTURE-DATES field on the Search by Example form in the following manner:

CAPTURE-DATES[033]:> 12/31/1919

The same command could be entered directly as:

SELECT ITEMS WITH CAPTURE-DATES AFTER "12/31/1919"

Using Search by Example, the default linkage between conditions in different fields is "AND", while between conditions in the same field the default connection is "OR". The example search shown above would retrieve records on the subject of either aqueducts or dams, but only if the county designation was not Los Angeles. To change the linkage between conditions, place the ampersand symbol "&" for AND or the exclamation mark "!" for OR in front of the object to search for. Thus, to require that both an aqueduct and a dam appear in the same photo, the SUBJECTS entry on the form would be filled out in the following manner:

SUBJECTS[650]:Aqueducts; & Dams

The same command could be entered directly as:

SELECT ITEMS WITH SUBJECTS = "Aqueducts" AND "Dams"

Truncation and wildcards can be employed with Search by Example or with direct searching. Use the left bracket "[" to truncate at the beginning of a word or phrase, and the right bracket "]" to truncate at the end. The caret symbol "^" serves as a wild card for a single character. To retrieve records for all corporations or other organizations whose names began with "Ford", place the following entry in the ORGANIZATIONS-SUBJECTS field on the Search by Example form:

ORGANIZATIONS-SUBJECTS[610]:Ford]

The same command could be entered directly as:

SELECT ITEMS WITH ORGANIZATIONS-SUBJECTS = "Ford]"

Utilities for database maintenance

The consistency and accuracy of a database cannot be maintained simply by spending more time on each individual record, in the hope that you can enter the data with such painstaking accuracy that it will stand forever. The goals of consistency and accuracy are better achieved by using automatic facilities for database maintenance.

For example, what happens if someone misspells the name of Aaron Burr ten thousand times? Will you have to comb through the database to make ten thousand individual corrections? With History Database, you can make the correction through the use of global search and replace facilities, which make a change to a selected field across the entire database. The program will keep a log of the changes made.

The History Database program's facilities for global search and replace have allowed historical societies and museums to use relatively unskilled staff or volunteers for first-pass cataloging, entering the basic information already written on the back of photographs, for example. More skilled staff can later very efficiently correct the entries, changing them to adhere to a standardized format and vocabulary. The program's global search and replace facilities allow hundreds or thousands of entries to be corrected in one pass.

The Methods for Global Search and Replace screen appears in FIG. 6-22. The menu lists the changes that can be made automatically. Some of the changes are most useful for textual material, while others are intended for cleaning up identification numbers that vary from your standard practice. If you wish to change your use of a subject heading, you can do so with a single command that will apply to all of the records in which that heading appeared. If you neglected to include a designation for the project under which records had been cataloged, you can insert the project name or abbreviated code automatically into your records.

```
F1: Help         METHODS FOR GLOBAL SEARCH AND REPLACE           ENTER: Next
Over-Type   Choose a change to make across the entire database   Page  1 of  1

REPLACE CURRENT VALUE                             INSERT A NEW VALUE

 1. Replace a Value                               16. Insert Text Typed by User
 2. Replace Embedded Text                         17. Insert Today's Date
 3. Replace an Empty Field                        18. Insert Current Project Code
                                                  19. Insert Current Project Name
CHANGE CURRENT VALUE
                                                  GET FROM OTHER FIELD, RECORD-ID
 4. Convert to Upper-Case
 5. Convert to Lower-Case                         20. Insert from Other Field
 6. Convert to Upper then Lower Case              21. Remove from Other Field
 7. Convert Years or Year-First to Dates          22. Extract from Record-ID
 8. Convert Years to Era Begin-End
 9. Extract Portion of Field                      USE CODES OR CUSTOM FACILITY
10. Trim Unwanted Characters
11. Trim Non-Numeric, Lead Zeroes from Number     23. Use Conversion Codes
12. Trim Leading, Ending, Double Spaces           24. Use Custom Field Definition
13. Change Value Not within Length Range          25. Use Custom Routine
14. Change Value Not Matching Pattern
15. Change Value Not Matching Format              26. Quit

                          Pick a Number:1
```

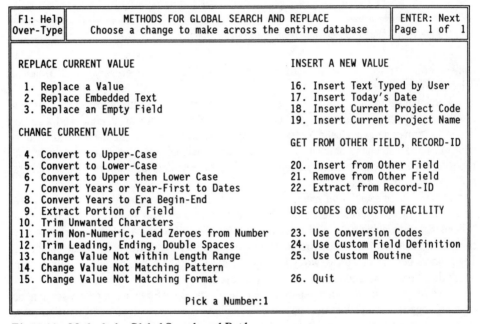

Fig. 6-22. Methods for Global Search and Replace

Additional facilities, not shown on the menu of field changes, are available through the options to use a custom routine, custom field definition, or conversion code. For example, if you wish to pull the name of an author or photographer from a collection-level file into item-level records, you can do so automatically with a custom field definition that will reach across to the appropriate collection-level record. If some names of people have not been typed in the correct form of last name, comma, space, first name, the correction can be made through the use of the "Put Last Name First" custom routine supplied with the History Database program.

If you wish, you can choose to inspect and then approve or cancel each change, rather than having all the changes made at once. After you have inspected a few, you can opt to have all of the remaining changes made automatically. You can also decide to intervene personally and edit a change. The screen used to approve changes appears in FIG. 6-23. In this case, the

```
F1: Help  |          APPROVE CHANGE FOR: SUBJECTS                       | Record 8 of 9
Over-Type | Choose to approve, not approve, or edit the change shown    | Page  1 of  1

RECORD-ID:LADWP-1-1-1-147

OLD:Port

NEW:Harbors


1. Approve change          3. Delete the value          5. Change all remaining
2. Do not change           4. Edit the change           6. Quit

                           Pick a Number:1
```

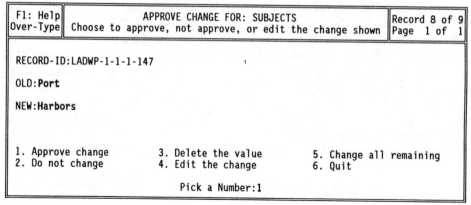

Fig. 6-23. Menu to approve change from old to new subjects entry

subject entry "Port" is changed to the correct Library of Congress Subject Heading "Harbors".

Cataloging standards are the key to creating and keeping a useful database. The History Database program provides automatic facilities for database maintenance, combined with the flexibility of making individual alterations at any point, in order to make it easier for you to maintain good cataloging standards. The automatic facilities will also enable an historical repository to utilize experienced catalogers to correct the work of less experienced catalogers in a quick and efficient manner.

Differences in search and replace in a database and a word processor Those who are already using word processors such as Wordperfect or Microsoft Word might at this point believe that the functions of global search and replace described above could be performed by transferring the data to a word processor, and then transferring it back again to the database. The process performed by the two types of programs is not the same, because the manner in which they hold information is fundamentally different.

A word processor does not separate data into fields, therefore a word processor cannot limit a change to a single field. Let us say that you have incorrectly used "Construction" as a subject term, when the official Library of Congress Subject Heading is "Building." In a database, you can limit the change to the SUBJECTS field. In a word-processor file, there would be no such limitation, thus the "Jones Construction Company" would become the "Jones Building Company."

A word processor could not apply other conditions, such as limiting a change according to information held elsewhere in each record. In a database, we could specify that the change should take place only if the record concerned a given time period, dealt with a particular industry, or included other conditions that would separate the records that we wanted to change from those that we wished to leave untouched. Such controlled change is essential for maintaining the consistency and accuracy of a large database.

Can you access and change individual values within a field? Just as the Pick operating system separates one field from another with a delimiting or boundary character, so Pick can distinguish individual values or sub-fields within a field in the same manner. Pick will even go a step further to individual entities within a subfield, thus providing a full three-dimensional data structure.

Because it can maintain separate values within a field, Pick can treat individual subject headings, entered into a SUBJECTS field, as separate entities for Global Search and Replace and for other purposes. Thus, if the Library of Congress changes a standard subject term from "Agricultural utensils" to "Farm tools" or from "Architecture, Baroque" to "Baroque architecture" you can make that change throughout your database with one command, even though your field contains multiple subject values.

The need to treat individual values within a field also applies to the fields used for the names of persons, the names of organizations, and the names of geographical places. The consistency and accuracy of the subjects and names fields is of paramount importance, because these are the fields that will be searched most frequently.

DOS database programs, such as dBase and R:base, will treat an entire field as only one entity, rather than separating the individual subject headings or names that you have placed there. Thus, with dBASE and R:BASE, the Global Search and Replace command is only useful for single-entry fields.

Data validation: the computer catches our mistakes A database program can greatly assist us in the task of keeping our subject headings and other terms used for searching consistent. For example, if the record includes a FILE-HEADING field, and we write a file heading that does not appear in the index file of previously-used terms that the program maintains, the program can display the unfamiliar term and ask "Did you mean to enter a new term, or did you make a mistake?" In this way, we can avoid the common error of introducing a small and unintended change.

In an institution, where more than one person is entering data, any introduction of a new term can also be flagged automatically. The person in charge of cataloging may then periodically ask the database program for a review of all the records that contain new file headings. As the records are granted final approval, they are removed from the new headings list.

The use of a database program to check our work introduces the concepts of *Data Integrity* and *Data Validation.* Data Integrity refers to the consistency of materials in a database. You must avoid referring to autos as automobiles in one SUBJECTS entry and as cars in another. Data Validation means that the program will help us to ensure the accuracy of our work. For example, we will not be allowed to enter February 29 as a date except for a valid leap year (a year divisible by 4, but not by 400). We will be warned when we enter a subject term that the program has not seen before. In this way we can use Library of Congress Subject Headings without having to refer to the big red books to check the accuracy of every entry.

Visual checks are also useful on occasion. For this purpose you would simply display or print the index file, with the entries in alphabetical order, and each entry identified by the Record-ID of the record in which the entry was held. The index will have the same appearance as the index at the back of a book. The index to the SUBJECTS field of a very small database might resemble the following:

SUBJECTS	RECORD-ID
Automobiles	2; 3
Ship	1
Ships	4; 5

Note the inconsistent use of the singular form "Ship" in record number 1. The term should be changed to the approved Library of Congress Subject Heading plural form "Ships."

Although a program with choices on menus is much easier for a novice operator to use, a program can never do everything that might possibly be required. Even without the use of a program and an index file, we can make a quick visual check of the entries in a single field, across the entire database, by displaying or printing the entries in alphabetical order. Under the Pick operating system, this operation can be performed even if the field contains multiple separate entries, as would be the case for a field holding topical subjects. The SUBJECTS field will be "exploded," with each separate subject term pulled out and listed separately. In addition, the command will "break" the listing whenever a new term appears in the SUBJECTS field, in order to highlight the difference for visual inspection. The following command would accomplish the same purpose as the index listing above. The command will send to the printer a listing, in alphabetical order, of all the subjects terms used, and identify the record in which each appeared.

```
SORT ITEMS BY-EXP SUBJECTS BREAK-ON SUBJECTS RECORD-ID (PI)
```

The response might be the following:

```
SUBJECTS . . . . . . . . . . . RECORD-ID.
Automobiles             2
Automobiles             3
***
Ship                    1
***
Ships                   4
Ships                   5
```

Note again the inconsistent use of the singular form "Ship" and the plural form "Ships."

Data normalization: let the computer handle the details In addition to warning us of errors, a database program can make the process of data entry far simpler and more convenient. Data Normalization refers to the database program feature whereby the program will allow us to enter a given piece of information in a variety of different formats. The program then "normalizes" the data, converting it to the format considered most normal and appropriate.

For example, the Pick operating system can allow us to enter a date in several different formats, as long as the entry can be interpreted as a valid date. Thus, some catalogers may find it more natural to write out a date, others to use numbers separated by dashes, and still others to use slashes as separators. For processing and action fields that would only contain twentieth century dates, some catalogers may write the year in four digits, others in two. The database program can accept the various forms as having the same meaning, and then display the entry in the format that you have defined for the field.

With regard to Library of Congress Subject Headings, the program can provide a list of related terms, including terms that are broader in scope and others that are narrower. If we have entered a term that is not used, such as "Cars," the program can suggest the correct term, in this case "Automobiles." This feature operates in a manner similar to a spelling checker or a thesaurus that you would use with a word processor. Whenever you are working with a previously-defined list of terms, you can pick terms off of a list rather than having to commit the list to memory. The use of a Controlled Vocabulary is greatly aided in this way.

Data Validation and Data Normalization facilitate the use of abbreviations to save typing time and storage space. For example, to identify California in a state location field, a database program can allow you to enter either the two-letter state abbreviation "CA" or the full name "California." If you try to enter either an abbreviation or a name that does not match any of the fifty states, the program will warn you of the error.

The same validation and normalization procedures can be applied to social security numbers, telephone numbers, zip codes, Library of Congress cataloging numbers, International Standard Book Numbers, or any other piece of information which has a defined format or that must be drawn from a limited list of possibilities. You could enter a phone number as "(818) 888-9371" or "818-888-9371" or "818 888-9371" and the program would take the first three digits as the area code. The area code most common to your location could be treated as the Default Choice, if no area code appeared with the number. The program would warn you if you accidentally entered too many digits, or too few. Data Validation and Data Normalization greatly reduce the amount of detail work that humans have to perform, while improving the accuracy and consistency of the information in a database.

How to assign an Accession Number One of the major aggravations of data entry is the need to assign an Accession Number, Record-ID, or other designation that must not be repeated. If two different photos are given the same Accession Number, confusion results. The most commonly used method to avoid the duplication of a number is the log book, in which each cataloger records the Accession Number of every photo cataloged. The time wasted by this redundant procedure is considerable, particularly with an increasing number of catalogers who must share the same log book. If the cataloger is entering the same information into a computer, there should be no need for a duplicate paper entry.

A computer database program can quite easily assign the Accession Number. For example, when filling out a data entry form with the History Database program, while at the Accession Number field, the operator would simply press CONTROL-N for Next Record-ID. The program will assign a number one greater than the largest number used so far. The need for log book entries has been eliminated.

Relational databases

Looking above the level of the individual record, a database may be thought of as a table. The simplest table to represent is two-dimensional. Each vertical column represents a field holding a particular kind of data, such as the name of the photographer or the date that the photo was taken. Each horizontal row represents a record, holding all of the field information for a particular entity such as photograph.

In the following examples from a PHOTOGRAPHERS file, the records contain only three fields, for the name of the individual photographer, the years when he was active, and the city in which he was located.

PHOTOGRAPHER	YEARS	CITY
Bledsoe, James W.	1900–1922	Los Angeles
Padilla, Julius L.	1920–1945	Los Angeles

A relational database can relate together information from different tables. For example, in many cases photographs are not dated. However, other information may be pulled out to construct an approximate date. If the photographer is known, and you can establish the beginning and ending dates of his activity, this information will narrow down the range of possible dates for the photograph.

Time periods can also be established for events, such as construction projects, or for structures, such as buildings or aqueducts. A relational database will allow you to tie this information together in meaningful ways. For example, you could make a search in the ITEMS file for all of the photos taken by photographers who were active in given city for a specified time period. The name of the photographer serves as the link between the two files.

An example from an ITEMS file was previously presented for a photo taken by James W. Bledsoe of the building of the Los Angeles Aqueduct. No date was available for that photo. But in the PHOTOGRAPHERS file, you'll find the years when Bledsoe was active. To find the records in the ITEMS file for photos taken by photographers based in Los Angeles during the period 1908-1913, when the Los Angeles Aqueduct was constructed, a searcher might enter the command:

```
LIST ITEMS WITH PHOTOGRAPHER-CITY = "Los Angeles"
  AND PHOTOGRAPHER-BEGIN BEFORE "1914"
  AND PHOTOGRAPHER-END AFTER "1907"
```

Relational database facilities have allowed us to browse through the database by time period, even though many of the records contained no specific date.

A relational database helps to maintain accuracy and consistency. The features that maintain the accuracy and consistency of our entries are made possible by the relational aspect of a database program. A database program can relate together information from different files in the database. Thus, a file containing the list of our Controlled Vocabulary of subject terms can be used to verify that the terms we are currently entering already appear on the appropriate list, or to offer alternative terms from that list. The same procedure applies to file headings, state abbreviations, or any other controlled material.

When producing invoices, database programs are used routinely to combine a customer name, address, and other information from a Customers file with up-to-date pricing and sales tax information from a Prices file. The program uses the Prices data to compute the total price. If a distinction is made in the Customers file between different categories of customers, such as between non-profit organizations and commercial accounts, the program will adjust the final price by applying any discounts indicated.

Providing a readable report The use of relationships among different files, such as among a collections level, an items level, and a file holding a list of state abbreviation codes, allows you to reduce your typing time without producing printed reports filled with cryptic and confusing abbreviations. Your printing and display for patrons can include the full names.

A database program can provide you with a complete and attractive printed report of your entire database, with indexes for subject headings, personal names, corporate names, geographical names, and other fields commonly used for searching. Such printed reports provide easy access to the materials, even when a computer is not available.

A relational database avoids redundancy and inconsistency. The relational database feature of pulling information from a collections level to supplement information on the items level saves you a great deal of work by eliminating the need to repeat information. It is perhaps more important however, that avoiding redundancy helps to prevent inconsistency.

For example, imagine the dreadful possibility that you are currently managing a photo collection, but you are not using a database program. On each individual invoice for the purchase of photographs from your collection you include all of the information that you need about the customer. You store not only the person's name, but also his address and telephone number. The same information for a given customer is repeated on many records. What happens when his address or phone number changes? You will have to make the change in each individual record in the Invoices file. What will probably happen in such circumstances is that some records will be updated, and others will not. The database has become inconsistent.

It is a standard rule of database management that no record should include a field that holds information only about another field, without relevance to the record as a whole. Fields that relate only to one another, such as customer name, address, and phone number in an Invoices file, should be split off into a separate Customers file, with the address and phone number stored under the customer's name.

Only the customer's name remains in the Invoices file. The customer's name in the Invoices file has now become a link from the Invoices file to additional information stored in the Customers file. In the same fashion, a number entered to identify a collection can give us access to all of the information stored at the collections level. Using that link, the program can draw information from the other file whenever the information is needed, without a special request from the operator. Thus, the printed invoice will automatically include the customer's address, and a printed report for an individual photograph will include the complete name of the collection.

A relational database will allow you to keep a given piece of information, such as the customer's address, in one place and one place only. You can draw upon that information for reports, invoices, and screen displays whenever needed. When the information must be updated, you will have only one change to make, not many.

Virtual Fields

A database program can also create *Virtual Fields* that contain no data of their own, but that display the results of manipulating other fields or that derive from the relationship between one file and another. Thus, although you stored a given piece of data, such as the full name of a collection, only at the collections level, you could still use that name as part of a search statement at the items level. When you use the field designator COLLECTION-NAME in your items-level search, the program knows to look for the complete name at the collections level.

A Virtual Field can also re-define your data in useful ways. For example, each record may contain a field named ENTRY-DATE, for the date when the record was entered. To chart the progress of our cataloging efforts or to check on the consistency of our entries, the date of entry might be employed as the basis of a search. But the manipulation of dates can soon become quite complex, and beyond the ability of a novice or occasional user.

You can define Virtual Fields with names such as ENTERED-THIS-WEEK, ENTERED-LAST-WEEK, ENTERED-LAST-MONTH, and so forth. That will make searching much easier. A field such as ENTERED-LAST-WEEK will check today's date, taken from the computer's internal clock, against the ENTRY-DATE field for each record and select only those records that were entered last week. You could retrieve all of the photo records entered during the previous week with the command:

```
SELECT ITEMS IF ENTERED-LAST-WEEK
```

Library and archival managers are often required to report the number of records cataloged during specific time periods, particularly if the cataloging project is grant-funded. How would you make such a count of your collection? Do you end up leafing through the pages of log books? It would be much simpler to enter a command such as:

```
COUNT ITEMS IF ENTERED-LAST-YEAR
```

What if a single photo record is used to catalog more than a single photo? How would you report on, not just the number of records, but the number of photographs cataloged? Say that the field NUMBER-UNITS (equivalent to MARC 330A: PHYSICAL DESCRIPTION—EXTENT) reports the number of photos or other separate physical units cataloged in a single record at the Items Level. You could return a count of the total number of photos cataloged last year with the command:

```
SUM ITEMS NUMBER-UNITS IF ENTERED-LAST-YEAR
```

Many other variations on these commands are possible. You could easily count the entries made by a particular cataloger or for a specific grant-funded project.

```
SUM ITEMS NUMBER-UNITS IF ENTERED-LAST-YEAR
  AND PROJECT = "National Endowment for the Humanities"
```

Free-text programs

Because free-text programs also store information, some researchers and libraries have mistakenly adopted free-text programs for database usage. But free-text programs lack the essential database features for maintaining the accuracy and consistency of a large body of information. For example, most free-text programs will not perform Global Search and Replace. To change an incorrect subject term or name that has been entered many times, you will have to make the change by hand in each individual record. A free-text program will not maintain relationships between different files. Therefore the program cannot check on the consistency and accuracy of your use of file headings, subject terms, corporate names, or other Controlled Vocabulary items.

The cataloging of materials, whether by an individual researcher, a library, or an archival center, is a very straight-forward database application. A free-text program is intended for another purpose entirely. Free-text programs are used to take in a body of uncataloged information, such as Congressional records, courtroom testimony, or wire service news reports, and to conduct searches for certain words or combinations of words within that free-text environment. Thus, General Westmoreland's attorneys used a free-text program to search for news reports discussing casualty figures in Viet Nam.

Free-text searching is a method for exploratory drilling into unknown territory, to be used on a body of previously-existing text for which no librarian or archivist has entered cataloging information. For example, when writing a history of the Avery corporation (best known for Avery labels), I conducted a free-text search among business reports offered through the Dialog on-line information service.

To find information about Stan Avery, the founder of the company, I finally used fifteen different variations of his name. If the information had been entered by a library or archival cataloger, the Controlled Vocabulary facilities of a database program would have been employed to maintain the consistent usage of a single version. To use a free-text program for cataloging is to defeat the central purpose of cataloging, which is to maintain control and consistency over a large body of data.

To adopt a free-text program for a database purpose is like using a cement truck to move furniture, or a furniture truck to move wet cement. A person who understood the difference between the two types of vehicles would not use them in that way.

Indexing: required or optional? On occasion, free-text programs have been adopted because they offer variable-length fields, in contrast to DOS database programs in which the fields are fixed in length. However, in most cases it is an error to adopt a free-text program in order to save space. Some free-text programs use very large and complex indexes for searching. The indexes are required, not optional. You cannot search a field unless the field is indexed.

The indexes used by free-text programs might wipe out the storage-space advantages hoped from variable-length fields. For example, the free-text program InMagic takes up three times more space for the indexes than for the data.[1] Recently I made a backup of an InMagic file. The backup for an entire file, including both data and indexes, took eighteen disks. A dump of just the data took only five disks. The indexes made up the difference.

Large indexes take time to build. In my own experience of using the free-text program InMagic, a new record with fifteen searchable fields and a total size of 500 characters took two minutes to store. When I subsequently loaded the same record into R:base or Pick, only two seconds were required for storage. If you entered thirty new records into InMagic in a day, you would waste an hour. If you were to make a slight editing change to many records, you would spend more time waiting than editing. The worst result of this inconvenience is that you would probably avoid making necessary changes and corrections.

Free-text programs are not simple. Since searching is performed on the indexes, rather than directly on the data, you must understand how the indexes are constructed for each field. It is not a simple case of "what you see is what you get." For example, although you had seen the name "U.C.L.A." in a printed report, you might not be able to retrieve the name in that form, depending on how the indexing system had been told to handle punctuation marks for that particular field. The indexing instructions may also include ignoring the word "The," as in *The Magic Mountain* and *Tender is the Night.* The index may also ignore "the" in the major European languages, as in the original German title of *The Magic Mountain*, which is *Der Zauberberg.* As a result, in some cases it has proven impossible to search for Los Angeles because "Los" means "the" in Spanish, and the index did not include it.

The complexity of the indexes makes them subject to damage. Since the data can be reached only through the indexes, if you lose your indexes you lose your data. In a case in which I was personally involved, the free-text program InMagic destroyed the data created for a library photo cataloging project nine times in three years.[2] Since I had created the data, I found this situation to be extremely aggravating. InMagic does not provide any method for fixing a file once it has become corrupted. The library's only recourse was to restore the data from backup copies, and then re-enter the data entered after the last backup. A better solution would be to choose a system that does not spoil its own data, and that provides the means of correcting any problems that may occur.

---

[1]This figure is based on my own experience, the InMagic manual, and Carol Tenopir and Gerald Lundeen, *Managing Your Information* (New York, New York: Neal-Schuman Publishers, 1988), page 189.

[2]A comparative study of free-text programs noted that InMagic experienced a "problem with files getting corrupted for unknown reasons." Carol Tenopir and Gerald Lundeen, *Managing Your Information* (New York, New York: Neal-Schuman Publishers, 1988), page 191.

Backup disks do not provide complete security. As explained below, backups created under the DOS operating system are of the "all or nothing" variety, which do not permit even the slightest error. Because it was personally unacceptable to me to have my work destroyed, I spent my own time and money backing up the records that I created. I put them onto a Pick database system.

The danger of the loss of data is not of great importance for a free-text program, as long as the program is used to search entries from news reports and other sources. The data could easily be reloaded from the same sources. The loss of cataloging data, however, would represent the loss of all the time and money spent on the cataloging process.

A database program will allow indexes for faster searching on selected fields, but it will not require them. The database can be searched sequentially, from start to finish, without an index. If an index should become damaged, the data is still intact, and a single command will rebuild the index. As mentioned earlier, the Pick operating system combines the advantage of variable-length fields with the necessary database maintenance features.

The inconveniences and disadvantages of a free-text program for cataloging purposes should not be blamed on the program. Free-text programs are not intended for cataloging. They are intended for searching free text.

Editing

Most database and free-text programs provide only limited editing facilities. In order to change a field, the simplest procedure is to re-type the entire field. The reason for this deficiency is that the programs are intended for short-entry fields. Re-typing is not onerous if a field contains only a few words. But the cataloging of historical materials usually includes one or more long descriptive fields, plus other fields with lists of subject terms or names. To handle the long fields, a program intended for historical cataloging should include the editing features common to word-processing programs.

You should be able to type new data in the Insert mode, in which each new character typed pushes over all those that follow it in the field, or in Over-Type mode, in which the new character replaces an existing character. A Cut and Paste facility should be available to move or copy text from one place to another, either within a field, between fields, or between records.

Your data entry form should not be restricted to the size of a single screen. The form should stretch over as many as twenty screens or pages. You should be able to jump immediately to any page within the form.

You should also be able to jump back and forth between records. In the History Database program, when you are entering, editing, or displaying data, you can jump back immediately to the previous record. You can also jump back to the first record added, edited, or displayed in the current session, and later resume with the record that you were using when you made the jump. The records used in your current session are held on a list. You can move back and forth through the list.

Restructuring the database

Change is inevitable and must be prepared for. Information will be used in ways that were not anticipated when the cataloging project began. A database program should allow you to restructure the database, adding new fields, deleting others, and changing the meaning of some fields, without requiring that information be re-typed or that the database be dumped out to a backup file and then reloaded.

If a program does not facilitate change, inertia and an unwillingness to face the task of making necessary corrections will grow as the database becomes larger. Change will be laborious if a free-text program or a filing program, which stores information in isolated files, has been used instead of a true database program. One change may also set off a chain reaction of other changes that must be made. The catalogers and searchers will drift into a state of passive resistance. They will try to ignore problems and inconsistencies with their computerized information, while they resort to the old methods of scanning through log books and rummaging through drawers.

The Pick operating system makes change far easier through Data Dictionaries, which maintain a distinction between the actual information held in a database and the order and meaning of that information. Each file holding data has two levels, a dictionary level and a data level. The dictionary level defines the meaning and order of the information in the data level below.

Several data files can share the same dictionary. The sharing of dictionaries allows you to quickly and easily create a second data file that will have exactly the same structure. The second file might be used to hold data on a different subject, to hold data that may require a security clearance to access, or, perhaps only for testing purposes, to try a new procedure.

The identifying field names for the fields contained in our records are stored at the dictionary level. Because of the independence that Pick maintains between dictionary and data, we can call the same field by several names, by including synonyms in our dictionary. For example, the MARC field for topics is number 650, officially entitled "SUBJECT ADDED ENTRY—TOPICAL HEADING." For the convenience of the computer user, we can allow several varieties of the MARC field name to be used in search statements. An experienced MARC user could simply ask for "650". Others would probably prefer to ask for "SUBJECTS" or "TOPICS". We can give them both. For our printed report, we might include both the MARC number and a helpful description by printing the field name as "SUBJECTS[650]".

The Pick system allows you to provide synonyms for anything, not only field names but also file names and even commands. Such renaming is possible because Pick is entirely dictionary-driven. The system looks for the meaning of each command and name in dictionaries. You need only change or add to the dictionaries to change the vocabulary. This feature has made it easy to adapt Pick to foreign languages. All of the commands, file names, and field names that the database uses can easily be provided in Spanish, French or another language.

Importing and exporting data

Because a database program can restructure a database at will, the program can easily convert the data for import and export. For export, the program will convert the data from your internal format to whatever format the receiver desires. For import, the program will accept the data in the sender's format, and then convert the information to the format that is most efficient for your needs.

A database program can readily convert its data for use by another program. For example, I use three different programs to manage and store information: Rbase, the History Database program running under Pick, and the free-text program InMagic. I often enter data on a small portable computer, the Radio Shack Model 100. When I am ready to transfer the information from the portable device to a larger machine, the Convert During Transfer Menu shown in FIG. 6-24 appears, to ask if and how the data is to be converted. In this manner, the same data can be converted for use by different programs. The data could also easily be converted for use by any other database program, such as dBase or Paradox, which treats data in a standard, structured manner.

```
            CONVERT DURING TRANSFER?

                1. No
                2. Rbase
                3. Pick
                4. Free Text (InMagic)

                  Pick a Number:1
```

Fig. 6-24. Convert During Transfer Menu

A database program will generally only require that each record and field fit a predetermined length, or that each record and field begin and end with certain special characters. For example, to convert a file with the History Database program to or from another database program, you need only tell History Database the beginning and ending characters that the other program uses to designate fields and records.

MARC is a format for Machine-Readable Cataloging. It is not a program. But the same conversion considerations apply. A database program can convert the information it holds from some other format to pure, orthodox MARC and then back again. It is important to understand that the MARC format is only a medium for exchange. The usefulness of the MARC format derives exclusively from the ability that it gives a library or archival center to exchange data with other repositories. It is a common medium for communication, like a trade language that might be spoken in the marketplace, but not necessarily at home.

MARC can be made much easier to use by providing descriptive field names and by presenting the fields in a data entry form grouped together in a way that will seem most natural to the cataloger or searcher. In addition, rather than requiring you to enter the MARC Leader, Directory, and Indicators, the program can assign these or use Default Choices that you can over-ride.

The database program will store the data in the manner that provides the greatest speed and flexibility for day-to-day operations, rather than in the orthodox MARC format. However, when you want to send the data to another repository or to an online network such as RLIN (Research Libraries Information Network) or OCLC (Online Computer Library Center), the database program will convert each record to MARC format before the record is transmitted.

The sort of conversion required to convert a record from your own internal storage format to MARC format is a typical database operation. A business subsidiary will often be asked to forward a copy of its records to the main corporate headquarters in a different format, to be used by a different hardware or software system. Since the MARC format does not lend itself to efficient computer storage or searching, nothing is to be gained by keeping the data in that format for day-to-day use.

In any case, to store all of your data in the MARC format would be impossible in practical terms, because the format continues to change. Presently the different MARC formats for various types of media are undergoing consolidation into a single format for all. You will not want to change your entire database each time that the MARC format undergoes a slight evolution. Instead of changing your database, you will only change the manner in which you export MARC format data.

A database program allows you to convert one or more records from the storage format that is most efficient for daily use into whatever format you require for transfer. You might send out your data in three different formats for three different purposes. You might also import data in three different formats from three different sources. The program can make the conversion from one or more external exchange formats into the internal format that is most convenient for you. In this way, a database program gives you flexibility for exchange, both for export and import, and flexibility for the future as the various formats evolve.

Easing the transition from manual to automated records

Pick's variable-length fields and database facilities ease the transition from a manual cataloging system to an automated one. It is common for a repository to have index cards, collected over many years, that contain only a few fields of information. The organization wishes to change to a more complete cataloging procedure using the MARC format. But the staff is faced with a long, painful transition period in which every search must be conducted twice because some materials will be referenced in the cards, others in the computer, and the terms and formats used will be different in each location.

Since Pick imposes no space penalties for leaving a field empty, you could use a record format that includes all the fields that you want for eventual use, but you would actually fill in at first only those fields that correspond to what you already have on the index cards. Under Pick, there would be no disadvantage to allowing the other fields to remain bare until you have the opportunity to complete them.

The information taken directly from the old index cards could be typed into the database by clerical staff. The use of Default Choices would speed that initial data entry task. You would then employ the database functions mentioned above, such as Global Search and Replace, Data Validation, and Data Normalization, to change the information to the form that you desire.

For example, if the staff has used a home-grown set of subject terms, you would use Global Search and Replace to change each term into the nearest equivalent from the Library of Congress Subject Headings. You could thereby change the subject term "Cars" to "Automobiles" in the SUBJECTS field across the entire database.

With regard to fields in which it is the format rather than the data that must be converted, it would probably not be necessary to retype the entries. For example, it would not be necessary to retype dates in order to convert the year from two digits to four. The program would first check that each date entered actually constitutes a valid and intelligible date. The program would then print or display that date in the format that you specified, without the need for any change in the data. Recall that under Pick, you can change the format of a field merely by changing the dictionary definition of the field. To change the format of a date field from

"04-25-45" to "04/25/1945" only requires changing the field definition. You do not have to change the data.

The process of copying your old index card information and transforming the data for use with a Controlled Vocabulary and standardized formats could be accomplished very quickly through the use of database management facilities. You would then complete the other fields for the MARC format as you have the opportunity. In the meantime, all of your data, however limited, would be stored in the same place and in the same format.

7

Keeping your data secure

As explained previously, a database file consists of individual records, each of which consist of individual fields. One record is separated from another, and one field is separated from another, either by fixed-length, or by special characters called delimiters.

Figures 7-1 through 7-3 show a database file for BOOKS as the file might look to a computer in a database of fixed-length fields, and in a Pick database of variable-length fields. Figure 7-1 shows information as it would appear in a report that would be displayed on a computer screen or printed. Separate fields contain the information for RECORD-ID, AUTHOR, TITLE, YEAR, and PUBLISHER.

```
RECORD-ID:1
AUTHOR:Clark, David L.
TITLE:Programming with IBM PC Basic and the Pick Database System
YEAR:1989
PUBLISHER:TAB Professional and Reference Books

RECORD-ID:2
AUTHOR:Sandler, Ian
TITLE:The Pick Perspective
YEAR:1989
PUBLISHER:TAB Professional and Reference Books

RECORD-ID:3
AUTHOR:Sisk, Jonathan
TITLE:Programmer's Guide to Pick Basic
YEAR:1987
PUBLISHER:TAB Professional and Reference Books
```

Fig. 7-1. BOOKS database report, printed or displayed

The information seems perfectly clear. Even if the field names did not appear on the report, you could assume that "1989" represented the year of publication and that "The Pick Perspective" was the title of a book. The computer is not so smart. To the computer, "1989" could just as well be the author or publisher. To distinguish one field from another, the database program must provide a map for the computer.

Database programs that use fixed-length fields allocate a fixed amount of space for each field within a record. The computer distinguishes one field from another and one record from another by position. For our example of the BOOKS database, the following fixed lengths in spaces have been allocated.

RECORD-ID: 10
AUTHOR: 20
TITLE: 60
YEAR: 4
PUBLISHER: 40
TOTAL FOR RECORD: 134

The program will take up the amount of space allocated for each field, whether or not the data requires it. Thus, the AUTHOR field will always be twenty spaces long. A fixed-length field is like the bed on which Procrustes forced his guests to lie. If the guest was too short, he was stretched to fit the bed. If he was too tall, he was chopped down to size. If our author's name is longer than twenty characters, we are out of luck.

The program using fixed-length fields will find each field and record by position. If the first record begins at character position 1, then the program will know that the RECORD-ID field occupies spaces 1-10, the AUTHOR field holds down spaces 11-30, TITLE takes up spaces 31-90, YEAR occupies 91-94, and PUBLISHER takes positions 95-134. By the same process, the program will know that the entire first record occupies spaces 1-134, the second record holds down 135-268, and the third record is located at positions 279-402. The program can quickly find any field in any record by adding up the allocated record and field lengths to calculate the starting and ending positions of the field. In FIG. 7-2, the BOOKS data file is shown as it would appear to a computer using a fixed-length fields program. The underline character "_" has been used to represent the blank spaces not needed by the data, but still allocated by the program for each field.

```
1_________Clark, David L._____Programming with IBM PC Basic and
the Pick Database System__1989TAB Professional and Reference Boo
ks____2_________Sandler, Ian________The Pick Perspective________
________________________________1989TAB Professional and Referen
ce Books____3_________Sisk, Jonathan______Programmer's Guide to
Pick Basic____________________________1987TAB Professional and R
eference Books____
```

Fig. 7-2. BOOKS data file, with fixed-length fields separated by position

Note the large amounts of blank space wasted by the fixed-length method, even though the lengths in this case were chosen for the examples. In practice, you would have to allocate much more space for AUTHOR and TITLE in order to hold long names without having to cut them off.

The Pick database system uses delimiters rather than fixed–lengths. In FIG. 7-3 the caret "^" represents the Field Delimiter that appears at the end of every field to mark the boundary point between the end of one field and the beginning of the next. To find a particular field, Pick will count Field Delimiters. The underline character "_" represents the Record Delimiter, which marks the end of each record.

```
007C1^Clark, David L.^Programming with IBM PC Basic and the Pick
 Database System^1989^TAB Professional and Reference Books^_0053
2^Sandler, Ian^The Pick Perspective^1989^TAB Professional and Re
ference Books^_00613^Sisk, Jonathan^Programmer's Guide to Pick B
asic^1987^TAB Professional and Reference Books^_
```

Fig. 7-3. BOOKS data file, with variable-length fields separated by delimiters

When a record is stored, Pick will also store a number for the actual length of the record. The number appears in hexadecimal in the first four character positions of the record. (Hexadecimal numbering, based on sixteen, is easier for a computer to understand than decimal numbering, based on ten. Computers do not have fingers and toes to count on.)

Note how much more compact and economical the Pick system of variable-length fields is, compared to the method of fixed-length fields. Pick stores the same amount of data in far less space. So what could go wrong with either of these very orderly schemes for distinguishing individual records and fields? The error most likely to occur is that a record will be stored on the disk in an incomplete form. Imagine that you have entered a record for the BOOKS database on a data entry form, and that you have told the program to store the record in the database. The program is writing the record onto the hard disk, but halfway through the TITLE field, electric power to the computer is cut off. Perhaps there was a power outage, or someone accidentally kicked out the plug, or the computer malfunctioned. When power is restored, the disk now holds a file that the computer cannot completely understand.

The extent of the damage will depend on how the data is stored, and the various remedies that might be available for fixing the problem. Under Pick, once you identify the record where the problem has occurred, you would compare the record length number, which is stored in the first four characters of the record, with the actual position of the Record Delimiter character "_". If the actual length and the length number stored do not match, a Group Format Error has occurred. You would change the record so that the record length number matches the actual length of the record.

In a database, indexes can be used to provide faster access. An entry in an index file points to the records holding a particular value in the same way that an index in a book points to the pages holding certain words. For example, an index in a book might tell you that information about "Oil-well drilling" appears on pages 13, 27, and 54. An index file in a database might tell the database program that the SUBJECTS file holds the Library of Congress Subject Heading "Oil well drilling," and that these records have the Record-IDs of 13, 27, and 54. Access to records on this subject will be faster because the database can look in the index rather than having to look through the SUBJECTS field of every record.

If a record has been written incompletely to disk, then the indexes might also be out of joint. Perhaps you deleted the heading "Oil well drilling" from a record, but the computer did not delete the index entry before power was shut off. The index still points to a record where the appropriate heading no longer occurs. The normal recourse in these circumstances is to issue a command that will cause the program to rebuild all of the index files. If you are using a free-text program that only provides access to the data through indexes, then to lose the indexes means that you have also lost the data.

The simplest solution to a problem is often to prevent it from happening. Take precautions to prevent power cut off. Make sure that the plug will not come out accidentally.

Use a surge suppressor to dampen the vagaries of the electric line. If power outages occur in your area, invest in a UPS (Uninterruptible Power Supply), which consists of a heavy duty battery that will give you about fifteen minutes to save your file and shut down the computer after the electricity has gone out.

Make regular backups of your data. If your database becomes corrupted, and the task of fixing the errors is beyond your experience, then you would restore the data from the backup and re-enter the information that was entered after the backup was made.

Backup and restore

Under the DOS operating system, when a file exceeds the size of a single floppy diskette, you must use the BACKUP command to store a backup copy of the file from a hard disk to a series of diskettes. As a database grows, the backup may stretch over twenty or more diskettes. The danger in this procedure is that the backup constitutes a chain that is only as strong as its weakest link. If a single error creeps into one of the diskettes, the whole backup will fail. There is no opportunity for a selective restore from diskettes and records that remain undamaged.

On two occasions, once with a DOS database program and once with a DOS free-text program, I discovered quite by accident that my backup was worthless. You would normally learn the horrible truth only when it's too late, when the backup is needed. If I had not made the discoveries in time, all of the data would have been lost. The Pick operating system provides for selective restoration. If only one record is damaged, then only one record would be lost, not the whole database.

Plan a schedule of backups

Do not copy over the same disk or tape each day. The more you use a disk or tape, the more quickly it will wear out. Rotate your disks or tapes on a schedule, always keeping several different backups preserved, rather than relying on one single set of disks or tapes. Another advantage of keeping several backups is that if you accidentally deleted data or changed it in a manner that you want to reverse, you can restore the data from your earlier backup versions.

Recommended schedule and forms

The following schedule is a recommended for backups:

- Use a different disk each day of the week. Label the disks "Monday", "Tuesday", etc.
- Keep a separate disk for each Friday in the month. Label the disks "1st Friday", "2nd Friday", etc.
- Keep a separate "End of month" disk, for the last workday in each month. Label the disks "End January", "End February", etc.
- At the end of the year, replace your daily and Friday disks with new disks. Recycle the old disks by reformatting them. Use them in DOS for less-important files.

If you receive error messages when using a disk, replace the disk. Reformat the disk and use it in DOS for less important files. Store the end-of-month disks in a safety deposit box or other secure location away from the site where the computer is located. Use an off-site location so that if a fire or other disaster destroys your computer, it will not destroy all of your backups also.

As your backup extends over several disks, number the disks clearly, so that they will be inserted in the proper order. Always keep extra disks on hand, already formatted and labeled, so that you will not be surprised by a message to insert another disk when you have no extra blank disk available.

When you purchase new disks, format and label them immediately, so that no one will accidentally insert the wrong type of disk for a backup. At the bottom of the label identify the type of disk, high-density or low-density, and its capacity. Also write down whether you are using the disk in the DOS operating system or in Pick. You can format a disk in DOS, and then use it in either DOS or Pick. But once you have used the disk in one system, you cannot use it in the other without reformatting the disk.

The Save Database procedure, which you begin from the main menu of the History Database program, will save your entire account, rather than saving only a single file. Your account contains all of your data files, as well as other information relating to your use of the computer. The name of your account will be "HISTORY.DATABASE" unless you have designated another name. The method for saving an entire account is known in Pick as an ACCOUNT-SAVE. This information has been included on the sample label to make sure that anyone who later tries to restore the data will know exactly what the disk contains.

The label shown in FIG. 7-4 is for disk number one, for the first Friday of the month. The disk is 3.5 inches in size. It is a high-density disk, holding 1.44 megabytes of data. When you put a label on a 3.5 inch disk, make sure that the label does not block the metal sleeve, which must slide back and forth when the computer reads your data.

```
HISTORY.DATABASE Account-Save
1st Friday, disk #1




Pick
3.5 inch High-Density (1.44 Mb)
```

Fig. 7-4. Sample backup disk label

Sample forms for your backup schedule are shown in FIG. 7-5. At the top of the form, write in the location of extra blank disks, and the type of disks that should be used, so that anyone making a backup will find and use the proper disks. The disks would be one of the following types:

- 3.5 inch, high-density (1.44 megabyte)
- 3.5 inch, low-density (720 kilobyte)
- 5.25 inch, high-density (1.2 megabyte)
- 5.25 inch, low-density (360 kilobyte)

HISTORY DATABASE
Computer Database Management for Research, Writing, and Cataloging
24851 Piuma Road. Malibu, California 90265-3036. Phone: (818) 888-9371

Keep a disk for each day of the week: Monday, Tuesday, etc.
Keep a disk for each Friday in the month: 1st Friday, 2nd Friday, etc.
Keep a disk for the last workday in the month: End May, End June, etc.
For each backup, write your initials and the number of disks used.

Month: Year:
Location of Extra Blank Disks:
Type of Disks Used for Backup:

1st Week:

Monday By: Disks:	Tuesday By: Disks:	Wednesday By: Disks:	Thursday By: Disks:	1st Friday By: Disks:

2nd Week:

Monday By: Disks:	Tuesday By: Disks:	Wednesday By: Disks:	Thursday By: Disks:	2nd Friday By: Disks:

3rd Week:

Monday By: Disks:	Tuesday By: Disks:	Wednesday By: Disks:	Thursday By: Disks:	3rd Friday By: Disks:

4th Week:

Monday By: Disks:	Tuesday By: Disks:	Wednesday By: Disks:	Thursday By: Disks:	4th Friday By: Disks:

5th Week:

Monday By: Disks:	Tuesday By: Disks:	Wednesday By: Disks:	Thursday By: Disks:	5th Friday By: Disks:

Last Workday of Month:

End of Month: By: Disks:

Fig. 7-5. History Database backup schedule

Of the types listed, the 3.5 inch high-density disks are strongly recommended. It is also recommended that all of the disks at your site be of the same type, to reduce the danger of someone mixing together low and high density disks in the same backup.

Each person who makes a backup should write down how many disks were used, and include his or her initials in the space provided. The person who makes the backup takes responsibility for following the instructions provided in this guide, and any supplementary instructions that you might add to the form.

Check the number of disks used to make sure that you keep extra blank disks on hand well ahead of the need for them. Photocopy an extra copy of the backup schedule form for each month in the year, and write in the month at the top of the form. Post the schedule next to the computer.

Who gets to change the data?

If an extra terminal is to be placed in a public area for use by patrons, you will want to allow the patrons to see the data, but not to change it. If you also use the computer to keep records for staff payroll, you would allow some people both to see and to change the data, others to see it only, and others not to see it or to change it.

Security procedures will make it possible to restrict access. However, it will not be productive to institute more security than you really need. The correct observance of security procedures adds an extra degree of learning inconvenience that seems to yield no tangible benefit. At a minimum, the operators will have to remember separate account names or passwords to access the system. Occasional users will tend to have difficulty remembering the names and passwords, and to leave the codes written on slips of paper in their desks. If security procedures are not followed strictly, they are worse than useless because you will think that your data is safe when it is not.

The Pick operating system makes security about as easy to observe as it can possibly be. When you log onto the Pick system from a terminal, Pick will ask for your account name. In addition, a password may also be required before you are logged onto Pick from that account. An account may be thought of as similar to a directory under the DOS operating system, but the Pick account method is far more powerful.

Under Pick different operators can be given different account names, with access to different files. Access may be permitted for reading the file, for changing it, or for both. For example, Tom may be allowed both to read and to change the Payroll file; Jane may be allowed to read it but not to change it; and Dick may be prevented from either reading or changing.

Separate accounts may vary, not only in what files they access, but also with regard to the commands that each account is allowed to use. Each account can be assigned a high, medium, or low-privilege level. The lower privilege levels have a more restricted list of commands available to them.

A user can also be prevented from using any specific command. As mentioned above, Pick is entirely dictionary-driven. Pick looks for the definition of each command word that you use in the Master Dictionary of your account. The dictionary method makes it possible to supply the same command words in Spanish and other languages by placing synonyms in the dictionary. The user of a given account can also be prevented from using certain commands simply by removing those command words from the account's Master Dictionary. For example, the Pick system has a built-in editor that you call up with the command "EDIT". To prevent someone from using the editor, simply remove the "EDIT" command from the Master Dictionary of that person's account.

An operator can also be restricted to using only a single program. When the individual logs onto an account, the program starts up automatically. When the user is finished with the program, then he or she is logged completely off of the system. If he or she tries to break out of the program by pressing the BREAK key, the program simply restarts at the beginning. A terminal set aside for patron use would presumably be restricted in this way to a program that allowed searching of the data, but not editing.

8

Cataloging strategies

The goal of this guide, to combine computer database and cataloging practices, will in some cases be stymied by conflicts in procedures between the two methodologies. Some cataloging rules have survived from the era of the typed card catalog to complicate the lives of computer database searchers. These conflicts will be resolved on a case-by-case basis.

In time, the conflicts will hopefully disappear as the methodologies merge. In the interim, the approach of this guide is to avoid creating nonstandard cataloging entries, and to attempt to use the facilities of computer database management to meet those cataloging standards that have any potential for future usefulness.

Filing strategies

When cataloging collections or gathering research materials, the various pieces of information and the objects described will differ in many ways. A very basic policy issue for you to decide is what categories of information you will place in the same file, and which you will store in separate files.

Materials can differ in many ways. The option of separate file storage should only be considered for differences that are so important and basic to the materials that when you are looking for information about one type of material, you would not want to also get information about the other. The following are examples based on the three types of differences: cataloging agency, subject, and form of material.

If several different cataloging agencies use the same computer system, they might want to keep their files separate to avoid confusion. The term "cataloging agency" in this context could refer to different departments in a library, or to a husband and wife, both putting data into the same computer. Separate files can help prevent marital disharmony in the same way that separate checking accounts can. Materials on different subjects might be kept in separate files if each subject-file had a cohesive unity and was completely different from the other subject file. This might occur in the case of separate and well-defined projects.

For example, imagine two different institutional history projects undertaken at the same time, with virtually no overlap in information. By keeping separate files, you could search for information on one organization under a given Library of Congress Subject Heading, such as

"Finance" or "Income," without having to wade through information on the other organization. The institution might be concerned about the confidentiality of the information collected. Separate files would avoid the embarrassment of accidentally including one organization's data in a printout meant for the other institution. In the case of a repository with an isolated collection on a particular subject, such as 17th century Dutch paintings, and with nothing else remotely similar to that topic, separate files could simplify searching.

The third type of difference is the form of the material. An example of separate files for different forms of material would be keeping information on your photographs in a file separate from information on manuscripts. The advantage of this arrangement is that when you are searching for a visual image on a given subject, you will not have to wade through the non-visual materials, or add to your search statement.

The issue of separation by form of material brings up the question of creating not only separate data files to hold the information, but also separate data dictionaries to define the fields that will be stored. The MARC format grew as a family of formats for the following seven different types of materials:

- Books (MARC-BK)
- Serials (MARC-SE)
- Maps (MARC-MP)
- Music (MARK-MU)
- Archives and Manuscripts Control (MARC-AMC)
- Visual Materials (MARC-VM)
- Machine-Readable Data Files (MARC-DF or MARC-MRDF)

The seven different formats are now being integrated into a single format. However, although a given field might be allowed for any of these types of material, what you would put into the field might differ. It might therefore be useful to have data dictionaries with different field names and explanations, for use by catalogers and searchers.

When you're considering separating material by form or any other criteria, such as subject, project, or cataloger, you must make a decision among the following three conditions. I have presented them in my own order of preference:

- Same dictionary, same file
- Same dictionary, different file
- Different dictionary, different file

Among the many advantages that Pick has over other database systems is the ability for several data files to share the same dictionary. Under Pick, this is a simple matter. When the data files are created, the same dictionary is specified.

The data for the separate files would be stored separately, without having to create and maintain a separate dictionary for each data file. The need to maintain separate-but-identical dictionaries would be time-consuming and aggravating, and it would almost inevitably lead to errors.

Taking advantage of Pick's provision for variable-length fields, in which fields left empty do not waste space, my preference is for "Same dictionary, same file". It will be easier to search for and handle the data if there is no confusion as to which file the data is in. In the case of differing forms of material, it may not be obvious whether a given item belongs with manuscripts or with visual materials. Subjects also tend to overlap. A cataloger is likely to search for a record and not find it because he or she is looking in the wrong file.

In my own case, I recently wrote two separate institutional histories at the same time, one for the Avery corporation and one for the California Club. I kept all the data in the same file without conflict. I made distinctions by adding to search statements the condition:

```
WITH PROJECT = "Avery"
```

or:

```
WITH PROJECT = "California Club"
```

Similar search distinctions could be made in regard to form of material. For example:

```
WITH GENRE = "Maps"
```

If the subject matter is absolutely distinct, as in the case of a museum holding a separate collection that pertains to nothing else in the institution, or if data files are most usefully separated by different departments responsible for the data, take advantage of Pick's common dictionary for several data files. The departments might later consolidate or decide to put their data into the same file. Then it will be a simple matter to copy the data from one file to another.

Differences between libraries and archives

When writing a history of Los Angeles, I researched the role played by women aircraft industry workers during World War II. When I visited the National Archives, however, I was told that I could not simply ask for materials according to a Library of Congress Subject Heading such as "Women aircraft industry workers". Instead, I had to ask for the materials according to the name of the agency that created or maintained them. In this case, the correct designation was "Office of War Information, 1942–1945".

The difference in points of access illustrates the differences between libraries and archives. In a library, each book is described in individual terms as to its author, title, and the subjects. In contrast, archivists are primarily concerned with controlling large quantities of material. The individual pieces of material might not have much meaning in isolation. For example, one letter in a correspondence file would not be easily comprehended without an understanding of the people, agencies, events, and prior communications to which the letter referred. The letter has far more value as part of the agency's administrative records than as an isolated correspondence. Conceptually, the archival parallel to a published book is not the individual letter, but the collection as a whole. The pieces of correspondence have meaning within the context of an entire collection, just as the individual pages of a book have meaning within the context of the entire work.

The nature of archival materials has led to the principle archival unity. Archival principles hold that a collection that was created or maintained as a whole should be kept intact, rather than separating out the individual items and storing them according to a classification scheme. The collection should be regarded as an organic whole, in which the parts derive most of their significance from their relation to other parts and to the entire collection.

According to archival principles, the meaning of each individual item may best be understood in context with other items. Thus, you would not pull out individual letters and scatter them about the repository according to subject matter, mixing them with letters and papers from other sources. An individual letter will probably be better understood if it is placed within the context of the correspondence that preceded and followed it.

The principle of archival unity (also called by the original French term, "*respect des fonds*") runs counter to the researcher's desire to have subject access. Computer cataloging can provide an answer, since a computer database will allow access to materials via many different paths. The materials need not be arranged by subject in order to access them by subject. A subject search can be conducted in the computer database. The database will show the locations of all the different materials that pertain to a given subject.

Database searching, however, presupposes cataloging. Archivists have traditionally used the collections level to describe the materials they hold. Researchers may be disappointed to learn that they cannot call up a search of all the letters in the Edward Dickson Papers file, in which the founder of UCLA made disparaging remarks about the hated rival, the University of Southern California. But it is clearly unrealistic to expect the archivist to go through all thirty-seven boxes of the Dickson Papers and to analyze each letter for all of the references and allusions that it contains.

In archival cataloging, the question is always how deep should you go. The answer is generally to establish basic control over the materials with collection-level descriptions, and to descend to greater levels of detail and specificity as time and opportunity allow.

Gaining basic control

It is a standard strategy to catalog materials first at the collections level, in order to gain basic control of your materials, and then to proceed downward to greater levels of detail as time and opportunity permits. That strategy assumes, of course, that your holdings do not consist of a myriad of small collections.

An emphasis on providing reference services would suggest that you next individually catalog those items that are likely to be in the greatest demand. However, that suggestion has a chicken-and-egg quality to it, since you might not know what you have until you go through and catalog the materials.

Simplified cataloging procedures using computer database management should greatly help the cataloging process. Take a good look at how much time, effort, and concentration is required for the various kinds of cataloging, and who is capable of doing it. Those staff members or volunteers with less skill and experience might be able to enter into the database the information that already appears on the backs of the photographs or on file folder labels. More knowledgeable individuals can later use database Global Search and Replace facilities to assign correct subject headings and to fill in other fields.

Collections, series, and items

Librarians generally catalog individual items, while archivists usually catalog groups of items together. The published book in a library will thus be described in the card catalog as a single item. Archivists will generally catalog an entire collection as one item, or break that collection down into various kinds of series and groups.

An archival collection, such as the papers of Edward Dickson held at UCLA Special Collections, will generally be stored in boxes. Each box will have some unifying factor, such as correspondence written by Dickson, correspondence received by Dickson, or papers and reports from the meetings of the Regents of the University of California. Within each box, the items are arranged in chronological order.

Cataloging, however, does not have to stop at the collection or the box level. There may be several appropriate levels of description, from records that describe the collection as a whole, to others that describe parts or series within the collection, to records that describe individual items.

A researcher taking notes on *Southern California Country: An Island on the Land*, by Carey McWilliams, might note that chapter 14, entitled "The Politics of Utopia," describes political movements in southern California. The researcher might go further to record that the story of the founding of the Thirty-Dollars-Every-Thursday movement appears on page 305 (of the original, 1946 edition).

In the same manner, a cataloger going through the Dickson papers might group together as a series the heated exchange of correspondence between Dickson and fellow regent Francis Neylan on the subject of the university's loyalty oath. Such a grouping would be particularly appropriate if researchers were likely to seek out either Dickson, Neylan, or the loyalty oath controversy as a focus of interest. The cataloger might even select a single crucial letter for item-level attention. However, the cataloging record for the letter would describe it within the context of the series, and the record for the series would place it within the context of the collection. Thus item-level cataloging takes place only within the context of previous collection-level cataloging.

Cataloging focus

The purpose of a cataloging activity determines the focal points and layout of the information in the cataloging record. Each method of intellectual control constitutes a conceptual framework for viewing the material. Different frameworks could be applied to the same material, and a single framework could be used to describe a wide variety of materials.

The kinds of institutions and individuals listed below each desire a different type of control over their materials:

- Archives: The materials are seen within the context of provenance, the history of the custody of those materials. The materials reflect the history of the agency that created them, and would have far less meaning if separated from that context.
- Library, Monographic: A book is identified by the information on its title page. The book stands alone, and does not require links with other materials in order to have meaning.
- Library, Serial: The individual issue of a periodical or other serial publication is recorded within the context of the sequence of publications. The library uses the cataloging record to manage its accession of additional issues.
- Historical museums: The object's use is of prime importance. The object is thus seen within the context of associations, including producer or manufacturer, owner, user, cultural practices, and other materials used with the object.
- Science museums: Physical features distinguish one object from another.

- Historical researchers: The individual unit of material is seen within the context of the themes and theses that the researcher is attempting to develop and prove. The researcher does not value the item simply because it is there, but because he or she can use it to prove something. Thus, figures on the declining patronage and revenues of the urban electric railway systems in the 1920s, 1930s, and 1940s for one researcher would have importance within the context of the theme of the growing dominance of the automobile, while another researcher would look for signs of a conspiracy against the trolley cars.[1]

Group like materials together

When you start cataloging, it will be slow at the beginning. It will seem that there are many different kinds of choices to make and many different types of information to enter. You will find, however, that as you continue to catalog the same kind of material, most of the choices become repetitive, and can be handled by the program as Default Choices. The only effort that you will need to make will be to look over the defaults to make sure that they will apply. For example, as long as you are cataloging photographs of airplanes, the term "Airplanes" can remain the SUBJECTS[650] field. You will also find that you will become more adept at applying the other terms related to aviation as you catalog more photos on the subject. Your work will become both faster and better.

When you switch to a different type of material, and the defaults are no longer appropriate, the operation will slow again. The effect will be greater in proportion to the areas of description involved. For example, if you are still cataloging nitrate 4 x 5 negatives, but the subject has shifted from aviation to agriculture, you must deal with different subject terms, but not with different terms for physical description. If you are moving from aviation photos to farm tools, then both subject content and physical description have changed.

Grouping like items together will greatly facilitate cataloging. My own personal observation is that a comparison of cataloging like items together, and cataloging those same items interspersed among very different kinds of material, would yield approximately a three-to-one differential. If like items are cataloged together, they will be cataloged faster, better, and more efficiently.

The cataloging will be faster because the cataloger will not have to search for the appropriate terms. The appropriate term will in many cases already be there from the previous record. The cataloging will be better because terms will be assigned more precisely and more consistently. Examining like items together makes their differences and their points in common much easier to identify.

The cataloging will be more efficient because duplicate and near-duplicate items will be spotted immediately. Items containing the same information will be grouped together in a single record, rather than being cataloged separately. David Bearman, formerly of the Smithsonian, relates the story of a project to catalog sheets of postage stamps, which began by separately cataloging each stamp on a sheet. If identical items are dispersed widely across a repository's holdings, the cataloger might inadvertently perform a similar feat of absurdity.

---

[1]The descriptions of the first five categories are paraphrased from: David Bearman, "Intellectual Control Methods," *Archival Informatics Newsletter*, Volume 2, Number 4 (Winter 1988/89), page 1.

Group materials together before cataloging, to the extent that it is practical to do so. You should not, however, violate the archival principles of keeping together items that share a common origin, and respecting the original arrangement of those items. Common origin and original arrangement will probably provide a degree of similarity between items that will aid cataloging. But if an original arrangement that would provide information about the materials does not really exist, as is often the case with photo collections, then group for cataloging efficiency.

9

Creating a database of names and addresses

The same data structure can be used for different purposes. This chapter will show how a database of names and address, similar to a personal address book, can also be utilized as a membership roster and as a system for tracking influential leaders within a community or profession. The same basic structure, with additional fields appended, could be used by a writer surveying publishers as potential outlets for his material, by a political aspirant looking for donors and supporters, by an investment counselor seeking clients, or by a football coach looking for a fast defensive linebacker.

In each case, the core of information describes the individual or institution, specifying name, address, phone number, and affiliations. Each database also highlights subject categories where your particular needs and requirements, and the interests and abilities of each individual or institution listed, intersect. These points of intersection might include a commitment to saving the whales, an interest in model railroads, influence on the local planning board, or the ability to help your historical society preserve a collection of photographs that, like John Brown's body, are presently "a-moldering in the grave".

The most common mistake made by those embarking on database management is to focus on the uniqueness of their needs, and not to recognize a common underlying structure. Cement is cement, whether you are building an outhouse or a cathedral.

The advantages of using the same data structure for different purposes come at the beginning, when the databases are defined, and later, during the continuing process of data entry and maintenance. At the beginning, if you can borrow an existing structure, you do not have to create your own. One of the most frustrating aspects of database management is that you are required to perform the most difficult task, which is to design a database, before you have sufficient experience to know where the booby traps are. If something is available that approximates your needs, it would be far better to adopt a tried and tested structure than to invent your own. You might want to alter the structure later.

Throughout the life of the database, if you have several databases that share the same structure, they can share a common pool of information. For example, the same individual might appear in your personal address book, in the membership roster of your organization, and in your list of community firebrands on a certain issue. If the databases exist on separate computers held by different individuals, the information can be copied from one database to another. As long as the databases shared a common structure, you can copy the information rather than re-typing it.

Everyone needs an address book

Every organization, institution, or individual needs an address book, whether to keep track of personal friends or corporate donors. Almost everyone already has an address book of some sort, written on paper. I have created a sample address book data entry form both as a practical service and as an exercise in database management. Some of the database concepts might be easier to understand when applied to an everyday activity.

Shown in FIG. 9-1 are the data entry fields that might be used in an address book meant for both business and personal use. Do not be concerned that the forms includes more fields than you might need to use. A database using the Pick operating system will take only the space that is needed for the data that you supply.

Consider whether you plan to print the names in the database on mailing labels. If so, you may need to limit the length of the name entries to the size of the labels. An alternative course would be to buy bigger labels. Try to plan ahead for any use of the data that might require that the data fit into a fixed format.

The RECORD-ID is simply a sequential number that should be assigned automatically by the data entry program. A number is more reliable than a name as a unique identifier for the record because several people might have the same name. You might search for or sort records by name. You will not have to remember the number.

Recall that Default Choices will fill in the blanks for you from the previous record on fields that always seem to remain the same. For example, a local historical society is not likely to have many members in foreign countries, but you never know. Until you obtain some foreign members, the entry in fields for country will simply be repeated automatically as "United States" from one record to the next.

Help messages, called up by pressing the F1 key, will show the suggested format for zip codes, telephone numbers, and other fields. In the case of a foreign country, the zip code fields would hold the mailing codes used by that nation, and the telephone numbers would differ in format from American practice. Therefore, although standard U.S. formats are suggested, they are not required.

Multiple entries can be made in any field with a plural name, with each entry separated by a semicolon and space. For example:

```
WORK-PHONES:(213) 888-9999; (714) 555-6666
```

A Pick database will store each of the phone numbers in a separate subfield.

The same form can be used for organizations and for individuals. For an organizational listing, you would not supply the personal name fields that are at the beginning of the form. Instead, you would list individuals in the company in the CONTACT-PERSONS field. The form might also be used by an organization to keep track of members and donors. Additional fields are shown for those purposes.

It might seem simpler to create three different forms for the three different cases of individuals, organizations, and membership lists. However, the forms would overlap on most fields. Searching and data entry will be easier if the fields used are exactly the same rather than

```
CTRL-O:Ins/OT  F1: Help  ENTER:Next Field     ADDRESS.BOOK           Record 5 of 9
 Over-Type     ESC:Done  TAB:  Prev Field  Names and addresses       Page  1 of  1

DATABASE[001]:LACHS                     ENTRY#[001]:111
LAST-NAME:Clark
FIRST-NAME:David
MIDDLE-NAMES:L.
TITLE:
SUFFIX:
GREETING:David
JOINT-GREETING:David and Suzanne
COMPANY:History Database
DEPARTMENT:
POSITION:
CONTACT-PERSONS:
OTHER-WORK-AFFILIATIONS:UCLA Extension; JES & Associates

WORK-STREET:24851 Piuma Road
WORK-CITY:Malibu
WORK-STATE:California
WORK-COUNTRY:United States
WORK-ZIP:90265-3036
WORK-PHONES:(818) 888-9371
WORK-FAX:
HOME-STREET:24851 Piuma Road
HOME-CITY:Malibu
HOME-STATE:California
HOME-COUNTRY:United States
HOME-ZIP:90265-3036
HOME-PHONES:(818) 888-9305
HOME-FAX:

ENTRY-DATE:01/20/1990                    EDIT-DATE:07/13/1990
CATALOGERS:Clark, David L.
SUBJECTS:History; Oral history; Photography; Computers; Cataloging
PERSONS-SUBJECTS:
ORGANIZATIONS-SUBJECTS:
PROJECTS:History Computerization Project
PERSONAL-DATES:04/25:Birthday
NOTE:Wrote "L.A. on Foot" historical guide book, "Los Angeles: A City Apart" for
the L.A. Bicentennial, histories of the California Club and Avery corporation,
"Programming with IBM PC Basic and the Pick Database System" on database
management. Cataloged the Security Pacific Photo Collection at the Los Angeles
Public Library and historical materials for the Los Angeles Department of Water
and Power. Teaches Los Angeles history for UCLA Extension, database management
for JES & Associates.
```

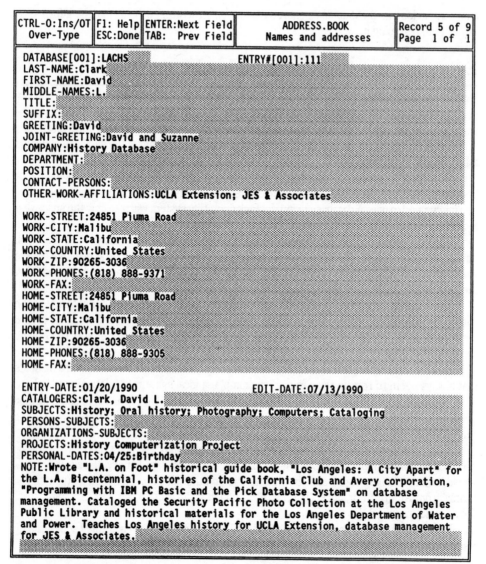

Fig. 9-1. Data entry form, address book

mostly the same. It is likely that information will migrate among the three purposes. If you are looking up your plumber, who owns his own business, would you look him up as an individual or as a company? If many of your friends are active in the historical society of which you are membership chairman, you would not want to enter the same information twice.

The SUBJECTS field would be used for searching when you wanted to find the people or organizations relating to a given subject. For example, you might be looking for the name of your auto mechanic. If you have become accustomed to using of Library of Congress Subject Headings to catalog historical materials, and if your address book is likely to become large, use the same subject headings list rather than making up your own terms. The SUBJECTS entry for your auto mechanic would be "Automobiles—Maintenance and repair".

The PERSONAL-DATES field would be used as a reminder to send cards for birthdays, anniversaries, and other special events of a personal nature. The field will contain two pieces of information separated by a colon. You would type the name of the event first, then a colon, then the month and day. If a person's birthday was on the Fourth of July, the entry would be:

"Birthday:07/04"

As explained earlier in the section on "Database Management," you can create Virtual Fields (also called Calculated Fields) to search for information in convenient ways. The Virtual Field PERSONAL-DATES-MONTH will return just the month of a personal date. To retrieve all the records with personal dates in the month of April, you would enter the search command:

SELECT ADDRESS.BOOK WITH PERSONAL-DATES-MONTH = "April"

The most commonly used personal date for sending cards would probably be Christmas. Because the format for this field includes both the date and the occasion, you could distinguish between those to whom you would send Christmas cards, Hanukkah cards, Druid Winter Solstice cards, and more generalized, nondenominational, cards of "Season's Greetings". The Virtual Field PERSONAL-DATE-EVENT would retrieve your Christmas card list with this command:

SELECT ADDRESS.BOOK WITH PERSONAL-DATE-EVENT = "Christmas"

Shown in FIG. 9-1 is a sample record, such as the Los Angeles City Historical Society might keep for me.

Membership roster

If the ADDRESS.BOOK database will also be used as a membership roster by an organization, other fields would be added, as shown in FIG. 9-2.

```
JOINED-DATE:10/01/1976
EXPIRE-DATE:01/01/1992
MEMBER-CATEGORY:Regular
OFFICES:Director; Chairman, History Computerization Project
OFFICES-PAST:Director:1976-1985, 1988-1991; Program Chairman:1983
COMMITTEES:
COMMITTEES-PAST:Nominating:1988-1989
VOLUNTEER-JOBS:Lecturers; Teachers; Photographers; Historians;
Computer programmers; Computers--Study and teaching; Catalogers
GIFTS:
```

Fig. 9-2. Data entry form, membership fields added

To facilitate the handling of our database as a membership roster, we will create a synonym name for our ADDRESS.BOOK file, calling it also MEMBERS. You can enter a search statement using either file name.

Pull volunteer workers from the membership database

Our membership roster form contains an element of redundancy that in most cases would be considered undesirable. The fields OFFICES, OFFICES-PAST, COMMITTEES, COMMITTEES-PAST, and VOLUNTEER-JOBS all describe work that the individual has done for the organization. In addition, the field VOLUNTEER-JOBS overlaps somewhat with the field SUBJECTS. Thus, the term "Photography" may appear in the SUBJECTS field, to indicate that the person knows about or has some relationship to photography, while the term "Photographers" appears in the VOLUNTEER-JOBS field to indicate that this person actually has taken photographs for the organization on a volunteer basis. Have you not repeated very similar information?

Yes, you have repeated the fact that the person can take pictures. But you are not creating your database merely as an exercise. Data entry takes too much time and work to accomplish unless you have a clear purpose in mind. Your purpose is to meet the needs of the organization. The needs of a voluntary organization can be stated succinctly, in the following order, as:

- Volunteer workers
- Money

There is a clear distinction between the two fields SUBJECTS and VOLUNTEER-JOBS. The SUBJECTS field indicates only that the person knows something about the subject. The VOLUNTEER-JOBS field tells us that the person has done volunteer photography in the past, and therefore presumably will do so again. Accordingly, the entries in the VOLUNTEER-JOBS field appear in the form of job descriptions, while those in the SUBJECTS field appear as general subjects.

For each field, the terms have been taken from the Library of Congress Subject Headings. If you are going to learn LCSH, you might as well use it for everything. The heading "Computers—Study and teaching" was employed as the closest available term to express the idea of a person who taught people how to use computers, since LCSH does not contain a heading such as "Computer instructors".

If you are looking for someone to take on a volunteer job, such as taking photos of an upcoming event, the first place to look would be the VOLUNTEER-JOBS field. You would enter a search statement such as:

```
SELECT MEMBERS WITH VOLUNTEER-JOBS = "Photographers"
```

Having retrieved your list, you would then take into consideration those factors that require human judgement rather than computer manipulation. Have you asked the same person to take photos at all of your events? Is he or she getting tired of taking pictures? Are the pictures out of focus?

To consider alternative photographers, you would treat the SUBJECTS field as the key to your secondary list. To find everyone in the organization who knows something about photography, enter the statement:

```
SELECT MEMBERS WITH SUBJECTS = "Photography"
```

If the matter at issue is financial, you would also look in the OFFICES-PAST field for former treasurers, and in the COMMITTEES-PAST field for former members of the finance committee.

For these fields, rather than using the Library of Congress Subject Headings, you would enter the exact office and committee names used by your organization.

The fields OFFICES-PAST and COMMITTEES-PAST each contain two elements: the name of the office or committee, and the years of service. The two elements are separated by a colon, similar to our field for PERSONAL-DATES shown before. The History Database program's MEMBERS database includes Virtual Fields named OFFICES-PAST-NAMES and COMMITTEES-PAST-NAMES to allow you to enter search statements on the basis of the name of the committee or office. Thus, to find those who have held financial responsibilities in the past:

```
SELECT MEMBERS WITH OFFICES-PAST-NAMES = "Treasurer"
  OR COMMITTEES-PAST-NAMES = "Finance"
```

If you have not created Virtual Fields, you can nevertheless restrict your retrieval to just a part of the field, in order to search according to the name of the office or committee. You are looking for an OFFICES-PAST field that starts with the word "Treasurer". If you are using a menu to enter your search statement, one of your choices will be "Starts with", as shown earlier in the section on "Search Methods" under "Simple Search".

If you are entering the search statement directly, you would use truncation operators. In the Pick system, brackets are used for truncation. You end the word that you are looking for with a right bracket, to indicate that you want any record in which the field begins with this word:

```
SELECT MEMBERS WITH OFFICES-PAST = "Treasurer]"
  OR COMMITTEES-PAST = "Finance]"
```

To find the sort of person that every organization is looking for, a person knowledgeable in the arcane art and science of fund raising, you would very politely ask the computer:

```
SELECT MEMBERS WITH SUBJECTS = "Fund raising"
```

Getting the person to do it is another matter.

What is the expiration date for a life member?

Reality often intrudes upon our plans for putting information into neat categories. What is the EXPIRE-DATE date for a life member? If you are careless, you may enter a search statement such as the following to find out who has fallen behind in their dues.

```
SELECT MEMBERS WITH EXPIRE-DATE BEFORE "03/01/1992"
```

If EXPIRE-DATE has been left blank for life members, they will receive dunning notices. The result will be to confirm suspicions that computers do not work properly. But, the computer did exactly what it was told. The search statement should have been:

```
SELECT MEMBERS WITH EXPIRE-DATE BEFORE "03/01/1989"
  AND MEMBER-CATEGORY # "Life"
```

(The operator "#" stands for "Not Equal".)

To avoid complicating the search statement with the life membership category, you could set the EXPIRE-DATE entry to a date far off in the future, such as "01/01/2100". However, there will always be the chance that someone will try to use the field in a way that you did not expect.

For example, a new computer enthusiast, wishing to show off his or her statistical prowess, might use the EXPIRE-DATE field to calculate an average for how far ahead or behind the members are on their dues. The calculations may show your membership to be far ahead in their payments, when in fact they are far behind and your organization is near bankruptcy.

For every field you must establish conventions, and those conventions must be documented. Anyone using the database should be willing to read the documentation. Hopefully, your field names will be descriptive and largely self-explanatory. But there will always be cases, such as the expiration date to apply for a Life member, where further explanation is required.

The recommendation of this guide is that conventions not be created that violate accuracy for the sake of temporary convenience. The expiration date for a Life member should be left blank. It's not nice to try to fool Mother Database.

Another solution for the life member complication affecting the use of the EXPIRE-DATE field would be to create a data field named CURRENT to store a "Yes" or "No" response indicating whether the individual's membership is paid up and current. You would only need to search for a "Yes" or "No" in the CURRENT field to find out who is behind in their dues. To locate the dead-beat members, you would ask:

```
SELECT MEMBERS IF CURRENT = "No"
```

But the CURRENT field is redundant. Its "Yes" or "No" is entirely derived from information already stored in other fields, the fields for EXPIRE-DATE and MEMBER-CATEGORY. It will lead to inaccuracies and extra work to store information redundantly. Someone must check the EXPIRE-DATE against the present date and manually change the entry in the CURRENT field to keep the field accurate. If that work is not done properly, members who have already paid their dues will be dunned, and they will not be amused. Organizations hard-pressed to find volunteer labor should not use the computer to create extra work and bad will.

Instead of creating a real CURRENT field to store redundant data, the History Database program's MEMBERS database employs CURRENT as a Virtual Field. Like other Virtual Fields, this CURRENT field will not hold anything. Rather, it will report on the holdings of other fields, checking the EXPIRE-DATE against the present date, and making sure that the MEMBER-CATEGORY field does not contain "Life". A Virtual Field may also be called a Calculated Field, because it performs calculations based on the data held in other fields.

You could have your new Virtual Field named CURRENT return an answer in the form of "Yes" or "No", just as if a real "Yes" or "No" had been stored in the field. Instead, you will further improve both simplicity and efficiency by making CURRENT a Boolean Flag Field.

If CURRENT returned an answer of "Yes" or "No", you would have to worry about the differences between "YES", "Yes", and "Y". Using a Boolean Field, also called a Flag Field, you need only check for existence. You do not need to look for a specific value.

A Boolean or Flag Field can hold only two possible values: something or nothing. The flag is either up, or it is down. There are no other possibilities that you need to consider. As a result, you can list the members who have paid their dues with the simple command:

```
SELECT MEMBERS IF CURRENT
```

To find the delinquents:

```
SELECT MEMBERS IF NOT CURRENT
```

Note in this example that you have combined the simplest methods of data entry with the simplest methods of searching. On data entry, the user is not required to draw conclusions, only to enter the dates and categories. Yet at the time of searching, you need only ask whose membership is current and whose is not. Most importantly, you have a clean database. You have not entered any bogus values, such as memberships expiring a hundred years hence, that would foul up other uses of the data.

You have accomplished ease of use and database integrity by using the Pick database management facilities of Virtual Fields and Boolean Fields. Learning such new concepts is extra work. The average data entry person and the average searcher will not have to learn all of the underlying concepts of the system. But at any installation, someone should understand what is going on. Someone must be the System Administrator. If you are a one-person installation, then the System Administrator is you.

Correlating member categories with amounts of dues

The field MEMBER-CATEGORY was used rather than recording the amount of dues paid because two very different categories of members might pay the same amount. For example, student members and senior citizens may both receive the same reduced rates.

To tie category names to amounts, you simply create a small DUES-AMOUNTS file with the records shown below. In each case, the RECORD-ID is the category name, and AMOUNT is the amount of dues for that category. If the amount required for a particular category is raised in the future, you need only change one entry in the DUES-AMOUNTS file, rather than changing the record for every member.

RECORD-ID	AMOUNT
Student	$10
Regular	$20
Sustaining	$50
Patron	$100
Life	$250

The two files will be tied together with a Virtual Field. The MEMBER-AMOUNT Virtual Field would return the amount of dues paid rather than the membership category. To return both the total amount of dues paid and the statistical average amount of dues paid for all the members of the organization, you would enter the statement shown below. (The field name MEMBER-AMOUNT at the end of the statement indicates the field on which the calculations are to be performed.)

```
STAT MEMBERS MEMBER-AMOUNT
```

A display such as the following would appear:

```
STATISTICS OF MEMBER-AMOUNT:
TOTAL = $13,099.52          AVERAGE = $27.52          COUNT = 476
```

Keeping track of potential donors

The GIFTS field holds two different types of data: the date of a gift, and the amount. The two pieces of information are to be separated by a colon. Multiple values can be entered into the field, as long as each contains a colon separator.

You use Virtual Fields to retrieve the information separately. Your Virtual Fields will look for the colon separator, and return GIFT-DATE and GIFT-AMOUNT. Other Virtual Fields named LARGEST-GIFT, LATEST-GIFT, TOTAL-GIFTS, and AVERAGE-GIFT will return information of use to fund-raisers. The Development Chairperson may scour the database for previous patterns of gift-giving to his or her heart's content, without putting the tedious burden of performing the calculations on the data entry staff. That is what computers are for.

List of community leaders

The same basic data structure employed for the address book can be put into service for the purpose of maintaining a list of community leaders. A database of this type might be used, for example, by the public affairs department of a local water and power utility. The department would be able to ask the database questions such as:

- Who are the current officers of influential groups such as the Los Angeles Chamber of Commerce and the Merchants and Manufacturers Association?
- Who are the individuals in the community leaders database with an interest in the issue of nuclear power reactors?
- Who are the individuals from the agricultural sector, which uses 85 percent of California's water resources? From the related food-processing industries?
- What individuals in the database serve on the boards of commissioners of other public utilities?

The SUBJECTS field explained previously would hold Library of Congress Subject Headings. The headings would serve as access points for the individual's interests, political positions, and the types of economic activities that he or she was involved in, such as "Agriculture" or "Petroleum industry and trade".

The added elements to keep track of are the offices that the individual holds and the organizations in which he or she is active. The fields shown in FIG. 9-3 would be added, just before the final NOTE field. The form has been filled out for a chamber of commerce president.

```
OFFICE:President
OFFICE-BEGIN-DATE:01/01/1991
OFFICE-END-DATE:01/01/1992
OFFICE-ORGANIZATION:Los Angeles Chamber of Commerce
ACTIVE-ORGANIZATIONS:Los Angeles Chamber of Commerce; Merchants
and Manufacturers Association
```

Fig. 9-3. Data entry form, community leader fields added

For political officeholders, the designation for organization would cover the political district or jurisdiction. The community leader data structure would serve just as well for the leaders of a profession. The database would hold information about the officeholders of the most prominent professional organizations.

10

Advice on creating your own database

Information must be broken down into small, discrete units. For example, it might seem simpler at first to create one field called "ADDRESS" and to put the entire address there, including street, city, state, and zip code. But it will not be easy to later select all the entries from California, or the entries with a zip code of 90024, or with zip codes between 90024 and 90049. You could not sort the file of addresses by zip code. Nor could you validate the information at the time of data entry by making sure that the zip code had the correct number of digits, or that a state code abbreviation appeared on a list of state codes.

Segregate data types

Not all information is of the same type. The main types that you will deal with are the following:

- Text, consisting of words, perhaps in the form of complete sentences
- Dates
- Numbers
- Dollar amounts

The different data types must be segregated, or you will not have a database. You will only have a free-form text document. To perform arithmetic on numbers, such as counting the number of photographs that you have cataloged, or to use ranges of dates, such as counting the number of photos that you have cataloged in the past six months, the number and date information must be placed in fields that have been defined for the appropriate data types.

Each data type has its own conventions that must be respected. For example, if you wish to enter the date "January 30, 1989" you might be required to type ""01/30/1989". When entering numbers and dollar amounts, you should not include the dollar signs and commas. These will be supplied automatically when the program displays or prints the information.

Group like fields together

When laying out your data entry form, try to group like pieces of information together, and to place them in logical sequences. If the physical description of an object is necessary, place the physical description fields together, for size, color, numbers of units, etc., and segregate the physical description data from the fields that require more conceptual thinking, such as the fields for subject content.

Place fields together that may repeat the same information. For example, the current custodian of the material and the cataloging agency supplying the information will probably be the same institution. The name of the custodian will probably also appear in the required credit line. The History Database program will allow you to press CONTROL-G to "get" the information from the previous field and place it in the current field.

In most cases a program should not bother you with details about how the information is stored physically. If you are creating your own database, however, you may wish to have some insight into issues of machine efficiency. Within a database record, the fields that are searched most often and the shorter fields should be placed at the beginning. The longer fields and the fields that are searched least often should be placed at the end. In other words, always place your textual fields for notes, summaries, and descriptions at the end of the record.

Assign field names that are descriptive and consistent

Do not use cryptic abbreviations for field names. Use field names that will be as self-explanatory as possible to someone entering data with a data entry form or reading a report. Even if you are the only person who will ever use the database, you are unlikely to remember the meaning of your own abbreviations six months later. What is "SS" supposed to mean? The field name SOCIAL-SECURITY would be more useful. Many database programs will limit the length of a name to eight characters, or limit the total number of characters that all your field names together may take. Pick imposes no such limitations. Do not include spaces in your field names. Most programs will not allow spaces, and in any case they cause confusion.

Adopt conventions for assigning names and apply the conventions consistently. The conventions should help you to remember the names when you must include a field name in a command. In addition, the conventions should give the field names a consistent appearance. The distinction between the name of a field and the data held in the field is not immediately apparent to a novice user or to someone reading a report. The conventions used in this guide are to spell out words completely, to put field names in all uppercase letters, and to connect separate words in a field name with hyphens. For example: ENTRY-DATE, EDIT-DATE. If MARC format definitions can usefully be applied to a field, I strongly recommend doing so. In such cases you might add the MARC Tag numbers to the field name in brackets.

I recommend that you also adopt naming conventions that tell you what type of data is contained in a field. The conventions adopted in this guide are:

- Singular or Plural: Use a singular or plural name to indicate whether only a single value can be entered into the field, or if multiple values can be entered. For example, the name PROJECTS indicates that multiple project names may be included, while FILE-HEADING indicates that only a single file heading is allowed.

- DATE for dates: If the field is used to store dates, end the name with DATE or DATES, depending on whether only one or several dates are allowed.
- # for a whole number: End the field name with the hash mark symbol "#" if the field is to store a whole number, without letters, commas, or decimal points.

Use the data validation features

A database program should provides features for checking that a particular type of data has been entered into a field. For example, if the field is meant to be a date, the program should check that a date has been entered, and warn the user if the program cannot recognize the entry as a valid date.

A database program can also check if a number falls within a certain range, or if an entry appears in an Authority File list. Use all of the features that are available to check on the accuracy of data entries.

Assigning a unique Record-ID

Every record in a database should have an identifier that applies to that record alone. Some systems, such as Pick, require a unique Record-ID. Other systems, such as R:base, do not make such a requirement. Whether required or not, assign an identifier that, when used for commands to copy or delete a record, will apply only to the record that you intend.

How will you use the database?

The hardest part of database management is that you must know exactly how you will use a database before you begin to set it up. It is quite aggravating to spend the time to create a database and to enter several hundred records, only to discover that you cannot accomplish what you had intended.

An example was given previously of putting all of the information on street, city, state and zip code into a single ADDRESS field. You would later find that you could not search or sort the information by the individual elements with the ADDRESS field, each of which should have been placed into a separate field. Placing the elements into separate fields will require a good deal of manual editing.

Rather than setting out to create your own database structures, you might first try to use those provided in this guide. Then modify those structures to suit your needs. If you must create an entirely new database, test your fields and structure thoroughly before entering significant amounts of data. Use the following steps for testing.

Test the database

Using a word processor, enter information for the types of items that you will be dealing with. For example, if you will be recording name and address information, take your present address file and enter the information that you would want to put in a database into a word processor.

Create names for the fields that you want to use. Place each field in a separate paragraph, starting with the name followed by a colon. Type in the data. For example:

```
NAME:Clark, David L.
COMPANY:History Database
STREET:24851 Piuma Road
STATE:California
ZIP:90265-3036
```

As you enter information, you will always find that reality is more complex than your original design. In the address file that you kept with pencil and paper, you often threw in other kinds of information, such as spouse's name, or separate phone numbers for work and home, directions to the person's house, names of projects you had worked together on, or a note that the person had an inside contact at a certain company. There is no substitute for actually entering data to discover what types of data you want to enter.

For each type of information that you can think of, or that you used previously in your manual address book, you must decide on one of the following three courses of action:

- Create a separate field for the information. For example, create a field called SPOUSE-NAME or PROJECTS. Information that would be used in a search statement, or by which a listing might be sorted, should be placed in a separate field. Data that you consider to be of primary importance should be placed in a separate field to remind you to include the information, and to facilitate changes later through database facilities such as Global Search and Replace. Consider also what types of reports you expect to produce, and whether you want everyone who reads the reports to see all of the information that you have collected. Information that may be personal or confidential must be placed in separate fields, so that you will have the option of including or not including that information in a report.
- Put the information into a general NOTES field. This solution would apply to information that is only collected occasionally, and that is free form in nature. For example, directions to the house of a person who lives in an out-of-the-way area. Avoid applying this solution as the lazy way to avoid making a decision. If you stick your most important information into note fields, jumbled together with other kinds of data, you will not have a database. You might as well use a word processor rather than a database program.
- Do not include the information. If you have only a few bits of information that might be personal or confidential, consider whether it is worth including it. You must take extra steps to exclude that information from a printed report, and you might not remember to do so. When you stored the information with pencil and paper, you did not have to make such decisions. When working with computers, it is best to establish regular procedures, and not to vary those procedures for cases that seldom occur.

Write sample reports

Still using a word processor, write out samples for each type of report that you expect to print. Does the report present all the information needed, in a clear manner? Will you want the reports or listings printed or displayed in a certain order, such as by the last name of the individuals and companies in an address book? Will the fields that you have set up allow sorting in the manner that you wish? To sort personal names, you must have either a PERSONAL-NAMES field in which you entered the first name last, or separate fields last, first, and middle names. To apply for bulk mailing rates, you must be able to sort the materials by zip code, and include a full nine-digit code.

Conduct sample searches

Conduct sample searches on the reports that you have created. If the database will be used to handle questions asked by other people, gather sample questions, either from records of past queries or by asking for input. Other people will always think of questions that did not come to mind for you, so go out of your way to solicit their contributions. For example, if you are putting your personal file of names and addresses into a database, your spouse might later ask, "Are there any birthdays or anniversaries coming up this month for which we need to buy presents?" That inquiry would require a separate field for significant dates.

Try out searches that have a reasonable probability of occurring. How will you find all the records for California? If you have included all the location information in one big ADDRESS field, it will be difficult to pick out the two-letter state abbreviation "CA". The search may retrieve any record in which the street or city name contains the two initials. Place the information most likely to be used for searching in separate fields.

Repeat the test

Repeat the process of entering data, printing sample reports, and conducting sample searches so that you are fairly sure that your database will have what you need. It will be much easier, and require much less learning, to make changes now rather than later.

The steps recommended here should make the database as robust and long-lasting as possible. If a database is worth creating your own database and filling with information, then it will probably outlast by a wide margin your original expectations for it, and will be used in helpful ways that you did not imagine.

11

Maintaining a distributed database

A distributed database allows organizations and individuals to share information without the expense and technical complications of maintaining an online system. In an online system, the person entering information is directly connected to the master database via telephone lines. The advantage of an online system is rapid access to the latest information in the master database. The disadvantages are the expense of telecommunications charges; the need for technical experts to keep the system running; the presence of telephone line noise that can disrupt communications, confuse novice operators and slow response times as each keystroke or command is sent back and forth over the telephone lines; and the lack of powerful database management features such as Global Search and Replace, which in an online system could allow a single participant to change the information contributed by others. In some situations it will not be possible to maintain the constant contact that an online system demands, therefore the distributed database method must be used instead.

In a distributed database system, a separate database is maintained by each contributor. Periodically, newly created records, and records to which the contributor has added more information, are uploaded from each contributor to the master database. The contributors will also download edited versions of their own records, which have been placed in a more standardized form or otherwise cleaned up by a database administrator.

As the use of portable computers increases, individuals will find themselves in the situation of maintaining a distributed database. The researcher setting out with a portable computer to collect information in the field might have on the portable device only a portion of the records contained in the larger and more powerful computer back home or in the office. This individual has a distributed database. The desktop computer holds the master database. The portable computer contributes records to that database.

Preserving record consistency

In a distributed database system, the master database and the individual contributing database will both hold copies of the same record. Database records, however, are not static. They change constantly as they are edited and updated to include new or more accurate information.

A distributed database system should include a database administrator whose job it is to maintain the consistency of the records in the master database. In a system for archival, library, or museum materials, the database administrator should be an experienced cataloger with access to the cataloging tools that the library and archival communities have developed for maintaining database consistency. These tools include the Anglo-American Cataloging Rules, the Library of Congress Name Authority File, the Library of Congress Subject Headings list, the specifications for the Library of Congress MARC format, and other guides and authoritative references directed toward particular types of material. The same guides and standards may also be of use outside of the library environment, for the purpose of maintaining database consistency.

When records are uploaded to the master database, the database administrator will check the entries for the names of persons and organizations against the Library of Congress Name Authority File, and otherwise standardize the database record according to accepted cataloging practices. This task is less onerous than it sounds, if database management features such as Global Search and Replace are available for making the changes. If the record is a mess because the contributor did not know how to catalog, then the record should be returned to sender.

At the same time that the database administrator is making changes to the record, the original contributor of the record might also be making changes. The person who wrote the original record might have acquired more complete information on who owned a particular house, or the date and location of a photograph, and on that basis changed the record.

After changes are made by the original contributor and the database administrator, the contributor and the Master Database no longer hold identical versions of the same record. The situation is presented in TABLE 11-1. You can track the changes made to the record by means of the fields EDIT-DATE, which holds the last date when the record was edited, and TRANSFER-DATE, which holds the date of the most recent transfer between the contributor of the record and the Master Database.

Table 11-1. Control of distributed records by dates of transfer and editing

Fields for Administrative Control by Date	**Original Record on Date of Transfer**	**Record Edited by Original Contributor**	**Record Edited by Database Administrator**
EDIT-DATE	01/01/1989	01/30/1989	01/29/1989
TRANSFER-DATE	01/15/1989	01/15/1989	01/15/1989

Because of editing changes made by the original contributor and by the database administrator, we now have three versions of the sme record. According to the entry in the field EDIT-DATE, the original record was created or last edited on 01/01/1989 by the contributor to the distributed database system. You can refer to this record as "Original-Record".

Original-Record was uploaded to the Master Database on 01/15/1989, according to the entry in the field TRANSFER-DATE. TRANSFER-DATE will always tell you the last date when you can be sure that the Master Database version and the original contributor's version were the same. If EDIT-DATE comes later than TRANSFER-DATE, then you know that you have a problem, because the Master Database version and the original contributor's version are no longer the same.

The original contributor changed the record on 01/30/1989, presumably to reflect new or better information. You can refer to this changed record as "Record-Edited-by-Contributor". The database administrator also changed the record, on 01/29/1989. You can refer to this version of the record as "Record-Edited-by-Administrator".

On 02/15/1989 the contributor and the Master Database again exchanged information. Some of the records no longer match, because of editing changes made by either or both parties. How can you reconcile these conflicting records? The program will take the following steps to create the final product, which you can all "Reconciled-Record".

When the person or organization contributing records to the distributed database system gathered together the data to be uploaded to the Master Database, the contributor included all of the records that had been added or changed since the last uploading. These records were selected very simly by comparing EDIT-DATE with TRANSFER-DATE. If EDIT-DATE comes after TRANSFER-DATE, then the record has been added to or changed since the last time that a transfer took place.

In the Pick database system, to compare EDIT-DATE and TRANSFER-DATE to capture all of the records edited or added since that last transfer. You use the Virtual Field in a search statement such as the following, to ask for all of the records for which the record has been added or edited since the last transfer:

```
SELECT ITEMS IF EDITED-SINCE-TRANSFER
```

The packet of records to be uploaded from the contributor will include the record named Record-Edited-by-Contributor. It will be included because in this record EDIT-DATE is later than TRANSFER-DATE. The database program will recognize a conflict between versions of a record if it sees that the Record-ID of a record from a contributor matches an already existing Record-ID in the Master Database. For each record, the program will then compare EDIT-DATE with TRANSFER-DATE to see which version of the record has been changed since the last transfer.

If only one version of the record has been changed, then you could simply allow the latest version to take precedence. For example, if the original contributor had made no changes, but the database administrator had made changes in order to standardize the subject vocabulary used, then the database administrator's version would prevail. At the time of transfer, the database administrator would give the revised record from the Master Database to the contributor. The contributor would use this record to update and standardize his own database.

In the same fashion, if the database administrator had made no changes, but the contributor had made changes, then the contributor's version would prevail. If only one version has been changed, then the changed record has precedence.

When both the Master Database version and the contributor's version of the record have been changed, matters grow more complicated. You cannot simply use the version that was changed most recently, since each was changed independently of the other.

The versions edited by the contributor and the database administrator will probably differ in the types of new or changed information that they contain. The original contributor knows more about the particulars of the document in hand. The database administrator is engaged in applying broad standards of consistency.

Because the types of information supplied by the two parties will vary, you cannot give a blanket precedence for the changes made by one party over the other. You cannot simply over-write the version from the contributor with that of the database administrator, or vice versa. In order to arbitrate between the versions, as far as it is possible for a computer to do, the database program must have access to the three different versions of the record, which were earlier named Original-Record, Record-Edited-by-Contributor, and Record-Edited-by-Administrator. These three versions will be compared in order to produce the final result, Reconciled-Record.

The program will have to retrieve Original-Record from another file, or perhaps from a backup tape or disk. In order to retain a copy of each Original-Record, an extra copy must be made of every record transferred between a contributor and the Master Database.

The program will now compare the three versions of the record, field-by-field. For each field, there are three possibilities:

1. Neither party has edited the field.
2. One party has edited the field.
3. Both parties have edited the field.

If no one has edited the field, then the program will find that the field is the same across all three versions. The field can stay as it is. No action is needed.

If the field has been edited by only one party, then that party's version of the field will conflict with the Original-Record version, while the other party's version of that field will remain identical to the field in Original-Record. The version of the field in conflict with Original-Record is the most recent version, and so has precedence.

If both parties have edited the field, then both versions of that field will conflict with Original-Record. At this point, human intervention will be necessary. The program will present all three versions of the field on the screen, ask the user to choose one version, and then give the user the opportunity to make editing changes to incorporate any desired features of the other versions.

More detailed levels of machine arbitration are possible. In the Pick database system, the database program could compare individual sub-fields (also called values) within a field, just as individual fields were compared before. For example, each individual subject heading within a SUBJECTS field would constitute a sub-field. If both parties had simply added new sub-fields to the end of the field, then both sets of additions could be included in the final Reconciled-Record. If sub-fields had been inserted or deleted in the middle of the field, then matching would be more difficult.

The same matching process would take place in the case of an individual who took part, but not all, of his or her database on the road. The database program would compare the records from the Master Database on the desktop machine and the records uploaded from a portable computer first on a Record-by-Record basis and then, if need be, field-by-field, to find the points of conflict between different versions of the same record. The individual, acting as his own database administrator, would make the final arbitration.

Pick dictionary definitions for maintaining a distributed database

The definition for EDITED-SINCE-TRANSFER states that if EDIT-DATE is greater than TRANSFER-DATE the field will return a result of "True". If EDIT-DATE is not greater than TRANSFER-DATE, the field will return null.

Note the distinction in the dictionary definitions for the date fields between dates that are to be shown in external format as "MM/DD/YYYY", and dates in internal format, which Pick will report as the number of days before or after December 31, 1967. The internal date fields do not carry the conversion "D/". The Virtual Field EDITED-SINCE-TRANSFER will use the internal dates for its comparison. (See FIG. 11-1 and FIG. 11-2.)

```
Record-ID:  EDITED-SINCE-TRANSFER
01          A
02          0
03
04
05
06
07
08          A;"True"["1","4"*(N(EDIT-DATE-INTERNAL)>N(TRANSFER-DATE-
              INTERNAL))]
09          L
10          4
```

Fig. 11-1. Dictionary definition for virtual field EDITED-SINCE-TRANSFER

```
Record-ID:  EDIT-DATE        EDIT-DATE-INTERNAL
01          A                A
02          1                1
03
04
05
06
07          D/
08
09          L                R
10          10               10

Record-ID:  TRANSFER-DATE    TRANSFER-DATE-INTERNAL
01          A                A
02          2                2
03
04
05
06
07          D/
08
09          L                R
10          10               10
```

Fig. 11-2. Dictionary definitions for date fields

12

Practical considerations

When considering how to proceed with the computerization of your present historical research and cataloging activities, it's easy to get confused by the many features offered by different pieces of hardware and software. In order to make a decision, you have to first understand your own purpose, and then understand the purposes of the various elements of hardware (equipment) and software (operating systems and programs).

The cataloging of historical materials, whether for research purposes or to make a collection of materials available to the public, is a classic database application. Therefore, you will need a database program and a computer that will run such a program.

With regard to hardware, again consider the basic purpose. The function of the hardware is to run the software. If the software that you need will not run on a given machine, then the machine is of no use to you, no matter what its technical merits. In the future, you might want to use a program that you are not aware of today. Therefore, you should choose a machine that is as standardized as possible, meaning that it operates in a standard manner that programs can anticipate, rather than throwing a curve-ball at them. Computers do not like surprises. The machine should be in widespread use, and widely supported, with plenty of documentation available.

Considering that your purpose is to create and store a database, and that the historical information that you collect will not lose value over time, the machine should have a serious storage capacity, with the possibility of enlarging that capacity in a standardized way in the future. The machines most commonly chosen to meet the requirements described are the IBM-compatible personal computers with hard disks. These machines include computers compatible with the IBM PC-XT, PC-AT, or one of the newer models based on the 80386 or 80486 chip. A hard disk size of at least 20 megabytes or preferably 40 megabytes is a reasonable starting point.

My own philosophy in respect to hardware is very conservative. When software products are improved, you can purchase an upgrade to the newer version for a fraction of the original cost. The same option is not available for hardware. Therefore, the main goal in choosing hardware is to leave doors open for the future, since changing the hardware will be expensive. Choose the hardware that is most widely used, because programmers will direct their efforts and attention to the hardware that offers the largest market. As Napoleon observed, God is on the side of the larger battalions.

With regard to software, it is most important to understand the purpose for which the program, and perhaps also the operating system, was designed. Then compare that purpose to your own, and decide how closely they match.

What happens when your data outgrows your present machine?

A cataloging project may be in for a rude surprise when its data outgrows the machine or program with which the information was originally collected. Transferring the data over to another machine or program might not be an easy matter. You might be left with the equally unpleasant choices of re-typing everything or hiring a custom programmer, who may have little understanding of what you are trying to accomplish. How would you transfer the data out of your present system into another? You should find out, before you get in any deeper.

Match what you expect to do with what you are willing to learn

There is no computer and no program so simple and obvious that no learning is required. The Macintosh computer offers a graphical interface intended to guide the user with images, yet a close friend lost an entire book on a Macintosh, because she had not spent the few minutes required to learn the command to copy a file.

First, read the manual. Do not assume that you already know what you want to do. If the manual is well-written, it should give you many new ideas for procedures that will make your work faster and better. Take a few notes on those techniques that seem most relevant to your purposes. Do not write your notes on the pages of the manual itself. When the program is revised and improved, you will receive a new manual.

Under time pressure, never try a new operation for the first time. Midnight the night before an important report is due is not the time to make your first experiment with Global Search and Replace. Experiment with those techniques that you want to use before you actually need to use them. Do not trap yourself into the sort of frustration that is common to computer users by committing yourself to accomplish something that depends on an untried procedure that may not work in the way that you expected. Create a test database with the same structure as your real database, but with only a hundred records. Use the test database to experiment without potential harm to your data.

After you have succeeded with an operation, document any special tricks or features that the manual did not make totally obvious. Keep such documentation in a special notebook or, better yet, write the instructions with a word processor, which will later allow you to modify them easily and to print them out for others to use. A small amount of writing time can save hours of retracing your steps later.

Should you automate?

When should you automate an operation, and when should you not bother? Recall the earlier statement regarding a trade-off between conceptual thinking and drudgery. To automate an operation successfully requires learning and thought. Failures of automation in almost all cases stem from not learning the concepts involved in a process and not thinking through the entire operation. It is not worth while to spend the time required for good-quality learning and thinking unless the alternative is repetitious drudgery. If you are going to perform the task a thousand times, then automate it. If the job need be done only once, then do it by hand.

If you don't want to do it, don't do it

The desirability of the trade-off of learning new concepts in order to escape drudgery may seem obvious, but be warned that not everyone considers it a bargain. Some people are very content with their drudgery. I have seen a library manager complain bitterly about having to learn the concept of a Default Choice. That person was happy to spend her time entering repetitive information.

The only unsolicited advice that I offer with regard to computers is: if you don't want to do it, don't do it. If an individual resents having to learn the concepts involved, then the computer will be used poorly, and the person will return to paper procedures whenever real work needs to be done. When the time comes to find a photograph, he or she will revert to log books and rummaging.

Is your computer guru hurting or helping?

Which of the following are you prepared to believe?

- The check is in the mail.
- I'm going to make you a star.
- You don't need to worry about this computer stuff. I'll take care of it for you.

Hopefully, you answered "none of the above."

Within an organization, it is common for an individual to become the computer guru of the unit, whom others turn to for help when the computer goes on strike. It is natural to wish to rely upon someone with more knowledge. But the goal should be to learn from that person, not simply to be taken care of.

There is a simple rule of thumb to determine if your computer advisor is really hurting or helping. Is he or she willing to give you advice that you do not want to hear, such as suggesting that you need to learn the fundamentals, rather than depending on someone for quick fixes? Does your advisor try to teach you how to solve a problem yourself? Does the advisor point you toward other sources of information, such as computer professionals whom the advisor knows? Does the advisor recommend books that could provide background information for understanding your computer operation?

If not, then the advisor is not helping you. The advisor is only trying to make himself or herself indispensable, and is probably avoiding exposing you to other sources of information because these will reveal how little the advisor really knows.

Simple for whom?

When the features of a powerful, flexible database program are described, occasionally someone asks if it would not be easier or simpler to use a program that is less powerful. The basic answer to that question is that the easiest program to use is one that is intended for what you need to do. The hardest program to use is one that is not meant for your application, and that requires you to use special tricks and gimmicks to try to make the program into something that it is not.

To return to the Kitchen Table test presented at the beginning of this guide, if all you need to do is to keep the scores for your bowling league or store a scrapbook of photos, then you do not need a database program. If you expect to catalog a sizable quantity of materials using the MARC format and a Controlled Vocabulary, then yours is a database application.

The question of simplicity also raises the question, "Simple for whom?" Among the following groups who will be affected by the program, who should decide the priorities for ease of use and simplicity?

- Managers, who decide which program to adopt.
- Catalogers and searchers, who actually use the program.
- Patrons, who use the information produced by the program.

It would seem that the priorities should be: patrons first, catalogers and searchers second, managers third.

A database program can clearly provide information in the most complete and readable form for a patron. A database program can take information from the collections level to supplement the information at the items level, and avoid the use of cryptic abbreviations.

A database program will also be easiest for catalogers and searchers. As explained above, a database program can provide Default Choices and automatic checking of terms from a Controlled Vocabulary that will reduce by more than half the work of cataloging. A database program can also provide simplified search procedures and Virtual Fields that will make retrieving information much easier for novice or occasional searchers.

The concepts presented here took only a short time to learn. Yet it can be very difficult to induce managers to take a deep breath, relax, and spend a half-hour or even five minutes learning new concepts. It is virtually impossible to convey new concepts to managers who are stressed-out with other concerns.[1]

It is to be hoped that the concepts of database management will spread throughout the library, archival, and historical professions whose cataloging tasks present natural applications for database management methods. The trade-off is between thinking and drudgery.

---

[1]Ann Gilliland found that the major stumbling blocks to archival automation were not technical, but educational and managerial. Ann Gilliland, Introduction to special issue on "Automating Intellectual Access to Archives", in *Library Trends*, Volume 36, Number 3 (Winter 1988), pages 501-518.

13

Estimating system requirements

Guidelines for calculating your future requirements for computing power and storage capacity appear in this chapter, as well as advice on the amount of time and work that it will take to complete a cataloging or research project. Using the History Database program, you will be able to call up reports, such as those presented earlier in the section "For Managers", that will show you current and past system usage, and the progress of your cataloging or research. You will be able to compare the results with your estimates to see if your estimates were correct, or if adjustments are necessary.

Speed requirements

An historical repository should put a terminal, or extra computer used as a terminal, on the desk of every staff member who wants to use the database. If you give everyone a terminal that they can use at any time, they will learn to use the computer, and they will make much more effective use of the information that you have spent time and resources to collect. Terminals should also be provided for knowledgeable patrons and researchers. They can search the data without having the ability to change it.

The Pick multi-user operating system makes it both practical and economical to give everyone a terminal. Pick will allocate system resources on demand. How much speed and power you need therefore depends not only on how many terminals you have attached, but also how they are used, and how often. You will not save much money by giving terminals only to your catalogers, who make the greatest demands on system resources, and denying terminals to occasional users, whose demands on the system are far less.

Calculate usage

Take into account the proportion of the time that the terminal will actually be in use. When a terminal is not in use, Pick will automatically shift computing resources to the other stations. If you give terminals to occasional users, both staff and patrons, as recommended here, you do not need to provide each of these users with as much power as a cataloger needs. A cataloger will keep a terminal busy constantly. A reference librarian or archivist helping patrons might not be at the keyboard more than one-fourth of the time.

For each person connected to the system, estimate the fraction of time that person would be actively using the system. Use the fraction for adding up your total number of users on the form shown in FIG. 13-1. A full-time cataloger would count as "1.00". If a person is employed full-time for reference work, but would use the system only about one-fourth of the time, that person would count for one-fourth of one full user, for a decimal fraction of ".25". If a person worked part-time cataloging, and part-time on reference, the proportions would be mixed.

CALCULATE SYSTEM USAGE

Include each person on the system, and add the fraction of time which that person would spend using the database actively:

	Fraction of Time Actively Using Database	Person, Activity
1.		
2.		
3.		
4.		
5.		
6.		
7.		
8.		
9.		
10.		
		TOTAL NUMBER OF FULL SYSTEM USERS

Fig. 13-1. Calculate system usage

After calculating total use, allow for periods of peak demand. If you have two half-time catalogers, they would add up to only one full user. But if they work at the same time, for purposes of training or pooling information, then for those time periods they must be counted as two full users. If you estimate that you will have significant fluctuations in the level of usage, recalculate for the period of greatest demand. Make an extra copy of the form for each ten users. Figure 13-2 provides an example of the calculations to make.

CALCULATE SYSTEM USAGE

Include each person on the system, and add the fraction of time which that person would spend using the database actively:

	Fraction of Time Actively Using Database	Person, Activity
1.	.50	Baldwin, cataloging and reference
2.	.25	Booth, reference
3.	1.00	Bourdet, cataloging
4.	1.00	Clark, cataloging
5.	.50	Hayes, cataloging
6.	.50	Kozo, cataloging and reference
7.	.25	Rudd, reference
8.	.75	Strottman, cataloging and reference
9.		
10.		
	4.75	TOTAL NUMBER OF FULL SYSTEM USERS

Fig. 13-2. Example of calculating full-system usage

Compromise between speed and economy

The level of resources that you decide upon will depend ultimately on the trade-off that you decide to make between speed and economy. Those using the computer will always want it to go faster and do more. As each new generation of IBM PC-compatible computers has been introduced, industry observers have predicted that the faster and more powerful equipment would be put to use only for scientific work-stations and other specialized applications. In each case the observers have been wrong. Everyone has wanted more speed.

Give as much power and speed as you can afford to those who will use the computer productively. The faster the system performs, the easier it will be to entice others into using computers. But do not restrict the number of users on your system for the sake of speed. Speed depends not only on the system resources, but on the knowledge and experience of the human being giving the commands. Those who are given only limited access to the system will never learn to use it efficiently. And do not put off computerization until you can afford something faster. The slowest computer is faster than three-by-five note cards.

Storage requirements

Pick is very economical in its use of storage space. Pick uses variable-length fields, and takes only the amount of space that the data requires. In contrast, DOS database programs such as dBASE and R:BASE take a fixed amount of space for each field, even when the field is left empty. To calculate your storage requirements for Pick, you will not have to make allowances for the padding of fixed-length fields.

Different types of cataloging and research

Estimate the number of records that you will add to your database, and the average size of the records. To do so, first consider the type of cataloging or research that you will be doing. Determining the content of photographs or manuscripts that are not already identified is the most important and the most time-consuming cataloging task to perform, and it requires the highest levels of skill and knowledge. Make an estimate of the proportion of your materials that already carry a satisfactory identification.

The writing of detailed descriptions of photos or documents, with explanations of their historical significance, greatly increases the value of a collection, but it also slows the pace of cataloging, expands average record size, and requires both an historical background and writing ability. Decide whether a short phrase will be satisfactory for purposes of description, or whether you are likely to want one or two paragraphs.

Factor in the time needed for any extra tasks or problems associated with handling the materials. Working with negatives is slower than working with prints. Buildings are easy to identify on negatives, but people are not. When dealing with negatives, especially nitrate negatives that are flammable, the cataloger may also be called upon to decide which photos to make into prints, which to discard, and how to combine negatives for printing on a single sheet. Each of these tasks requires time and skill.

Repeating material from previous records

The History Database program's use of default choices to automatically repeat those elements that remain the same from one record to another will save from one-half to over 90 percent of the typing needed to catalog an object. The program will present the data for each field from a preceding record as a default choice, to accept or to change. The program will first offer as default choices the data from the immediately preceding record. If this data is not relevant, you can instead opt to use as your source any other record in the database.

Default choices will boost cataloging speed considerably, if you have many photos, documents, or other items on similar themes. Catalogers have been clocked at speeds of over 100 records per hour when only a few elements required changing from one record to the next. Make an estimate of the proportion of the material in your typical cataloging record that could be repeated automatically from the immediately preceding record, or from another record already in the database. Cataloging will be faster and more accurate if similar materials are grouped together. Not only will the default choices from the immediately preceding record be available automatically, but information on one photo or document will help to identify another, and the assignment of subject headings, place names, names of organizations, and other descriptive terms will be more consistent.

Group similar items into a single record

Will each item be cataloged separately, or will nearly identical items be grouped together into a single record? The most efficient procedure is to combine into a single record a group of photos taken at the same time and place, by the same photographer, of the same subject. However, if your photos already carry accession numbers that you intend to maintain, then you will need to create a separate record for each photo. Default choices will make the process fast, but considerable space will be used.

When cataloging 8 × 10-inch historical photographs, there are few instances of nearly-identical photos that can be combined usefully into a single record. Photographers working with heavy glass plates and long exposure times tended to take a single, carefully-planned shot of an event. Photojournalists today, armed with 35 millimeter film and motor drives, will take several hundred shots where a turn-of-the century photographer would have taken only one. The photographers of the 1920s and 1930s, using 4 × 5-inch and 5 × 7-inch film, represent an intermediate stage, often taking 5 to 20 photos of the same activity.

The importance of grouping items together will vary, therefore, according to the time period of your collection. Avoid adopting an absolute policy of one photo per record, or you will be swamped when you acquire more recent materials.

Also avoid judging productivity solely on the basis of the number of photographs accounted for. A catalog record describing one 8 × 10 photograph is approximately the equivalent, in work and amount of useful information, of a record describing five 4 × 5 photos or two rolls of 35 mm film. To judge the size of the cataloging task before you, estimate not only of the number of photos or other items to describe, but also the degree to which the items overlap closely in content and origin. Will 10,000 photographs require 10,000 records or 1,000 or 100?

Estimate future record size and number by type of cataloging

When cataloging photographs from the 1920s that carried little or no identification, that required descriptions of historical significance, that were in nitrate negative form, and for which decisions were made on whether to print or discard and how to combine for printing on a single sheet, the average speed of cataloging was 25 records per day, with an average size of 750 bytes (characters) per record. On average, four photos were combined per record, for a daily average of 100 photographs. When there was no opportunity to combine like photographs into a single record, the speed and volume of data entered remained the same, although the number of photographs accounted for dropped to a figure equal to the number of records, 25 per day.

When cataloging photos from the 1970s that carried identification, that required only short descriptions, with an average of 20 photos combined per record, and with considerable repetition in content from one group of photos to the next, a speed of 50 records per day prevailed, with an average size of 400 bytes. The number of photographs cataloged in a day averaged 1,000. When nearly-identical photos carried separate accession numbers, and were cataloged individually but in sequence, the number of records and the number of photographs cataloged in a day both averaged 300, with an average record size of 350 bytes. In one day a cataloger added 170,000 bytes of data to the database, cataloging nearly-identical photos into separate records. If you are trying to estimate either data storage needs or the time required to complete a cataloging project, decisions on grouping together closely-similar items are clearly of major importance.

Data for research use

For a researcher entering data to be used later for a book or article, record size may vary considerably. In some cases several pages of information will be typed into the long DESCRIPTION field. If, however, you view the database record as the successor to the three-by-five note card, and limit each record to information on a single subject or event, then research data can be compared in size and speed of entry to item-level cataloging.

When entering data from minutes of boards of directors and other organizational documents for historical articles and books, a typical pace was thirty records per day, with an average size of 1,000 bytes per record. These records were the equivalent of first-draft manuscript text, and included conclusions drawn from the material. In cases where material was merely copied, the average speed was one hundred records per day.

Collection-level descriptions

Collection-level descriptions, whether for research or cataloging, vary much more widely in speed and size of entry than item-level descriptions. The proportion of material repeated automatically through default choices is smaller at the collection-level than at the item-level, thus more typing is required for the same amount of data entry.

Table 13-1. Cataloging results, daily averages

Records per Day	Bytes Average /Total	Items Average /Total	Type of Cataloging or Research
25	750 18,750	4 100	Item-level cataloging: The items required identification, description and decisions. Nearly identical items were combined.
25	750 18,750	1 25	Item-level cataloging: The items required identification, description and decisions. There were no nearly identical items.
50	400 20,000	20 1,000	Item-level cataloging: The items were already identified, description was short. Nearly identical items were combined.
300	350 105,500	1 300	Item-level cataloging: The items were already identified, description was short. Nearly identical items bearing accession numbers were cataloged separately.
30	1,000 30,000	1 30	Item-level research data: Description was equivalent to a first-draft manuscript.
100	1,000 100,000	1 100	Item-level research data: Mostly copy work rather than original writing.
10	3,000 30,000		Collection-level cataloging: Included the origin and arrangement of the materials, using information already at hand.
100	325 32,500		Collection-level research data: Gathered for bibliographical use, with little description.

For an archivist including information such as the history of the ownership of the materials and their arrangement in the repository, but not describing the contents of the materials in detail, and with all of the information required already at hand, fluctuations in speed and size tended to even out to an average of 10 records per day, and 3,000 bytes per record. An archival cataloger who describes the materials primarily at the collection-level rather than at the item-level will proceed at a much slower pace, and produce much larger records. In that case, daily averages rather than record averages should be used.

Collection-level descriptions entered by a researcher primarily for bibliographical use, and without commentary, will be much smaller than those created by an archivist. The average speed and size of entry was 100 records per day, and 325 bytes per record. The daily total of data entered by the researcher was approximately the same as that entered by the archivist.

Estimating future size

The estimates provided in TABLE 13-1 are based solely on personal experience. Use them as a starting point, and adjust them according to your own experience. Calculate the speed and volume of entry for your previous work. Use these figures to fill out the form shown in FIG. 13-3.

Your speed will at least double when using the History Database program, due to the use of default choices and other features. The size of your entries will probably also increase, as

CALCULATE PROJECT REQUIREMENTS FOR STORAGE AND MANPOWER

Fill in the estimates based on the table of cataloging results above, and the speed and volume of entry of your previous work:

	Estimate	Description
1.		Number of items to catalog or research.
2.		Average number of nearly-identical items which can be combined into a single record.
3.		Number of records to create: Divide 1 by 2.
4.		Average record size, from daily averages above, based on the amount of description needed.
5.		Total data storage required: Multiply 3 by 4.
6.		Average number of records per day, from daily averages above, based on need for identification, description, and decisions, and the use of default choices to repeat automatically data from previous records.
7.		Total days cataloging: Divide 3 by 6.

Fig. 13-3. Calculate project requirements for storage and manpower

these features wean you away from the use of cryptic abbreviations toward the use of a more complete and standardized descriptive vocabulary.

Do not try to economize by using abbreviations or truncating your descriptions. Hard disks today cost less than $10 per million bytes of storage, for an average of about 30 cents per cataloger or researcher, per day. Figure 13-4 provides an example of the estimates to make. The person filling out the form has chosen figures for estimates intermediate between some of those that appeared in TABLE 13-1. Note that the key elements in the example are the forecast that, on average, 10 nearly-identical items can be combined into a single record, and that the availability of identifying information already on hand and default choices from preceding records will permit a rate of 50 records per day.

CALCULATE PROJECT REQUIREMENTS FOR STORAGE AND MANPOWER

Fill in the estimates based on the table of cataloging results above, and the speed and volume of entry of your previous work:

	Estimate	Description
1.	100,000	Number of items to catalog or research.
2.	10	Average number of nearly-identical items which can be combined into a single record.
3.	10,000	Number of records to create: Divide 1 by 2.
4.	500	Average record size, from daily averages above, based on the amount of description needed.
5.	5,000,000	Total data storage required: Multiply 3 by 4.
6.	50	Average number of records per day, from daily averages above, based on need for identification, description, and decisions, and the use of default choices to repeat automatically data from previous records.
7.	200	Total days cataloging: Divide 3 by 6.

Fig. 13-4. Example of calculating project requirements for storage and manpower

Comparison of multi-user and single-user systems

To assess your system requirements accurately, and to fully comprehend the hardware issues involved, you should have an understanding of the differences between multi-user and single-user systems. System resources are far more efficiently employed when they are shared rather than isolated. Those not familiar with multi-user systems might have the impression that a computer with 10 or 20 terminals attached would be slower than 10 or 20 separate computers. The opposite is true, because all computers are not created equal. On a dollars-per-user basis, the more powerful versions of the IBM PC-compatible desktop computer, with inexpensive terminals attached, will give better performance for database usage than will individual but less powerful computers.

Features that would prove too expensive to place on a single-user system become affordable when they can be shared. For database usage the critical advantages provided by a more powerful desktop machine include a larger and faster hard disk, a disk cache controller with its own processor and memory to reduce the need for disk access, increased system memory, a faster and more powerful Central Processing Unit (CPU), and a memory cache that gives the central processor almost-immediate access to certain information.

Each step in the ladder of data storage facilities holds more-frequently used information in slots giving faster access. The difference between one level and the next in speed of access can be on the order of 10, 100, or 1,000 to one.

For example, the hard disk supplied with the original IBM PC-XT was rated as having an average access time of 90 milliseconds, a little less than one-tenth of a second. Hard disks available on the more powerful desktop systems today feature access times rated as low as 10 milliseconds. The memory cache employed by Everex desktop computers has an access time of 7 nanoseconds (billionths of a second), for access a million times faster than on the fastest hard disk. Regular system memory chips, and the memory chips on the disk cache controller card, are not as fast as the memory cache, but they are many times faster than having to read the data from the hard disk.

You use a similar system for your own personal objects, keeping frequently used items closer at hand, and storing less used objects further away. You would not keep your car keys and wallet in a trunk in the basement, nor would you carry your winter ear muffs around with you in summer. For both you and the computer, there is not simply one storage location, but a series of locations, with varying speeds of access, and with priority given to the objects used most recently or most often.

You can easily observe this principle in operation on a Pick database system. If you turn on the system and bring up a particular database record twice in succession, the same record will come up much faster the second time than the first. The first time, it was brought up from disk. The second time, it was brought from memory. If the entire staff is using the same historical database, the information in that database needs to be placed in memory only once, for use by everyone. The information that is needed the most, and used most often, will be the fastest to obtain.

The exception to the rule of faster access for frequently-used information would be if the amount of memory on the system is not sufficient to meet the demands that you are making of it. This situation can be compared to moving books from boxes in a warehouse to bookshelves. If you had enough shelving, you would keep the books that you had already called up on the shelves, for faster access to them the next time. If you ran out of shelf space, you would have to move books back and forth between the shelves and the boxes. The second time that you needed a book, it might have been sent back to the warehouse. As a result access the second time would take as long as the initial access. Thus, it is far more efficient for the staff to share a common multi-user memory pool, which will be large enough to hold a large portion of the institution's database, than to divide system resources between separate single-user machines.

In regard to the comparative efficiency of multi-user and single-user systems, common sense would suggest that on an hourly or daily basis, everyone at a repository is not using his or her computer, or using it for equally-intensive tasks. On single-user systems, if half of the staff are not using their computers, the computing resources locked up in those machines is lost. Even those sitting at their computers are not typing on the keyboards or searching the database at every moment, and for a computer, time is measured in units of thousandths of a second or less.

When cataloging historical data, much of the cataloger's time is normally spent examining the photograph or document, looking through reference sources, or thinking. When searching a database, time is spent reading the data displayed on the screen. On a multi-user system, the full amount of system resources is always available, and will be quickly allocated on demand.

If someone needs to accomplish a task that is particularly demanding on computing resources, such as a global search and replace function performed across the entire database, that person can choose a time when there are few competing demands, and thus have available all the power of the system for a single task. A multi-user system can shift computing power between assignments. It can alternately disperse system resources between many small tasks or concentrate resources for a few big jobs in a fashion not possible on single-user platforms.

The best compromise between single-user and multi-user operation is to allocate to each type of system those tasks for which it is best suited. Most of those working in an historical repository will be primarily engaged in database tasks, adding to the database or searching the information already there. For these users, terminals connected to the Pick multi-user database management system should be provided.

Managers and administrative personnel will need word processors to write letters and reports. These users could be supplied with computers running the DOS operating system, to run WordPerfect, Microsoft Word, or whatever word processor the staff prefers. Terminal emulation programs will allow these computers also to act as terminals attached to the Pick database.

Managers can search the database directly from the computers in their offices, and download information from the Pick database to their DOS word processors for inclusion in letters, articles, and reports. Documents created on the DOS word processors can also be stored in the common Pick database, if desired, and passed back and forth through Pick to the other staff. As an alternative, word processors are available that run entirely under Pick. The Pick word processors could be used from inexpensive terminals.

Printers can also be shared on a multi-user system. Anyone on a terminal, or extra computer acting as a terminal, can send material to the printer. Pick will automatically referee the different printing requests, taking them in the order in which they were received. Printing requests can be marked special priority for immediate printing. Even those staff members using DOS word processors can send their printing requests through Pick to a shared printer.

There are many advantages to sharing printers. Laser printers are much faster, quieter, and easier to load with paper than dot-matrix printers. Laser printers also produce output that is far more attractive and easier to read. The only disadvantage of the laser printer is that, with a starting price of about $1,000, it is more expensive than a dot-matrix machine. In this case also, a multi-user system can make a feature affordable. 10 or 20 staff members can easily share a laser printer, producing better and more pleasing results at a lower price than providing each person with a dot-matrix device.

The sharing of printing resources will also make it feasible to reserve certain printers for certain tasks. Thus, one printer would hold regular paper, and another would hold labels. Printing requests would be sent automatically to the appropriate printer, without any need for manual reloading and adjustment.

14

Estimating costs

The following recommended system configurations have been carefully selected for the best match of price and performance for database usage. Many other configurations in addition to those listed are possible. The systems are presented in order of price, from lowest to highest. Each section details the advantages of one unit over those preceding it.

You could mix and match elements if you wished. For example, you could include a VGA color monitor, a mouse, or an uninterruptible power supply with the mid-range system, or choose a smaller hard disk for a high-performance system.

Everex equipment was chosen for the examples. Everex computers occupy the mid-range between the most expensive systems, sold by IBM and Compaq, and the least expensive systems imported from Korea and Taiwan. The least expensive systems are also the least reliable.

The computers listed below are completely compatible with the IBM PC, and will run both the DOS and Pick operating systems. The two systems will reside in different partitions on the hard disk. You can easily transfer information back and forth between Pick and DOS.

All of the Everex systems described below include the following:

- A front-access control panel
- One parallel port for a printer
- One serial port, for connection to a terminal, to another computer used as a terminal, or to a mouse, modem, or other device
- A 5.25 inch, 1.2 megabyte diskette drive
- A controller card for the hard and floppy disks
- A 101-key keyboard
- Everex disk cache and RAM disk software
- A one-year warranty on all Everex components

Lowest entry level

The following are usage recommendations.

- Pick, Multi-User: 1-2 users only
- DOS, Single-User: Word processing, without graphic displays

Description

A computer based on the 80286 processor and compatible with the IBM PC-AT represents the lowest level of equipment for use of the current version of the Pick operating system. Although Pick will run on the older IBM PC-XT computer, which is based on the 8088 processor, Pick has not been updated for that machine for the past three years. The configuration suggested here will run either Pick or DOS applications approximately six times faster than an XT.

System unit

- System: Everex AGI model, 80286 processor, 12 megahertz speed, small footprint chassis
- Main memory: 1 megabyte
- Ports included: one parallel port, one serial port
- Diskette drive included: 5.25 inch, 1.2 megabyte
- Room for disk drives: the small footprint chassis includes room for three half-height disk drives
- Expansion slots: 8 total (6 are 16 bit, 2 are 8 bit.)
- Warranty: one year, walk-in

DOS

- DOS operating system, for word processing and other DOS programs

Monitor

- Everex monochrome monitor and adaptor

Hard disk

- Everex ST251-1 MFM controller, 40 megabytes, average access time of 28 milliseconds

Table 14-1. Price list: lowest entry level

Equipment	**Price**
Everex AGI 80286, 12 Mz speed, 1 Mb memory	919.00
Everex Monochrome Monitor	153.50
Everex Monochrome Adaptor	77.00
Everex MFM 40 Mb hard disk	399.50
Total	$1,549.00

Medium range with extended memory, more reliable backup

The following are usage recommendations.

- Pick, multi-user: 1-3 users
- DOS, single-user: word processing, without graphic displays

Description

If possible, take the small step in price between the low and medium configurations in order to take advantage of the following differences between the two systems:

- The 80386SX processor, rather than the 80286
- Two megabytes of memory, for faster speed and less disk usage, rather than one megabyte
- A 3.5 inch floppy disk drive, which will provide more reliable backup copies of your database than will a 5.25 inch drive

The major importance of the 80386 processor is that it facilitates access to extended memory. Computer software is increasingly becoming directed specifically to the capabilities of the 80386 processor for handling greater amounts of memory. As a result, the 80386 processor is a much better investment than the 80286. The medium-range configuration presented uses the 80386SX processor, which combines the 80386 processor's internal architecture (moving data 32 bits at a time) with the use of low-priced components designed originally for the 80286 processor used in the IBM PC-AT (which moves data 16 bits at a time).

The 3.5 inch floppy disk is encased in a hard plastic shell. Therefore, the disk is less subject to damage and reliability problems than is the exposed 5.25 inch disk. The 3.5 inch size is presently becoming the industry standard. Use of this size will be necessary to exchange disks with the current IBM computers. A 5.25 inch disk drive is included at no extra charge on all of the Everex models, thus you will still be able to exchange data with machines using the older type of disk drive.

System unit

- System: Everex AGI model, 80386SX processor, 16 megahertz speed, small footprint chassis
- Main memory: 2 megabytes
- Ports included: one parallel port, two serial ports
- Diskette drive included: 5.25 inch, 1.2 megabyte
- Room for disk drives: (The small footprint chassis includes room for three half-height disk drives.)
- Expansion slots: 8 total (6 are 16 bit, 2 are 8 bit.)
- Warranty: One year, walk-in

DOS

- DOS operating system, for word processing and other DOS programs

Monitor

- Everex monochrome monitor and adaptor

Hard disk

- Everex ST251-1 MFM controller, 40 megabytes, average access time of 28 milliseconds

Additional diskette drive

- 3.5 inch, 1.44 megabyte. (The 3.5 inch drive will be configured as drive A, and the 5.25 inch AT-compatible drive will be configured as drive B.)

Table 14-2. Price list: medium range, with extended memory, more reliable backup

Equipment	Price
Everex AGI 80386SX, 16 Mz speed, 2 Mb memory	1,376.50
Everex Monochrome Monitor	153.50
Everex Monochrome Adaptor	77.00
Everex MFM 40 Mb hard disk	399.50
DOS operating system	115.00
Everex 3.5 inch, 1.44 Mb drive	147.50
Total	$2,269.00

High performance with faster speed, greater capacity

The following are usage recommendations.

- Pick, multi-user: 1-6 users. (For 1-3 users, this system will provide noticeably faster speed than the medium-range system.)
- DOS, Single-User: word processing. (With the addition of a color monitor and adapter, this system will provide good speed for graphic displays and Windows.)

Description

The high-performance system has faster speed and greater capacity due to the following advantages, which distinguish it from the medium-range system:

- A full 80386 processor and data bus, rather than the 80386SX, running at a speed of 25 megahertz rather than 16
- A 64 kilobyte memory cache and advanced memory management architecture
- 4 megabytes of system memory, rather than two megabytes
- 90 megabytes of hard disk capacity, rather than 40 megabytes, and an average access time of only 18 milliseconds, rather than 28 milliseconds
- A full size chassis, with room for additional disk or tape drives and expansion cards

The full 80386 processor and data bus, the 64 kilobyte memory cache and advanced memory management architecture, the larger amount of memory, and the faster hard disk drive bring noticeable speed improvements. The processor and bus move data through the system 32 bits at a time. The memory cache and advanced memory management architecture provide the fastest possible access to information used repetitively to carry out a series of instructions, with an incredible access time of seven nanoseconds (billionths of a second). The larger allotment of regular system memory keeps more information at a time in memory, rather than taking the information from the disk. The larger and faster hard disk drive will hold more data, and give you faster access to it.

The speed difference will prove most important as additional catalogers or searchers are attached at the same time to the multi-user History Database program. You can give more users access to the data by adding terminals, or extra computers employed as terminals, connected through additional serial ports. The use of terminals will be explained shortly in the section on other hardware and software.

System unit

- System: Everex AGI model, 80386 processor, 25 megahertz speed, 64 kilobyte memory cache, full size chassis
- Main memory: 4 megabytes
- Ports included: one parallel port, one serial port
- Diskette drive included: 5.25 inch, 1.2 megabyte
- Room for disk drives: (The full size chassis includes room for five half-height disk drives.)
- Expansion slots: 8 total. (6 are 16 bit, 1 is 8 bit, and 1 can be used as either 32 bit or 8 bit.)
- Warranty: one year, walk-in

DOS

- DOS operating system, for word processing and other DOS programs

Monitor

- Everex monochrome monitor and adaptor

Hard disk

- Disk: Everex CDC ESDI 90 megabyte hard disk with an average access time of 18 milliseconds
- Controller: ESDI hard disk controller

Additional diskette drive

- 3.5 inch, 1.44 megabyte. (The 3.5 inch drive will be configured as drive A, and the 5.25 inch AT-compatible drive will be configured as drive B.)

Table 14-3. Price list: high performance with faster speed, greater capacity

Equipment	Price
Everex AGI 80386, 25 Mz speed, 4 Mb memory, 64 Kb memory cache	3,198.50
Everex Monochrome Monitor	153.50
Everex Monochrome Adaptor	77.00
Everex 90 Mb ESDI hard disk	912.50
Everex ESDI disk controller	171.20
DOS operating system	115.00
Everex 3.5 inch, 1.44 Mb drive	147.50
Total	$4,775.20

High performance for heavy usage

The following are usage recommendations.

- Pick, multi-user: 1-6 users. For more than 3 users, or for constant usage, this system is recommended over the preceding system. For more than 6 users, add a disk cache controller with additional memory.
- DOS, single-user: word processing. With the addition of a color monitor and adapter, this system will provide good speed for graphic displays and Windows.

Description

The high performance system for heavy usage is an Everex STEP model computer. STEP is the top Everex line for speed and reliability. Peter Norton's System Information utility rated this system at 30.6 times faster than an IBM PC-XT. A horn concerto that we had played on an XT sounded like a blip on this computer.

The added features of this system are directed towards increasing data security and reliability for situations in which the computer will be used for data entry and database searching all day long every day, perhaps by several users. The advantages that distinguish this system are the following:

- The Everex STEP system unit, the company's top-of-the line unit for system speed and reliability
- A one year on-site warranty, rather than a walk-in warranty
- 160 megabytes of hard disk capacity, with an average access time of 16.5 milliseconds, rather than ninety megabytes with an average access time of 18 milliseconds for the previous model
- An uninterruptible power supply rated at 450 volts, which will provide reliable power in the event of blackouts, surges, or spikes

Most of the advantages of this model over the previous one are not immediately visible, but they are highly recommended for systems that may be called upon for continuous, heavy usage for data entry and database searching, particularly as greater numbers of users are attached to the system.

An uninterruptible power supply (UPS) is an important investment to make to protect your database. It is an absolutely essential investment if your area is subject to power problems. A sudden loss of power, however brief, or a power spike or surge, can easily cause a corrupted database. The greater the amount of data entry or editing activity going on at the time, the greater the chances for problems, as the new data is written to the disk in an incomplete form. The result is an error message warning you of a Group Format Error. When this problem strikes, you must reload the data from your most recent backup, losing whatever has been added since. It is possible to repair a corrupted database using the Pick operating system, a feat generally impossible in DOS, but repair requires on-site technical expertise and several hours of work. It is cheaper to purchase a UPS.

The UPS from Unipower is three inches in height, with a width of thirteen and one-half inches and a depth of eighteen inches. It will fit under a computer or printer. In the event of a power loss, the unit comes on immediately, providing approximately twenty minutes of power to the computer, and sounding a warning. You will thus have plenty of time for an orderly shut-down of the system.

To determine the size of the UPS needed, the standard formula is to divide the size of the computer's power supply by ".7". For simpler calculation, and an extra margin of safety, pick a UPS with a voltage rating approximately double your computer's power supply. A 450 volt UPS will cover the 200 Watt power of a standard PC.

Note that the inexpensive surge suppressors purchased with most personal computers do not provide adequate protection. On one occasion we blew out a monitor by powering-up the computer at the same time that a blender was turned off and on. The computer was connected to a $35 surge suppressor.

Improvements in speed and system durability will prove more important as more users are attached. You would give more users access to the data by adding terminals, or extra computers employed as terminals, connected through additional serial ports. The use of terminals will be explained shortly in the section on other hardware and software. If more than six users will be attached to the system at the same time, a disk cache controller is strongly recommended, which will further reduce the need to read from and write data to the hard disk. For large databases, a quarter-inch tape drive will save the time spent loading floppy disks when making backups.

System unit

- System: Everex STEP model, 80386 processor, 25 megahertz speed, 64 kilobyte memory cache, full-size chassis
- Main memory: 4 megabytes
- Ports included: one parallel port, one serial port
- Diskette drive included: 5.25 inch, 1.2 megabyte
- Room for disk drives: (The full size chassis includes room for five half-height disk drives.)
- Expansion slots: 8 total. (6 are 16 bit, 1 is 8 bit, and 1 can be used as either 32 bit or 8 bit.)
- Warranty: one year, on-site
- DOS: included with system at no extra charge.

Monitor

- Everex monochrome monitor and adaptor

Hard disk

- Disk: everex CDC 160 megabyte hard disk with an average access time of 16.5 milliseconds
- Controller: ESDI hard disk controller

Additional diskette drive

- 3.5 inch, 1.44 megabyte. (The 3.5 inch drive will be configured as drive A, and the 5.25 inch AT-compatible drive will be configured as drive B.)

Uninterruptible power supply

- Unipower PS4.5 450 volts

Table 14-4. Price list: high performance for heavy usage

Equipment	**Price**
Everex STEP 80386, 25 Mz speed, 4 Mb memory, 64 Kb memory cache	3,525.50
Everex Monochrome Monitor	153.50
Everex Monochrome Adaptor	77.00
Everex 160 Mb ESDI hard disk	1,312.50
Everex ESDI disk controller	171.20
Everex 3.5 inch, 1.44 Mb drive	147.50
Unipower PS4.5 450 Volt UPS	637.00
Total	$6,024.20

High performance for desktop publishing

The following are usage recommendations.

- Pick, multi-user, same as the preceding system, "High Performance for Heavy Usage"
- DOS, single-user. (The color monitor and adapter and the mouse equip this system for graphic displays, desktop publishing, and Windows.)

Description

The full 80386-based, Everex STEP system, VGA color monitor configuration provides a powerful system for both Pick multi-user database management and for DOS desktop publishing. This system represents the best long-range value, for usage over the next five years.

For desktop publishing or use with Microsoft Windows, it would not be practical to use a less powerful system. Even full-featured DOS word processors such as Microsoft Word and WordPerfect are greedy of system resources when the programs are used in the graphics mode to show italics, a mouse printer, and differences between fonts. The specific features of this system not included in the preceding unit are the following:

- VGA (Video Graphics Adaptor) color monitor and adaptor. The VGA type represents the most standardized and widely-used high-resolution system for word processing and desktop publishing. The adaptor card includes 256 Kilobytes of extra memory for video display. Additional video memory can be added for Super-VGA capability.
- A mouse, for point-and-shoot capability with word processors and desktop publishing programs. The latest mouse from Microsoft has higher resolution and better control than previous versions.

You would give more users access to the Pick database by adding terminals, or extra computers employed as terminals, connected through additional serial ports. An additional serial port can also be utilized to attach a mouse, modem, serial printer, scanner, or other device.

System unit

- System: Everex STEP model, 80386 processor, 25 megahertz speed, 64 kilobyte memory cache, full size chassis
- Main memory: 4 megabytes
- Ports included: one parallel port, one serial port
- Diskette drive included: 5.25 inch, 1.2 megabyte
- Room for disk drives: (The full size chassis includes room for five half-height disk drives.)
- Expansion slots: 8 total. (6 are 16 bit, 1 is 8 bit, and 1 can be used as either 32 bit or 8 bit.)
- Warranty: One year, on-site
- DOS: included with system at no extra charge

Monitor

- Type: Everex VGA color monitor and adapter including 256 Kb of extra memory for video display. (The video memory can be increased to 512 Kb for Super-VGA capability for an additional $50.)

Hard disk

- Disk: Everex CDC 160 megabyte hard disk with an average access time of 18 milliseconds
- Controller: ESDI hard disk controller

Additional diskette drive

- 3.5 inch, 1.44 megabyte. (The 3.5 inch drive will be configured as drive A, and the 5.25 inch AT-compatible drive will be configured as drive B.)

Uninterruptible power supply

- Unipower PS4.5 450 volts

Mouse

- The mouse would be attached to a serial port.

Table 14-5. Price list: high performance for desktop publishing

Equipment	Price
Everex STEP 80386, 25 Mz speed, 4 Mb memory, 64 Kb memory cache	3,525.50
Everex VGA Color Monitor	502.00
Everex VGA Color Adapter	199.50
Everex 160 Mb ESDI hard disk	1,312.50
Everex ESDI disk controller	171.20
Everex 3.5 inch, 1.44 Mb drive	147.50
Unipower PS4.5 450 Volt UPS	637.00
Microsoft Mouse	126.00
Total	$6,621.20

High performance for up to thirty-three users

The following are usage recommendations.

- Pick, multi-user, 6–33 users. For fewer users, reduce the amount of hard disk storage and memory. For a smaller database, reduce the amount of hard disk storage and eliminate the tape drive.

- DOS, single-user. With the addition of the color monitor and adapter and the mouse included in the preceding system for desktop publishing, this system would handle the most intense graphic applications, such as Computer-Aided Design for architects or for the preservation of historic buildings and sites.

Description

The latest 80486 processor has its own special memory pocket and math co-processor, running at a faster clock speed, with larger amounts of memory and memory cache. The 80486 also includes a disk cache controller to reduce hard disk usage to a minimum, a quarter-inch tape drive for quick and convenient backups of large databases, and a larger, faster hard disk drive. The 80486 will support 33 users simultaneously at a high level of performance. The advantages that distinguish this system from the "High Performance for Heavy Usage" system described above are the following:

- The 80486 processor, rather than the 80386, running at a speed of 33 megahertz, rather than 25
- A memory cache of 128 kilobytes, rather than 64 kilobytes
- Sixteen megabytes of system memory, rather than four megabytes
- An intelligent disk cache controller card with its own processor and 8.5 megabytes of memory, to reduce disk access without using the resources of the central processor or system memory
- A hard disk capacity of 330 megabytes, with an average access time of 10.7 milliseconds, rather than 160 megabytes of capacity and an access time of 16.5 milliseconds for the previous model
- A 375 watt power supply, rather than 200 watts for the units described above
- An uninterruptible power supply rated at 650 volts, rather than the unit rated at 450 volts. (The larger UPS is needed to cover the larger power supply, and will provide a longer interval of time on battery power to shut down the system.)
- A quarter-inch tape drive with a capacity of 150 megabytes, to back up the entire database in one operation

The 80486 processor, running at a speed of 33 megahertz, has a rating of over 20 MIPS (Million Instructions per Second), compared to a rating of 6 MIPS for the 80386 processor running at 25 megahertz. The 80486 chip puts mainframe power on the desktop. It has outdistanced the IBM 3083 mainframe computer in selected benchmark tests (according to *PickWorld* magazine, September 1990 issue, page 68). The 80486 holds a special memory pocket of 8 kilobytes, allowing it to execute a series of instructions entirely within the processor chip, without the need to look elsewhere for the information. The 80486 also includes a math co-processor, to speed up mathematical functions. Everex has enhanced the chip with 128 kilobytes of memory cache and Advanced Memory Management Architecture.

The larger allotment of regular system memory and the intelligent disk cache controller will work together to reduce the need for disk access to a minimum. Information retrieved previously will be held in memory, rather than read from and written back to the disk each time. The disk cache controller carries its own processor and its own memory, allowing it to perform some data management tasks without the need for intervention by the computer's central processing unit. A ratio of two-to-one between system memory and memory on the disk cache controller is recommended. The use of the disk cache controller makes unnecessary the purchase of the regular disk controller.

A quarter-inch tape drive for backup is recommended for large databases, to eliminate the chore of feeding in a series of floppy disks when making a backup. The tape drive will fit below the floppy disk drives in the system unit.

You could scale down your configuration from the system described here if you are not likely to have as many users on the system simultaneously, or if you need at this time to trade a degree of performance or convenience for economy. The areas in which it would be easiest to reduce system cost now, and to upgrade later, are the quarter-inch tape drive, the number of serial ports and the number of terminals to which they are attached, and the amount of memory placed on the system and on the disk cache controller.

If all of your users are not entering data intensively, you could employ one of the smaller and slower hard disks recommended for the systems described above. You do not need to purchase now the total amount of storage space that you will need five years from now. You can add a second hard disk later.

Processors are available that are intermediate in power and price and that fall between the 80386, at a speed of 25 megahertz, and the 80486, at 33 MHz. An example is the 80486, at 25 MHz. However, the strategy recommended here is instead to vary those components that are easier and more economical to upgrade later. It is a simple matter to drop in more serial ports or memory chips or to install a tape drive or second hard disk, and no existing components need be discarded.

For those needing to attach more than 33 users, a version of the Pick system will soon be released to support 66 users on an IBM PC-compatible computer. System memory can be increased to 64 megabytes, and disk cache controller memory can be increased to 16 megabytes. Multiple hard disks can be combined, holding up to 677 megabytes of data each. Digital tape drives will store backups of over a billion bytes. For larger sites, hundreds of users can be supported, with complete software compatibility, on the IBM RS/6000 system.

System unit

- System: Everex STEP model, 80486 processor, 33 megahertz speed, 128 kilobyte memory cache, full size chassis
- Main memory: 16 megabytes
- Ports included: One parallel port, one serial port
- Diskette drive included: 5.25 inch, 1.2 megabyte
- Room for disk drives: (The full size chassis includes room for five half-height disk drives.)
- Expansion slots: 8 total. (6 are 16 bit, 1 is 8 bit, and 1 can be used as either 32 bit or 8 bit.)
- Warranty: One year, on-site
- DOS: Included with system at no extra charge

Monitor

- Everex monochrome monitor and adaptor

Hard disk

- Disk: Everex CDC 338 megabyte hard disk with an average access time of 10.7 milliseconds

Disk cache controller

- Controller: Distributed Processing Technology SmartCache Intelligent Disk Cache Controller (DPT PM3011/70) for the ESDI disk, with Motorola 68000 processor and 512 kilobytes of memory. (The disk cache controller is employed in place of the Everex ESDI disk controller.)
- Memory module: 4 megabyte cache memory module (DPT MM3011/4) on the controller card
- Memory board: 4 megabytes of cache memory on an additional card (DPT MX3011/4), bringing the total memory of the disk cache controller unit to 8.5 megabytes

Additional diskette drive

- 3.5 inch, 1.44 megabyte. (The 3.5 inch drive will be configured as drive A, and the 5.25 inch AT-compatible drive will be configured as drive B.)

Uninterruptible power supply

- Unipower PS6.5 650 volts

450 watt power supply

- High Step 450 watt power supply

Quarter-inch tape drive

- Everex 150 megabyte tape drive, placed in the system unit below the floppy disk drives

Other hardware and software

The Wyse 60 terminal with PC-Enhanced keyboard presents exactly the same screen appearance and keyboard as IBM PC-compatible computers, making it easy for a user to switch back and forth between a computer and a terminal. On both the terminal and the main computer the History Database program provides a full-screen editor with the same functions as a word processor for efficient data entry and editing. Each terminal is attached to the computer through a serial port and serial cable.

Terminal emulation programs

For those who wish to use DOS word processors such as WordPerfect and Microsoft Word, extra computers can be used both as terminals to access the multi-user Pick database, and as

Table 14-6. Price list: high performance for up to thirty-three users

Equipment	Price
Everex STEP 80486, 33 Mz speed, 16 Mb memory, 128 Kb memory cache	7,953.50
Everex Monochrome Monitor	153.50
Everex Monochrome Adaptor	77.00
Everex 330 Mb ESDI hard disk	2,112.50
DPT ESDI Disk Cache Controller, 512 Kb memory	977.50
DPT Disk Cache 4 Mb memory module	761.00
DPT Disk Cache 4 Mb memory card	902.50
Everex 3.5 inch, 1.44 Mb drive	147.50
Unipower PS6.5 650 Volt UPS	729.50
High Step 450 Watt power supply	402.50
Everex 150 Megabyte tape drive	1,412.00
Total	$15,629.00

Table 14-7. Price list for terminals

Equipment	Price
Wyse 60 terminal with PC keyboard	537.00

stand-alone computers to run DOS programs. Even when using DOS, Pick can be employed to pass data between computers or to handle printing requests from many users simultaneously. You can also download data from the Pick database on the main computer to a DOS file on the individual PC.

For use as extra computers, the medium-range system employing the 80386SX processor previously described is recommended. Any old IBM PC-XTs or ATs that you happen to have on hand can also be pressed into service. Each computer used as a terminal will be attached to the main computer through a serial port and serial cable. The terminal emulation program is distributed free of charge by Columbia University.

Table 14-8. Price list for terminal emulation programs

Equipment	Price
Kermit	Free

Serial ports

Serial ports can be installed individually, or on expansion cards in groups of four, eight, or sixteen. Thirty-two serial ports will take up only two expansion slots on the system unit, utilizing two 16-port cards. A serial port has many uses, in addition to attaching a terminal. A serial port can also be utilized to attach a mouse, modem, serial printer, scanner, or other device. (The 16-port boards employ a connector similar to a telephone jack, the RJ45. The 4 and 8-port boards can employ the same type of connector as an option, or they can use the DB25 or DB9 connectors usually employed for IBM PC or AT serial ports.)

Table 14-9. Price list for serial ports

Equipment	Price
Everex Second Serial Port	29.50
Digiboard 4-port serial board	373.00
Digiboard 8-port serial board	552.50
Digiboard 16-port serial board	1,030.00

Serial cables

The serial cable, with appropriate connectors on each end, connects the serial port on the back of the main computer to the serial port on the terminal, or extra computer used as a terminal. The cable for short distances has approximately the thickness of a telephone cord. Beyond fifty feet, a thicker type of cable would be used. As a rule-of-thumb for cable price, whether below or above 50 feet, figure $10 for the two connectors on the ends, and $1 per foot of cable.

Tape backup

A quarter-inch tape drive is recommended for backup for large databases, to eliminate the chore of feeding in a series of floppy disks when making a backup. The tape drive will fit next to the floppy disk drives in the system unit. The list price of a 3M 60 megabyte tape cartridge is $36.00, for a 3M 150 megabyte tape cartridge the list price is $38.00. A quarter-inch tape drive should be purchased only through a Pick dealer, to ensure compatibility. There are no industry-wide standards for quarter-inch tape drives.

Table 14-10. Price list for tape backup

Equipment	Price
Everex 60 Megabyte Tape Drive	962.00
Everex 150 Megabyte Tape Drive	1,412.00

Modems

With a modem connected, you can provide access to your database to remote computers or terminals, and you can reach other online databases, including services such as Historical Abstracts, America: History and Life, and Dissertation Abstracts. You could download data from these services over the telephone line and then transfer the data to your own database files. You can also receive software product support and upgrades over the telephone line.

If you have a group of catalogers or searchers at another location, they can use terminals connected to a single modem with a multiplexor, which will transmit multiple signals over a single communications line, in a manner similar to the stereo transmission of FM radio. Only external modems can be employed with Pick.

Table 14-11. Price list for modems

Equipment	Price
Everex 2400 Baud External Modem with Error Correcting Code	253.50

Part II

Data entry fields

15

Cataloging with a computer database

For the history database described in this guide, data will be entered and stored at two different bibliographic levels, corresponding to two related files: COLLECTIONS and ITEMS. An ITEMS record describes an individual photo or document or a group of like photos or documents. A COLLECTIONS record describes the characteristics of an entire collection of photos or documents. A record in the COLLECTIONS file can pertain to many different records stored in the ITEMS file. Items are contained within collections.

A collection can be divided into parts and further divided into sub-parts, designated by the fields PART and SUB-PART. Archivists generally describe entire collections, or parts of collections, rather than individual items. If a collection is divided into five different parts of series of related items, one collection-level record would be created for the entire collection, and then five collection-level records would be created for the five parts into which the collection has been divided.

Linking items and collections

Information such as the name of the donor of a collection or the credit line required for use of photographs from the collection need be typed only once, at the COLLECTIONS level. The information can be called up automatically whenever an ITEMS entry is printed or displayed. The program will draw the information from the corresponding COLLECTIONS entry. If a collection has been divided into parts, the information will be drawn from the appropriate part of the collection. The capability of combining information automatically from different sources is a standard part of relational database management, which allows a program to "relate" records from different files to each other.

Information that remains the same from one ITEMS record to another within a collection (or a subdivision of a collection) does not have to be re-typed repeatedly, but could be drawn from the COLLECTIONS entry. Considerable time, effort and disk space can be saved by avoiding the repetition of information that remains the same for many items. For example, you would not have to fill in the name of the photographer for each photo if the entire collection was shot by one person, or the name of the author if all of the letters or manuscripts were written by one person.

When the same field appears for both ITEMS and COLLECTIONS, the field in ITEMS can be left blank if information at the COLLECTIONS level is to be used, or filled in if information for the individual item is meant to over-ride the information supplied for the entire collection. Thus, if nearly all of the photos in a collection were taken in California, you could identify California in the STATE field at the COLLECTIONS level, and fill in the STATE field only at the individual photo level when the location is not California.

Who or what is the main entry?

The practice of assigning a Main Entry has been inherited from library card catalogs, which required a master card for each book. That card would be stored in alphabetical order in the catalog under the Main Entry for the book. Although you will probably not be creating a card catalog, it may still be convenient on occasion to print or display your database records in order of Main Entry.

In library practice, the Main Entry is traditionally the author. For visual materials, it is easy to translate that concept to the photographer. For archival materials and collections, the concept of Main Entry occasionally must be stretched. The Main Entry would preferably be the person or the institution responsible for creating the collection of personal papers or administrative documents.

If the documents originated from many sources, the Main Entry could be the person who collected them. An example is C. C. Pierce, who collected photographs for sale to tourists in Los Angeles at the turn of the century. These materials are commonly known as the C. C. Pierce Collection.

For the following recommended data entry fields, the Main Entry will be taken from the following fields, in the following order: AUTHORS[100,700], PHOTOGRAPHERS[100,700], or AGENCIES-OF-ORIGIN[110,710]. The first entry that you make in this sequence will become the Main Entry. If you place more than one name in the field, the first name entered will be the Main Entry.

Different types of materials

The fields listed below were chosen primarily for collections of photographs and manuscripts. The selection of fields, out of those offered by MARC, can be expanded to accommodate other materials such as maps and recorded music. Different data entry forms could be constructed for the different types of materials.

Any format that is intended to accommodate different kinds of materials, and perhaps also the needs of different repositories, will contain fields that are used in some circumstances and left blank in others. Under the Pick operating system there is no penalty for leaving a field blank. The variable-length nature of fields under Pick is one of the prime reasons for choosing that system. The database records can include all of the fields required for each repository and each type of material.

Cataloging and technical issues

Do not include variant forms of name in the bibliographic record. An Authorities File will hold the preferred and variant forms of name for persons and organizations, as well as the headings to be used in subject heading lists and the relationships between terms, such as Broader Term and Narrower Term. For example, an Authority Record for Mark Twain will contain the information that the form of name to be used is "Twain, Mark" and that variant forms of the name include "Clemens, Samuel Langhorne" and "Clemens, Samuel L." The Authority Record will also hold the birth and death dates, 1835-1910.

It is a basic principal of database management that a piece of information should be stored only once. The variant forms for a name should appear only in the Authority Record for that name, they should not be repeated elsewhere in the database. Storing information redundantly is wasteful, time consuming, and eventually leads to discrepancies between the various records, as some are updated for needed changes and others are not.

Place expressions of uncertainty in the note fields

Expressions of uncertainty over matters such as whether an individual reputed to be the author of a work actually wrote it, or whether the attributions of place and time for a photograph are correct, should be segregated into the note fields. I strongly recommend that you do not clutter up the fields for persons, organizations, dates, and places with qualifications.

The conventions for expressing uncertainty used by catalogers on manual systems have included the use of brackets, a question mark, or "ca." for "circa" with date fields. A cataloger who inferred that a particular photograph was taken by Ansel Adams at Yosemite in 1925 might use some combination of the conventions for uncertainty such as the following:

```
PHOTOGRAPHERS:[Adams, Ansel]
PLACE-NAMES:Yosemite?
CAPTURE-DATES:ca. 1925
```

It is easy for a human being to understand the conventions. But the question marks, brackets, and "ca." will create problems in a computer database. At the very least, these conventions will make searching more difficult for the novice.

An entry such as "ca. 1925" will make it difficult for the searcher to find all of the photos taken before 1925 or after 1925, without special provisions for eliminating the "ca. ". In contrast, if only the year were placed in the field, with uncertainty expressed elsewhere, then the searcher could find the information with a simple search statement such as:

```
SELECT ITEMS WITH CAPTURE-DATES AFTER "1925"
```

Conventions such as brackets, question marks, and "ca." will create confusion at the time of sorting and in printed indexes. The entry "[Adams, Ansel]" might be placed in a different location than "Adams, Ansel", as would "ca. 1925" be located differently than "1925". Brackets, used by some catalogers to indicate uncertainty, are employed by some database systems for truncation.

Among the fields presented in this guide for a database of historical materials, uncertainties over time and place should be written in the field DATE-PLACE-NOTE[518]. These types of uncertainties are the most common. Other types of uncertainty, over matters such as authorship, should be placed in the more general notes field NOTE[500].

Express the reasons for the attribution that you gave, and your uncertainty about it, as completely as possible. For example, when identifying a photograph, you might be sure that the photo was taken in Los Angeles county, in California. Furthermore, the appearance of the buildings, automobiles, and clothing styles shown in the photo suggest 1925 as a probable date and Hollywood, which is within the municipality of Los Angeles, as a location. The suggested entries are shown in FIG. 15-1.

```
CAPTURE-DATES[033]:01/01/1925
ERA[045B]:1920-1930
COMMUNITIES[651]:Hollywood
CITIES[651]:Los Angeles
DATE-PLACE-NOTE[518]:Date and place are approximate. The
buildings, automobiles, and clothing styles shown suggest
Hollywood around 1925.
```

Fig. 15-1. Recording uncertainty for date and place

An alternative method for indicating uncertainty would be to put into the DATE-PLACE-NOTE[518] field notations such as "ca." and "?". For printing catalog cards or information transfer, the contents of the field could be used for date and place. (See FIG. 15-2.)

```
CAPTURE-DATES[033]:01/01/1925
ERA[045B]:1920-1930
COMMUNITIES[651]:Hollywood
CITIES[651]:Los Angeles
DATE-PLACE-NOTE[518]:ca. 1925; Hollywood (Los Angeles, Calif.)?
```

Fig. 15-2. Recording uncertainty for date and place, alternative version

Agency-assigned elements

An *Agency-Assigned Data Element* is an element that has been defined by an agency that maintains the list of possible terms or the rules that must be applied. For example, the field CATALOGING-AGENCY[040] is used to identify the organization that cataloged the record. Into this field should be placed the National Union Catalog symbol for the cataloging institution. The symbol must be taken from the Library of Congress publication *Symbols of American Libraries*. To obtain a designation for your organization, write to the Library of Congress at the address listed in the Bibliography under the publication.

The control number appearing in MARC field 010, Library of Congress Control Number, would be assigned by the Library of Congress. The cataloger would merely type in the number that the Library of Congress had already assigned.

Cataloging manuals and vocabulary lists

The following manuals and vocabulary lists should be consulted when filling out the various fields. For a description of these publications, and other more detailed publications and coding lists that are also recommended for use, see the Bibliography.

- Betz, Elisabeth W. *Graphic Materials: Rules for Describing Original Items and Historical Collections*. Washington, D.C.: Library of Congress, Prints and Photographs Division, 1982. Supplements AACR2 (*Anglo-American Cataloging Rules*, Second edition) as a standard source of descriptive practice for photographs, paintings, posters and other non-projected visual materials.
- Evans, Linda and Margaret O'Brien Will. *MARC for Visual Materials: A Compendium of Practice*. Chicago, Illinois: Chicago Historical Society, 1988. A compendium on the practices of various organization using the MARC-VM (Visual Materials) format.
- Evans, Max J. and Weber, Lisa B. *MARC for Archives and Manuscripts: A Compendium of Practice*. Madison, Wisconsin: State Historical Society of Wisconsin, 1985. Examples of the usage of each MARC field for manuscripts and archives by different institutions. Some of the examples have been made obsolete by rule changes, but this is still a useful guide.
- Gorman, Michael and Paul W. Winkler, *editors. Anglo-American Cataloguing Rules*. Second edition, 1988 revision. Chicago, Illinois: American Library Association, 1988. Commonly referred to as AACR2, it is the authoritative style reference for library catalogers throughout the English-speaking world.
- Hensen, Steven L. *Archives, Personal Papers, and Manuscripts: A Cataloging Manual for Archival Repositories, Historical Societies, and Manuscript Libraries*. Second edition. Chicago, Illinois: Society of American Archivists, 1989. An addition to and modification of the rules of AACR2, as applied to manuscripts and archives. Commonly known as APPM, the first edition of this publication was mandated as the standard for describing manuscripts and archives by the online networks RLIN and OCLC and was widely accepted by the archival profession. The second edition has been greatly expanded to serve as a more complete cataloging guide.
- Library of Congress. *Library of Congress Subject Headings*. Thirteenth edition. Washington, DC: Library of Congress, Cataloging Distribution Service, 1990. By far the most comprehensive collection of subject terms available.
- Library of Congress. *Subject Cataloging Manual: Subject Headings*. Third edition. Washington, DC: Library of Congress, Cataloging Distribution Service, 1988. A guide to the use of Library of Congress Subject Headings.
- Library of Congress. *USMARC Format for Bibliographic Data: Including Guidelines for Content Designation*. Washington, D.C.: Cataloging Distribution Service, Library of Congress, 1988. The authoritative reference to the MARC format.
- Sahli, Nancy. *MARC for Archives and Manuscripts: The AMC Format*. Chicago, Illinois: Society of American Archivists, 1985. A guide to the MARC format for archives and manuscripts.
- Zinkham, Helena and Parker, Elisabeth Betz. *Descriptive Terms for Graphic Materials: Genre and Physical Characteristic Headings*. Washington, D.C.: Library of Congress, 1986.

Rules for field entries

If a field name appears in plural form, then multiple separate values can be entered into that field. Each individual value should be separated by a semicolon and space, like a list in a normal

English sentence. For example, to include several subjects in the SUBJECTS field having to do with water:

SUBJECTS[650]:Water-supply; Water consumption; Water conservation

The multiple values shown above will each be treated individually. For example, you could give a command to change, in the SUBJECTS field, "Water consumption" to the simpler term "Water use" without causing any change to the other entries or to other fields.

Dates and numbers

If the field name ends with the word "DATE," then a date should be entered in the form MM/DD/YYYY. If a field name ends with the hash mark symbol "#" for number, then a whole number should be entered. In other cases mentioned below, a number is preferred as an entry, but not required.

Punctuation and spacing

Do not place special punctuation at the beginning or end of the field. If such punctuation is desired, it can be supplied by the program at the time of information transfer. In the meantime, it would serve no purpose to store a comma at the end of a name, or to place a fuller form of a name in parentheses.

Initials in a personal name should each be separated by a space. For example:

AUTHORS[100,700]:Mencken, H. L.
PERSONS-SUBJECTS[600]:Goodrich, B. F.; Penney, J. C.

But if the name of a company happens to include the name of an individual, in direct word order, there are no spaces between the initials:

ORGANIZATIONS-SUBJECTS[610]:B.F. Goodrich; J.C. Penney Co.

There are no spaces in initials for academic degrees, such as "M.A." or "R.N.". In the case of an abbreviation, there is a space between the abbreviation and the initial that follows. For example: "Ph. D.".

The ampersand character "&" should be included as used by an organization in its name, rather than replaced with "and". For example:

ORGANIZATIONS-SUBJECTS[610]:O'Melveny & Myers

When the name of an organization includes a subordinate unit, separate the elements with a period and two spaces. Consult examples among the Library of Congress Subject Headings. For example:

ORGANIZATIONS-SUBJECTS[610]:United States. Army. Infantry

Sentences in a long text field such as DESCRIPTION should also be separated by a period and two spaces. The punctuation will make it possible for a database program later to divide the entry into separate sentences.

Subdivisions of Library of Congress Subject Headings are separated by a dash, which should be typed as two hyphens, not one. Thus, for equipment used by bakers you would enter the heading:

SUBJECTS[650]:Bakers and bakeries—Equipment and supplies

Requirements set by the repository

Requirements and limits can be placed by the individual repository on any field. For example, you could limit entries in the FILE-HEADING field to an Authority File of headings previously used. If the operator entered a heading that did not already appear on the list, the program would ask if a new heading was intended, or if the operator simply made a mistake. It may also be desirable to limit a field to a range of values. You might require that the values in a numerical field be limited to the range of zero to one-hundred.

Pattern matching will require than an entry match a particular pattern of numbers or characters. For example, the required pattern for a social security number would be "###-##-####". For a phone number, one might require "(###) ###-####", if no foreign phone numbers would be included. Pattern matching helps to prevent mistakes.

Although Pick provides variable-length fields, it may be desirable for administrative convenience to limit the length of a field. For example, you might limit the length of a field for file headings to the size of the labels to be attached to the photographs.

Null fields

The only fields that can never be left blank are those that are required to create a unique RECORD-ID. A particular system, such as one of the national bibliographic utilities, might also require that other fields be filled in. A Main Entry for the person or organization that created the work, or the title of the work, is generally required.

Field descriptions

For the following fields, the field name is shown first, followed by an explanation of how the field is used. For technical details on how the program handles each of the fields and carries out default choices, see the subsequent section on "Simplifying the MARC Format".

MARC Tag numbers appear in brackets after the descriptive field name. For example: "SUBJECTS[650]". The field name will make the system easy to use for those who are not professional archivists, while the MARC Tag provides a reference to the national standard for cataloging practice.

The field name including the MARC Tag is informative, but it may seem long and unwieldy. Because Pick allows us to create synonyms for a field name, we can refer to the field by a shorter version of the field name. In a search statement, you could use the full field name with the MARC Tag in brackets. In most cases, it will be simplest to use just the name without the MARC Tag. A person familiar with the MARC format might use the bracketed MARC Tag alone, without the descriptive name. Any of the following search statements will have the same result:

```
SELECT ITEMS WITH SUBJECTS[650] = "Parades"
SELECT ITEMS WITH SUBJECTS      = "Parades"
SELECT ITEMS WITH [650]         = "Parades"
```

In the following field definitions, the field name used in the MARC manuals and additional notes on the MARC definition appear after the subheading "MARC Tag:". For more complete definitions of the fields, consult the cataloging manuals cited, according to the MARC Tag number.

Sources to consult for each field

Consult the MARC format manuals under the MARC Tag number that appears in brackets with the field name. For example, for field SUBJECTS[650], look in the MARC manuals under MARC Tag 650.

Manuals for descriptive conventions

In the explanation section for each field, a note marked "Consult:" will indicate authoritative sources to consult for guidance in filling in the field. Because this guide emphasizes the cataloging of archival and photographic materials, reference sources for those types of materials will be most heavily represented.

Each source is represented by its common acronym. The sources are organized into numbered paragraphs. Following the acronym for the source, the numbers of the appropriate paragraphs in the cataloging manual will appear. The first part of each paragraph number designates the chapter. Note that many cataloging manuals and guides are organized according to the paragraph numbers of AACR2 (*Anglo-American Cataloging Rules*, Second edition). The acronyms are listed in TABLE 15-1.

Table 15-1. Acronyms for cataloging reference manuals

Initials	Reference
AACR2	Anglo-American Cataloguing Rules
APPM	Archives, Personal Papers, and Manuscripts
FTAMC	Form Terms for Archival and Manuscripts Control
GIHC	Graphic Materials Rules for Describing Original Items and Historical Collections
GMGPC	Descriptive Terms for Graphic Materials: Genre and Physical Characteristic Headings
MIM	Moving Image Materials

Order of fields

Fields are grouped together, and pairs of fields are juxtaposed, to help the cataloger gather similar pieces of information, and to highlight the distinctions between types of information that are often mixed together. Examples of distinctions include the difference between physical form and genre, or between subjects that are the name of an organization or the name of a geographical place.

The following technical considerations have also affected field placement:

- The fields that are searched most often should be placed near the front of the record. Those that are searched infrequently, especially the long, descriptive fields for notes, should be placed at the end of the record. The more fields and text that the computer has to scan through to find a field, the longer the search will take. This speed consideration affects only sequential searches, and not indexed searches.
- The History Database program allows information from one field to be re-used in the next field with a single keystroke. Information can also be placed in a buffer for re-use with the Cut and Paste function. Therefore, fields have been juxtaposed that might use the same corporate or personal name or other heading.

16

Subject analysis

Unlike text, photos provide no title page or table of contents to specify subject matter. The cataloger must look at the photo and make judgements. In addition, what the photo is "of" might be very different from what it is "about".[1] A photo, cartoon, painting, or other visual representation can have more than one level of meaning.

As an example of a visual image with an underlying message, consider the favorite political cartoon of William Jennings Bryan's 1896 presidential campaign. The cartoon depicted a giant cow that stretched across the United States. The cow was fed by the farmers of the West, Midwest, and South, but milked by the bankers of Wall Street. The Library of Congress Subject Heading "Dairy farming" would cover the feeding and milking of the cow that the cartoon depicted, but would give the searcher no access point for the message that the cartoon was meant to convey. Deciding on the most appropriate terms in such cases is not easy. The subjects and genre fields might be filled in as follows:

SUBJECTS[650]:Dairy farming;
  Presidents-United States-Election-1896;
  Farmers—Political activity; Wall Street
GENRE[655]:Editorial cartoons

Note that in the subjects field, Wall Street, although it is a geographic location, is treated here as a concept. The geographic location would have been indicated as "Wall Street (New York, N.Y.)". Also note that the year "1896" for presidential elections is not a Chronological Subdivision. Rather, it pinpoints a specific event.

It is difficult when assigning headings to political materials not to make subjective and partisan judgements. I would argue, however, that avoiding the introduction of political subjects does as great a disservice as partisanship. For example, one of the best photos that I have seen of child labor depicts a Japanese boy, about eight years of age, carrying a bunch of

[1]For a clear and useful discussion of subject analysis applied to photographs, see the introduction by Jackie Dooley in: Elisabeth Betz, compiler, *Library of Congress Thesaurus for Graphic Materials: Topical Terms for Subject Access*, Washington, D.C.: Library of Congress, Prints and Photographs Division, 1987.

carrots that is almost as big as he is. The photo was cataloged only under "Carrots". I would have added "Children—Employment", "Agricultural laborers", and "Japanese Americans".

Older photographs of industrial activities often show practices that were taken for granted at the time, but that we might regard as unsafe. For example, a photo of a worker painting a building, perched precariously on a tall ladder, might warrant the subject heading "Industrial safety".

The cataloger must decide upon the relative significance of the various elements in a photograph, manuscript, or any other type of material that does not include a specific indication of an author's intent. Among the factors to consider are the following:

- How clearly and prominently is the element shown? The subject heading "Automobiles" would clearly apply to an auto showroom, but not to a photo that showed an automobile dimly visible in the background.
- Is the depiction novel, or could it almost be taken for granted? You would assume, for example, that in photos of people, the people are wearing clothes. You might reserve the heading "Clothing and dress" for photos that best illustrate a particular style, period, or set of circumstances. If a collection includes thousands of photos of Spanish dancers decked out for the Southern California tourist trade, you might reserve the heading "Costume, Spanish" for only the best, unless you wanted to avoid losing the combination of that heading with other significant concepts.
- Does the photo carry an underlying intent that was typical of the time and place? For example, the intention of photographers who work for a chamber of commerce is normally to promote the trade and industry of that locality. Headings such as "Boards of trade", "Tourist trade", and "Industrial promotion" should be kept in mind when cataloging such photographs. A Southern California promotional photo of "Miss Venice" in a bathing suit picking oranges does not show agricultural harvesting, except whimsically. The clear intent of the photo, borne out by notes from the photographer and photo captions supplied by the chamber, was to encourage the tourist trade.

The whimsical aspect of a photograph might constitute a useful access point. Someone might want a photo that depicts orange picking in a humorous way. The notion of humor could be indicated by the heading "Wit and humor" or "Photography, Humorous". Other possibilities are to use the Topical Subdivision "Humor" or to employ the term "Humorous pictures" as a genre heading. For the photo of Miss Venice picking oranges, the following entries might be made:

```
SUBJECTS[650]:Orange—Harvesting; Bathing suits;
  Beauty contestants; Wit and humor; Tourist trade
ORGANIZATIONS-SUBJECTS[610]:Los Angeles Chamber of Commerce
```

Distinguish subject from form and genre

Distinguish the subject of the photo from the photo's physical form or genre. Subjects are placed in MARC 650, Genre in 655, and Physical form in 755. For example, a photo might illustrate the preservation of nitrate negatives, although the photo itself was not nitrate, but safety. The following terms were taken from *Descriptive Terms for Graphic Materials: Genre and Physical Characteristics Headings*, by Helena Zinkham and Elisabeth Betz Parker.

SUBJECTS[650]:Cellulose nitrate photonegatives;
  Photographs-Conservation and restoration
PHYSICAL-FORMS[755]:Cellulose triacetate photonegatives

If a postcard carried an illustration of tourists buying postcards, then the term "Postcards" would be appropriate both as a subject heading and as a genre heading:

SUBJECTS[650]:Postcards
GENRES[655]:Postcards

In 1972 I wrote the historical guide book *L.A. on Foot.* For this work the term "Guide-books" should appear in the field GENRES, not under SUBJECTS. If a topical usage is intended, it would be preferable to use a term that is clearly topical rather than a type of material. Rather than "Maps", use "Cartography". Rather than "Photographs", use "Photography".

17

Library of Congress Subject Headings

The Library of Congress Subject Headings reflect their history. The headings were created as needed, rather than developed as a unified whole based on a general plan. The system did not spring into being full-blown, like Athena from the head of Zeus. Rather like Topsy, it "just growed".

As a result of the process by which the headings were created, many gaps appear where you would expect to see a corresponding term. The appearance of a term such as "Architecture, Spanish colonial" should not lead you to expect to see "Architecture, Streamline moderne", if no occasion has arisen to catalog a book on the latter subject.

The level of specific detail varies from one subject to another, depending on what works have been written on the subject. In some cases the level of specificity seems perfect. Photos of Rosie the Riveter can be cataloged under "Women aircraft industry workers". In other instances the level of detail seems absurd, as in the case of "Cat litter boxes". Has someone written a book about cat litter boxes? How much is there to say?

The Library of Congress Subject Headings generally cover the terms that one could expect an educated person to understand. It is my recommendation that you use other vocabularies only if you are operating in a very specialized setting for which the Library of Congress Subject Headings do not provide the specific terms that are needed. For example, if you were cataloging photographs of the sign language used by the deaf, you would need terms not provided on the Library of Congress list.

If your usage is not terribly specialized, before reaching the conclusion that you will have to go outside the Library of Congress Subject Headings list, examine the following sections on "Free-Floating Subdivisions" and "Subdivisions Controlled by Pattern Headings". You might be able to cover the concepts that you need by attaching Free-Floating Subdivisions to the terms that appear in the big red books.

Form of the headings

The form of the Library of Congress Subject Headings is generally singular for concepts and plural for objects. Thus, the concept of government known as "Democracy" is singular, but the objects used for transportation, "Railroads", are listed in the plural.

Headings can consist of one or several words. For headings consisting of an adjective and noun, natural word order is preferred, but there are many exceptions. Thus "Electric railroads" reflects natural word order, while "Electric railroads, Miniature" includes inversion. The subject of lunchrooms maintained for employees is represented by the unappetizing rubric, "Industrial feeding".

Inversion is most often used to keep closely related terms together in cases where it will seem more natural to search on the noun rather than on the adjective. For example, when looking for the appropriate term for a style of architecture, it is much easier to go down the "Architecture, . . ." list from "Architecture, Anglo-Saxon" to "Architecture, Visigothic" than to look for the adjective first.

Headings might also consist of terms joined by "and" to indicate a relationship or to combine two similar terms. Thus, the headings "Libraries and publishing", "Libraries and readers", and "Libraries and schools" all indicate relationships that would not be as adequately conveyed by two separate headings. The terms "Banks and banking" and "Boats and boating" indicate an industry and a sport by combining the terms for the objects and the activity.

Scope notes

Library of Congress Subject Headings sometimes carry scope notes to explain the intended range of a term and distinctions between closely similar terms. Thus, the scope note for "Women in advertising" indicates that the term refers to the portrayal of women in advertisements, whereas the careers of women advertising executives and other aspects of involvement by women in the field would be placed under "Women in the advertising industry".

Scope notes distinguish between the terms "Conjuring" and "Magic". The heading "Magic" is to be employed for the use of charms and spells believed to have supernatural powers, whereas "Conjuring" refers to tricks of so-called magic performed by an entertainer.

The scope note under "Actresses" explains that the term is to be used for women actors collectively. Works on individual stage actors, whether men or women, are to be entered under "Actors". Thus, even though the photo shows an actress, the appropriate heading is "Actors".

Relationships between terms

Indications of relationships to other terms might appear under a heading. The other terms might be broader, narrower or otherwise closely associated, or the reference might indicate which of two similar terms is preferred.

Use and used for

The term "USE" directs the cataloger to the approved heading from the term that was first consulted. "UF", an abbreviation for "Used For", is displayed with the approved heading, to show the terms with similar meanings that the correct term replaces. USE and Used For are thus reciprocal. The following USE and Used For notes explain that rather than utilizing the term "Shops", a more specific designation should be employed, to distinguish between a workshop and a retail store:

Shops
  USE Stores, Retail
    Workshops

Stores, Retail
  UF Shops

Workshops
  UF Shops

(Editions of the *Library of Congress Subject Headings* before the Eleventh edition in 1988 used "x" instead of Used For.)

Broader term and narrower term

Broader Term and Narrower Term, abbreviated to "BT" and "NT", represent reciprocal choices within a hierarchical relationship. Broader term indicates the broader category of which the more specific term is a member. Narrower term gives a more narrowly defined subject within that category. For example:

Motor vehicles
  NT Automobiles

Automobiles
  BT Motor vehicles

In each direction, there are terms that are still broader and terms that are even narrower. Thus, there are narrower definitions for the type of automobile, and broader definitions of transportation. For example, proceeding from the broadest to the most narrow:

Locomotion
  NT Transportation

Transportation
  BT Locomotion
  NT Vehicles

Vehicles
  BT Transportation
  NT Motor vehicles

Motor vehicles
  BT Vehicles
  NT Automobiles

Automobiles
  BT Motor vehicles
  NT Station wagons

Station wagons
  BT Automobiles

You can follow the hierarchy one step at a time from the concept of movement or locomotion down to the favorite vehicle of 1950s suburbia, or from Ozzie and Harriet Nelson's car up to the idea of locomotion. Each individual term carries both upward and downward links, as long as additional levels exist.

At each stage of the hierarchy, only the levels immediately above or below are usually included. The entire hierarchy is not laid out with every term. Exceptions to the one-level rule reflect an obsolete practice. In most cases, a term will have many more narrower definitions below it than broader usages above it. (Editions of the *Library of Congress Subject Headings* before the Eleventh edition in 1988 used "sa", an abbreviation of "See Also", for Narrower Term and the very informative "xx" for Broader Term.)

Related term

Related Term, abbreviated as RT, indicates a relationship that is not as clearly defined as that of a hierarchy. For example, the following are Related Terms for "Transportation":

Transportation
  RT Commerce
    Communications and traffic
    Storage and moving trade

The terms below have some sort of relationship with "Boats and boating":

Boats and boating
  RT Boatbuilding
    Ships

In each case, the Related Terms seem akin to the heading that appears with them, but you could not categorize that relationship as one of broader and narrower terms within a hierarchy. The current direction in Library of Congress cataloging is to examine whether terms considered in the past to be related could logically fit into a hierarchy, and to emphasize hierarchical relationships over side excursions.

See also

See Also references, abbreviated as "SA", are now used mainly to avoid listing all of the narrower and more specific terms that might apply. For example:

Automobiles
  SA headings beginning with the word Automobile

The See Also note for "Automobiles" thus directs the cataloger to "Automobile industry and trade", "Automobile racing", and many other terms, without making the big red subject heading books even bulkier by repeating each term. In other cases, a See Also reference will point to specific breeds for a type of animal, in order to avoid listing all of the breeds.

Subdivisions

Library of Congress Subject Headings may be extended to greater degrees of specificity through the use of subdivisions. Subdivisions allow terms to be extended in uniform ways. Thus, "Equipment and supplies" can be employed as a subdivision for "Automobiles" and for any other type of land vehicle. Examples of the combined terms are:

Automobiles—Equipment and supplies
Motorcycles—Equipment and supplies
Bicycles-Equipment and supplies

The subdivision is separated from the main term by a long dash, which in typewritten copy should appear as two hyphens. A subdivision can in turn be subdivided, leading to combinations such as:

Automobiles—Motors—Carburetors
Automobiles—Motors—Crankshafts
Automobiles—Motors—Mufflers—Acoustic properties

Before applying a subdivision, make sure that no term appears in the Library of Congress Subject heading list that already covers the matter. For example, it would seem correct to say "Buildings-Design and construction". But the Scope Notes under the heading "Buildings" inform you that for the subject of the designing of buildings, you should use the term "Architecture". For the construction of buildings, you should use "Building".

Subdivisions for form, time period, and geographical place

The only type of subdivision described so far has been topical, used to narrow down a general concept. However, there are three other types in use, designating form, time period, and geographical place. These additional types would be counter-productive to use in a computer database. The information can be much more efficiently conveyed in individual fields.

The form, chronological, and geographic subdivisions have been and continue to be employed when all of the subject information must be conveyed in a single field, most often because of the limitations of the computer or manual system in use. Thus, to categorize information about the automobile industry in Los Angeles, you might enter the heading "Automobile industry and trade—Los Angeles (Calif.)". But it would be extremely tedious to include "Los Angeles (Calif.)" after every topical subject. And to further subdivide by time period and the form of material would in most cases become unworkable. The introduction to the eleventh edition of Library of Congress Subject Headings refers to use of subdivisions under names of places as "problematic" and states that no general rule exists as to whether geographic or topical headings are to appear first.[1] Rather than lumping the types of subdivision together, the non-topical subdivisions should be placed in the subsequent separate fields. The MARC field number follows the field name in brackets.

Form subdivisions describe the genre of the material, such as "Periodicals", "Diaries", "Dictionaries", or "Pictorial works". These should be placed in GENRES[655]. For the physical form of the material, the designated field is PHYSICAL-FORMS[755].

---

[1]*Library of Congress Subject Headings*, Eleventh edition (Washington, D.C.: Library of Congress, 1988), page xiv.

Chronological subdivisions represent time periods relevant to a geographical area or topical subject. For example:

California—History—To 1846
—1846-1850
—1850-1950
—Civil War, 1861-1865
—1950–

The chronological subdivisions provided for California are not very useful. The closest approximation that they allow for a description of the 1920s would be "1850-1950". The time period should be placed in a separate field, with beginning and ending dates, using ERA[045b].

Geographical subdivisions specify the place, and would be best put in a hierarchy of separate fields for the type of locality. For example, country, state or province, county, city, community name, and perhaps even street, could be used to indicate the location of a photograph.

A database record for aerial photographs of factories owned by Litton Industries in the 1960s in Los Angeles, California would contain the following:

SUBJECTS[650]:Factories
SUBJECTS-ORGANIZATIONS[610]:Litton Industries
CITIES[651]:Los Angeles
STATES[651]:California
ERA[045B]:1960-1969
PHYSICAL-FORMS[755]:Aerial photographs

Note the distinction between aerial photographs as a description of the form of material, and as a topical subject. If the material in hand was a technical manual on the handling, maintenance, and indexing of aerial photographs, then the following field entries would appear:

SUBJECTS[650]:Aerial photographs
GENRES[655]:Technical manuals

Individual names

Personal, corporate, and other specific names also appear in the Library of Congress Subject Headings. These are used primarily as pattern examples. Names for individuals and organizations should not appear in the topical subjects field SUBJECTS[650], but under the fields designated for persons or organization that are treated as subjects: PERSONS-SUBJECTS[600], and ORGANIZATIONS-SUBJECTS[610].

For example, when cataloging material related to the accounting procedures used by General Motors, the database record would contain:

SUBJECTS[650]:Accounting
SUBJECTS-ORGANIZATIONS[610]:General Motors

Free-floating subdivisions

When you look up a term such as "Automobiles", you will not find all of the permissible subdivisions listed there. To list all of the possible combinations of terms would make the printed editions of *Library of Congress Subject Headings* too bulky. Considerations of size will become less important as the terms are referenced electronically rather than on paper. Until that Brave New World arrives, the concept of a Free-Floating Subdivision describes a term such as "Equipment and supplies", which may be appended to many different headings for the purpose of creating more specific references.

If you cannot find an appropriate subdivision under the main heading, consult these sources, in the following order:

- *Library of Congress Subject Headings*, under a subdivision term such as "Equipment and supplies".
- The Table of Pattern Headings. The table appears in the introduction to *Library of Congress Subject Headings* and in the *Subject Cataloging Manual.* Use the source that is most current.
- The tables of Free-Floating Subdivisions. The tables appear in the *Subject Cataloging Manual.*

Listed under a subdivision heading

Many eligible subdivisions appear in the Library of Congress Subject Headings list as independent headings. These subdivisions are listed with Scope Notes that indicate how the term should be used.

In the case of "Equipment and supplies", if you look under that term you will find the following note indicating the types of headings to which the subdivision may be applied:

Equipment and supplies
  USE subdivision Equipment and supplies under names of
    disciplines, types of processes, industries, services,
    laboratories, institutions, individual wars, names of
    individual corporate bodies, and phrase headings for
    particular types of equipment

Controlled by pattern headings

Pattern Headings control the use of subdivisions, which may be applied to any subject term that fits the pattern. If you cannot find a term that is sufficiently specific under the main heading or under the subdivision term that you have in mind, your next step would be to look up the Pattern Heading that is most closely related to the concept that you are dealing with. Thus, to find the subdivisions appropriate for "Bicycles", look under "Automobiles", which is the Pattern Heading for Land Vehicles. To find the subdivisions appropriate for "Wheat", look under "Corn", which is the Pattern Heading for Plants and Crops. For subdivisions to be used with "High schools", look under the Pattern Heading for types of Educational Institutions, which is "Universities and colleges".

In some cases there is a choice of Pattern Headings under a category, and you should select the heading that comes closest to term that you are trying to extend. For example, in the category of Industries the two Pattern Headings are "Construction industry" and "Retail trade".

In most cases the appropriate Pattern Heading will be obvious. If it is not, find it by tracing through the Broader Terms or Related Terms. Under the category of Materials the choice of

Pattern Heading lies between "Concrete" and "Metals". As a Pattern Heading for "Cement", you would adopt "Concrete", which appears as a Related Term under "Cement", as shown below:

Cement
  RT Concrete

As a Pattern Heading for "Aluminum" you would choose "Metals". Under "Aluminum" appears "Light metals" as a Broader Term, and under "Light metals" appears the Broader Term "Metals", as shown below:

Aluminum
  BT Light metals

Light metals
  BT Metals

For general use

The *Subject Cataloging Manual* provides lists of Free-Floating Subdivisions that are not controlled by Pattern Headings. An example of a Free-Floating Subdivision for general use is the subdivision "Study and teaching", which can be applied to any subject that can be studied and taught. Examples include:

Architecture—Study and teaching
Engineering—Study and teaching

The Free-Floating Subdivision "Design and construction" would apply to anything that could be designed and constructed. Structures of all sorts would be eligible for this subdivision. For example:

Aqueducts—Design and construction
Factories—Design and construction

Note the difference between the kind of term to which the subdivision "Study and teaching" would apply and the sort of heading to which "Design and construction" would be applicable. Engineers design aqueducts, but it would clearly be incorrect to say, "Engineering—Design and construction" or "Aqueducts—Study and teaching". "Engineering" is not something to be constructed, it is something to be studied and taught. "Aqueducts" are not studied and taught, they are constructed. You would study engineering in order to construct an aqueduct.

One good clue to the type of term involved in the Library of Congress Subject Headings is whether the term is singular or plural. Remember that concepts and intellectual subjects are singular, such as "Engineering", while objects are plural, such as "Aqueducts".

Not included in the examples presented here are subdivisions such as "Memoirs" and "Diaries", which describe the form of the material rather than the subject of the material. Also not included are subdivisions for use under the name of individual corporate bodies, persons, families, and geographic place names. As stated above, it is the recommendation of this guide that the names of individuals, organizations, and geographic places, and terms for the form of material, not be placed in the topical subjects field, but instead be placed in other, more specific fields. It is also recommended that topical subdivisions not be included after the names of individuals, organizations, and geographic places, and terms for the form of material. To combine a topic with the name of an individual, you would include two different fields in your search statement, rather than expecting to find all of the information in one field.

Used under classes of persons

Free-Floating Subdivisions can be applied to classes of persons. Classes of persons include age and sex groups, social, economic, and political categories, members of religious groups, and occupational groups.

An example of a subdivision to use with classes of persons is the heading "Conduct of life", which refers to standards of ethics and moral behavior. The subdivision would be employed in cases such as:

Youth—Conduct of life
Librarians—Conduct of life

Used under ethnic groups

Free-Floating Subdivisions can be applied to ethnic groups and nationalities. The nationality headings should not be used when the name of a country could be used instead. For example, one should use:

SUBJECTS[650]:Mental health—United States

rather than:

SUBJECTS[650]:Americans—Mental health

If you follow the procedure recommended in this guide, separating geographic place names from topical subjects, the record would contain:

SUBJECTS[650]:Mental health
COUNTRIES[651]:United States

Subdivision under ethnic group or nationality would be used in cases such as:

SUBJECTS[650]:Japanese Americans—Mental health

Attach 'in art' or 'in literature' to topics

The *Subject Cataloging Manual* for the Library of Congress Subject Headings specifies Free-Floating Terms and Phrases that may be attached to topical headings. The phrases "in art" and "in literature" can be added to a topical heading to indicate that the subject of the work being cataloged is how a particular topic is treated in art or in literature.

As an example, consider the topical term "Women". If you were cataloging a scholarly article on how women have been depicted in art you would apply the heading, "Women in art". If the subject of the article was how women have been depicted in literature, you would apply the heading, "Women in literature".

Note carefully that you are using the heading "Women in art" for a work of art criticism that talks about how women have been represented in art and that compares various current artistic works depicting women. The actual item that you are cataloging is not a painting, it is a work of art criticism. Your entries would be:

SUBJECTS[650]:Women in art
GENRES[655]:Art criticism

In contrast, if you were cataloging a portrait painting of a woman, you would not assign the heading "Women in art". The subject of the painting is not "Women in art", it is a particular woman. You might assign the following entries:

SUBJECTS[650]:Women
GENRES[655]:Portraits
PHYSICAL-FORMS[755]:Paintings

If the heading to which you are attaching "in art" or "in literature" contains a comma, then you should insert an additional comma before "in art" or "in literature". For example, the subject heading to apply to hotels and taverns is "Hotels, taverns, etc.". If the work that you are cataloging describes how Prohibitionist tracts depicted a fanciful variety of sordid acts taking place in barrooms, a relevant subject heading would be, "Hotels, taverns, etc., in literature".

Inverted headings, such as "Architecture, Spanish colonial", contain commas. If you were cataloging an article that discussed how Spanish Colonial architecture had been depicted in art, the appropriate heading would be, "Architecture, Spanish colonial, in art".

Precoordination and postcoordination

Using the method of precoordination, separate concepts are combined before any search is conducted, at the time of data entry. With postcoordination, the concepts are combined after data entry, when giving a search command. The disadvantage of precoordination is that it leads to long lists of lengthy, complicated terms. If the precoordinated terms are to be created by the cataloger, rather than listed explicitly, no two catalogers are likely to combine various concepts in exactly the same way. To combine the concepts of "Water" and "Politics", should you choose "Water and politics" or "Politics and water"? It seems simpler and more reliable to postcoordinate. Thus, the searcher, using Library of Congress Subject Headings, would ask for:

SELECT ITEMS WITH SUBJECTS = "Water-supply" AND "Politics, Practical"

The great advantage of precoordination is in providing a printed index. The reference librarian or patron could look under "Water and politics" or "Politics and water", whereas it might not be practical to look up all of the records that had "Water" as a subject to see if any had a connection with political matters. As a compromise, the cataloger might enter the Library of Congress Subject Heading with the subdivision that comes closest to combining the two concepts: "Water-supply—Law and legislation".

Postcoordination is generally the easier method, because only simple, single-concept terms are used, rather than employing a set of rules to combine terms in a hierarchical sequence. But postcoordination sometimes brings confusing results. For example, imagine a photo of a bicycle next to an automobile. The automobile is being repaired. If the cataloger entered three separate subject headings, for "Automobiles", "Bicycles", and "Repairing", you would not know whether the bicycle or the automobile was undergoing repair. A search statement such as:

```
SELECT ITEMS WITH SUBJECTS = "Bicycles" AND "Repairing"
```

would retrieve unwanted photos of auto repairs. Instead, the topical subdivision "Maintenance and repair" should be applied for mechanical objects. The subjects field would be filled in as follows:

```
SUBJECTS[650]:Bicycles; Automobiles—Maintenance and repair
```

Specific and direct entry

The rule of Specific and Direct Entry is that you should enter only the heading that provides the most specific and direct coverage of the subject available. For example, when cataloging a photo of a dog, you would enter the Library of Congress Subject Heading "Dogs". The cataloger would not also enter the broader term "Domestic animals" or the still broader heading "Animals". If the cataloger recognizes the breed of dog, the specific breed name should be entered instead. For example, "Bloodhounds" could be used.

Now that the rule is clear, consider how it may work in practice. If the only subject heading that you enter is "Bloodhounds", how will you find all the photos for dogs? Will you enter a search statement that includes every conceivable breed of dog, such as:

```
SELECT ITEMS WITH SUBJECTS = "Basset hound" OR "Bloodhounds"
  OR "Collies" OR "Doberman pinschers" OR . . .
```

And how would you retrieve documents relating to subjects further up in the hierarchy, such as "Domestic animals" or "Animals"? To retrieve all photos of animals, will you have to enter a search statement that includes the name for every breed of animal?

To search on a level above that of the Specific and Direct Entry term placed in the field, you have two choices:

- Break the rule of Specific and Direct Entry by also making entries for broader terms. Thus, the cataloger would enter all of the terms: "Bloodhounds; Dogs; Domestic animals; Animals". This method requires extra work on the part of the cataloger to enter the terms, and extra storage space to store them. This procedure also leads to questions about how far up a hierarchy you should go. A policy change later will require editing all of the records affected.
- The second method would be to use an Authority File to document the hierarchy. The Authority File would show that each term in the following series, proceeding from the most specific to the most general, is broader than the term before and narrower than the term after: "Bloodhounds; Dogs; Domestic animals; Animals". When the searcher asked for "Animals", the records including "Bloodhounds" would automatically be included. The disadvantage of this procedure is that someone has to create and maintain the Authority File that contains the hierarchies. Shared cataloging efforts, conducted through information exchange networks, can lighten the load of authority work.

18

The Record-ID

The primary and absolutely essential function of a Record-ID is to provide a unique identification for each record in the database. Pick requires that each Record-ID in a file be unique. Even though some systems allow duplicate IDs, avoid that practice at all costs.

If you create duplicate IDs, you will not have complete control over your database. You will delete records that you did not mean to delete, because more than one record had the same ID. Records sharing the same ID might be over-written on top of each other. And you will not be able to export your records to a system requiring unique IDs.

Arguments for a simple, numerical Record-ID

The Record-ID serves a variety of useful purposes. Beware, however, of the tendency inherited from manual systems to attempt to load too much information into the ID. Users of a manual system try to put much of the information that they need into the Record-ID in order to avoid the trouble of looking up the complete record in the card catalog or inventory.

The tendency to cram information into the Record-ID has been perpetuated into the computer age by single-user database systems. Even though the complete record for the item can be retrieved electronically, such retrieval is still not convenient as long as only one person at a time has access to the database.

A multi-user computer database management system should eliminate most of the reasons that prevailed in the past for stuffing data into the item ID. A low-cost computer terminal can be supplied to each person who needs database access, making it easy and convenient for anyone to retrieve all of the information recorded for the item.

The most common disadvantages of cramming the item identifier full of information about the item it identifies are that you will produce a long and convoluted ID, and a long and convoluted procedure for assigning it. The more complicated the procedure, the more errors will occur in making the assignments.

I have had many occasions to listen while a library manager explained to someone a system for assigning identification numbers. There really was no system. There was only a set of idiosyncrasies.

The longer the identifier, the more likely are errors in transcription. In addition, more processing will be required from the computer. In tests that I conducted, I found that the computer processed a list of simple numerical Record-IDs more than twice as fast as IDs composed of textual elements joined together by hyphens.

Disadvantages of using meaningful data for a Record-ID

At first glance, it seems more sensible to use real data for your Record-ID, rather than assigning numbers that have no particular meaning except to identify the record. For example, for a file of names and addresses, you could use each person's name, rather than assigning numbers to your friends and relations. But real data has important disadvantages. Because it reflects the outside world, the data may not meet the requirements for creating and maintaining simple, convenient, orderly Record-IDs.

If the data changes, you must change the Record-ID. Information changes as the world changes. If the information on which a Record-ID is based changes, then the Record-ID must change also. For example, if you assigned Record-IDs to your address file from personal names, you must change a Record-ID every time a woman marries and changes her last name. The experience could turn you against the institution of marriage.

Changing a Record-ID is more complicated and slower than merely changing the data in a field, even if the database program handles the operation for you. You have probably made printouts of your database records, in order of Record-ID. The database will no longer correspond to the printouts.

If you have created any references to a specific Record-ID, the references will no longer be valid after the ID changes. The reference will be an "orphan", because it refers to a "Mother Record" that no longer exists under the same name.

Duplicate information creates duplicate Record-IDs. Two records should not have the same Record-ID. But what if two people have the same name, and you have used names as Record-IDs in your address file? That is why most personnel files and other database files for people use numbers rather than names.

If the information is missing, there is no Record-ID. You may not use a null value as a Record-ID. For your database of names and addresses, if you decided to use phone numbers as Record-IDs, and you did not have a phone number for a person whom you wanted to include in the database, you would have a problem. The same problem would occur if you used Social Security numbers, which not everyone would have.

A very unsatisfactory solution to the problem of a null Record-ID would be to make up a bogus value for the missing information. When you see a printout with a phone number listing such as "(000) 000-0000", you know that someone did not think through the fundamentals before setting up the database.

Other uses for the Record-ID

Having made the arguments for short, simple, numerical Record-IDs, I will nevertheless cite cases in which the Record-ID could be used to provide additional utility. For records on the lower levels of a clear, distinct hierarchy, the Record-ID should identify the higher levels. The database structure for historical materials recommended in this guide divides records into two types: collection-level and item-level. A collection-level record will provide information that would apply to an entire collection of materials. The item-level records will describe the individual items, without needing to repeat information that would apply to every item in the collection.

The Record-ID for a collection-level record might be "6", for collection number 6. The Record-ID for an item within that collection might be "6-2000", indicating item number 2000 within collection number 6.

Provide direct access to photo negatives

An informative Record-ID provides direct access to original items that are frequently retrieved to make copies. The most common case is a collection of photo negatives. Every time a patron or customer makes an order, the negative must be fetched. The fetching is generally performed by clerical staff who have no need for other information about the photo. The order in which the negatives are stored will probably be dictated by considerations of space and preservation, rather than by numerical simplicity. Negatives can be placed according to size in drawers built to accommodate each size. Negatives can further be broken down for preservation purposes by type of material, such as nitrate, safety, and glass.

A Record-ID of "1-N-45-2000" would allow the clerical staff to go directly to collection number 1, nitrate section, drawer for 4 x 5 inch images, item number 2000. The information on the type of photographic material (nitrate, safety, glass, etc.) and size could be stored below the collection level at the levels of PART and SUB-PART.

Sort the materials in convenient order

The Record-ID cited above of "1-N-45-2000" would not only provide direct access to an individual photo negative, it would also allow easy sorting on the computer of a list of negative numbers to retrieve. If a person is to pick out 100 negatives, the task will be made much easier by a list in which each collection is grouped together, and then each photographic material is grouped by type and image size. In this case, a sequential number has been used for the final ENTRY# field that designates the individual item.

In other cases the original items themselves possess a natural order that might usefully be reflected in the Record-ID. The classic case is for a collection consisting of a series of items produced over time, such as monographs or reports produced in a series that have each been assigned a sequential number by the producing agency or publisher. You might group the monographs or reports into a collection and use the series number for field PART.

In many cases, however, the items produced over time do not carry sequential numbers. The information demonstrating sequence is the date. Examples would include the minutes of the board of directors of an organization or daily issues of a newspaper. The date of the board meeting or of publication is our most important piece of identifying information about the materials, after the name of the organization or newspaper.

From my experience in writing the histories of three organizations, the Avery corporation, the California Club, and UCLA, I believe that the minutes of boards of directors and most other administrative information should be sorted by date of creation. When you review the board minutes, for editing of the database records or to trace the development of a trend, to read the material in any sequence other than date proves extremely confusing.

Of course, you do not have to reflect the date in the Record-ID in order to sort the records by date. You can add a sorting clause to the search statement. But the extra clause will complicate your commands. When you print out records from the database, you will have to distinguish the board minutes records from the others, and much of the time you will forget to do so. The additional requirement will make useful searching more difficult for novice users, which is a result to be avoided at almost any cost.

If an entire database consisted of nothing but newspaper editions, board minutes, and other items to be sorted by date, you could let the program handle the matter automatically for you. You would tell the program to take your first entry for the field CAPTURE-DATES[033] and use it to designate the part of the collection from which the item came, or to attach the date as a prefix to the item number.

In order to sort correctly, you could ask that the date be represented in the Record-ID in the format "YYYYMMDD". Thus December 7, 1941 would appear in the Record-ID as "19411207". Alternatively, you could tell Pick to store the date in the system's standard internal format, which is the number of days before or after December 31, 1967. Pick's method is better for manipulation, but would not allow you to read the date from the Record-ID. If the entire database will not consist of date-sequenced items, then you must either perform the sequencing manually, or make provision in the collection-level record for indicating whether the collection is to be date-sequenced or not.

History database record sorting

The History Database program will adopt the following procedures to facilitate the sorting of records in a particular desired sequence.

Default sorting for an entire database

When defining a database, the user may designate a default sorting sequence for printing and display. For example, if all of the records in your database of historical materials will consist of administrative materials, then you can designate that for printing or display the records will be sorted automatically by COLLECTION, then CAPTURE-DATE.

For your ADDRESS.BOOK database of names and addresses, specify a default sorting sequence of LAST-NAME, FIRST-NAME, MIDDLE-NAME, COMPANY. For this database, in the case of a listing for a company rather than for an individual, the personal name fields would be null. The default sorting sequence can be overridden by placing a specific sort clause in the search statement.

19

Fields

The Record-ID constitutes the full and unique identification for a record in a database file. The Record-ID is not entered directly by the user. It will be created by the program from the entries in the first four or five fields in the record: DATABASE[001], COLLECTION[001], PART[001], SUB-PART[001] and for item-level records, also ENTRY#[001].

The program will insert hyphens to separate the elements that make up the Record-ID. The default choice of the hyphen as a separator can be changed by the repository. It is strongly recommended, but not required, that simple numbers only, without a decimal point, be used for the fields COLLECTION, PART, and SUB-PART. Numbers alone must be used for the field ENTRY#. The field DATABASE can consist of both letters and numbers.

The use of characters other than letters and numbers should be strictly avoided in the fields that make up the Record-ID. The Record-ID must not contain spaces. If one of the fields that will be used to make up the Record-ID has been taken from another system under which the item was previously cataloged, and that field contained spaces in the other system, then either close up the spaces, or substitute the underline character "_" for spaces when filling in the field.

None of the fields that make up the Record-ID can contain the character used as a separator between the elements of the Record-ID. If a hyphen is used as the Record-ID separator, then a number or name taken from a previous system, and containing a hyphen, cannot be placed in any of the fields that will be used to make up the Record-ID. Either the field entry must be changed, perhaps replacing the hyphen with the underline character, or the default Record-ID separator must be changed.

Bibliographic level

Collection: The Record-ID will be formed by concatenating the first four fields: DATABASE, COLLECTION, PART, and SUB-PART, each separated by a hyphen.

Item: The Record-ID will be formed by concatenating the first five fields: DATABASE, COLLECTION, PART, SUB-PART, and ENTRY#, each separated by a hyphen.

MARC Tag: 001 Control Number

DATABASE[001]

Enter a unique name, abbreviation, or initials for your database of information. Do not use spaces, hyphens, or any other characters except letters and numbers. The field cannot be left blank. The entry in this field will be used as the first segment of the Record-ID.

In most cases, the entry in this field will be the same National Union Catalog symbol for the repository used in the field CATALOGING-AGENCY[040]. If you do not have a National Union Catalog symbol, pick a set of initials or an abbreviation that will be unique. It will be preferable to obtain a National Union Catalog symbol, in order to ensure uniqueness.

Within the same institution, you might use the DATABASE field for the purpose of distinguishing between two separate databases. For example, the museum and the photo lab of the Los Angeles Department of Water and Power could both use the initials: "LADWP", or the museum could use the initials "LADWPM" and the photo lab the initials "LADWPP". If you decided to keep, in separate files, separate databases for different forms of material, such as photographs, manuscripts, and maps, or separate files for different projects, you could add initials for the form-of-material or project to the end of the DATABASE field.

The DATABASE field is vital for the purpose of allowing the exchange of records between different databases, including databases kept at different repositories. In each individual database, the meaning of a particular designation in the COLLECTION field or the ENTRY# field will be different. COLLECTION number "3" in one database will be different from COLLECTION number "3" in another. The DATABASE field will distinguish one database from another. Since the DATABASE field is the first component of the Record-ID, one database might hold a record with the ID: "LADWP-3-1-1-150" while another database held a record with the ID: "LACHS-3-1-1-150". If records were exchanged between the two databases, these two records would still each keep their individual identity.

Bibliographic levels: all

MARC Tag: 001 Control Number. For an item-level record, the collection-level information, consisting of DATABASE[001], COLLECTION[001], PART[001], and SUB-PART[001], also represents MARC 773w: Control Number of Host Item.

COLLECTION[001]

Enter a number or other designation for the collection. A whole number is preferred, but not required. The field may not be left blank. The entry in this field will be used as the second segment of the Record-ID [001].

It is anticipated that nearly all of the cataloging done will be of primary source materials that have not been cataloged previously. A control number taken from another institution, or from a previously-used system at the same institution, would be placed in the field OTHER-IDS[035], preceded by the National Union Catalog symbol of the institution that assigned the number.

If one of the numbers in OTHER-IDS[035] represents a control number with prominent official standing, which would commonly be used to represent the bibliographic item, then that number should be used for the COLLECTION[001] field. Control numbers from the following sources would be employed for the COLLECTION[001] field, in the listed order of preference:

- Custodian's call number: For an item that is not held by the agency writing the cataloging record, use the call number employed by the repository that holds the item.

For example, a researcher or an archival center might create a cataloging record for an item that is used for reference purposes, and which is stored at the UCLA library. The UCLA library's call number should be used.

- Predominant call number: If the item is held by the cataloging agency, but copies of the same item appear elsewhere, use the call number under which the item would most commonly be listed.

If the number taken from another system contains spaces, the spaces should be closed up, or an underline character "__" should be substituted for each space. If the number from another system contains hyphens, but the hyphen is used to separate elements in the Record-ID[001], then another character should be substituted for the hyphen in the COLLECTION[001] entry. For more information on IDs taken from other systems, see: OTHER-IDS[035].

Bibliographic levels: all

MARC Tag: 001 Control Number. For an item-level Record, the collection-level information, consisting of DATABASE[001], COLLECTION[001], PART[001], and SUB-PART[001], also represents MARC 773w: Control Number of Host Item.

PART[001]

Enter a number or other designation for a part within the collection. If the collection is not divided into parts, enter 1 (one). If a collection is divided into parts, for a collection-level record describing the collection as a whole, enter 0 (zero). A whole number is preferred, but not required. The field may not be left blank. The entry in this field will be used as the third segment of the Record-ID.

A collection might be subdivided into parts according to the origin of the materials, the type of materials, or subject matter. For example, in a photo collection, all of the photographs taken by an individual photographer, originating from a specific agency, utilizing a particular format size such as 4 x 5 inches or 8 x 10, or depicting a clearly-defined subject such as the building of the Los Angeles Aqueduct, can be grouped together as a specific PART of a larger COLLECTION.

Bibliographic levels: all

MARC Tag: 001 Control Number

SUB-PART[001]

Enter a number or other designation for a subdivision within a part of a collection. If the part is not subdivided, enter 1 (one). If a part is divided into sub-parts, for a collection-level record describing either the collection as a whole or the part as a whole, enter 0 (zero).

A whole number is preferred, but not required. The field may not be left blank. The entry in this field will be used as the fourth segment of the Record-ID.

Bibliographic Levels: all

MARC Tag: 001 Control Number

ENTRY#[001]

Enter a number 1 greater than the number for the previous record. Use whole numbers only. The program should automatically provide a unique sequential number for you.

The entry in this field will be used as the fifth segment of the Record-ID for item-level records. ENTRY# distinguishes an individual record within the ITEMS file from other records that may share the same information for fields DATABASE, COLLECTION, PART, and SUB-PART. The same ENTRY# must not be repeated, it must be unique for each record. During data entry, the program will supply a new number automatically, and will warn if the user tries to enter a number that has been used before.

Bibliographic levels: items only

MARC Tag: 001 Control Number

ACCESSION#[099]

If you are using previously-assigned codes to identify or locate the items, rather than using COLLECTION and ENTRY#, then enter the identifier here.

Title of the materials

For TITLE[245], enter the title assigned to the item or collection by its creator. Do not leave the field blank. If no title has been assigned, write a short descriptive title such as: "Los Angeles Aqueduct construction". Place at the beginning of the title the most important identifying words and the words that you would want to use for sorting, to group like materials together.

The process of assigning titles might seem artificial at first for original source materials such as manuscripts and photographs, as if those items were to be treated like books. But the title will provide a handy reference point for quickly browsing through a list of items.

Bibliographic levels

Collections: For primary source materials, use the name given to a collection, such as the "Security Pacific National Bank Photographic Collection". For publications, use the title of the book or journal.

Items: Use a title assigned to the individual item, as in the case of art photographs. If no title has been assigned, construct a short title descriptive of the item.

MARC Tag: 245 Title Statement. (Consult: AACR2 1.1B; APPM 1.1B.)

Creator of the materials

For AUTHORS[100,700], enter the names of those who wrote the documents or who otherwise provided the intellectual content of the material. For example, a person interviewed. List the most important contributor first.

If you wish to specify the relationship of the individual to the material, you may use a Relator Term. After the person's name, place a colon and then the Relator Term. As a Relator Term, use the singular form of a Library of Congress Subject Heading or use the *USMARC Code List for Relators, Sources, Description Conventions* (Washington, DC: Library of Congress, 1988). For example:

```
AUTHORS[100,700]:Avery, R. Stanton:Interviewee;
  Clark, David L.:Interviewer
TITLE[245]:Avery, R. Stanton, Oral History Interview
```

Bibliographic levels: all

MARC Tag: 100 Main Entry—Personal Name. If more than one name is supplied, those after the first are demoted to MARC 700: Added Entry—Personal Name. The program automatically creates an entry for MARC 100e or 700e: Relationship of the person to the Item, with the designation "Author". (Consult: AACR2 22.1-22.17; APPM 3.1-3.17. In cases where more than one person may be responsible for the work, also consult AACR2 21.1, 21.4-21.30.)

PHOTOGRAPHERS[100,700]

Enter the names of the those who shot the photos or who otherwise provided the visual content of the material. For example, a painter. List the most important contributor first.

If you wish to specify the relationship of the individual to the material, you may employ a Relator Term. After the person's name place a colon and then the Relator Term. As a Relator Term use the singular form of a Library of Congress Subject Heading or use the *USMARC Code List for Relators, Sources, Description Conventions* (Washington, DC: Library of Congress, 1988). For example:

PHOTOGRAPHERS[100,700]:Rousseau, Henri:Painter
PHOTOGRAPHERS[100,700]:Pierce, C. C.:Collector

Note the distinction between original photography and copy work. Before the widespread use of photocopy machines, cameras were often used in their place. When cataloging materials from the 1920s, I have found many copy photographs of written documents. Although the physical form in hand is a photograph, the material should be considered textual and attributed to the author who wrote it, rather than to the photographer who made the copy. The same would apply to a photographic copy of an architectural drawing. The work should be attributed to the architect.

In the case of a photo of a building, the work that you are cataloging is the photograph, not the building. Attribute the work to the photographer, and place the name of the architect in the field SUBJECTS-PERSONS[600].

Bibliographic levels: all

MARC Tag: 100 Main Entry—Personal Name. If an entry has also been made for AUTHOR, then the entry in this field will be demoted to MARC 700: Added Entry—Personal Name. If more than one name is supplied, those after the first are demoted to MARC 700: Added Entry—Personal Name. The program automatically creates an entry for MARC 100e or 700e: Relationship of the person to the Item, with the designation "Photographer". (Consult: AACR2 22.1-22.17; APPM 3.1-3.17. In cases where more than one person may be responsible for the work, also consult AACR2 21.1, 21.4-21.30.)

AGENCIES-OF-ORIGIN[110,710]

Enter the names of the organizations or conferences from which the materials came or who commissioned their creation. The names of conferences or meetings should be entered in this field, under the name of the organization sponsoring the conference. No separate field for conference names has been included.

It will be assumed that the documents originated with the agency named, in the sense that administrative records or annual reports derive from an agency. If the organization is not the originator, and you wish to specify the relationship of the organization to the material, you can employ a Relator Term. After the agency's name, place a colon and then the Relator Term. As a Relator Term use the singular form of a Library of Congress Subject Heading or use the *USMARC Code List for Relators, Sources, Description Conventions* (Washington, DC: Library of Congress, 1988). For example:

AGENCIES-OF-ORIGIN[110,710]:Security Pacific National Bank:Donor
TITLE[245]:Security Pacific National Bank Photographic
  Collection

AUTHORS[100,700]:Clark, David L.
AGENCIES-OF-ORIGIN[110,710]:Avery:Sponsor
TITLE[245]:Avery 50-Year History: 1935-1985

Bibliographic levels: all

MARC Tag: 110 Main Entry—Corporate Name. If MARC 100: Main Entry—Personal Name has been used, then the entry in this field will be demoted to MARC 710: Added Entry—Corporate Name. If more than one name is supplied, those after the first are demoted to MARC 710: Added Entry—Corporate Name. The program automatically creates an entry for MARC 110e or 710e: Relationship of the organization to the Item, with the designation "Originator". (Consult: AACR2 24.1-24.27; APPM 5.1-5.27. To determine if personal authorship or corporate authorship should apply, also consult AACR2 21.1, 21.4.)

Subject content of the materials

For SUBJECTS[650], enter subject terms from *Library of Congress Subject Headings*. Include the main topics that the photos, documents, or objects could be used to illustrate. For collection-level entries, limit yourself to a broad overview of the subjects included in the collection. SUBJECTS is the most important single field for searching. Judgement must be used in determining the relative importance of various possible topic entries.

I strongly recommend that you take your entries for the SUBJECTS field exclusively from the Library of Congress Subject Headings list. The entries should consist only of topical headings, and not include the names of persons, places, or organizations, whose names should be placed instead in fields specifically designated for persons, places, and organizations.

If you wish to use more than one subdivision after a subject term, then repeat the term. For example:

SUBJECTS[650]:Automobiles—Equipment and supplies;
  Automobiles—Maintenance and repair—Study and teaching

Note that in the example, "Study and teaching" represents a further subdivision of "Maintenance and repair". The material cataloged provides instruction in how to repair automobiles. "Study and teaching" could also be used as a subdivision directly after "Automobiles", to indicate instructional materials having to do with automobiles in general, rather than with how to repair automobiles.

Bibliographic levels: all

MARC Tag: 650 Subject Added Entry—Topical Heading. (Consult: *Library of Congress Subject Headings* and *Subject Cataloging Manual: Subject Headings*.)

PERSONS-SUBJECTS[600]

Enter the names of the individuals who appear in a photograph, are described in a document, or who otherwise have subject relevance. For collection-level entries, limit yourself to those who appear most prominently in the collection.

Bibliographic levels: all

MARC Tag: 600 Subject Added Entry-Personal Name. (Consult: AACR2 22.1-22.17, APPM 3.1-3.17.)

ORGANIZATIONS-SUBJECTS[610]

Enter the names of the organizations or conferences that appear in a photo, are described in a document, or that otherwise have subject relevance. For collection-level entries, limit yourself to those organizations that appear most prominently in the collection.

The distinction between conferences and organizations will be made in an Authority File for Agencies. Note that a photograph could have UCLA as its subject, because of an event with which the university was connected, even though the photograph was not taken on the UCLA campus. Do not confuse the usage of the PLACE-NAMES field with the ORGANIZATIONS-SUBJECTS field.

Bibliographic levels: all

MARC Tag: 610 Subject Added Entry—Corporate Name. (Consult: AACR2 24.1-24.27, APPM 5.1-5.27.)

TITLES-SUBJECTS[630]

Enter the title of the work or legal case that the materials describe. For documents that have as their subject a legal case, the title of the case would be stored in this field. For example: "Brown versus the Board of Education of Topeka, Kansas". For a work of criticism describing a book, film, or painting, the title of the book, film, or painting would appear in this field. For example: "Gone with the Wind".

Bibliographic levels: all

MARC Tag: 630 Subject Added Entry—Uniform Title. (Consult: AACR2 25.1-25.35, APPM 6.1-6.11.)

Subject content, time periods

In most cases the CAPTURE-DATES[033] of the document will coincide with the ERA[045B] of the document's subject content. Note, however, that a photo of a California mission might be said to illustrate an era different from that in which the photo was taken, thus the entries for CAPTURE-DATES[033] and ERA[045B] would be different. The movie "Gone with the Wind" was made in the 1930s, but its subject time period is the Civil War and Reconstruction. The fields CAPTURE-DATES[033] and ERA[045B] are juxtaposed to lead the cataloger to consider whether the entries for the two fields should be the same or different. If different entries are created, it will be possible, for example, to search for all the documents created in the 1930s that had as their subject the events of the 1860s.

In practice if not in theory, the degree of precision of the distinctions applied will most often correlate to how closely the item comes to the central interests of the person applying the distinctions. If the cataloger is required to apply distinctions that are more precise than his knowledge, the entries will be erroneous. It is preferable that an entry be broader than desired, rather than that it be incorrect.

In the following example, a group of photographs was taken on June 30, 1923. The cataloger has judged the photos to provide a representative view of the clothing styles of the 1920s.

```
SUBJECTS[650]:Clothing and dress
CAPTURE-DATES[033]:06/30/1923
ERA[045B]:1920-1930
```

If you are cataloging a collection of a million photos taken of 1920s clothing styles, you would want to apply much finer distinctions than would seem relevant to a person with only a few shots on the subject. The cataloger in the example listed the era's range as "1920-30". Another person might list the range more broadly as covering the inter-war period of "1920-1940". A cataloger specializing in the subject of 1920s clothing might define the time period more narrowly as covering only the early part of the decade, with the entry "1920-1923".

How is the searcher to find all of the 1920s clothing photographs, when the three catalogers have defined the time period covered so differently? The searcher could ask for the beginning and ending dates of ERA[045B] separately, as ERA-BEGIN and ERA-END. A searcher looking for 1920s clothing would be sure to retrieve all of the relevant photographs with the command:

```
SELECT ITEMS WITH SUBJECTS = "Clothing and dress"
  AND ERA-BEGIN BEFORE "1930"
  AND ERA-END AFTER "1919"
```

Virtual Field dictionary definitions can be created for time periods, such that a novice using the system could enter a simpler search statement, such as:

```
SELECT ITEMS WITH SUBJECTS = "Railroads" AND DURING-CIVIL-WAR
```

Note that no conventions for expressing uncertainty as to dates are to be used in the fields CAPTURE-DATES[033] and ERA[045B]. The field DATE-PLACE-NOTE[518] is used to record uncertainty or qualifications for the date and geographic place fields. DATE-PLACE-NOTE[518] is located at the end of the geographic fields.

CAPTURE-DATES[033]

Enter individual dates or first and last dates in the format MM/DD/YYYY, with the dates or period when the materials were created or found. In the case of a natural object, such as a fossil or a meteorite, enter the date when the object was found, not when it was created. If you are uncertain of the exact date, also use the field DATE-PLACE-NOTE.

A series of specific single dates, if known, should be entered in preference to a range of dates. For the item-level cataloging of discrete individual objects, such as photographs, it would be preferable to place photos taken on different dates in separate records, even if the photos shared the same subject content. An exception to this rule would be the case of a series of photographs taken over time that were meant to be used together to show a process of change. An example would be a series of photos of the construction of a building, all taken from the same vantage point, in order to illustrate the building process.

You will be able to search separately for the first and last dates entered into this field as CAPTURE-DATE-BEGIN and CAPTURE-DATE-END. If only the boundaries for beginning and ending dates can be established, place those dates in the field to provide a range of possible dates. For example, if a photograph shows a building constructed in 1960 and torn down in 1980, the photo must fall between those two dates. Enter the time period as "01/01/1960; 12/31/1980". Enter the two dates separately, rather than placing a hyphen between them.

If the date is approximate or uncertain, rather than using conventions such as hyphens, brackets, "ca.", or a question mark, which would prevent the efficient computer manipulation of the date for selecting ranges or time periods, put the reasons for qualifying the information in the field DATE-PLACE-NOTE[518]. Into the DATE-PLACE-NOTE[518] field you could place the date and location information with qualifiers included, in catalog-card format, or you could give a textual description of the reasons for believing that a particular date or place might apply when no precise information was available. For example:

CAPTURE-DATES[033]:01/01/1933; 12/31/1935
ERA[045B]:1933-1936
DATE-PLACE-NOTE[518]:The photo appears to have been shot during the early New Deal period, judging from the National Recovery Administration blue eagle visible in the store window.

Bibliographic levels: all

MARC Tag: 033 Date and Place of Capture. MARC does not provide for B.C. dates in this field. (Consult: AACR2 1.4F, 4.4B; APPM 1.1B5. For graphic materials: AACR2 8.4F; GIHC 2H. For three-dimensional artefacts and naturally occurring objects: AACR2 10.4F. For translation between the Julian and Gregorian calendars, consult AACR2 22.17A, footnote 18.)

ERA[045B]

Enter begin-end dates for the era that the material illustrates in a subject sense. For example: "1920-1940". For natural objects, enter the time period when the item originated. Record uncertainties about the time period in the field DATE-PLACE-NOTE[518].

For the sake of simplicity, always enter a range of dates, rather than single dates, and use only the years, without reference to month or day. For example, for a photo taken in 1923 that illustrates some aspect of the 1920s: "1920-1930". You will be able to search for the beginning and ending dates separately, as ERA-BEGIN and ERA-END.

It will be assumed that all the dates entered are A.D. For a B.C. date, enter "B.C." after the date. For example, for the reign of Hammurabi: "1792 B.C.-1750 B.C.".

Bibliographic levels: all

MARC Tag: 045b Range of Dates. The MARC format will not allow more than one range of dates.

Subjects, geographical places

The identification of exact location, in a manner that may easily be computer-searched, is extremely important in the cataloging of photographs. For other types of materials, such information should be included when a document describes or an object came from a particular location.

PLACE-NAMES[651]

Enter the names by which locations shown or described are known, particularly when there is no street address. For example: "Vasquez Rocks; Owens Lake". If you are uncertain of the exact place, also use the field DATE-PLACE-NOTE.

Bibliographic levels: all

MARC Tag: 651 Subject Added Entry—Geographical Name. (Consult: AACR2 23.2-23.5.)

STREET-ADDRESSES[651]

Enter street names and addresses, without abbreviations, for locations shown. For example: "Wilshire Boulevard and Fairfax Avenue; 123 North First Street". If you are uncertain of the exact place, also use the field DATE-PLACE-NOTE.

Bibliographic levels: all

MARC Tag: 651 Subject Added Entry—Geographical Name

COMMUNITIES[651]

Enter the names by which the communities shown or described are known, whether or not they are incorporated municipalities. For example: "Hollywood; San Pedro". (Hollywood and San Pedro are legally a part of the municipality of Los Angeles, but each community has a distinctive identity and is generally known by its community name.) If you are uncertain of the exact place, also use the Field DATE-PLACE-NOTE.

Bibliographic levels: all

MARC Tag: 651 Subject Added Entry—Geographical Name. (Consult: AACR2 23.2-23.5.)

CITIES[651]

Enter only the official, legal names of incorporated municipalities. For example: "Los Angeles; San Diego; City of Commerce". If you are uncertain of the exact place, also use the field DATE-PLACE-NOTE.

Bibliographic levels: all

MARC Tag: 651 Subject Added Entry—Geographical Name. (Consult: AACR2 23.2-23.5.)

COUNTIES[651]

Enter the names of the counties shown or described, for U.S. locations. For foreign countries use equivalent jurisdictions. If you are uncertain of the exact place, also use the field DATE-PLACE-NOTE.

Bibliographic levels: all

MARC Tag: 651 Subject Added Entry—Geographical Name. (Consult: AACR2 23.2-23.5.)

STATES[651]

Enter the names of the states shown or described, for U.S. locations. For foreign countries use equivalent jurisdictions. If you are uncertain of the exact place, also use the field DATE-PLACE-NOTE.

Bibliographic levels: all

MARC Tag: 651 Subject Added Entry—Geographical Name. (Consult: AACR2 23.2-23.5.)

COUNTRIES[651]

Enter the full names of the countries shown or described. Take the names from *Library of Congress Subject Headings*. If you are uncertain of the exact place, also use the field DATE-PLACE-NOTE.

Bibliographic levels: all

MARC Tag: 651 Subject Added Entry—Geographical Name. (Consult: AACR2 23.2-23.5.)

DATE-PLACE-NOTE[518]

If you are uncertain of an exact date or place, repeat the information from the date and location Fields, in catalog-card format, with qualifications or notes. For example: "1927; ca. 1927; ca. 1925-1927; San Diego (Calif.)?".

An alternative practice, if you did not intend to use this information on printed catalog cards, would be simply to record your uncertainty, perhaps including the basis on which you judged a particular date and place assignment to be probable. For example: "Date approximate; Location not certain".

This field should only be used to record reasons for uncertainty, rather than used for free-form descriptive information, which belongs in the field DESCRIPTION[545]. A user might search field DATE-PLACE-NOTE[518] not for content, but for existence or non-existence, as an indication of whether the information in the date and place fields was exact or uncertain. For example, a supervisor or subject specialist might call up the records with an entry in the field DATE-PLACE-NOTE[518] for review, in order to supply more exact information, with the search statement:

```
SELECT ITEMS IF DATE-PLACE-NOTE
```

Bibliographic levels: all
MARC Tag: 518 Date and Place of Capture/Finding Note

Physical description

For NUMBER-UNITS[300a], enter the number of photos, maps, manuscripts, or other separate but closely-related items whose descriptions have been combined in a single record. If the number is approximate, place a number in this field, and indicate in the NOTE[500] field that an approximate number was used. Do not use a question mark, "ca.", or brackets to indicate approximation. This field is important from an administrative standpoint, because it will be used in constructing progress reports on the total number of items cataloged.

Bibliographic levels:

Collection: Total number of items in the collection. For printed materials, number of pages. For archival materials, boxes or linear feet.

Item: Indicates either a single item or that a number of items have been grouped together. If more than one document or photo is included in a record, they should either be duplicates, or they should share, not only a common subject matter, but also a common point of creation. For example, do not simply group together a number of different airplane photographs. But you might include in a single record photos taken of the same airplane on the same day by the same photographer, who shot the plane from a number of different angles. Within the narrative DESCRIPTION[545] field, you might distinguish between the different photos. A label placed on the mylar sleeve holding the photograph would identify the photo first by RECORD-ID and then by UNIT#.

MARC Tag: 300a Physical Description—Extent. (Consult: AACR2 1.5B; APPM 1.5B. For graphic materials: GIHC 3B.)

FORMATS[300C]

Enter height followed by width. Include depth for three-dimensional objects. Inches: "in.". Centimeters: "cm.". Millimeters: "mm." For example: "8 x 10 in.; 35 mm.".

Bibliographic levels: all

MARC Tag: 300c Physical Description—Dimensions. (Consult: AACR2 1.5D; APPM 1.5D. For graphic materials: GIHC 3D.)

COLORS[300B]

For black and white, use "b&w". For color, use "col." (Include the period.) To these choices AACR2 paragraph 8.5C2 adds "sepia". GIHC does not use "sepia", but for hand-colored materials GIHC adds "hand col.". Consistent standards are wonderful. My suggestion is to use only "b&w" and "col.".

Bibliographic levels: all

MARC Tag: 300b Physical Description—Details. (Consult: AACR2 1.5C. For graphic materials: AACR2 8.5C2, GIHC 3C4.)

RECORD-TYPE[L/06]

A help message will offer the cataloger the following abbreviated list of choices:

> Text, Graphic, Projected medium, Three-dimensional, Archival,
> Kit, Manuscript map, Printed map, Nonmusical sound recording,
> Musical sound recording, Computer file

This field may not be left blank. The cataloger can either enter a term from the simplified and abbreviated list, or enter one of the official codes or terms taken from *USMARC Bibliographic Format.* At the time of information transfer, the database program will convert the simplified terms to the official codes or terms. The official designations are listed in TABLE 19-1.

Bibliographic levels: all

MARC Tag: Leader /06 Type of Record. (Consult: *USMARC Bibliographic Format.*)

Table 19-1. Codes and terms for record type

Code	Term
a	Text (Official term: Language material)
b	Archival (Official term: Archival and manuscripts control. This category describes the kind of control, not the type of material.)
c	Printed music
d	Manuscript music
e	Printed map
f	Manuscript map
g	Projected medium (Examples: slides, films.)
h	Nonmusical sound recording (Example: Oral history tapes.)
j	Musical sound recording
k	Graphic (Official term: Two-dimensional nonprojectable graphic. Examples: photoprints, photonegatives, drawings, paintings, charts, postcards.)
m	Computer file
o	Kit (A mixture of several types, with none predominant.)
r	Three-dimensional (Official term: Three-dimensional artifact or naturally occurring object.)

GENRES[655]

Enter terms for the types of material, from *Library of Congress Subject Headings* and other guides. For example: "Advertisements; Architectural drawings; Portraits". The GENRES and PHYSICAL-FORMS fields are juxtaposed to lead the cataloger in distinguishing two different types of information that are often confused.

Bibliographic levels: all

MARC Tag: 655 Genre/Form. (Consult: *Library of Congress Subject Headings* for terms describing the form of material. Additional sources: For graphic materials: *Descriptive Terms for Graphic Materials* (GMGPC). For archival materials: *Form Terms for Archival and Manuscripts Control* (FTAMC). For motion pictures: *Moving Image Materials* (MIM).)

PHYSICAL-FORMS[755]

Enter terms for the physical form of the materials, from *Library of Congress Subject Headings* and other guides. For example: "Photoprints, Photonegatives". More specific terms to enter would include: "Glass photonegatives; Film photonegatives; Dry plate photonegatives; Cellulose nitrate photonegatives."

Bibliographic levels: all

MARC 755: Physical Characteristics. (Consult: *Library of Congress Subject Headings* for terms describing the physical form of material. Additional sources: For graphic materials: *Descriptive Terms for Graphic Materials* (GMGPC). For archival materials: *Form Terms for Archival and Manuscripts Control* (FTAMC). For motion pictures: *Moving Image Materials* (MIM).)

LANGUAGES[008/35-37,041]

The languages used in the collection. When several languages appear, list the most predominant first. For example: "English; Spanish". If only a few minor instances occur of words in languages other than the predominant language, record only the predominant language. The program will initially supply a Default Choice of "English" as the language.

Bibliographic levels: collections only

MARC Tags: 008/35-37 Language, 041 Language Code.

Administrative control, present

For PROJECTS[692], enter the name of the project for which the material is cataloged. The database program should fill in this field from information given at the initial setup. The cataloger can change or add to the Default Choice.

This field is important from an administrative standpoint, to keep track of work performed under different funding arrangements. For example, the initials "NHPRC" might be entered to keep track of the items cataloged under a grant from the National Historical Publications and Records Commission. In combination with the fields NUMBER-UNITS[300A] and ENTRY-DATE[008/00-05], a progress report would show how many records were created and how many individual items were brought under control in a given time period. An individual researcher might use this field to indicate the book or article for which a photo or piece of information was intended. A consultant would use the field for the name of a client.

Bibliographic levels: all

MARC Tag: 692 Local Subject Added Entry

FILE-HEADING[693]

Enter locally-defined terms for the location where the material is filed or the heading under which it is managed administratively. Try to choose a single term. If the physical item is placed in a file drawer by subject designation, enter the designation here. In this case, only one file heading entry should be made per record, because the physical item will be stored in only one place. The great disadvantage of storing and retrieving items by subject file heading is that although an item such as a photograph may contain many subjects, the photo itself can be placed in only one location. In the photo cataloging that I have done as an historical consultant, more than 95 percent of the changes made to the records that I created were in the file heading field. When the collection is completely computer-cataloged, it will be much more convenient to store the physical items by Record-ID, and look up records by subject content in the computer database.

An individual researcher might use this field to designate the chapter in a future book for which the material was intended. When the researcher was ready to write that chapter, the material that contained that file heading would be transferred to a word processor.

Bibliographic levels: all

MARC Tag: 693 Local Subject Added Entry. (Consult: For subject file headings, use terms from *Library of Congress Subject Headings* if possible.)

ENTRY-DATE[008/00-05]

This is the date when the record was first entered, in the format MM/DD/YYYY. The program should automatically assign the current date. The difference between ENTRY-DATE[008/00-05] and EDIT-DATE[005] is that EDIT-DATE is changed each time that a record is edited, while ENTRY-DATE remains the same.

Bibliographic levels: all
MARC Tag: 008/00-05 Date Entered on File

EDIT-DATE[005]

This is the date when the record was last changed, in the format MM/DD/YYYY. The program should automatically assign the current date. If you are going through your collection and making modifications, EDIT-DATE[005] will tell you whether or not your editing process has reached a particular record yet. For example, if you were in the middle of revising personal names according to more current information, you could use EDIT-DATE to differentiate between records holding the old names and records holding the new names.

When you have two copies of the same record, EDIT-DATE will tell you which record is the most current. For example, if you are restoring records from a backup, the EDIT-DATE field would tell you if the hard disk or the backup had the more current information.

Rather than taking the time to backup your entire database at the end of the day, you might choose to make copies of only those records with today's date in the EDIT-DATE field. If you are contributing records to a shared database, you would transmit only those records for which the EDIT-DATE field indicated that the record had been added or edited since the last time that you sent records to the shared database.

Bibliographic levels: all

MARC Tag: 005 Date and Time of Latest Transaction. Time is not used here. MARC defines this field as not repeating, therefore the field will be changed to the latest date, rather than adding on a new date each time the record is edited.

ACTIONS[583]

These are actions that should be taken to preserve or copy the materials or to add to the information in the database record. Include unit numbers for grouped items. For example: "Information needed; Preserve: 7, 14".

If the field is to be searched or used for producing summary reports to show, for example, how many nitrate negatives remain to be copied to safety film, then a controlled list of terms must be applied to the field. If more information is needed, begin the field with the word "Information". If preservation actions are required, begin the field with the word "Preserve". A truncation operator can be employed to examine only the first portion of the field.

To retrieve all of the records that indicated that some action was needed, you would enter the search command:

```
SELECT ITEMS WITH ACTIONS
```

To retrieve the records for which more information was required:

```
SELECT ITEMS WITH ACTIONS = "Info]"
```

To retrieve the records for of materials which needed preservation:

```
SELECT ITEMS WITH ACTIONS = "Preserv]"
```

Bibliographic levels: all

MARC Tag: 583 Actions. (Consult: Examples of Controlled Vocabularies for the ACTIONS[583] field appear in *MARC for Archives and Manuscripts: A Compendium of Practice,* Appendix F.)

ARRANGEMENT[351]

This is the order in which the physical items are stored, by Record-ID, by FILE-HEADING, etc.

Bibliographic levels: collections only

MARC Tag: 351 Organization and Arrangement. (Consult: APPM 1.7B5; GIHC 5B16.)

CATALOGERS[593]

Enter the names of the individuals who wrote or edited the record. The program should automatically fill in the name of the person who first wrote the record. A person editing the record should add his or her name only when significant new information has been added to the identification of the materials.

Bibliographic levels: all

MARC Tag: 593 Local Note for Persons Providing Information. (Consult: For the catalogers' names use the standard conventions for personal names in AACR2 22.1-22.17, APPM 3.1-3.17.)

CATALOGING-AGENCY[040]

This is an identification of the organization that cataloged the record. The identification should be the National Union Catalog symbol for the repository. The symbols appear in the Library of Congress publication *Symbols of American Libraries*. To obtain a National Union Catalog symbol, write to the Library of Congress at the address listed in the Bibliography.

The fields CATALOGING-AGENCY, CUSTODIAN, and CREDIT are juxtaposed because the CUSTODIAN will most often be the same as the CATALOGING-AGENCY, and the name of the CUSTODIAN will generally appear in the CREDIT. Use the database program feature of repeating information from a previous field to provide the information without re-typing.

Bibliographic levels: collections only

MARC Tag: 040 Cataloging Source. (Consult: If a National Union Catalog symbol is not employed, then use the standard conventions for the names of organizations in AACR2 24.1-24.27 and APPM 5.1-5.27.)

CUSTODIAN[851A]

This is the repository now holding the collection. Information such as the street address of the custodian should not be placed in the bibliographic record. If the address should change, all of the records would have to be changed. A database program can retrieve information such as the address and phone number from a separate REPOSITORIES or ADDRESS.BOOK file, using the name of the custodian.

Bibliographic levels: collections only

MARC Tag: 851a Holdings Location—Custodian. The street address (MARC 851c: Holdings Location—Street address) will be held in a separate file. (Consult: For the name of the repository holding the materials, use the standard conventions for the names of organizations in AACR2 24.1-24.27 and APPM 5.1-5.27.)

CREDIT[524]

This is the credit line that should appear with the photo caption when a photo is used for publication, or that is required for other materials.

Bibliographic levels: collections only

MARC 524: Preferred Citation. (Consult: APPM 1.7B15.)

RESTRICTIONS-ON-ACCESS[506]

These refer to restrictions that would inhibit the opportunity for a researcher to examine the materials. The field for RESTRICTIONS-ON-ACCESS is juxtaposed with TERMS-FOR-USE to make a clear distinction between restrictions that would prevent a researcher from examining the materials and restrictions on the use of those materials for publication.

Bibliographic levels: collections only

MARC Tag: 506 Restrictions on Access. (Consult: AACR2 1.7B20, 4.7B14; APPM 1.7B11; GIHC 5B24.)

TERMS-FOR-USE[540A]

These are terms attached to the use of photographs or information for publication. The terms limiting use will often originate from the previous owner, therefore the information about the previous owner follows this field.

Bibliographic levels: collections only

MARC Tag: 540a Terms Governing Use and Reproduction. (Consult: APPM 1.7B12; GIHC 5B24.)

Administrative control, past

For OTHER-IDS[035], enter any identification codes previously placed on the item that might prove useful later for reference. For example, a number assigned by a photo studio. The number might have been assigned by another institution, or by the same institution under a previous numbering system. In the case of archival materials, the identification will most likely have been applied by the previous owner, therefore the PREVIOUS-OWNER[541] field follows OTHER-IDS.

The criterion for filling in this field is whether the information is likely to be useful. For example, photographs collected by C. C. Pierce appear in libraries and archives throughout Southern California. The number assigned by C. C. Pierce is often visible on the print. The number could be used to find duplicates of the photo in other repositories, or to locate the original negative held in the Title Insurance Collection of the California Historical Society. The National Union Catalog symbol or name of the organization that assigned the number should be placed in parentheses before the number, with no intervening spaces. For example: "(C.C. Pierce)2401".

The MARC format provides separate fields for placing call or control numbers assigned by several prominent institutions or under widely-used classification schemes. For the sake of simplicity, these numbers will be placed in the field OTHER-IDS[035] rather than in separate fields. If the call or control number derives from one of the sources listed below, place in parentheses either the MARC Tag number or the abbreviation shown. To make an entry for a MARC field whose Tag number begins with zero, and that does not appear on the list, supply the Tag number in parentheses.

010a LCCN: Library of Congress Control Number

010b NUCMC: National Union Catalog of Manuscript Collections Control Number

020 ISBN: International Standard Book Number

022 ISSN: International Standard Serial Number

027 STRN: Standard Technical Report Number

030 CODEN: CODEN Designation (for scientific periodicals)

050 LC Call: Library of Congress Call Number

060 NLM: National Library of Medicine Call Number

070 NAL: National Agricultural Library Call Number

074 GPO: Government Printing Office Item Number

082 Dewey: Dewey Decimal Call Number

If the call number applied by another institution would commonly be used to represent the bibliographic item, then that number, without the institutional name, should also be used for the COLLECTION[001] field.

Bibliographic levels: all

MARC Tag: 035 System Control Number. (Consult: AACR2 1.7B19, 1.8B; GIHC 5B19.)

SOURCE-OF-ACQUISITION[541A]

This is the immediate source of acquisition of the collection. Place here one name only for the person or institution from whom the collection was obtained. The names of all of the previous owners of the collection will appear in the HISTORY-OF-OWNERSHIP[561] field. Other details, such as the date of the acquisition and the purchase price, should also be placed in the HISTORY-OF-OWNERSHIP[561] field.

Bibliographic levels: collections only

MARC Tag: 541a Immediate Source of Acquisition. (Consult: AACR2 4.7B7; APPM 1.7B10; GIHC 5B26. For the names of individuals, use the standard conventions for personal names in AACR2 22.1-22.17 and APPM 3.1-3.17. For the names of organizations, use the standard conventions for organizational names in AACR2 24.1-24.27 and APPM 5.1-5.27.)

OWNERSHIP-RETAINED[541F]

This is to be used only in cases where the repository does not own the collection. Name the person or institution that retains ownership. The person or institution listed in the field SOURCE-OF-ACQUISITION[541A] might have only placed the collection on deposit, without relinquishing legal ownership. If the repository holding the collection has legal ownership, leave this field blank. Only one name for a person or institution should appear in this field.

An administrator or curator could quickly check to see if there was a complication in regard to ownership by simply asking whether anything had been placed in this field, with the following type of search statement:

SELECT COLLECTIONS IF OWNERSHIP-RETAINED

The following entries in the fields SOURCE-OF-ACQUISITION[541A] and OWNERSHIP-RETAINED[541F] indicate that the Avery corporation has placed the materials on deposit, while retaining ownership:

SOURCE-OF-ACQUISITION[541A]:Avery
OWNERSHIP-RETAINED[541F]:Avery

Bibliographic levels: collections only

MARC Tag: 541f Immediate Source of Acquisition—Owner. (Consult: AACR2 4.7B7; APPM 1.7B10; GIHC 5B26. For the names of individuals, use the standard conventions for personal names in AACR2 22.1-22.17 and APPM 3.1-3.17. For the names of organizations, use the standard conventions for organizational names in AACR2 24.1-24.27 and APPM 5.1-5.27.)

HISTORY-OF-OWNERSHIP[561]

This is the provenance of the collection, including a description of the history of the creation, acquisition, and transference of the collection through all of its previous owners.

Bibliographic levels: collections only

MARC Tag: 561 Provenance. (Consult: AACR2 4.7B7; APPM 1.7B9; GIHC 5B25. For the names of individuals, use the standard conventions for personal names in AACR2 22.1-22.17 and APPM 3.1-3.17. For the names of organizations, use the standard conventions for organizational names in AACR2 24.1-24.27 and APPM 5.1-5.27.)

PUBLISHER[260B]

For a book, periodical, or other published work, enter the name of the publisher.

Bibliographic levels: collections only

MARC Tag: 260B Name of publisher, distributor, etc. (Consult: AACR2 2.4D, 12.4D.)

PUBLICATION-PLACE[260A]

For a book, periodical, or other published work, enter the place of publication.

Bibliographic levels: collections only

MARC Tag: 260A Place of Publication, distribution, etc. (Consult: AACR2 2.4C, 12.4C.)

PUBLICATION-DATE[260C]

For a book, periodical, or other published work, enter the date of publication. Use the same format employed for dates elsewhere in the record: "MM/DD/YYYY".

Bibliographic levels: collections only

MARC Tag: 260C Date of Publication, distribution, etc. (Consult: AACR2 2.4F, 12.4F.)

SERIAL-VOLUME-DATE[362]

This is for serials, and it gives the volume, number, and date. For example: "Vol. 2, no. 3 (April 1972)".

Bibliographic levels: collections only

MARC Tag: 362 Dates of Publication and/or Volume Designation. (Consult: AACR2 12.3.)

EDITION[250A]

This field is for books, and it gives the number of the edition. For example: "2nd ed." or "2nd ed., revised, 1974".

Bibliographic levels: collections only

MARC Tag: 250a Edition Statement. (Consult: AACR2 2.2.)

REVISED-BY[250B]

This field tells the persons or agencies responsible for the revision. For example: "Edited by Ezra Pound, annotations included."

Bibliographic levels: collections only

MARC Tag: 250b Remainder of edition statement. (Consult: AACR2 2.2E.)

DISSERTATION-NOTE[502]

This is for theses and dissertations, and it tells the degree, institution, and year the degree was granted. For example: "Thesis (doctoral)—Sorbonne, Paris, 1968".

Bibliographic levels: collections only

MARC Tag: 502 Dissertation Note. (Consult: AACR2 2.7B13.)

BIBLIOGRAPHY-INDEX-NOTE[504]

Indicate the presence of a bibliography or index in the work. For example: "Includes bibliography and index."

Bibliographic levels: collections only

MARC Tag: 504 Bibliography Note. (Consult: AACR2 2.7B18.)

TABLE-OF-CONTENTS[505]

This field contains the table of contents of a work. For archival materials, this field gives the table of contents of a finding aid, which can be used to help locate items in a collection.

Bibliographic levels: collections only

MARC Tag: 505 Formatted Contents Note. (Consult: AACR2 2.7B18.)

NOTE[500]

Enter comments for internal administrative and cataloging use. Include suggestions for sources of additional information about the materials. On the collections level, include leads to information about a previous owner.

The database program should not include the NOTE field in screen displays and printouts for patrons. A useful distinction to make between NOTE and DESCRIPTION[545] is whether a researcher is likely to have an interest in the information. Put the information of general interest in the DESCRIPTION[545]. Put information only of interest for processing purposes, or information concerning private individuals, in the NOTE.

Bibliographic levels: all

MARC Tag: 500 General Note. (Consult: AACR2 1.7; APPM 1.7B17.)

Other sources of information

FINDING AIDS[555] contains descriptions of any aids that can be used to look up items in the collection. For example: "The items have been cataloged into a computer database and may be searched on any field. In addition indexes have been printed for the fields: SUBJECTS, PERSONS-SUBJECTS, and ORGANIZATIONS-SUBJECTS".

Bibliographic levels: collections only

MARC Tag: 555 Cumulative Index/Finding Aids. (Consult: APPM 1.7B13; GIHC 5B18.)

CITATIONS[510]

These are published references to the collection, which may be useful in providing a detailed description.

Bibliographic levels: collections only

MARC Tag: 510 Citation Note. (Consult: AACR2 1.7B15, 4.7B15; APPM 1.7B14; GIHC 5B12.)

Summary and description

SCOPE and DESCRIPTION are the longest fields in the record. They consist of text in narrative form, and would seldom be searched. No Authority File or other measures of control are applied to these fields.

SCOPE[520]

This gives a descriptive summary of the extent of the collection. Just as the DESCRIPTION field in the ITEMS file should be able to stand alone as a caption for the item in a book or exhibit, so the SCOPE field in the COLLECTIONS file should have the capability of standing alone as a summary of the most important aspects of the collection. For example: "The collection deals principally with the economic development of Los Angeles in the 1920s and 1930s, especially the spread of branch-plant manufacturing as eastern auto and rubber firms built plants on the west coast".

Bibliographic levels: collections only

MARC Tag: 520 Scope and Summary. (Consult: AACR2 1.7B1, 1.7B17, 4.7B1, 4.7B17, 8.7B1, 8.7B17; APPM 1.7B7; GIHC 5B14.)

DESCRIPTION[545]

For an item, describe the item's most significant aspects. Distinguish different items in the group by unit number. Summarize the information in the first sentence. For a collection, enter biographical information about the individual or historical background about the organization that is the main focus of the collection.

The DESCRIPTION[545] field places the item or collection within an historical context. The field is occasionally computer-searched for details that it contains that appear nowhere else. The field is most often scanned by sight, after a computer search has yielded a group of records with similar subject identifications.

The first sentence should contain a succinct description that could be scanned quickly by a person looking through the file for a particular kind of information. For example, as a first sentence: "An outstanding collections of photos of aircraft production at the Douglas plant in Santa Monica in 1936".

Some information from the individual fields can be repeated here for the convenience of patron scanning and to allow this field to be employed as a complete caption for use in a book, journal, or exhibit by transferring the database information directly into a word processor.

Bibliographic levels:

Collection: Biographical information about the individual or historical background about the organization that is the main focal point of of the collection. For example, for the Edward Dickson papers, in additional to providing biographical information on Dickson, the note would highlight his role in founding UCLA, since university relations are the major subject of the collection.

Item: A description, in the form of a caption, of the photograph, document, or other item. The note might also describe the item's importance and the potential uses to which it could be put. The description should include the names of all the individuals and organizations depicted or mentioned to a significant extent. The description might also distinguish between different items grouped together. For example: "Photo 1 Exterior view of the Douglas plant. 2 Donald Douglas. 3-9 Building a DC-3." When different photos are grouped together, start with the pictures that give the best overall view, and then proceed to the more detailed images.

MARC Tag: 545 Biographical or Historical Note. (Consult: APPM 1.7B6; GIHC 5B15.)

20

Simplifying The MARC format

The 80-20 Rule is a rule of thumb for computer application programs. The rule states that approximately 80 percent of a user's time is spent using only 20 percent of the features that a program offers. For a novice user the proportion is higher, in the range of 90-10.

This rule provides a rough guide for computer programmers and instructors. To make a program more accessible, or to teach the use of a program, identify and concentrate on those features that are used most frequently.

For those users with more experience, more interest, or special needs, provide additional facilities that will allow them to learn and to utilize the program's more esoteric features. But do not allow the tools for creating elaborate page layouts to clutter the path of someone who simply wants to write a letter or print a report. If the user wants to graduate to desktop publishing and electronic teleconferencing, he or she should be willing to undertake the extra learning involved. The 80-20 rule is thus perhaps only a corollary of the broader guideline of focusing on "the greatest good for the greatest number." Make those facilities that the greatest number of people need the most easily accessible.

The same rule of 80-20 or 90-10 will guide you in simplifying the MARC format. Focus on those parts of a bibliographic description that have the greatest applicability, such as identifying the author who wrote the work or the photographer who took the picture. Allow the user to enter this information in the most natural manner that you can provide. The special coding instructions that MARC requires will be supplied by the computer database program.

Those features of MARC that are used less often, or that are of interest to a smaller group of catalogers and researchers, will still be available. But to use them, you will have to learn considerably more than how to type in the name of an author.

In this chapter, I hope to provide a broad, well-lighted central highway, with road signs and guide posts clearly marked. Travel on this highway will be possible with minimum knowledge and experience. The person who seeks a destination that is not of interest to many of his or her fellow travelers will need to carry a map and a full tank of gas. Human beings might be created equal, but destinations are not. No department of transportation would provide as many highways leading to Mojave Flats as to Los Angeles.

Methods used

The program employed will allow you to enter information on a data entry form. In most cases you will not be bothered with the technical details of the MARC format. The program will simplify MARC through the use of the following methods:

Default Choices: The program will assume certain Default Choices, such as the use of Library of Congress Subject Headings as the only source of topical terms. The Default Choice can be over-ridden by an experienced cataloger.

Data Normalization: The program will convert the information into the format required. For example, MARC requires that in field 008, bytes 00-05 contain the Date Entered on File in the format "YYMMDD". "January 31, 1989" would be entered as "890131". The program will take the Default Choice for the date automatically from the computer clock. The date will be displayed to the user in the commonly-used and readable format "MM/DD/YYYY". "January 31, 1989" will appear as "01/31/1989". The program will convert the date to MARC's required format when exporting MARC records.

Data Validation: The program will warn if the user tries to enter invalid data, such as information that does not constitute a valid date.

Authority Files: The program will automatically check entries against Authority Files provided for the fields most critical for searching. The program will warn if an entry for a field such as SUBJECTS[650] does not already appear in the Authority File for that field. Authority File information will also be used for the codes required by MARC.

Limited Choices: The default data entry form made available will not include all of the fields and options available in MARC. It will only include those that have been judged to be most important. The user can add other fields.

Is it justifiable to simplify MARC?

What is wrong with the MARC format is that it does not follow the 80-20 rule. The format is democratic in the wrong sense. It treats all purposes as equal. The degree of difficulty for entering the most commonly-used information is the same as for information that might be called upon once in a blue moon.

At the 1986 annual meeting of the Society of American Archivists, there was still a great deal of hand-wringing about standardization and the MARC format. The complaints took the form of special pleading. The complainant alleged that MARC would not allow him to achieve some very unique purpose in quite the manner that he was accustomed to.

MARC stretched itself as much as possible to accommodate all such objections. In the process MARC-AMC (MARC for Archival and Manuscripts Control) bloated out to 77 fields with up to 20 sub-fields each. David Bearman, chairman of the National Information Systems Task Force, which created the MARC-AMC format, makes very clear in the series of task force reports published by the Society of American Archivists that the format was stretched to accommodate everyone's special needs and pet fields for political reasons, in order to secure the format's approval.

The NISTF papers explain that the MARC-AMC standards are descriptive rather than prescriptive. The standards simply sanctioned existing practice with a consistent vocabulary. The data dictionary was inclusive and "Inclusion meant everything." In order to win acceptance by the archival profession, the dictionary included virtually any data element in use by anyone. Including everything does not make for an efficient cataloging process. It was anticipated that most repositories would choose a limited subset out of all the possibilities allowed by MARC-AMC.[1]

Let the computer make the translations

The task of entering data compatible with the MARC format can be greatly simplified by employing a computer database program to translate between human-readable data entries and the appropriate MARC codes. Professor Frank Burke, of the University of Maryland's School of Library and Information Science, has forcibly presented the case for leaving the codes to the computer: "Why anyone would want to confront a display of numeric codes instead of . . . simple statements in plain English is puzzling . . . . Let [the programmers] do whatever they want with numeric tags and transmission or reception of data, but don't bother us with all of these obscure codes; we want plain language or at least code words that are meaningful. Archivists need to know MARC-AMC about as much as they need to know COBOL or PL/1."[2]

On the last point, note that COBOL, an acronym for Common Business-Oriented Language, was initially conceived as a vehicle by which non-programmers could direct a computer. Instead, COBOL became a language for programmers. In the same manner, MARC could become a language for technicians, without a need for the user to learn the underlying intricacies.

Simplified cataloging will encourage the use of subject specialists

A more difficult cataloging process means that fewer people can do it, or do it well. Today, there is a shortage of librarians, and among librarians, there is a still more severe shortage of capable catalogers.[3]

It would seem appropriate, therefore, to make maximum use of computer database management facilities and simplified procedures to facilitate the cataloging process. From my own personal standpoint as an historian, I hope that facilitating the cataloging process will encourage using subject specialists as catalogers who have content knowledge of the materials.

Default choices

Default choices will greatly simplify your use of the MARC format. Rather than requiring that you enter the various MARC Indicator and Sub-Field codes, the program will furnish the values that would apply in most or nearly all cases. If a particular default choice does not apply to your situation, you will have two options:

---

[1]*NISTF Papers*, pages 5–6, 82, 99.

[2]Frank G. Burke, "Real Archivists Don't Use Marc," *Archives and Museum Informatics*, Volume 3, Number 1 (Spring 1989), pages 7-12.

[3]In March 1989 the Council on Library Resources sponsored a symposium on the difficulty which libraries across the United States have experienced in finding qualified catalogers. Janet Swan Hill, "Stalking the Elusive Cataloger", in *American Libraries*, Volume 20, Number 5 (May 1989), pages 458, 460.

- Over-ride the default for the individual case by writing in the desired value yourself.
- Change the default in the parameters file, from which the defaults are taken.

The names of two different parameter files will appear in descriptions of alternative default choices for the data fields. The file simply named PARAMETERS holds general program parameters, such as the character that the user would type as a Sub-Field Delimiter, to separate one sub-field from the next. The suggested choice is a semicolon, but you could choose something else.

The second file, named MARC.PARAMETERS, holds the default choices that will be used when converting a database record to MARC exchange format. For example, the user will not be required to enter an Indicator value for a field. The program will use the Indicator value specified for that field in the MARC.PARAMETERS file as the default choice.

Parameter files can be changed in the same way that you enter or edit data, through the use of a data entry form. For each parameter the form will display a descriptive name and the present value. The user can change the value shown. The following example shows the default choice for Sub-Field Delimiter, which is a semicolon. The user could change the value shown.

```
SUB-FIELD-DELIMITER:;
```

21

Authority Files

An experienced cataloger has the option of entering MARC Indicator and Sub-Field Codes directly into the record on the data entry form. A better use of that experienced cataloger's time, however, would be to create and maintain an Authority File that would provide the necessary translations to supply the MARC codes.

The Authority Record will make the correlation between the name as it would be entered by the user, and the additional MARC codes and information to apply for translation. The entry in the following data record is for Pope John Paul II. (The form of name with title following after a comma is taken from AACR2 1988, paragraph 22.16B.)

```
RECORD-ID:John Paul II, Pope
INDICATOR:00
NAME[A]:John Paul
NUMERATION[B]:II
TITLE[C]:Pope
DATES[D]:1920-
FULLER-FORM[Q]:
```

Using the information in the Authority Record, the program will convert "John Paul II, Pope" to:

```
100 00+aJohn Paul+bII+cPope+d1920–
```

For a person with a compound surname, such as the French Premier Pierre Mendès-France:

```
RECORD-ID:Mendès-France, Pierre
INDICATOR:20
NAME[A]:Mendès-France, Pierre
NUMERATION[B]:
TITLE[C]:
DATES[D]:1907–1982
FULLER-FORM[Q]:
```

For a simpler case, such as that of William Mulholland, builder of the Los Angeles Aqueduct:

RECORD-ID:Mulholland, William
INDICATOR:10
NAME[A]:Mulholland, William
NUMERATION[B]:
TITLE[C]:
DATES[D]:1855-1935
FULLER-FORM[Q]:

For the case of a person who was commonly known by a shortened form of his name, such as E. F. Scattergood, the builder of the system that created electric power from the Los Angeles Aqueduct:

RECORD-ID:Scattergood, E. F.
INDICATOR:10
NAME[A]:Scattergood, E. F.
NUMERATION[B]:
TITLE[C]:
DATES[D]:1871-1947
FULLER-FORM[Q]:Scattergood, Ezra Frederick

Control of data fields

The database program should create and maintain Authority Files for the categories and specific fields indicated in TABLE 21-1. For example, a personal name might appear in one of the fields for the creator of the materials, or in a field for individuals who are the subjects of the materials. In a database record for a photograph, a personal name would designate the photographer, while another personal name would indicate who was shown in the photo. In either case, the program would refer to the PERSONS Authority File to see if the name had appeared previously.

Table 21-1. Data fields controlled by Authority Files

Category & Filename	**Fields Controlled**
SUBJECTS	SUBJECTS[650]
PERSONS	AUTHORS[100,700] PHOTOGRAPHERS[100,700] SUBJECTS-PERSONS[600]
ORGANIZATIONS	AGENCIES-OF-ORIGIN[110,710] SUBJECTS-ORGANIZATIONS[610]
PLACE-NAMES	PLACE-NAMES[651]

Retrieving Authority Records

The authorized heading will be used as the Record-ID for the Authority Record. For the subject heading "Automobiles," the SUBJECTS Authority File will contain a record with the Record-ID "Automobiles". This record can be retrieved with a search statement, just like any data record. To retrieve the "Automobiles" Authority Record by Record-ID you would enter the search statement shown below. The Record-ID is surrounded by single right quote marks. To select the Authority Record for "Automobiles", enter the command:

SELECT SUBJECTS 'Automobiles'

Each Authority Record heading will be complete. In the case of the SUBJECTS file, the topical subject heading will include topical subdivisions, such as "Automobiles—Maintenance and repair". The headings for persons, places, and organizations will not have subdivisions. To select the Authority Record for "Automobiles—Maintenance and repair", enter the command:

SELECT SUBJECTS 'Automobiles—Maintenance and repair'

To select all of the Authority Records for which the main heading was "Automobiles", whether or not subdivisions were included, you would use the right truncation operator, which is the right bracket mark. The Record-ID would be surrounded by double quote marks, and preceded by the "=" sign. To select the Authority Records for which "Automobiles" is the main heading, with or without subdivisions, enter the command:

SELECT SUBJECTS = "Automobiles]"

To find all of the Authority Record for which "Maintenance and repair" was a subdivision, you would use the left truncation operator, which is the left bracket mark. You would also use the right truncation operator, in case this subdivision was followed by a further subdivision. The Record-ID would be surrounded by double quote marks, and preceded by the "=" sign.

SELECT SUBJECTS = "[Maintenance and repair]"

At the time of data transfer, the program will convert the information in the Authority Records to orthodox MARC Authorities format. The only type of Authority Record employed, as designated in MARC 008/09, will be type "a", for an established heading.

Authority File for SUBJECTS

The Authority File for topical subjects is named SUBJECTS. The authorized form of the subject heading will be used as the Record-ID for that topic's record. The Authority File will be applied to the field SUBJECTS[650], which contains topical subject headings, in the same manner as was previously described for the fields holding personal names. An experienced cataloger can over-ride the values held in the SUBJECTS Authority File by entering specific MARC Indicator and Sub-Field codes. The default Indicator for SUBJECTS[650] will be a blank followed by a zero: " 0". This Indicator signifies that no information has been provided as to a specific level for the subject term, and that the Library of Congress Subject Headings list is the source for the term.

The default condition regarding sub-fields will be that no Chronological or Geographic subdivisions are to be used, because that information is contained in other fields. The only type of subdivision employed will be Topical subdivision, which MARC designates with Sub-Field Code "x". A cataloger familiar with Library of Congress Subject Headings would separate the subdivision from the main term with a dash, represented in typing as two hyphens: "--". Thus, a cataloger might fill in the SUBJECTS[650] field on the data entry form in the manner shown in FIG. 21-1. The program's conversion to MARC coding for information exchange would yield what is shown in FIG. 21-2. (Note that the Indicator position before the zero is a blank, and that extra spaces have been added for readability.)

```
SUBJECTS[650]:Automobiles--Equipment and supplies; Automobiles--
Maintenance and repair--Study and teaching; Express highways;
Petroleum industry and trade--Safety regulations
```

Fig. 21-1. SUBJECTS field on data entry form, without MARC Codes

```
650 _0 ǂa Automobiles ǂx Equipment and supplies
650 _0 ǂa Automobiles ǂx Maintenance and repair ǂx Study and
          teaching
650 _0 ǂa Express highways
650 _0 ǂa Petroleum industry and trade ǂx Safety regulations
```

Fig. 21-2. SUBJECTS field after translation to MARC codes

Authority Record structure for SUBJECTS

Each Authority Record in the SUBJECTS file will contain the fields shown in TABLE 21-2. The field names are in uppercase.

Table 21-2. Authority Records for SUBJECTS: fields

```
Record-ID:
     HEADING

Tracings, Relationships with Other Terms:
     USED-FOR
     BROADER-TERM
     NARROWER-TERM
     RELATED-TERM

Explanations, Source of Information:
     SCOPE-NOTES
     SOURCE

Administrative Control:
     ENTRY-DATE
     EDIT-DATE
     CATALOGING-AGENCY
```

Authority file for persons

The Authority File for the names of persons is named PERSONS. The authorized form of the name of the person will be used as the Record-ID of that person's record. The personal names Authority File will make it possible to store the full MARC information for a field containing personal names, without the need for a novice cataloger to learn MARC codes. Of course, someone must create and maintain such an Authority File. An experienced cataloger's time will probably be more productive if spent placing the information in an Authority File, than repeating the information each time that the same name appears. The Authority File will also promote consistency, which is vital for searching. Within an information network of repositories sharing an interest in the same subject matter, Authority Files can be shared, greatly reducing the amount of authority work that a single institution has to do.

Each time a personal name is entered that does not already appear in the Authority File for Personal Names, the user will be asked if he or she wished to change the entry. If the answer is no, then the user will be asked to fill in an Authority Record for the name. In the example of the name Pierre Mendès-France, the experienced cataloger inserted an Indicator to designate that a compound last name appeared, and also supplied the dates of birth and death, marked off by the MARC Sub-Field code "d". Entering data in this manner follows standard library practice, but it violates the fundamental database principle that dependent information should not be entered redundantly.

The birth and death dates for Mendès-France are a dependent data element. The dates are dependent on the controlling data element "Mendès-France, Pierre". There is no need to enter the birth and death dates every time that a person's name is entered, except in the case of two individuals with the same name. Storing redundant information will almost inevitably lead to inconsistencies in the database. The Indicator value indicating a compound last name is also a dependent data element. There should be no need to repeat this information every time that the same name appears.

Information that is dependent on a personal name should be stored in the separate Authority File for Personal Names. The Record-ID for each record in the file will be a personal name. One field will include the birth and death dates for the individual. Another field will designate the Indicator value that is to be employed for that name.

Different forms of name

The most commonly-used name should be employed as the main heading. A fuller form of the name, which might include the entire middle name rather than an initial, should be kept in the Authority Record. The fuller form should be written in its entirety, as in the following example:

```
MAIN-HEADING:Nixon, Richard M.
FULLER-FORM[Q]:Nixon, Richard Milhous
DATES[D]:1913-
```

The program will use the Authority Record to fill in MARC Sub-Field "q" with the fuller form of the name at the time of conversion to the full MARC format. The fuller form of name may be searched for as a "USE" entry which points to the authorized heading. Thus a search on the name "Nixon, Richard Milhous" will retrieve the records for "Nixon, Richard M."

Types of personal names

The code for personal name is stored in Indicator position one. For the type of personal name, the program will offer the following choices:

Single surname in inverted order (Code: 1)
Forename or direct-order name (Code: 0)
Multiple surname (Code: 2)
Family name (Code: 3)

The Default Choice, appearing first in the list, will be "Single surname in inverted order", unless the following analysis of the name entry indicates otherwise:

Entry contains a comma:
  Entry contains a hyphen before the comma: Multiple surname.
Entry does not contains a comma:
  Entry contains the word "family": Family name.
  Entry does not contain the word "family": Forename or direct-order name.

The cataloger can override the program's Default Choice. The program will store the code that represents the form of the name.

A prefix does not create a compound surname. Note that a surname that begins with a prefix that is an article (Le, La), a preposition (De, Von, Van), or a combination of an article and preposition (Du, De La, Del) is considered a single rather than a multiple surname, unless the prefix if followed by more than one word, as in the case of the author De La Tour Du Pin. Thus "De Gaulle, Charles" is a single surname heading.

Authority File for agencies

The Authority File for the names of agencies and organizations is named AGENCIES. The authorized form of the name of the organization will be used as the Record-ID of that organization's record.

Different forms of name

Use the latest form of the name of the organization that is applicable to the collection. If there is a possibility that the collection will receive additional entries, use the contemporary form of the organization's name. The previous names of the organizations, and the time periods when they applied, should be kept in the Authority Record.

The following example presents the company names that have been used by the Avery corporation. After the colon, the dates of each former name appears. An additional field LEGAL-NAME contains the current legal name of the corporation, which differs from the name commonly used.

MAIN-HEADING:Avery
FORMER-NAMES:Kum-Kleen Products: 1935-1936;
  Avery Adhesives: 1936-1946;
  Avery Adhesive Label Corporation: 1946-1958;
  Avery Adhesive Products, Inc.: 1958-1964;
  Avery Products Corporation: 1964-1976;

Avery International Corporation: 1976-1986
LEGAL-NAME:Avery International Corporation

Types of names

Within the record, the field TYPE-OF-NAME will be used to fill in the first Indicator position for those fields containing corporate names, MARC fields 110 Main Entry—Corporate Name, 610 Subject Added Entry—Corporate Name, and 710 Added Entry—Corporate Name. The following choices are available for the type of name:

Name in direct order (Code: 2)
Jurisdiction name (Code: 1)
Inverted name (Code: 0)

The Default Choice will be name in direct order. Inverting the order of words in a name conflicts with AACR2 (Anglo-American Cataloging Rules, Second edition). Thus, you should enter:

John Randolph and Dora Haynes Foundation

rather than:

Haynes, John Randolph and Dora, Foundation

Subordinate units

Entries in the Authority Record fields MAIN-HEADING[A] and SUBORDINATE-UNIT[B] will be used to separate the parts of the name that should be entered into MARC Sub-Field "a" for corporate name or jurisdiction and Sub-Field "b" for subordinate unit. For meetings or conferences, the name of the sponsoring organization should be placed in MAIN-HEADING[A] and the name of the meeting in SUBORDINATE-UNIT[B]. In addition, in the case of a meeting or conference, entries should also be supplied for the fields LOCATION-OF-MEETING[C] and DATE-OF-MEETING[D]. This information will be used for MARC Sub-Fields "c" and "d". For example:

MAIN-HEADING[A]:American Library Association
SUBORDINATE-UNIT[B]:Annual Meeting
LOCATION-OF-MEETING[C]:Los Angeles (Calif.)
DATE-OF-MEETING[D]:1983

The field REFERENCE will indicate the reference source for the form of name chosen. The Default Choice will be: "Library of Congress Name Authority File".

Distinguish between organizations and conferences

The MARC format makes a distinction between conferences that are administered by an organization, which should be placed in fields 110, 610, and 710, and conferences that are listed only under a conference name, which should be entered in fields 111, 611, and 711. In order to avoid confusion for the searcher and the creation of additional fields, the names of conferences will be stored in the same fields as the names of organizations, whether or not the conference was sponsored by an organization. The distinction between organizational and conference status will be carried in the Authority Record. The field CONFERENCE-STATUS will hold a "Y" for True, null for False. The Default Choice will be null. The program will use the CONFERENCE-STATUS field to place the entry into the appropriate MARC format field at the time of conversion.

If the heading is a conference, whether entered under a sponsoring body or under the name of the conference, then the fields CONFERENCE-LOCATION[C], CONFERENCE-DATE[D], and CONFERENCE-NUMBER[N] should also be filled out. The following entries are for the 1984 Olympic Games, held in Los Angeles. The form of the heading is mandated by AACR2. The following would appear in the data record:

```
SUBJECTS-ORGANIZATIONS[610]:Olympic Games (23rd : 1984 :
  Los Angeles, Calif.)
```

The following would appear in the Authority Record. Note that the Record-ID of the Authority Record is the same as the field entry in the data record.

```
RECORD-ID:Olympic Games (23rd : 1984 : Los Angeles, Calif.)
NAME[A]:Olympic Games
CONFERENCE-STATUS:Y
CONFERENCE-NUMBER:23rd
CONFERENCE-DATE:1984
CONFERENCE-LOCATION:Los Angeles (Calif.)
```

The program will convert these entries into the following MARC format entry. Note that although the data record field was identified as MARC 610, the program has shifted the entry to MARC field 611 for conferences.

```
611 20 ‡a Olympic Games ‡n 23rd ‡d 1984 ‡c Los Angeles (Calif.)
```

No Relator Code would be included for the entry. MARC does not provide the Sub-Field "e" for Relator Term for the meeting fields that the format provides for persons and organizations.

Authority File for titles

The Record-ID will be the authorized title. The field NON-FILING-CHARACTERS[I2] will be used by the program to fill out the second Indicator position. Into this field enter the number of characters that should be ignored for sorting. For example:

```
RECORD-ID:Fall of the House of Usher
NON-FILING-CHARACTERS[I2]:4
```

The Default Choice for the field will be a null entry, which will be treated as zero.

Part III

For more information

22

History computerization project

The Los Angeles City Historical Society is beginning a History Computerization Project to develop the use of computer database management methods with historical materials, to encourage the application to local historical materials of nationally-standardized methods of description, and to facilitate the exchange of information between researchers, librarians, and archivists, particularly among those who share an interest in California history.

The History Computerization Project will provide computer assistance and support for the society's program to update the volume *Los Angeles: A Bibliography of a Metropolis*. The material collected will be made available in both printed and computer database form.

The project will also offer a series of courses on the use of computer database management for:

- Cataloging historical materials, including photographs, manuscripts, oral history interviews, books, and journals
- Historical research and writing
- Collecting information on historic sites
- Maintaining a membership roster

For more information on the project or on the History Database program please fill out the Request for Information Form shown in FIG. 22-1 and send it to: David L. Clark, History Database, 24851 Piuma Road, Malibu, California 90265-3036. Telephone: (818) 888-9371.

Request for Information Form

I have an interest in taking the course that the History Computerization Project will offer in the computer-cataloging of historical materials. Please send me information on the course.

NAME:

ADDRESS:

CITY: ZIP: PHONE:

ORGANIZATION:

POSITION, RESPONSIBILITIES IN ORGANIZATION:

DESCRIPTION OF HISTORICAL MATERIALS:

Mail to:

David L. Clark
History Database
24851 Piuma Road
Malibu, California 90265-3036
Phone: (818) 888-9371

Fig. 22-1. Request for information form

Bibliography

To learn archival procedures, the simplest first steps would be to join the local or state archival organization, to join the national Society of American Archivists (listed below under "Publishers, Distributors, and Organizations"), and to order those items from the society's Basic Manual series or new Archival Fundamentals series that best fit your needs. If you are already familiar with cataloging and automation, and you want to add some extra excitement into your life, subscribe to *Archives and Museum Informatics*.

Abell-Seddon, Brian. *Museum Catalogues: A Foundation for Computer Processing*. London, England: Clive Bingley, Ltd., 1987. Distributed in the U.S. by the American Library Association.

Access: Microcomputers in Libraries. San Diego, California: D.A.C. Publications. A quarterly newsletter.

Adams, Judith A. "The Computer Catalog: A Democratic or Authoritarian Technology?" *Library Journal*, Volume 113, Number 2 (February 1, 1988), pages 31–36.

Adler, Anne G. and Elizabeth A. Baber. *Retrospective Conversion: From Cards to Computer*. Ann Arbor, Michigan: Pierian Press, 1984. Fourteen case histories from U.S. libraries.

Advanced Technology/Libraries. Boston, Massachusetts: G. K. Hall and Company. A monthly newsletter on the subject of library automation.

Aitchison, Jean, and Alan Gilchrist. *Thesaurus Construction: A Practical Manual*. Second edition. London, England: Aslib, 1987.

Akers, S. G. *Akers' Simple Library Cataloging*. Seventh edition, revised by A. V. Curley and J. Varlejs. Metuchen, New Jersey: Scarecrow Press, 1984. A useful basic text.

Alberico, Ralph and Marry Micco. *Expert Systems for Reference and Information Retrieval*. Supplement to *Computers in Libraries* Number 10. Westport, Connecticut: Meckler Publishing Co., 1990.

American Archivist. Quarterly journal of the Society of American Archivists.

American Archivist Volume 52, Number 4 (Fall 1989). Special issue on "Standards for Archival Description." The section of "Checklist of Standards for Archival Description" contains a list of guides to the use of archival standards and the addresses and phone numbers of the organizations that produce the guides.

American Libraries. The general-interest monthly magazine of the American Library Association.

American Library Association. *American Library Association Publications Checklist 1989*. A list of all publications produced by the American Library Association. Chicago, Illinois: American Library Association, 1989.

American Library Association, Association of College and Research Libraries, Rare Books and Manuscripts Section. *Genre Terms: A Thesaurus for Use in Rare Book and Special Collections Cataloguing*. Chicago, Illinois: American Library Association, 1983.

American Library Association, Association for Library Collections and Technical Services, Preservation of Library Materials Section. *Standard Terminology for USMARC Field 583*. Chicago, Illinois: American Library Association, 1988. A three-page list of terms to use to describe prservation actions taken with library materials.

American Library Association, Resources and Technical Services Division. *Guidelines for the Subject Analysis of Audiovisual Materials*. Chicago, Illinois: American Library Association, 1978.

American Library Association, Resources and Technical Services Division. *Guidelines on Subject Access to Microcomputer Software*. Chicago, Illinois: American Library Association, 1986.

American National Standards Institute. *Guidelines for Thesaurus Structure, Construction and Use: Approved June 30, 1980*. New York, New York: ANSI, 1980.

Angell, Carolyn. *Information, New Technology, and Manpower: The Impact of the New Technology on Demand for Information Specialists*. London, England: British Research and Development Publications, 1987. Distributed in the U.S. by the American Library Association.

Archives and Museum Informatics. Pittsburgh, Pennsylvania: Archives and Museum Informatics. Formerly *Archival Informatics Newsletter*. A quarterly newsletter which provides an incredibly wide-ranging coverage and listing of reference sources for issues of archival cataloging, description, and automation.

Archives and Museum Informatics Technical Reports. Pittsburgh, Pennsylvania: Archives and Museum Informatics. Formerly *Archival Informatics Technical Reports*. One report is produced each quarter dealing with an issue connected to archival automation. The reports published or announced consist of the following:

Optical Media. Volume 1, Number 1 (1987).

Collecting Software. Volume 1, Number 2 (1987).

Functional Requirements for Collection Management Systems. Volume 1, Number 3 (1987).

Automated Systems for Archives and Museums. Volume 1, Number 4 (1987).

Directory of Software for Archives and Museums. Volume 2, Number 1 (1988).

Archives and Authority Control. Volume 2, Number 2 (1988). Proceedings of a seminar sponsored by the Smithsonian Institution, October 27, 1987. Edited by Avra Michelson.

Archival Appraisal of Online Information Systems. Volume 2, Number 3 (1988).

Functional Requirements for Exhibits Managements Management Systems. Volume 2, Number 4 (1988).

Archival Methods. Volume 3, Number 1 (1989). The subjects treated are: 1. Selection and Appraisal, 2. Retention and Preservation, 3. Arrangement and Description, 4.

Access and Use, 5. Structures for Intellectual Control, 6. Recorded Memory and Cultural Continuity.

Archives and Museum Data Model and Dictionary. Volume 3, Number 2 (1989).

Functional Requirements for Membership, Development, and Participation Systems. Volume 3, Number 3 (1990).

1990 Directory of Software for Archives and Museums. Volume 3, Number 4 (1990).

Archivaria. Ottawa, Ontario, Canada: Association of Canadian Archivists. An archival journal published twice yearly.

Ascher, Robert. "Tin* Can Archaeology," in *Material Culture Studies of America.* Edited by Thomas J. Schlereth. Nashville, Tennessee: American Association for State and Local History, 1982. Ascher proposes that museums should collect actively, seeking out what he calls "superartifacts" which offer insights into the mind-set of a period. Examples of such superartifacts are the automobile and the coke bottle. Note that the asterisk is part of the title, thereby creating problems for any computer cataloging program that uses the asterisk as a delimiter or control character.

Association for Recorded Sound Collections. *Rules for Archival Cataloging of Sound Recordings.* Silver Spring, Maryland: Association for Recorded Sound Collections, 1980.

Attig, John. "The USMARC Formats: Underlying Principles." *Information Technology and Libraries.* Volume 1, Number 2 (June 1982), pages 169–174. The paper appears with annotations as Appendix A of Walt Crawford's MARC for Library Use.

Avram, Henriette D. *MARC: Its History and Implications.* Washington, D.C.: Library of Congress, 1975.

Baker, Barry B., editor. *The USMARC Format for Holdings and Locations: Development, Implementations, and Use.* New York, New York: Haworth Press, Inc., 1988.

Baker, Barry B. and Lynne D. Lysiak. *From Tape to Product: Some Practical Considerations on the Use of OCLC-MARC Tapes.* Ann Arbor, Michigan: Pierian Press, 1985. Papers presented at a 1982 conference. Includes an overview and a tutorial on the MARC tape format.

Barnett, Patricia. "The Art and Architecture Thesaurus as a Faceted MARC Format." *Visual Resources,* Volume 4, Number 3, page 237. Barnett describes the use of AAT (Art and Architecture Thesaurus) facets as extensions of MARC sub-fields. She explains the seven facets of the thesaurus, each representing a broad area of knowledge, and the thirty-six hierarchies of terms under the facets.

Bartle, Rachel, and Michael Cook. *Computer Applications in Archives.* Liverpool, England: University of Liverpool, Archives Unit, 1983.

Baskerville, Peter A. and Chad W. Gaffield, editors. *Archives, Automation, and Access: Proceedings of a Conference at the University of Victoria, British Columbia, March 1–2, 1985.* Victoria, British Columbia, Canada: University of Victoria Press, 1986.

Bawden, David. *User-Oriented Evaluation of Information Systems and Services.* Brookfield, Vermont: Gower Publishing Company, 1990.

Bearman, David. "Archival Description Standards: A Framework for Action." *American Archivist,* Volume 52, Number 4 (Fall 1989), pages 514–519.

Bearman, David. "Archives and Manuscript Control with Bibliographic Utilities: Challenges and Opportunities." *American Archivist,* Volume 52, Number 1 (Winter 1989), pages 26–39. Includes an explanation of how the MARC (Machine-Readable Cataloging) format, developed originally for libraries, was expanded to include the collection management information used by archives. The same process of expansion may bring MARC to the museum world and to other communities collecting historical information.

Bearman, David. "Automated Access to Archival Information: Assessing Systems." *American Archivist,* Volume 42 (April 1979), pages 179–190.

Bearman, David. *Electronic Records Guidelines: A Manual for Policy Development & Implementation.* New York, New York: United Nations, projected publication. Distributed by Archives and Museum Informatics.

Bearman, David. *Towards National Information Systems for Archives and Manuscript Repositories: The National Information Systems Task Force (NISTF) Papers.* Chicago, Illinois: Society of American Archivists, 1987. The NISTF papers are a must for anyone planning an information network. Although the title refers to national systems, the papers are equally relevant for systems based on locality or on a unique subject focus. Bearman lays out a conceptual framework and a matrix of issues and implications within which any networking plan can usefully situate itself. Be forewarned that Bearman's writings are not for the timid of mind or heart. In his usual forthright style, he challenges the archival community to identify its mission in society with assertions such as, "Archivists are guilty of failing to make archival programs important."

Bearman, David. "'Who about what' or 'From whence, why and how': Establishing Intellectual Control Standards to Provide Access to Archival Resources." *Conference on Archives, Automation and Access: Proceedings of a Conference at the University of Victoria, British Columbia, March 1–2, 1985.* Edited by Peter A. Baskerville and Chad W. Gaffield. Victoria, British Columbia, Canada: University of Victoria Press, 1986, pages 39–47.

Bearman, David, and Richard H. Lytle. "The Power of the Principle of Provenance," *Archivaria* Volume 21 (Winter, 1985–1986), pages 14–27.

Bearman, David and Peter Sigmond. "Exploration of Form of Material Authority Files by Dutch Archivists," *American Archivist,* Volume 50, Number 2 (Spring 1987), pages 249–253. Report on a project of the Society of Dutch Archivists to standardize and to expand upon descriptions of forms of materials, in order to use form of material as an alternative access point. A researcher could then search for a particular form of material, such as school registers or voting registers, across jurisdictional lines, without having to know the names of the various agencies responsible for creating or maintaining the records.

Bearman, David and Richard Szary. "Beyond Authority Headings: Authorities as Reference Files in a Multi-disciplinary Setting," *Proceedings of the ARLIS/NS Symposium on Authority Control.* Edited by Karen Muller. Tucson, Arizona: Art Libraries of North America, 1987, pages 69–78.

Bellamy, Lois and Linda Bickman. "Thesaurus Development for Subject Cataloging." *Special Libraries,* Volume 80, Number 1 (Winter 1989), pages 9–15.

Bellardo, Lewis and Lynn Bellardo, editors. *The Vocabulary of Archives and Manuscripts.* Chicago, Illinois: Society of American Archivists, to be published as part of the new Archival Fundamentals Series.

Benedict, Karen M., compiler and editor. *A Select Bibliography on Business Archives and Records Management.* Chicago, Illinois: Society of American Archivists, 1981.

Benson, James A. and Bella Weinberg. *Gateway Software and Natural Language Interfaces.* Ann Arbor, Michigan: Pierian Press, 1988. Comparisons of thirteen software packages providing access to databases.

Berman, Sanford. *The Joy of Cataloging: Essays, Letters, Reviews, and Other Explosions*. Phoenix, Arizona: Oryx Press, 1981. An iconoclastic view of cataloging practices.

Berman, Sanford, editor. *Subject Cataloging: Critiques and Innovations*. New York, New York: Haworth Press, Inc., 1985.

Berner, Richard C. *Archival Theory and Practice in the United States: A Historical Analysis*. Seattle, Washington: University of Washington Press, 1983.

Betz, Elisabeth W. *Graphic Materials: Rules for Describing Original Items and Historical Collections*. Washington, D.C.: Library of Congress, Prints and Photographs Division, 1982. Supplements AACR2 as a standard source of descriptive practice for photographs, paintings, posters and other non-projected visual materials.

Bilindex: A Bilingual Spanish English Subject Heading List: Spanish Equivalents to Library of Congress Subject Headings/Bilindex: une lista bilingüe en español e inglés de ebcabezan-uebtis de materia. Oakland, California: Spanish Language Database, 1984.

Blackaby, James R. "Creating Common Databases," in *A Common Agenda for History Museums: Conference Proceedings, February 19–20, 1987*. Edited by Lonn W. Taylor. Nashville, Tennessee: American Association for State and Local History, and Washington, DC: Smithsonian Institution, 1987. Pages 44–49.

Blackaby, James R. and Patricia Greeno. *The Revised Nomenclature for Museum Cataloging*. Nashville, Tennessee: American Association for State and Local History, 1988. A revised and expanded edition of Robert G. Chenhall's system for classifying man-made objects in hierarchical fashion. Nomenclature is based on the model of scientific naming systems, such as those used in botany and biology, which provide a hierarchy of relationships between the terms that it standardizes. Thus, a species of plant or animal is always defined as part of a larger family. The hierarchy used for Nomenclature is based on the original function of the object, since all man-made objects were presumably created for some particular purpose. All objects are initially separated into three major divisions according to whether they are intended to provide shelter, to act as tools, or to serve as a means of communication. The divisions are then each broken down into categories and finally into individual terms. As in the natural sciences, Nomenclature provides only a list of preferred terms, rather than incorporating the many terms that might be used in daily speech. The format for each term that carries an adjective is inverted, with the noun first, followed by a comma, space, and adjective. The singular form is used for nouns, rather than the plural form generally employed by the Library of Congress Subject Headings. The style of capitalization is all upper case, rather than the upper and lower case style of LCSH. Thus, Nomenclature will use the term "AUTOMOBILE", while Library of Congress Subject Headings would employ "Automobiles." Continued updates to the Nomenclature list will take place through the AASLH's Task Force on Common Data Bases, which is part of the Common Agenda for History Museums Project.

Blamberg, Donald L., Carol L. Dowling, and Claudia V. Weson, compilers and editors. *Proceedings of the Conference on the Application of Scanning Methodologies in Libraries*. Beltsville, Maryland: National Agricultural Library, 1989. A collection of papers presented at a conference organized by the National Agricultural Library. Librarians making use of scanning technology presented the advantages and disadvantages of using scanning devices to transcribe bibliographic information during the process of cataloging and indexing.

Blixrud, Julia. *A Manual of AACR2 Examples for Serials*. Second edition. Lake Crystal,

Minnesota: Soldier Creek Press, 1986. Examples from AACR2 (Anglo-American Cataloguing Rules, Second edition) applied to serial publications such as periodicals.

Blixrud, Julia and Edward Swanson. *A Manual of AACR2 Examples Tagged and Coded using the MARC Format.* Lake Crystal, Minnesota: Soldier Creek Press, 1982. Examples from AACR2 (Anglo-American Cataloguing Rules, Second edition), tagged according to the MARC (Machine-Readable Cataloging) Format.

Boehm, Eric H. and Michael K. Buckland, editors. *Education for Information Management: Directions for the Future. Record of a Conference Cosponsored by the Information Institute, International Academy of Santa Barbara, and the Association of American Library Schools, May 6–8, 1982.* Santa Barbara, California: International Academy at Santa Barbara, 1983. Available through ISIM (International School of Information Management) in Santa Barbara, California. This book makes me want to cry. Eric Boehm, founder of the ABC-CLIO online bibliographic databases Historical Abstracts and America: History and Life, organized a conference in 1982 to urge librarians and library schools to establish themselves at the forefront of the emerging field of information management. The trumpet was sounded, but the troops stayed in their tents. As a result, by the end of the decade library schools were closing while the education in information management that the library schools were the best-equipped institutions to provide was instead subsumed under the expanding departments and schools of computer science and business.

Boles, Frank and Julia Marks Young. *Archival Appraisal.* New York, New York: Neal-Schumann Publishers, 1990. A guide to appraising material for archival selection and retrieval.

Boss, Richard W. *Library Manager's Guide to Automation.* Third edition. Boston, Massachusetts: G.K. Hall, 1990.

Boss, Richard W. and Hal Expo, "Standards, Database Design, and Retrospective Conversion." *Library Journal,* Volume 112, Number 15 (October 1, 1987), pages 54–58.

Bowers, Fredson. *Principles of Bibliographical Description.* Brookfield, Vermont: Gower Publishing Company, St. Paul's Bibliographies, 1986.

Bradsher, James Gregory, editor. *Managing Archives and Archival Institutions.* Foreword by Frank B. Evans. Chicago, Illinois: University of Chicago Press, 1989. A collection of nineteen essays on the management of archives. Includes an extensive bibliography.

Brandt, Scott. "Authority Files for Microcomputer Databases." *Special Libraries.* Volume 79, Number 4 (Fall 1988), pages 296–301. Provides a simple example of the use of a database management system to maintain an Authority File. Brandt demonstrates that relationships must be drawn, an authority source determined, interpretations made, and decisions documented prior to inputting the first data record.

Bratcher, Perry and Jennifer Smith. *Music Subject Headings, Compiled from Library of Congress Subject Headings.* Foreword by Richard Smiraglia. Lake Crystal, Minnesota: Soldier Creek Press, 1988. The use of music subject headings is explained in the introduction.

Bressor, Julie P. *Caring for Historical Records: Workshop Curriculum and Resource Materials.* Chicago, Illinois: Society of American Archivists, 1990.

Brichford, Maynard. *Appraisal and Accessioning.* Chicago, Illinois: Society of American Archivists, 1977.

British Library. *Name Authority List.* London, England: British Library, Bibliographic Services, 1981 and monthly updates.

British Library. *Subject Authority Fiche.* London, England: British Library, Bibliographic Services, bimonthly updates.

British Standards Institution. *Guidelines for the Establishment and Development of Monolingual Thesauri.* London, England: British Standards Institution, 1985.

Brophy, Peter. *Management Information and Decision Support Systems in Libraries.* Brookfield, Vermont: Gower Publishing Company, 1986.

Brottman, May and Mary Loe. *The LIRT Library Instruction Handbook.* Englewood, Colorado: Libraries Unlimited, 1990. A handbook and training manual developed by the Library Instruction Round Table.

Brown, Alan, with D. W. Langride and J. Mills. *An Introduction to Subject Indexing.* Second edition. London, England: Clive Bingley, Ltd., 1982. Distributed in the U.S. by the American Library Association. A primer on verbal subject analysis.

Bulletin of the American Society for Information Science. Newsletter of the society. Each issue includes an excellent annotated list of recent books and reports, with publisher information included.

Burcaw, G. Ellis, editor. *Introduction to Museum Work.* Second edition. Nashville, Tennessee: American Association for State and Local History, 1983.

Burgett, Teresa Hensley and Catherine W. Robert, compilers. *Library of Congress Subject Headings Significant Changes 1974–1988.* Lake Crystal, Minnesota: Soldier Creek Press, 1988.

Bureau of Canadian Archivists. *Toward Descriptive Standards: Report and Recommendations of the Canadian Working Group on Archival Descriptive Standards.* Ottawa, Ontario, Canada: Bureau of Canadian Archivists, 1985. By those who would prefer to make up their own standards, the title Toward Descriptive Standards has been abbreviated to T.D.S., pronounced "tedious".

Burger, Robert H. *Authority Work: The Creation, Use, Maintenance, and Evaluation of Authority Records and Files.* Englewood, Colorado: Libraries Unlimited, 1985. An introduction to the creation, maintenance, and use of a Controlled Vocabulary or Authority File. Includes a discussion of the first edition of the MARC Authorities Format.

Burke, Frank G. "Real Archivists Don't Use Marc." *Archives and Museum Informatics.* Volume 3, Number 1 (Spring 1989), pages 7–12. Burke declares that computer database programs should be employed to translate between human-readable data entries and MARC (Machine-Readable Cataloging) codes, relieving the cataloger of the burden of having to learn all of the codes.

Burton, Paul. *Microcomputer Applications in Academic Libraries II.* London, England: British Research and Development Publications, 1987. Distributed in the U.S. by the American Library Association.

Carey, Gabriele Gonder. *Orange County Archives Manual.* Santa Ana, California: Orange County Archives, Orange County Public Library, 1987. Includes many examples of forms for processing archival materials.

Carpenter, Michael and Elain Svenonius, editors. *Foundations of Cataloging: A Sourcebook.* Englewood, Colorado: Libraries Unlimited, 1985. An anthology that traces the development of cataloging theory and practice.

Carter, Carolyn and Jenny Monaco. *Learning Information Technology Skills*. London, England: British Research and Development Publications, 1987. Distributed in the U.S. by the American Library Association.

Carter, Ruth C., editor. *Education and Training for Catalogers and Classifiers*. New York, New York: Haworth Press, Inc., 1987.

Case, Mary, editor. *Registrars on Record: Essays on Museum Collections Management*. Washington, DC: American Association of Museums, 1988. An introduction to and overview of practices of museum registration.

Cataloging and Classification Quarterly. New York, New York: Haworth Press, Inc. A special issue, devoted to "Authority Control in the Online Environment", appeared as Volume 9, Number 3 (1989).

Catalogue and Index. Quarterly publication of the Library Association, Cataloging and Indexing Group.

Cataloguing Australia. Quarterly journal of the Library Association of Australia.

Cawkell, A. E. *Survey of Image Processing and Document Delivery Technology*. London, England: British Research and Development Publications, 1987. Distributed in the U.S. by the American Library Association.

Chan, Lois Mai. *Cataloging and Classification: An Introduction*. New York, New York: McGraw-Hill, 1981.

Chan, Lois Mai. *Library of Congress Subject Headings: Principles and Application*. Second edition. Englewood, Colorado: Libraries Unlimited, 1986. A guide to subject cataloging, utilizing the tenth edition of LCSH.

Chan, Lois Mai. *Theory of Subject Analysis: A Sourcebook*. Englewood, Colorado: Libraries Unlimited, 1985. An anthology of thirty-one contributions on the theory of subject analysis.

Chan, Lois M. and Richard Pollard. *Thesauri Used in Online Databases: An Analytical Guide*. Westport, Connecticut: Greenwood Press, 1988. This guide lists 122 controlled vocabularies used for bibliographic databases, with examples of entries and analytical descriptions. The fact that 122 different lists exist may indicate that catalogers, like the computer industry, are so fond of standards that they keep inventing new ones. Most of the lists do not have the structure of cross references necessary for a true thesaurus.

Chapman, Liz. *How to Catalogue: A Practical Handbook Using AACR2 and Library of Congress*. Second edition. London, England: Clive Bingley, 1990. Distributed in the United States by the American Library Association. A practical manual describing standard cataloging procedures, using the Anglo-American Cataloguing Rules, Second Edition, 1988 Revision, and Library of Congress cataloging practice.

Chenhall, Robert G. and David Vance. *Museum Collections and Today's Computers*. Westport, Connecticut: Greenwood Press, 1988. Intended to serve as an introduction to computers for museum curators. The book examines the nature of museum collections and the use of computer database management systems and information networks. The work includes a technical glossary and bibliography. Unfortunately, for their example of a small museum automation project the authors chose a system with fixed-length fields of a single line each. There is simply no good reason to use inadequate systems when good and inexpensive systems are available.

Clayton, Marlene. *Managing Library Automation*. Brookfield, Vermont: Gower Publishing Company, 1987. Advice for middle-level library managers.

Cloud, Patricia. "The Cost of Converting to MARC-AMC (MARC format for Archives and Manuscripts Control)" *Library Trends*, Volume 36, Number 3 (Winter 1988). A case study of archival automation.

Coates, Eric. *Subject Catalogues: Headings and Structures*. London, England: Library Association Publishing, Ltd., 1960, 1988 re-issue with introductory comments. Distributed in the U.S. by the American Library Association.

Cochrane, Pauline A. *Improving LCSH for Use in Online Catalogs*. Englewood, Colorado: Libraries Unlimited, 1986. A discussion of how the usage of Library of Congress Subject Headings might be modified for utilization in on-line catalogs with regard to form, scope notes, cross-reference structure, subdivision access, and relationships between terms.

College and Research Libraries. Journal of the Association of College and Research Libraries, distributed by the American Library Association.

Computers in Libraries. Westport, Connecticut: Meckler Publishing Co. A monthly journal on the use of desktop computers in libraries. Formerly *Small Computers in Libraries*.

Conservation Information Network. *Conservation Information Network Data Dictionary*. Marina del Rey, California: Conservation Information Network, Getty Conservation Institute, 1990.

Cook, Michael. *Archives and the Computer*. London, England: Butterworths, 1986.

Cook, Michael. *The Management of Information from Archives*. Brookfield, Vermont: Gower Publishing Company, 1986. A guide oriented to the use of information management techniques for archival description.

Cook, Michael and Margaret Proctor. *A Manual of Archival Description*. Second edition. Brookfield, Vermont: Gower Publishing Company, 1990. A guide to descriptive and cataloging practices for archivists.

Cook, Michael and Margaret Proctor. *MAD User Guide*. Brookfield, Vermont: Gower Publishing Company, 1989. A simplified manual for applying the principles of the *Manual of Archival Description*.

Corbin, John. *Directory of Automated Library Systems*. New York, New York: Neal-Schumann Publishers, 1989.

Cortez, Edwin M. and Edward J. Kazlauskas. *Managing Information Systems and Technologies: A Basic Guide for Design, Selection, Evaluation, and Use*. New York, New York: Neal-Schumann Publishers, 1985.

Cox, Richard J. *American Archival Analysis: The Recent Development of the Archival Profession in the United States*. Chicago, Illinois: Society of American Archivists, 1990.

Craven, Timothy C. *String Indexing*. Orlando, Florida: Academic Press (Harcourt Brace Jovanovich), 1986. Describes and compares thirty different systems for string indexing.

Crawford, Walt. *Bibliographic Displays in the Online Catalog*. With Lennie Stovel and Kathleen Bates. Professional Librarian Series. White Plains, New York: Knowledge Industry Publications, 1986.

Crawford, Walt. *MARC for Library Use: Understanding Integrated USMARC*. Second edition. White Plains, New York: Knowledge Industry Publications, Inc., 1989. Also distributed by G.K. Hall. An introduction to the MARC (Machine Readable Cataloging) format for storing information. The second edition discusses the integration of the MARC formats for different types of materials into a single, integrated format.

Current Research in Library and Information Science. A quarterly journal of the Library Association, in England.

Daily, Jay E. *Organizing Nonprint Materials*. Second edition. New York, New York: Marcel Dekker, Inc., 1986. A general introduction to organizing materials other than printed books and periodicals.

Daniels, Maygene F. and Timothy Walch, editors. *A Modern Archives Reader: Basic Readings on Archival Theory and Practice*. Washington, D.C.: National Archives and Records Service, U.S. General Services Administration, 1984. (Also distributed by the Society of American Archivists.) A series of readings that provide a basic introduction to archival practice.

Day, Joan M. *Computer Literacy and Library and Information Studies: A Literature Review*. London, England: British Research and Development Publications, 1987. Distributed in the U.S. by the American Library Association.

Dearstyne, Bruce W. *The Management of Local Government Records: A Guide for Local Officials*. Nashville, Tennessee: American Association for State and Local History, 1988.

Debons, Anthony, Esther Horne, and Scott Cronenweth. *Information Science: An Integrated View*. Boston, Massachusetts: G.K. Hall, 1988. An overview of the past twenty years of research in information science.

Dempsey, Lorcan, editor. *Influencing the System Designer: Online Public Access to Library Files*. Oxford, England: Elsevier Advanced Technology Publications, 1988. An edited collection of fifteen papers from the third national conference of Britain's Centre for Bibliographic Management, held at the University of Bath in 1987.

Dewe, Michael, editor. *Manual of Local Studies Librarianship*. Brookfield, Vermont: Gower Publishing Company, 1987. A collection of 17 essays from the British Isles on managing local history libraries and archives.

Dewey, Melvil. *Dewey Decimal Classification, Edition 20*. Albany, New York: Forest Press, a division of OCLC, 1989. Edited by John P. Comaromi. Lois M. Chan was chair of the Editorial Policy Committee. The most widely-used book classification and shelving system for libraries. In the United States, Dewey is used in 95 percent of school and public libraries and 25 percent of academic, research, and special libraries. The new edition includes a manual to assist in applying the classification system. A MARC format for the Dewey Decimal Classification system is now under development. Purchase by the national online bibliographic utility OCLC will lead to greater use and adaptation of Dewey in an electronic environment.

Dial In: An Annual Guide to Library Online Public Access Catalogs in North America. Compiled by Michael Schuyler. Westport, Connecticut: Meckler Publishing Co. An annual guide issued each September.

Diess, William A. *Museum Archives: An Introduction*. Washington, DC: American Association of Museums, 1984. A guide to establishing archives within a museum setting.

Documentaliste: Science de l'Information. Bimonthly journal of the *Association Française des Documentalistes et des Bibliothécaires Specialisés*.

Documentation et Bibliothèques. Quarterly journal of the *Association pour l'Avancement des Sciences et de Techniques de la Documentation*.

Dodd, Sue. A. *Cataloguing Machine-readable Data Files: An Interpretive Manual*. Chicago, Illinois: American Library Association, 1982.

Dodd, Sue. A. *Cataloguing Microcomputer Files: A Manual of Interpretation for AACR2*. Chicago, Illinois: American Library Association, 1985. A detailed manual for cataloging computer files according to AACR2 (Anglo-American Cataloguing Rules, Second edition).

Dudley, Dorothy H. and Irma Bezold Wilkinson. *Museum Registration Methods*. Washington, DC: American Association of Museums, 1979. A basic reference work for museum registration procedures.

Dyer, Hilary and Alison Gunson, compilers. *Directory of Library and Information Retrieval Software for Microcomputers*. Fourth edition. Brookfield, Vermont: Gower Publishing Company, 1990.

Dykstra, Mary. "Library of Congress Subject Headings Disguised as a Thesaurus." *Library Journal*. Volume 113 (March 1, 1988), pages 42–46. A Canadian subject indexer points out that Library pf Congress Subject Headings lack the underlying structure of a thesaurus.

Dykstra, Mary. "Can Subject Headings Be Saved?" *Library Journal*, Volume 114, Number 15 (September 15, 1988), pages 55–58. A follow-up to her earlier article.

Dym, Eleanor D., editor. *Subject and Information Analysis*. New York, New York: Marcel Dekker, 1985.

Edgar, Neal L., editor. *AACR2 and Serials: The American View*. New York, New York: Haworth Press, Inc., 1983.

Enyingi, Peter, Melody B. Lembke, and Rhonda L. Mittan. *Cataloging Legal Literature: A Manual on AACR2 and Library of Congress Subject Headings for Legal Materials with Illustrations*. Littleton, Colorado: Rothman, 1984. The application of AACR2 (Anglo-American Cataloguing Rules, Second edition) to legal literature.

Ercegovac, Zorana, and Wendy Culota, editors. *Microcomputer Power: Option or Necessity?* Medford, New Jersey: Learned Information, 1989. Proceedings of the 1985 Annual Continuing Education Seminar of the Los Angeles Chapter of the American Society for Information Science, updated for publication.

Evans, Frank B., compiler. *The Administration of Modern Archives: A Select Bibliographic Guide*. Washington, DC: National Archives and Records Service, 1970. Chapter 3 discusses "Archival Concepts, Terminology, and Principles".

Evans, Frank B., Donald F. Harrison, and Edwin A. Compson, compilers. *A Basic Glossary for Archivists, Manuscript Curators, and Records Managers*. Edited by William L. Rofes. Chicago, Illinois: Society of American Archivists. Reprinted from the American Archivist, Volume 37, Number 3 (July 1974), pages 415–433.

Evans, Linda and Maureen O'Brien Will. *MARC for Visual Materials: A Compendium of Practice*. Chicago, Illinois: Chicago Historical Society, 1988. A compendium on the practices of various organization using the MARC-VM (Visual Materials) format.

Evans, Max J. "Authority Control: An Alternative to the Record Group Concept." *American Archivist*. Volume 49 (Summer 1986), pages 249–261. Evans argues for access to archival materials via Authority Files containing information about the agencies that created the materials.

Evans, Max J. and Weber, Lisa B. *MARC for Archives and Manuscripts: A Compendium of Practice*. Madison, Wisconsin: State Historical Society of Wisconsin, 1985. (Also distributed by the Society of American Archivists.) Examples of the usage of each MARC field for manuscripts and archives by different institutions.

Fenly, Charles and Howard Harris. *Expert Systems: Concepts and Applications*. Advances in

Library Information Technology series, Number 1. Washington, DC: Library of Congress, Cataloging Distribution Service, 1988. An overview of expert systems and artificial intelligence, with discussion of how they may be used to aid subject cataloging, shelf listing, and series cataloging.

Fink, Eleanor E. and Christine M. Hennessey. "Testing the Flexibility of the MARC Format." *Visual Resources,* Volume 4, Number 4, page 373. A description of the use of the MARC-VM (Visual Materials) format for the Inventory of American Sculpture, a national database of information on works of sculpture. The authors concluded that limitations to cataloging with MARC do not come from the format itself, but from the types of computer programs with which it is usually implemented.

Foskett, A. C. *The Subject Approach to Information.* Fourth edition. London, England: Clive Bingley, 1982. Distributed in the United States by the American Library Association.

Freeman, Elsie. "In the Eye of the Beholder: Archives Administration from the User's Point of View." *American Archivist,* Volume 47 (Spring 1984), pages 111–123.

Frost, Carolyn O. *Cataloging Nonbook Materials: Problems in Theory and Practice.* Littleton, Colorado: Libraries Unlimited, 1983. A detailed text for all types of materials other than printed books and periodicals. Arranged by the rule numbers of AACR2 (Anglo-American Cataloguing Rules, Second edition.)

Gardner, Richard K. *Education of Library and Information Management Professionals: Present and Future Prospects.* Littleton, Colorado: Libraries Unlimited, 1987.

Gagnon-Arguin, Louise. *An Introduction to Authority Control for Archivists.* Ottawa, Canada: Bureau of Canadian Archivists, 1989.

Getty Art History Information Program. *Art and Architecture Thesaurus.* Williamstown, Maryland: Getty Art History Information Program, 1987. Known as the AAT, this thesaurus provides subject headings for use in art history.

Gibbs, George E. and Diane Bisom. "Creating an Interactive Authority File for Names in the UCLA Orion System: Specifications and Decisions." *Cataloging and Classification Quarterly,* Volume 9, Number 3 (1989), pages 153–169. A description of the conversion of MARC bibliographic records to authority records. The article is part of a special issue devoted to "Authority Control in the Online Environment: Considerations and Practices."

Gill, Arthur T. *Photographic Processes: A Glossary and Chart for Recognition.* Museum Association Information Sheets, Number 21. London, England: Museum Association, 1978.

Gorman, Michael and Paul W. Winkler, *editors. Anglo-American Cataloguing Rules.* Second edition, 1988 revision. Chicago, Illinois: American Library Association, 1988. Prepared by the American Library Association, the Australian Committee on Cataloguing, the British Library, the Canadian Committee on Cataloguing, the Library Association (Great Britain), and the Library of Congress. Commonly referred to as AACR2, it is the authoritative style reference for library catalogers throughout the English-speaking world. Note the British spelling of "cataloguing."

Gorman, Michael, editor. *The Concise AACR2, Being a Rewritten and Simplified Version of Anglo-American Cataloguing Rules, Second Edition.* Chicago, Illinois: American Library Association, 1981. Co-published by the Canadian Library Association and the Library Association.

Gould, Constance C. *Information Needs in the Humanities: An Assessment.* Stanford,

California: Research Libraries Group, 1988. Prepared for the Program for Research Information Management of the Research Libraries Group. Identifies existing sources of information and explores the role that a bibliographic utility such as RLIN could play in expanding its database beyond the present scope of bibliographic information.

Gracy, David B., II. *An Introduction to Archives and Manuscripts*. New York, New York: Special Libraries Association, 1981.

Gracy, David B., II. *Archives and Manuscripts: Arrangement and Description*. Chicago, Illinois: Society of American Archivists, 1977.

Greenburg, Alan M. and Carole R. McIver. *LC and AACR2: An Album of Cataloging Examples Arranged by Rule Number*. Metuchen, New Jersey: Scarecrow Press, 1984. The rules of AACR2 (Anglo-American Cataloguing Rules, Second edition) are illustrated with LC (Library of Congress) catalog cards.

Grinell, Stuart F. "Reference Service, Online Bibliographic Databases, and Historians: A Review of the Literature." *RQ* (Reference Quarterly), Volume 27, Number 1 (December 1987), pages 106–111.

Gurnsey, John. *The Information Professions in the Electronic Age*. London, England: Clive Bingley, Ltd., 1985. Distributed in the U.S. by the American Library Association.

Haas, Joan K., Helen Willa Samuels, and Barbara Trippel Simmons. *Appraising the Records of Modern Science and Technology: A Guide*. Cambridge, Massachusetts: Massachusetts Institute of Technology, 1985. Distributed by the Society of American Archivists.

Hallam, Adele. *Cataloging Rules for the Description of Looseleaf Publications: With Special Emphasis on Legal Materials*. Washington, DC: Library of Congress, Office for Descriptive Cataloging Policy, 1986. Arranged by the rule numbers of AACR2 (Anglo-American Cataloguing Rules, Second edition).

Ham, F. Gerald. "Archival Choices: Managing the Historical Record in the Age of Abundance." *American Archivist*, Volume 47 (Winter 1984), pages 11–22.

Ham, F. Gerald. "Archival Strategies for the Post-Custodial Era." *American Archivist*, Volume 44 (Summer 1981), pages 207–216. Ham subsequently chaired the group which produced *Planning for the Archival Profession: A Report of the Society of American Archivists Task Force on Goals and Priorities*. Chicago, Illinois: Society of American Archivists, 1986.

Ham, F. Gerald. *Selecting and Appraising Archives and Manuscripts*. Chicago, Illinois: Society of American Archivists, to be published as part of the new Archival Fundamentals Series.

Harrod, Leonard Montague. *Harrod's Librarians' Glossary and Reference Book of Terms Used in Librarianship, Documentation and the Book Crafts*. Sixth edition. Compiled by Raymond John Prytherch. Brookfield, Vermont: Gower Publishing Company, 1987.

Harter, Stephen P. *Online Information Retrieval: Concepts, Principles, and Techniques*. Orlando, Florida: Academic Press (Harcourt Brace Jovanovich), 1986.

Hedstrom, Margaret L. *Archives and Manuscripts: Machine-Readable Records*. Chicago, Illinois: Society of American Archivists, 1984. A manual for the handling of materials, such as census records, that are kept in computer rather than in printed form.

Hensen, Steven L. *Archives, Personal Papers, and Manuscripts: A Cataloging Manual for Archival Repositories, Historical Societies, and Manuscript Libraries*. Second edition. Chicago, Illinois: Society of American Archivists, 1989. Commonly known as APPM, this manual provides additions and modifications for the Anglo American Cataloguing Rules, as applied to manuscripts and archives. The first edition, published in 1983 by the Library of Congress, was mandated as the standard for describing manuscripts and archives by the online bibliographic networks RLIN and OCLC and was widely accepted by the archival profession. The second edition has been greatly expanded to serve as a more complete cataloging guide.

Hensen, Steven L. "Squaring the Circle: The Reformation of Archival Description in AACR2 [Anglo-American Cataloguing Rules, Second edition]." *Library Trends*, Volume 36, Number 3 (Winter 1988), pages 539–552.

Hensen, Steven L. "The Use of Standards in the Application of the AMC Format." *American Archivist.* Volume 49, Number 1 (Winter 1986). Pages 31–40. A discussion of the use of library standards for name authorities and subject headings when cataloging archival materials with the MARC format for Archival and Manuscripts Control.

Hiatt, Robert C. and Ben R. Tucker. *Library of Congress Rule Interpretations.* Washington, D.C.: Library of Congress, Cataloging Distribution Service, 1988. Interpretations of the Anglo-American Cataloguing Rules, second edition, by the Library of Congress and approved revisions to AACR2.

Hickerson, H. Thomas. *Archives and Manuscripts: An Introduction to Automated Access.* Chicago, Illinois: Society of American Archivists, 1981.

Hickerson, Thomas and Elaine Engst. *Form Terms for Archival and Manuscripts Control.* Stanford, California: Research Libraries Group, 1985.

Hildreth, Charles R. *Intelligent Interfaces and Retrieval Methods: For Subject Searching in Bibliographic Retrieval Systems.* Advances in Library Information Technology series, Number 2. Washington, DC: Library of Congress, Cataloging Distribution Service, 1989. A survey and discussion of intelligent front-end design approaches and software for improving access and subject searching in large online bibliographic retrieval systems.

Hipgrave, Richard. *Computing Terms and Acronyms.* London, England: Library Association Publishing, Ltd., 1985. Distributed in the U.S. by the American Library Association.

Hjerppe, Roland and Birgitta Olander. "Cataloging and Expert Systems: AACR2 as a Knowledge Base." *Journal of the American Society of Information Science*, Volume 40, Number 1 (January 1989), pages 27–44. Description of a project where expert systems were built for library cataloging. Includes an analysis of the structure of AACR2.

History News. Bimonthly journal of the American Association for State and Local History. Includes many articles on museum activities. The Association's newsletter, *History Dispatch*, includes bulletins on the Common Agenda for History Museums project.

Hlava, Marjorie M. K. *Private File Creation/Database Construction: A Processing with Five Case Studies.* Washington, DC: Special Libraries Association, 1984. A guide to creating online databases, with a focus on planning questions and potential difficulties of implementation.

Holbert, Sue E. *Archives and Manuscripts: Reference and Access.* Chicago, Illinois: Society of American Archivists, 1977. Contains the following standard guidelines for policies on access to and use of archival materials:

"Standards for Access to Research Materials in Archival and Manuscripts Repositories." Prepared by the Society of American Archivists' Committee on Reference, Access, and Photoduplication and approved by the Society's Council in December 1973. Printed in Appendix 1, as well as in the American Archivist, Volume 37 (January 1974), pages 153–154.

"Statement on the Reproduction of Manuscripts and Archives for Reference Use."

Prepared by the Society of American Archivists' Committee on Reference and Access policies and approved by the Society's Council in April 1976. Printed in Appendix 2 as well as in the American Archivist, Volume 39 (July 1976), page 411.

Holley, Robert P., editor. *Subject Control in Online Catalogs*. New York, New York: Haworth Press, Inc., 1990. A collection of essays. Also published in *Cataloging & Classification Quarterly*, Volume 10, Numbers 1 and 2.

Holzberlein, Deanne. *Cataloging Sound Recordings: A Manual with Examples*. New York, New York: Haworth Press, Inc., 1989.

Holzberlein, Deanne, editor. *Computer Software Cataloging: Techniques and Examples*. New York, New York: Haworth Press, Inc., 1986.

Houghton, Bernard and John Convey. *Online Information Retrieval Systems*. Second edition. London, England: Clive Bingley, Ltd., 1984. Distributed in the U.S. by the American Library Association.

Humanities Communication Newsletter. Leicester, England: Office of Humanities Communication. A biannual journal on humanities computerization projects in Europe.

Humanities Data Dictionary. Documentation Research Publication, Number 1. Ottawa, Canada: Canadian Heritage Information Network, 1985.

Hunter, Eric. *Anglo-American Cataloguing Rules, Second edition, 1988 Revision: An Introduction*. London, England: Clive Bingley, Ltd., 1989. Distributed in the U.S. by the American Library Association.

Hunter, Eric. *Computerized Cataloguing*. London, England: Clive Bingley, Ltd., 1985. Distributed in the U.S. by the American Library Association.

Hunter, Eric and K. G. B. Bakewell. *Cataloguing*. Second edition. London, England: Clive Bingley, Ltd., 1982. Distributed in the U.S. by the American Library Association.

IASSIST Quarterly. Journal of IASSIST, the International Association for Social Science Information Services and Technology. Volume 12, Number 2 (Summer 1988) was devoted to the subject of "Educating the Data User." Each article in the issue was contributed by a member of the Library Instruction Division of Baruch College, City University of New York. The library instructional program began at Baruch fifteen years ago, with the goal of improving the level of "information literacy" among the colleges faculty and students. The division incorporates instruction in the use computer database files into a varied bibliographic informational program.

IMC Journal. Journal of the International Information Management Congress.

Index to Personal Names in the National Union Catalog of Manuscript Collections, 1959–1984. Volume 1, Letters A–K. Volume 2, Letters L–Z. Alexandria, Virginia: Chadwyck-Healey, 1987.

Inform. Journal of the Association for Information and Image Management.

Information Center. Boston, Massachusetts: Weingarten Publications, Inc. A monthly publication.

Information Intelligence: Online Libraries and Microcomputers. Phoenix, Arizona: Information Intelligence. Published ten times yearly.

Information Retrieval and Library Automation. Mount Airy, Maryland: Lomond Publications, Inc. A monthly publication.

Information Standards Quarterly. Newsletter of NISO (National Information Standards Organization).

Information Technology and Libraries. Quarterly journal of the Library and Information Technology Association, which is a division of the American Library Association.

International Bulletin for Photographic Documentation of the Visual Arts. Journal of the Visual Resources Association.

International Cataloguing. A quarterly journal published by the International Federation of Library Associations, and distributed by the Library Association.

Intner, Sheila S. and Jane Anne Hannigan. *The Library Microcomputer Environment: Management Issues.* Phoenix, Arizona: Oryx Press, 1988.

Jensen, Patricia E. *Using OCLC: A How-To-Do It Manual for Libraries.* New York, New York: Neal-Schuman Publishers, 1989. A guide for librarians on using the database of the Online Computer Library Center, a national bibliographic utility.

Jones, Keith E. and Gavin A. Rea. *URICA: A Guide for Librarians and Systems Managers.* Brookfield, Vermont: Gower Publishing Company, 1989. A guide to the URICA library management system, which runs on the McDonnell-Douglas (MicroData Reality) version of the Pick operating system.

Journal of Academic Librarianship. Ann Arbor, Michigan: Mountainside Publishing, Inc. A bimonthly journal.

Journal of the American Society for Information Science.

Journal of Information Science: Principles and Practice. London, England: Institute of Information Scientists. Published six times yearly.

Journal of Librarianship. London, England: Library Association.

Judge, Peter and Brenda Gerrie, editors. *Small Scale Bibliographic Databases.* Orlando, Florida: Academic Press (Harcourt Brace Jovanovich), 1986. Compares options for computer control of small databases.

Kellen, James D. *A Manual of AACR2 Examples for Liturgical Works and Sacred Scriptures.* Second edition. Lake Crystal, Minnesota: Soldier Creek Press, 1987. The rules of AACR2 (Anglo-American Cataloguing Rules, Second edition), applied to scriptures.

Kershner, Lois M. *Forms for Library Automated Systems: An Illustrated Guide for Selection, Design, and Use.* New York, New York: Neal-Schumann Publishers, 1988. Contains hundreds of forms used by libraries, primarily for administrative functions.

Kesner, Richard M. "Automated Information management: Is There a Role for the Archivist in the Office of the Future?". *Archivaria,* Volume 19 (Winter 1094–1985), pages 162–172. Kesner warns that the archival profession will be subsumed by other professions and disappear unless archivists confront the current technological revolution and abandon the familiar "passive role of recipient of documents" and take "a more active role in the creation, distribution, and preservation of information." (page 164)

Kesner, Richard M. *Automation for Archivists and Records Managers: Planning and Implementation Strategies.* Chicago, Illinois: American Library Association, 1984.

Kesner, Richard M. *Information Management, Machine-readable Records, and Administration: An Annotated Bibliography.* Chicago, Illinois: Society of American Archivists, 1983.

Kesner, Richard M. *Information Systems: A Strategic Approach to Planning and Implementation.* Chicago, Illinois: American Library Association, 1988. Also distributed by the Society of American Archivists. Examines the design of information systems in relation to the objectives and structure of the organization, with the goal of incorporating the system into the organizational structure.

Kilpatrick, Thomas L. *Microcomputers and Libraries: A Bibliographic Sourcebook.* Metuchen,

New Jersey: Scarecrow Press, Inc., 1987. Includes a section on archives, pages 110–11 and 122.

Kimberley, Robert. *Text Retrieval: A Directory of Software.* Third edition. Brookfield, Vermont: Gower Publishing Company, 1990.

Kovacs, Bertrice. *Decision-Making Process for Library Collections: Case Studies in Four Types of Libraries.* Westport, Connecticut: Greenwood Press. Case studies of the collection development process, including decisions of which materials to keep or discard.

Lancaster, F. Wilfird. *Vocabulary Control for Information Retrieval.* Second Edition. Arlington, Virginia: Information Resources Press, 1986. The original 1972 edition became a classic on the subject of Controlled Vocabularies and Authority Files.

Larsen, John C., editor. *Museum Librarianship.* Hamden, Connecticut: Shoe String Press, 1985. Also distributed by the American Association of Museums. Eleven essays by museum librarians provide a basic guide for small museum libraries. The topics include organizing and cataloging materials.

Larsen, John C., editor. *Researcher's Guide to Archives and Regional History Sources.* Foreword by John Y. Cole. Hamden, Connecticut: Shoe String Press, 1988. Essays by twelve experienced professional archivists and librarians provide advice for collections managers and researchers. Includes a bibliography and index.

LASIE. Bimonthly journal of the Library Automated Systems Information Exchange, in Australia.

Learn, Larry L. *Telecommunications for Information Specialists.* Dublin, Ohio: Online Computer Library Center, 1989. A guide to telecommunications technology as it relates to library and information science. Includes a glossary of telecommunications terms and acronyms, a comprehensive bibliography, and a study guide for instructors.

Leong, Carol. *Serials Cataloging Handbook: An Illustrated Guide to the Use of AACR2 and LC Rule Interpretations.* Chicago, Illinois: American Library Association, 1989.

Library High Tech. Ann Arbor, Michigan: Pierian Press. Quarterly journal on the use of computer technology in libraries. Walt Crawford's series, originally entitled "Common Sense Personal Computing," now renamed "The Trailing Edge," is particularly useful.

Library Hi Tech Bibliography. Volume 1: 1986. 2: 1987. 3: 1988. 4: Projected for 1989. Ann Arbor, Michigan: Pierian Press. Annotated bibliographies that survey the literature on subjects related to library automation.

Library Hi Tech News. Ann Arbor, Michigan: Pierian Press. A monthly publication that supplements the Library Hi Tech journal with shorter pieces on new developments.

Library Journal. New York, New York: Bowker Magazine Group, Cahners Magazine Division.

Library Micromation News: News and Views for Micro Users in Libraries. London, England: Library and Information Technology Centre. A quarterly journal.

Library of Congress. *Archival Moving Image Materials: A Cataloging Manual.* (See under: "White-Hensen, Wendy".)

Library of Congress. *Bibliographic Description of Rare Books.* Washington, DC: Library of Congress, Cataloging Distribution Service, 1981.

Library of Congress. *Cataloging Rules for the Description of Looseleaf Publications: With Special Emphasis on Legal Materials.* Washington, DC: Library of Congress, Cataloging Distribution Service, 1986.

Library of Congress. *Cataloging Service Bulletin*. Washington, DC: Library of Congress, Cataloging Distribution Service. Issued quarterly. The bulletin describes current cataloging practices at the Library of Congress.

Library of Congress. *Catalogs and Technical Publications*. Washington, D.C.: Library of Congress, Cataloging Distribution Service. Annual brochure of publications.

Library of Congress. *CDMARC Bibliographic*. Washington, DC: Library of Congress, Cataloging Distribution Service, 1989, updated quarterly. The Library of Congress cataloging records for book, serials, maps, music, and visual materials on seven CD-ROM disks.

Library of Congress. *CDMARC Names*. Washington, DC: Library of Congress, Cataloging Distribution Service, 1989, updated quarterly. The Library of Congress Names Authority File on three CD-ROM disks.

Library of Congress. *CDMARC Subjects*. Washington, DC: Library of Congress, Cataloging Distribution Service, 1989, updated quarterly. The Library of Congress Subject Authority File on CD-ROM disk.

Library of Congress. *Descriptive Terms for Graphic Materials: Genre and Physical Characteristic Headings*. (See under: "Zinkham, Helena and Elisabeth Betz Parker".)

Library of Congress. *Expert Systems: Concepts and Applications*. (See under: "Fenly, Charles and Howard Harris".)

Library of Congress. *Format Integration and Its Effect on the USMARC Bibliographic Format*. Washington, D.C.: Library of Congress, Cataloging Distribution Service, 1988. A description of the new integrated MARC format, which supersedes the separate formats for books, serials, archival materials, visual materials, maps, music, and computer files.

Library of Congress. *Graphic Materials: Rules for Describing Original Items and Historical Collections*. (See under: "Betz, Elisabeth W.".)

Library of Congress. *Intelligent Interfaces and Retrieval Methods: For Subject Searching in Bibliographic Retrieval Systems*. (See under: "Hildreth, Charles R.".)

Library of Congress. "Legislative Indexing Vocabulary." Washington, DC: Library of Congress, Congressional Research Service. Used currently by the Congressional Research Service to supply subject headings for contemporary political and social issues.

Library of Congress. *Library of Congress Name Authority File*. Washington, DC: Library of Congress, Cataloging Distribution Service, 1977 with updates. Known as LCNAF, the file provides an authoritative list of personal and corporate names. The list is available on microfiche, CD-ROM, magnetic tape, and online through RLIN and OCLC.

Library of Congress. *Library of Congress Rule Interpretations*. Second edition. Washington, DC: Library of Congress, Cataloging Distribution Service, updated quarterly. Interpretations of the cataloging rules of AACR2, as applied at the Library of Congress. The basic volume is followed by quarterly updates.

Library of Congress. *Library of Congress Subject Headings*. Thirteenth edition. Washington, DC: Library of Congress, Cataloging Distribution Service, 1990. Updated annually. By far the most comprehensive collection of subject terms available. The use of standardized subject terms is essential for cataloging information into a database. Published in three volumes, the list is also available on microfiche, CD-ROM, magnetic tape, and online through RLIN and OCLC.

Library of Congress. *Library of Congress Subject Headings Weekly Lists*. Washington, DC: Library of Congress, Cataloging Distribution Service, weekly lists issued monthly. Lists of headings that have been added, changed, or deleted by the Subject Cataloging Division.

Library of Congress. *Library of Congress Thesaurus for Graphic Materials: Topical Terms for Subject Access*. (See under: "Parker, Elisabeth Betz, compiler".)

Library of Congress. *Moving Image Materials: Genre Terms*. (See under: "Yee, Martha, compiler".)

Library of Congress. *Multiple Thesauri in Online Library Bibliographic Systems*. (See under: "Mandel, Carol A.".)

Library of Congress. *National Union Catalog of Manuscript Collections*. Washington, DC: Library of Congress, Special Materials Cataloging Division, Manuscripts Section. New editions are issued periodically.

Library of Congress. *Newspaper Cataloging Manual. CONSER/USNP (Conservation of Serials/U.S. Newspaper Program) Edition*. Washington, DC: Library of Congress, Cataloging Distribution Service, 1984. An authoritative reference for cataloging newspapers for the U.S. Newspaper Program and the OCLC Conservation of Serials database.

Library of Congress. *Select MARC: Retrospective Conversion—Here's How*. Washington, DC: Library of Congress, Cataloging Service Division, 1988. 23 pages.

Library of Congress. *Serials Accessioning Manual*. Washington, DC: Library of Congress, Cataloging Distribution Service, 1985.

Library of Congress. *Subject Cataloging Manual: Subject Headings*. Third edition. Washington, DC: Library of Congress, Cataloging Distribution Service, 1988. The authoritative guide to the use of Library of Congress Subject Headings.

Library of Congress. *Symbols of American Libraries*. Washington, DC: Library of Congress, Cataloging Distribution Service, updated regularly. Every repository uploading data to a shared database should acquire a National Union Catalog Symbol. The NUC symbol will identify the cataloging agency that created the records. To obtain an NUC symbol for your organization, write to: Library of Congress, Catalog Management and Publications Division, Symbols of American Libraries, Washington, DC 20540.

Library of Congress. *USMARC Code List for Countries*. Washington, DC: Library of Congress, Cataloging Distribution Service, 1988.

Library of Congress. *USMARC Code List for Geographic Areas*. Washington, DC: Library of Congress, Cataloging Distribution Service, 1988.

Library of Congress. *USMARC Code List for Languages*. Washington, DC: Library of Congress, Cataloging Distribution Service, 1987.

Library of Congress. *USMARC Code List for Relators, Sources, Description Conventions*. Washington, DC: Library of Congress, Cataloging Distribution Service, 1988.

Library of Congress. *USMARC Concise Formats for Bibliographic, Authority, and Holdings Data*. Washington, DC: Library of Congress, Cataloging Distribution Service, 1988. A quick reference tool which lists the MARC field Tags, Indicators, and Sub-Field Codes.

Library of Congress. *USMARC Format for Authority Data: Including Guidelines for Content Designation*. Washington, DC: Library of Congress, Cataloging Distribution Service, 1988.

Library of Congress. *USMARC Format for Bibliographic Data: Including Guidelines for Content Designation*. Washington, D.C.: Cataloging Distribution Service, Library of Congress, 1988. The authoritative reference to the MARC format. LC produces many supplemental guides to individual elements in the format.

Library of Congress. *USMARC Format for Holdings Data: Including Guidelines for Content Designation.* Washington, DC: Library of Congress, Cataloging Distribution Service, 1989.

Library of Congress. *USMARC Specifications for Record Structure, Character Sets, Tapes.* Washington, DC: Library of Congress, Cataloging Distribution Service, 1990.

Library Quarterly: A Journal of Investigation and Discussion in the Field of Library Science. Quarterly journal of the University of Chicago Graduate Library School. Distributed by the University of Chicago Press.

Library Resources and Technical Services. Quarterly journal of the American Library Association, Resources and Technical Services Division.

Library Software Review. Westport, Connecticut: Meckler Corporation. A journal published six times yearly on the use of computer software in libraries.

Library Systems Newsletter. Chicago, Illinois: American Library Association, Library Technology Reports. A newsletter on library automation systems. See: "Processing OCLC Tapes" in Volume 8, Number 6 (June 1988), pages 41–45.

Library Technologies, Inc. *Library Database Preparation Services.* Abingdon, Pennsylvania: Library Technologies, Inc., 1988. An eight-page pamphlet on MARC tape formats, extracting records, exchanging data with OCLC, and authority control.

Library Technology Reports. A bimonthly publication of the American Library Association.

Library Trends. Quarterly journal of the University of Illinois at Urbana-Champaign, Graduate School of Library and Information Science. Distributed by the University of Illinois Press. In particular see the special issue on "Automating Intellectual Access to Archives," Volume 36, Number 3 (Winter 1988).

Library Workstation Report. Westport, Connecticut: Meckler Publishing Co. A monthly publication.

Lilley, Dorothy B. and Trice, Ronald. *A History of Information Science, 1945–1985.* Orlando, Florida: Academic Press (Harcourt Brace Jovanovich), 1989.

Longley, Dennis and Michael Shain. *Dictionary of Information Technology.* New York, New York: John Wiley and Sons, 1982. Also distributed by the Association for Information and Image Management.

Lucas, Amy and Annette Novallo, editors. *Encyclopedia of Information Systems and Services.* Eighth edition. Detroit, Michigan: Gale Research Company, 1988. A two-volume set with descriptions of information organizations and systems, as well as databases and database producers.

Lytle, Richard H. "An Analysis of the Work of the National Information Systems Task Force." *American Archivist,* Volume 47 (Fall 1984), pages 357–365.

Lytle, Richard H. "Intellectual Access to Archives: I. Provenance and Content Indexing Methods of Subject Retrieval." *American Archivist,* Volume 43 (Winter 1980), pages 64–75. "Intellectual Access to Archives: II. Report of an Experiment Comparing Provenance and Content Indexing Methods of Subject Retrieval." *American Archivist,* Volume 43 (Spring 1980), pages 191–207.

Lytle, Richard H., editor. *Management of Archives and Manuscript Collections for Librarians.* Chicago, Illinois: Society of American Archivists, 1980.

Lytle, Richard H. "Subject Retrieval in Archives: A Comparison of the Provenance and Content Indexing Methods." Doctoral dissertation, University of Maryland, 1979.

MacDonald, David R. "Data Dictionaries, Authority Control, and Online Catalogs: A New Perspective." *Journal of Academic Librarianship*. Volume 11, Number 4 (September 1985), pages 219–222. Compares concepts of authority control from the fields of computer database management and library cataloging.

Makepeace, Chris E. *Ephemera: Its Collection, Conservation and Use*. Brookfield, Vermont: Gower Publishing Company, 1985.

Malinconico, S. Michael. "Bibliographic Data Base Organization and Authority File Control." *Wilson Library Bulletin*. Volume 54, Number 1 (September 1979), pages 36–45. Describes the need to use relational database management systems in order to maintain Authority File control.

Maloney, James J., editor. *Online Searching Technique and Management*. Chicago, Illinois: American Library Association, 1983.

Mandel, Carol A. *Multiple Thesauri in Online Library Bibliographic Systems*. Washington, DC: Library of Congress, Cataloging Distribution Service, 1987. Analyzes problems of developing an online system which uses multiple thesauri for subject authority control and subject searching.

Manheimer, Martha L. *OCLC: An Introduction to Searching and Input*. Second edition. New York, New York: Neal-Schumann Publishers, 1986.

Marion, Phyllis. *A Manual of AACR2 Examples for Legal Materials*. Edited by Marilyn H. McClaskey and Edward Swanson. Lake Crystal, Minnesota: Soldier Creek Press, 1981. An application to legal materials of AACR2 (Anglo-American Cataloguing Rules, Second edition).

Markey, Karen. *Subject Access to Visual Resources Collections: A Model for Computer Construction of Thematic Catalogs*. New Directions in Information Management, Number 11. Westport, Connecticut: Greenwood Press, 1986.

Marmion, Dan. *The OCLC Workstation*. Volume 9 in the series *Essential Guide to the Library IBM PC*. Westport, Connecticut: Meckler Publishing Co., 1987.

Matthews, Joseph R., editor. *The Impact of Online Catalogs*. New York, New York: Neal-Schumann Publishers, 1986. For libraries considering the use of an online information system.

Maxwell, Margaret. *Handbook for AACR2, 1988 Revision: Explaining and Illustrating the Anglo-American Cataloguing Rules*. Chicago, Illinois: American Library Association, 1989.

McAninch, Glen. *Automated Records and Techniques in Archives: A Resource Directory*. Chicago, Illinois: Society of American Archivists, Committee on Automated Records and Techniques, scheduled for publication in winter 1989–1990. Descriptions of organizations, training programs, databases, journals, books, and terms relevant for archival automation.

McCarthy, Paul, editor. *Archives Assessment and Planning Workbook*. Chicago, Illinois: Society of American Archivists, 1989. A workbook with exercises to assess the resources, functions, and responsibilities of a small to medium-sized repository.

McCrank, Lawrence J., editor. *Archives and Library Administration: Divergent Traditions and Common Concerns*. New York, New York: Haworth Press, 1986. To the volume McCrank contributed, "The Impact of Automation: Integrating Archival and Bibliographic Systems."

McCrank, Lawrence J., editor. *Automating the Archives: Issue and Problems in Computer Application.* White Plains, New York: Knowledge Industry Publications, 1981. In his article, "The Status Quo", McCrank criticizes archivists for not taking a more active role in automation.

McCrank, Lawrence J., editor. *Databases in the Humanities and Social Sciences 4: Proceedings of the International Conference on Databases in the Humanities and Social Sciences, Auburn University, July 1987.* Medford, New Jersey: Learned Information, 1989.

McCrank, Lawrence J. "Prospects for Integrating Historical and Information Studies in Archival Education." *American Archivist,* Volume 42 (October 1979), pages 443–455.

Michelson, Avra. "Description and Reference in the Age of Automation." *American Archivist.* Volume 50, Number 2 (Spring 1987). Pages 192–208. In the course of a survey conducted in 1986 of the forty repositories inputting data into the Research Library Information Network (RLIN) with the MARC-AMC format, Michelson found a zero rate of subject indexing consistency among the catalogers.

Microcomputers for Information Management. Norwood, New Jersey: Ablex Publishing Corp. A journal on the use of computers in libraries.

Microcomputers for Libraries. Powell, Ohio: James E. Rush Associates. A product guide, updated quarterly.

Mid-Atlantic Archivist. Quarterly journal of the Mid-Atlantic Regional Archives Conference.

Midwestern Archivist. Semiannual journal of the Midwest Archives Conference.

Miksa, Francis. *The Subject in the Dictionary Catalog from Cutter to the Present.* Chicago, Illinois: American Library Association, 1983.

Miller, Frederic. *Arranging and Describing Archives and Manuscripts.* Chicago, Illinois: Society of American Archivists, 1990.

Miller, Rosalind E. and Jane C. Terwillegar. *Commonsense Cataloging: A Cataloger's Manual.* Fourth edition. New York, New York: H. W. Wilson, 1989. A simplified and widely-used introduction to cataloging, including the use of AACR2, Sears subject headings, and Dewey Decimal and Library of Congress classification.

Milstead, Jessica L. *Subject Access Systems: Alternatives in Design.* Orlando, Florida: Academic Press (Harcourt Brace Jovanovich), 1984.

Moline, Judi. *Document Interchange Standards: Description and Status of Major Document and Graphics Standards.* Gaithersburg, Maryland: National Institute of Standards and Technology, 1988.

Moore, Barbara N. *A Manual of AACR2 Examples for Cartographic Materials.* Lake Crystal, Minnesota: Soldier Creek Press, 1981. Application of the rules of AACR2 (Anglo-American Cataloguing Rules, Second edition) to maps.

Morris, Leslie R., editor. *Choosing a Bibliographic Utility: User Views of Current Choices.* New York, New York: Neal-Schumann Publishers, 1989. Comparisons of OCLC (the Online Computer Library Center) with other bibliographic utilities available to libraries.

Morton, Katherine D. "The MARC Formats: An Overview." *American Archivist.* Volume 49, Number 1 (Winter 1986). Pages 21–30. A description of the development of the MARC (Machine-Readable Cataloging) by the Library of Congress for bibliographic data and authority records. The article also outlines and explains the structure of a MARC cataloging record.

Muller, Karen, editor. *Authority Control Symposium.* Occasional Papers Number 6. Fourteenth Annual Art Libraries Society of North America Conference, New York, February 10, 1986. Tucson, Arizona: Art Libraries Society of North America, 1987.

Museum Computer Network. *A MARC-Based Structure and Data Dictionary for the Syracuse University Art Collection.* Syracuse, New York: Museum Computer Network, 1989. Description of a system based on the MARC (Machine-Readable Cataloging) format for cataloging information about museum collections. The system was developed by the staff of the Museum Computer Network in conjunction with the staff of the Syracuse Art Collections and the Syracuse University Academic Computing Services, and was implemented on the SPIRES database system. The book includes a discussion of each MARC field considered applicable to the task, a data dictionary including detailed rules of entry, and the entry screens developed for the application. The project and book were intended to provide information applicable to other museums.

Museum News. Washington D.C.: American Association of Museums. A journal published six times yearly, covering issues of interest to museums.

National Archives and Records Administration. *Archival and Records Information Sources of the National Archives Library.* Washington, D.C.: National Archives and Records Administration, Archives Library Information Center. Updated quarterly. A list of publications available at the Archives Library Information Center of the National Archives. One may order photocopies of many publications.

National Archives and Records Administration. *The MARC [Machine-Readable Cataloging] Format and Life Cycle Tracking at the National Archives: A Study.* Washington, DC: National Archives and Records Administration, 1986.

National Information Standards Organization (NISO). *Guidelines for Thesaurus Structure, Construction and Use (ANSI Z39.19).* Transaction Publishers: Rutgers University, New Brunswick, New Jersey, 1980.

National Information Standards Organization (NISO). *Information Retrieval (ANSI Z39.50-1988): Information Retrieval Service Definition and Protocol Specification for Library Applications.* Transaction Publishers: Rutgers University, New Brunswick, New Jersey, 1990. Defines a protocol for the exchange of messages between computers for information retrieval. Includes guidelines for the format of queries and the transfer of database records.

National Information Standards Organization (NISO). *System for the Romanization of Japanese (ANSI Z39.11).* Transaction Publishers: Rutgers University, New Brunswick, New Jersey, 1972. Similar guidelines are published for writing other non-roman languages with roman characters.

National Library of Canada. *Canadian Authorities.* Ottawa, Ontario, Canada: National Library of Canada, 1976–.

National Library of Canada. *Canadian Subject Headings.* Second edition. Ottawa, Ontario, Canada: National Library of Canada, 1985.

National Library of Medicine, Medical Subject Headings Section. *Medical Subject Headings Annotated Alphabetic List.* Springfield, Virginia: National Technical Information Service (NTIS), U.S. Department of Commerce, 1990.

National Library of Medicine. *National Library of Medicine Classification.* Distributed by the Superintendent of Documents, U.S. Government Printing Office.

National Online Meeting. *Proceedings of the 10th National Online Meeting: New York City,*

May 9–11, 1989. Medford, New Jersey: Learned Information, 1989. Papers dealing with issues related to maintaining online databases.

Nelson, Nancy Melin, series editor. *Essential Guide to the Library IBM PC.* Westport, Connecticut: Meckler Publishing Co. A series of spiral-bound guides on subjects such as hardware and software for library use.

Olsgaard, John, editor. *Principles and Applications of Information Science for Library Professionals.* Chicago, Illinois: American Library Association, 1989.

Olson, Nancy B. *Audiovisual Material Glossary.* Dublin, Ohio: OCLC (Online Computer Library Center), 1988. Covers terms for maps, music, sound recordings, motion pictures, video recordings, graphic materials, computer files, three-dimensional materials, and microforms.

Olson, Nancy B. *Cataloging of Audio-Visual Materials: A Manual Based on AACR2.* Second edition. Edited by Edward Swanson and Sheila S. Intner. Mankata, Minnesota: Minnesota Scholarly Press, 1985. Also: *Supplement: Coding and Tagging for OCLC.* Mankata, Minnesota: Minnesota Scholarly Press, 1985.

Olson, Nancy B. *Cataloging Microcomputer Software: A Manual to Accompany AACR2.* Englewood, Colorado: Libraries, Unlimited, 1988. Contains over 100 examples and an extensive list of subject headings.

Olson, Nancy B., compiler. *Cataloging Service Bulletin Index.* Lake Crystal, Minnesota: Soldier Creek Press, 1989. The Library of Congress Cataloging Service Bulletin contains the interpretations of the rules of AACR2 (Anglo-American Cataloguing Rules, Second edition) applied by the Library of Congress in its cataloging. The Bulletins are used by many other repositories in their own cataloging activities. The index is presently available for the Bulletin from Summer 1978 to Spring 1989. A standing order can be made for the annual cumulative index. An index for the years 1945–1978 is also available as *Index to the Library of Congress Cataloging Service Bulletin, No. 1–125 (1945–1978).*

Olson, Nancy B. and Edward Swanson. *The Complete Cataloging Reference Set—Collected Manuals of the Minnesota AACR2 Trainers.* A compilation of manuals dealing with printed materials, with the following chapters: Printed Materials, Technical Reports, Early Printed Materials, Cartographic Materials, Manuscripts, Music, Sound Recordings, Motion Pictures and Video Recordings, Graphic Materials, Three Dimensional Artefacts and Realia—Kits, Computer Files, Microsoforms, Serials, "In" Analytics, Legal Materials, Liturgical Works. The examples include MARC field entries tagged according to OCLC usage. The examples do not include subject headings or classifications.

Olson, Nancy B. *A Manual of AACR2 Examples for Microcomputer Software, with MARC Tagging and Coding.* Third edition. Lake Crystal, Minnesota: Soldier Creek Press, 1988. The application to computer software of the 1987 rules of AACR2 (Anglo-American Cataloguing Rules, Second edition) and the MARC (Machine-Readable Cataloging) format. The examples are coded and tagged for input on the national bibliographic utility OCLC (Online Computer Library Center).

The One-Person Library. A newsletter for special librarians working in small information centers. New York, New York: OPL Resources, Ltd.

Online Audiovisual Catalogers. *OLAC Newsletter.* Quarterly newletter of the Online Audiovisual Catalogers, Inc.

Online Computer Library Center (OCLC). *Name Authority: User Manual.* Second edition. Dublin, Ohio: OCLC, 1983.

Online Computer Library Center (OCLC). *OCLC Archives and Manuscripts Control Format.* Dublin, Ohio: OCLC, 1986 and updates. A manual for the MARC format for archives and manuscripts for users of the OCLC national online bibliographic service.

Online Computer Library Center (OCLC). *OCLC Micro.* Dublin, Ohio: OCLC. A bi-monthly magazine with advice to users of the OCLC national online bibliographic service.

Online Computer Library Center (OCLC). *Online Systems: Archives and Manuscript Control Format.* Dublin, Ohio: OCLC, 1984.

Online Computer Library Center (OCLC). *Online Systems: Audiovisual Media Format.* Second edition. Dublin, Ohio: OCLC, 1986.

Orbach, Barbara. "Integrating Concepts: Corporate Main Entry and Graphic Materials." *Cataloging and Classification Quarterly,* Volume 8, Number 2 (1988), pages 71–88. A discussion of the problems encountered by the catalogers of archival and graphic materials in applying the Anglo-American Cataloguing Rules.

Orna, Elizabeth. *Build Yourself a Thesaurus: A Step by Step Guide.* Norwich, England: Running Angel, 1983.

Orna, Elizabeth. *Information Policies for Museums.* Museum Documentation Association Occasional Paper #10. Leeds, England: W.S. Manley & Sons, 1987. Distributed by the Museum Documentation Association. A pamphlet on information policies for museum directors.

Orna, Elizabeth and Charles Pettitt. *Information Handling in Museums.* London, England: Clive Bingley, Ltd., 1980. Distributed in the U.S. by the American Library Association.

Orna, Elizabeth and Graham Stevens. *The Presentation of Information.* London, England: Aslib, 1987.

O'Toole, James. *Understanding Archives and Manuscripts.* Chicago, Illinois: Society of American Archivists, to be published as part of the new Archival Fundamentals Series.

Palmer, Roger C. *Online Reference and Information Retrieval.* Second edition. Littleton, Colorado: Libraries Unlimited, 1987. A clear and simple introduction to online database searching.

Palmer, Roger C. *Understanding Library Microcomputer Systems.* Studio City, California: Pacific Information Inc., 1988. Includes a disk with the Book Acquisitions System.

Paris, Marion. *Library School Closings: Four Case Studies.* Metuchen, New Jersey: Scarecrow Press, 1988. Paris found that "pedagogical turf" wars played a greater role than tight budgets in closing two private and two public university library programs.

Parker, Elisabeth Betz, compiler. *Library of Congress Thesaurus for Graphic Materials: Topical Terms for Subject Access.* Introduction by Jackie Dooley. Washington, D.C.: Library of Congress, Prints and Photographs Division, 1987. Subject terms specific to visual materials. In contrast to the LCSH (Library of Congress Subject Headings) the set of terms known as LCTGM emphasizes the visual image rather than the underlying subject content. For historical photographs I prefer LCSH as providing a more complete list and a list that gives a handle on the subjects that I might use the photo to illustrate. A curator of art photographs would probably find LCTGM more useful. For example, to describe a photo of children playing on the lawn of a day-care center, both lists would offer the term "Children." LCTGM would then provide phrases such as "Children playing outdoors", while LCSH would emphasize the underlying subjects such as "Day care centers" and "Children—Welfare." You must make a clear choice between the two lists, because they do not always use identical terms, even when they logically should. For example, LCSH speaks of "Carriages and carts", while LCTGM uses "Carts and wagons" for hauling materials and "Carriages and coaches" for carrying people. I doubt that a cataloger could reliably remember the distinctions between the subject lists. To compare the size and completeness of the lists, the Thesaurus for Graphic Materials contains 3,567 authorized terms and 2,569 cross reference terms. Library of Congress Subject Headings contains 162,750 authorized headings, of which 131,000 are topical subject headings. LCSH has 130,000 cross references from unauthorized to authorized headings. LCTGM includes subject categories only. It does not incorporate names of people, organizations, events, or places. The introduction to LCTGM, by Jackie Dooley, is very useful because it deals, not just with this specific thesaurus, but with issues in the subject cataloging of visual images, such as deciding what the image is really "about".

Parks, Janet. "Return to Sender—Addressee Unknown." *Visual Resources*, Volume 4, Number 4, page 389. A description of the use of the MARC format for the Avery Videodisk Index of Architectural Drawings on RLIN (known by the acronym AVIADOR). Includes details about the problems encountered in fitting information into the MARC fields. For example: assigning an author and title for an architectural drawing. Also employed were the cataloging rules of AACR2 and Elisabeth Betz's Graphic Materials.

Pao, Miranda Lee. *Concepts of Information Retrieval*. Englewood, Colorado: Libraries Unlimited, 1989. An introductory text on document retrieval systems, presenting the basic concepts of information science.

Paul, Sandra K. and Johnnie E. Givens. "Standards Viewed from the Applications Perspective." *Library Trends*, Volume 31 (Fall 1982), pages 325–341.

Peace, Nancy E., editor. *Archival Choices: Managing the Historical Record in an Age of Abundance*. Published by Lexington Books, distributed by the Society of American Archivists.

Pederson, Ann, editor. *Keeping Archives*. Sydney, Australia: Australian Society of Archivists, Inc. 1987. (Also distributed in the U.S. by the Society of American Archivists.) An excellent basic archival manual from Australia.

Penn, Ira A., and Anne Morddel, with Gail Pennix and Kelvin Smith. *Records Management Handbook*. Brookfield, Vermont: Gower Publishing Company, 1989.

Peterson, Toni, editor. *Art and Architecture Thesaurus*. New York, New York: Oxford University Press, 1990. A list of subject terms for art and architecture begun in 1981 by the Getty Art History Information Program.

Peterson, Toni and Pat Molholt, editors. *Beyond the Book: Extending MARC for Subject Access*. Boston, Massachusetts: G.K. Hall, 1990. A collection of essays on the use of the MARC format for art, arhitecture, music, and photography.

Petrie, J. Howard. *Overview of Image Processing and Image Management Systems and Their Application*. London, England: British Research and Development Publications, 1988. Distributed in the U.S. by the American Library Association.

Piggott, Mary. *The Cataloguer's Way through AACR2: From Document Receipt to Document Retrieval*. Chicago, Illinois: American Library Association, 1990. Background studies and essays on practical cataloging problems and the use of the Anglo-American Cataloging Rules.

Piggott, Mary. *Topography of Cataloging.* London, England: The Library Association, 1988. Distributed in the U.S. by the American Library Association.

Primary Sources and Original Works: A Quarterly Professional Journal for Archives, Museums, and Special Library Collections. New York, New York: Haworth Press. Journal of the Association for the Bibliography of History.

Program: Automated Library and Information Systems. Quarterly journal of the Aslib Association for Information Management. Distributed in the U.S. by Learned Information.

Prologue. Journal of the National Archives.

Provenance. Journal of the Society of Georgia Archivists, published twice yearly. Formerly *Georgia Archive.*

Provincial Archives of Alberta. *Provincial Archives of Alberta Subject Headings.* Revised edition. Edmonton, Alberta, Canada: Provincial Archives of Alberta, 1984. According to the instructors of the Society of American Archivists workshop on Descriptive Standards, "A good example of the application of LCSH in a specific locale."

Public Historian. Berkeley, California: University of California Press Journals. A quarterly journal sponsored by the National Council on Public History.

Pugh, Mary Jo. "The Illusion of Omniscience: Subject Access and the Reference Archivist," in Maygene F. Daniels and Timothy Walch, editors, *A Modern Archives Reader: Basic Readings on Archival Theory and Practice.* Washington, DC: National Archives and Records Service, 1984, pages 264–277. The article first appeared in: *American Archivist,* Volume 45 (Winter 1982), pages 33–44. Mary Jo Pugh calls into question the time-honored system of depending on the knowledge in the head of the archivist for access to research materials: "The myth of the immortal, omniscient, indispensable reference archivist must ... be examined. Current practice relies too heavily on the subject knowledge and memory of the individual archivist, and is too dependent on the personalities of the researcher and the archivist." (page 270) "It is folly to expect the reference archivist to remember all administrative histories, biographical sketches, series descriptions, and container lists required to translate subject requests into names of record groups or collections. Archivists need to be able to build on the work of predecessors and colleagues. Reference archivists need an alphabetical, updatable, multi-subject approach." (page 273).

Pugh, Mary Jo. *Using Archives and Manuscripts.* Chicago, Illinois: Society of American Archivists, to be published as part of the new Archival Fundamentals Series.

Rare Books and Manuscript Librarianship. A journal of the Association of College and Research Libraries and the American Library Association, distributed by the ALA.

Research Libraries Group. *RLIN Bibliographic Field Guide.* Stanford, California: Research Libraries Group, 1985 and updates. A guide to the use of the MARC format fields on the RLIN national bibliographic utility.

Research Libraries Group. *RLIN Supplement.* Stanford, California: Research Libraries Group, 1989 and updates. A supplement to the USMARC Format for Bibliographic Data, for users of the RLIN national bibliographic utility.

Resource Sharing and Information Networks. New York, New York: Haworth Press, Inc. A semi-annual publication.

Richardson, Zelda and Sheila Hannah, editors. *Introduction to Automation.* Second printing. Harrisonburg, Virginia: Visual Resources Association.

Ritzenthaler, Mary Lynn, Munoff, Gerard J. and Long, Margery S. *Archives and Manuscripts: Administration of Photographic Collections*. Chicago, Illinois: Society of American Archivists, 1984. Includes a glossary of photographic terms and many sample drawings and photos.

Ritzenthaler, Mary Lynn. *Preserving Archives and Manuscripts*. Chicago, Illinois: Society of American Archivists, to be published as part of the new Archival Fundamentals Series.

Roberts, D. Andrew, editor. *Collections Management for Museums: Proceeding from the First Annual Conference of the Museum Documentation Association*. Cambridge, England: Museum Documentation Association, 1988. The conference took place September 26–29, 1987.

Roberts, D. Andrew. *Planning the Documentation of Museum Collections*. Cambridge, England: Museum Documentation Association, 1985.

Rogers, JoAnn V. and Jerry D. Saye. *Nonprint Cataloging for Multimedia Collections: A Guide Based on AACR2*. Second edition. Littleton, Colorado: Libraries Unlimited, 1987. A detailed guide arranged by the rule numbers of AACR2 (Anglo-American Cataloguing Rules, Second edition).

Rowley, Jennifer. *The Basics of Information Technology*. London, England: Clive Bingley, Ltd., 1988. Distributed in the U.S. by the American Library Association.

Rowley, Jennifer. *Computers for Libraries*. Second edition. London, England: Clive Bingley, Ltd., 1985. Distributed in the U.S. by the American Library Association.

RQ (Reference Quarterly). A quarterly journal published by the American Library Association.

Rush, James E. "The Library Automation Market: Why Do Vendors Fail? A History of Vendors and Their Characteristics." *Library High Tech*. Ann Arbor, Michigan: Pierian Press, Inc. Volume 6, Number 3 (1988), pages 7–33

Russell, Keith W., editor. *Subject Access*. Washington, DC: Council on Library Resources, 1982.

Safady, William. *Introduction to Automation for Librarians*. Second edition. Chicago, Illinois: American Library Association, 1989.

Sahli, Nancy. "Automation and Archives/Records Management." *Bowker Annual of Library and Book Trade Information*, compiled and edited by Filomena Simora, New York, New York: R.R. Bowker, 1986, pages 74–80.

Sahli, Nancy. *MARC for Archives and Manuscripts: The AMC Format*. Chicago, Illinois: Society of American Archivists, 1985. A guide to the MARC format for archives and manuscripts.

Sahli, Nancy. "Interpretation and Application of the AMC Format." *American Archivist*. Volume 49, Number 1 (Winter 1986). Pages 9–20. A history and description of the MARC format for Archival and Manuscripts Control.

Salinger, Florence A. and Zagon, Eileen. *Notes for Catalogers: A Sourcebook for Use with AACR2*. White Plains, New York and London: Knowledge Industry Publications, Inc., 1985, reprinted 1988. A collection of examples of the use of the Anglo-American Cataloguing Rules.

Sarasan, Lenore, and A. M. Neuner, compilers. *Museum Collections and Computers: Report of an ASC Survey*. Lawrence, Kansas: Association of Systematics Collections, 1983.

Saye, Jerry D. and Sherry Vellucci. *Notes in the Catalog Record Based on AACR2 and LC Rule Interpretations*. Chicago, Illinois: American Library Association, 1988. The use of notes to describe the scope and summary of materials or their historical and biographical background, according to the rules of AACR2 (Anglo-American Cataloguing Rules, Second edition) and LC (Library of Congress) Rule Interpretations.

Schamm, A. M. *Managing Special Collections.* New York, New York: Neal-Schuman Publishers, 1986.

Schellenberg, Theodore R. *Modern Archives: Principles and Techniques.* Chicago, Illinois: University of Chicago Press, 1956. On pages 126–127, Schellenberg contended that archivists should be subject specialists.

Schellenberg, Theodore R. *The Management of Archives.* New York, New York: Columbia University Press, 1965. Schellenberg's two principal works did much to determine the shape of archives today.

Schuller, Nancy, editor. *Guide to Management of Visual Resources Collections.* Harrisonburg, Virginia: Visual Resources Association, 1979.

Schuyler, Michael. *Now What? How to Get Your Computer Up and Keep It Running.* New York, New York: Neal-Schumann Publishers, 1988. Guidance for libraries in maintaining computer systems.

Schuyler, Michael. *PC Management: A How-To-Do-It Manual for Selecting, Organizing, and Managing Personal Computers in Libraries.* New York, New York: Neal-Schumann Publishers, 1990.

Scott, Randall W. "An Original Catalog Librarian's Perspective on Library Automation." *Library Journal,* Volume 112, Number 18 (November 1, 1987), pages 48–54.

Sears List of Subject Headings. Thirteenth edition. Bronx, New York: H. W. Wilson Co., 1986. A list of subject heading terms often used by book indexers. The list is shorter and simpler than the Library of Congress Subject Headings.

Sharif, Carolyn A. Y. *Developing an Expert System for the Classification of Books using Micro-Based Expert System Shells.* London, England: British Research and Development Publications, 1988. Distributed in the U.S. by the American Library Association.

Shatford, Sara. "Analyzing the Subject of a Picture: A Theoretical Approach." *Cataloging and Classification Quarterly.* Volume 6, Number 3 (1986).

Sloan, Bernard G. *Linked Systems for Resource Sharing.* Boston, Massachusetts: G.K. Hall, 1990. A guide to planning, funding, implementing, and evaluating systems for linking together automated library catalogs.

Small Computers in Libraries. See: *Computers in Libraries.*

Smiraglia, Richard P. *Cataloging Music: A Manual for Use with AACR2.* Second edition. Lake Crystal, Minnesota: Soldier Creek Press, 1986, reprinted 1988. The application to printed music and second recordings of the rules of AACR2 (Anglo-American Cataloguing Rules, Second edition). The manual is intended to serve as a textbook for the beginning music cataloger.

Smiraglia, Richard P., editor. *Describing Archival Materials: The Use of the MARC AMC Format.* New York, New York: Haworth Press, Inc., 1990. Also published in *Cataloging & Classification Quarterly,* Volume 11, Numbers 3 and 4.

Society of American Archivists. *College and University Archives: Selected Readings.* Chicago, Illinois: Society of American Archivists, 1979.

Society of American Archivists. "Library Descriptive Standards: An Introduction for Archivists." Chicago, Illinois: Society of American Archivists, Library Descriptive Standards Workshop, September 26–27, 1988. Readings and examples prepared for the workshop.

Society of American Archivists, National Information Systems Task Force. "Data Elements Used in Archives, Manuscripts and Records Repository Information Systems: A Dictionary of Standard Terminology." Chicago, Illinois: Society of American Archivists, 1984.

Society of American Archivists. The society is currently producing a book of examples of archival descriptions in MARC-AMC (Archives and Manuscripts Control) format. Chicago, Illinois: Society of American Archivists, projected publication 1990.

Society of American Archivists. The society is currently producing replacements for its Basic Manual Series, now to be called the Archival Fundamentals series, under the general editorship of Mary Jo Pugh. Chicago, Illinois: Society of American Archivists, projected publication 1990–1991.

Society of Archivists Journal. Quarterly journal of the Society of Archivists, in England.

Sources File: Resources for Computer Industry Marketers. Phoenix, Arizona: Applied Computer Research, Inc. A bimonthly publication.

Speakman, Mary N. "The User Talks Back." *American Archivist.* Volume 47 (Spring 1984), pages 164–171. Letters from archivists and Speakman's reply to them appeared in, "The Forum," American Archivist, Volume 47 (Fall 1984), pages 352–353. A researcher's criticism of the reference services provided at certain archives.

Special Collections. New York, New York: Haworth Press, Inc. A semiannual publication.

Special Libraries Association. *From the Top: Profiles of U.S. and Canadian Corporate Libraries and Information Centers.* Washington, DC: Special Libraries Association, 1989. This Special Library Association research study portrays many variations of the corporate information center function.

Special Libraries Association. *Global Ties through Information.* Washington, DC: Special Libraries Association, 1989. A selection of papers and articles on global information flow.

Special Libraries Association. *Tools of the Profession.* Washington, DC: Special Libraries Association, 1988. A collection of bibliographies compiled by the seventeen divisions of the Special Libraries Association. The book lists the publications that would form the core of an industry-specific library in fields such as advertising, publishing, and broadcasting. The bibliography for the publishing industry includes the major reference works that you would use to track down an author, publisher, serial publication, or book.

Special Libraries Association. *User and Information Dynamics: Managing Change.* Washington, DC: Special Libraries Association, 1989. Proceedings of the 1989 Special Libraries Association Annual Conference.

Special Libraries. Journal of the Special Libraries Association.

Spectra: The International Journal of Computer Applications in Museums. Journal of the Museum Computer Network.

Stibbe, H. L. P., editor. *Cartographic Materials: A Manual of Interpretation for AACR2.* Ottawa, Ontario, Canada: Canadian Library Association, 1982. Distributed in the United States by the American Library Association.

Stielow, Frederick J. *The Management of Oral History Sound Archives.* Westport, Connecticut: Greenwood Publishing Group, Inc., 1986. Also distributed by the Society of American Archivists. Guidelines for creating, organizing, and managing archives for oral history and folklore collections.

Studwell, William E. *Library of Congress Subject Headings: Philosophy, Practice, and*

Prospects. New York, New York: Haworth Press, Inc., 1990. A comprehensive theoretical treatise on Library of Congress Subject Headings.

Subject Access and Bibliographic Instruction: Two Sides of the OPAC Problem. Halifax, Nova Scotia, Canada: Dalhousie University Occasional Paper Series Number 45, 1988. OPAC is an acronym for Online Public Access Catalog: The book consists of the following:

Dykstra, Mary. Introduction.

Dewer, Marged. "Restructuring the Library of Congress Subject Headings." Examines methods for making Library of Congress Subject Headings more effective for online searching.

Nowakowski, Frances C. "Bibliographic Instruction for the Online Public Access Catalog." An annotated bibliography for materials published between 1980 and 1986 on the subject of how Online Public Access Catalogs were utilized for library instruction.

Subject Authorities: A Guide to Subject Cataloging. New York, New York: R.R. Bowker, 1981.

Svenonius, Elaine, editor. *The Conceptual Foundations of Descriptive Cataloging*. Orlando, Florida: Academic Press (Harcourt Brace Jovanovich), 1989. The proceeedings of a conference by the same name held at UCLA in 1987. Includes a section on "Standardization and the Proliferation of Rule Interpretations."

Svenonius, Elaine. "Design of Controlled Vocabularies." Paper presented at the 1988 annual meeting of the Special Libraries Association. Copy provided by the author, a professor at the UCLA Graduate School of Library and Information Science. An excellent description of the requirements of a controlled vocabulary.

Swanson, Edward. *A Manual of Advanced AACR2 Examples*. Second edition. Lake Crystal, Minnesota: Soldier Creek Press, 1985. Examples of less frequently used rules from AACR2 (Anglo-American Cataloguing Rules, Second edition).

Swanson, Edward. *A Manual of AACR2 Examples for Manuscripts*. Lake Crystal, Minnesota: Soldier Creek Press, 1981. Illustrates the rules of AACR2 (Anglo-American Cataloguing Rules, Second edition) for manuscripts.

Swanson, Edward. *A Manual of AACR2 Examples for Microforms*. Lake Crystal, Minnesota: Soldier Creek Press, 1982. Illustrates the rules of AACR2 (Anglo-American Cataloguing Rules, Second edition) for microfilm and microfiche.

Swanson, Edward. *A Manual of AACR2 Examples for "In" Analytics, with MARC Tagging and Coding*. Lake Crystal, Minnesota: Soldier Creek Press, 1985. Illustrates the use of the MARC (Machine-Readable Cataloging) format and the rules of AACR2 (Anglo-American Cataloguing Rules, Second edition) for cataloging articles from periodicals, selections from collected works, items from annual reports, a hymn from a hymnal, and other cases where an item is cataloged as an element of a larger whole.

Swanson, Edward. *A Manual of AACR2 Examples for Technical Reports*. Lake Crystal, Minnesota: Soldier Creek Press, 1984. Illustrates the use of the MARC (Machine-Readable Cataloging) format and the rules of AACR2 (Anglo-American Cataloguing Rules, Second edition) for technical reports. The examples are coded and tagged for input on the national bibliographic utility OCLC (Online Computer Library Center).

Swanson, Edward, compiler. *Changes to the Anglo-American Cataloguing Rules, Second Edition*. Lake Crystal, Minnesota: Soldier Creek Press, 1988. A compilation of the changes appearing in the 1988 revision of the Anglo-American Cataloguing Rules.

Taylor, Hugh A. *The Arrangement and Description of Archival Materials*. New York, New York: K.G. Saur, 1980. Distributed by Gale Research of Detroit, Michigan.

Taylor, Lonn W., editor. *A Common Agenda for History Museums: Conference Proceedings, February 19–20, 1987*. Nashville, Tennessee: American Association for State and Local History, and Washington, DC: Smithsonian Institution, 1987. This report notes that the number of history museums in the United States has grown rapidly in the last decade, and that the increased emphasis on social and cultural history has renewed interest in the study of the sorts of objects held in museums, while also causing a shift in emphasis among museums toward providing a social background for the objects that the museums display. The report calls for the sharing of computerized information among museums, and for the creation of standardized data fields that would make such sharing feasible. In his essay on "Creating Common Data Bases," James Blackaby notes that for most museums, registration and cataloging practices continue to be "as much a matter of folklore as a matter of science." The resulting variations in the form of information recorded make the sharing of that information with other institutions extremely difficult.

Technical Services Quarterly. New York, New York: Haworth Press, Inc.

Thomas, Nancy G. and Rosanna O'Neil. *Notes for Serials Cataloging*. Edited by Arlene Taylor. Littleton, Colorado: Libraries Unlimited, 1986.

Thompson, Enid. *Local History Collections: A Manual for Librarians*. Nashville, Tennessee: American Association for State and Local History, 1987.

Thompson, John M. A. *Manual of Curatorship: A Guide to Museum Practice*. London, England and Boston, Massachusetts: Butterworths, revised 1986. Includes essays by Sheila M. Stone and D. Andrew Roberts on the process of documenting the objects that come into a museum.

Tillett, Barbara B., editor. *Authority Control in the Online Environment: Considerations and Practices*. New York, New York: Haworth Press, Inc., 1989. Also published in *Cataloging & Classification Quarterly*, Volume 9, Number 3.

Todeschini, Claudio and Michael P. Farrell. "An Expert System for Quality Control in Bibliographic Databases." *Journal of the American Society for Information Science*, Volume 40, Number 1 (January 1989), pages 1–11. A description of the use of an expert system to flag bibliographic entries for which there was a high probability that the cataloger had placed the entry into the wrong subject category.

Tucker, Ruth, editor. *Authority Control in Music Libraries. Proceedings of the Music Library Association Preconference, March 5, 1985*. Canton, Massachusetts: Music Library Association, 1990.

Turner, Chris. *Organizing Information*. London, England: Clive Bingley, Ltd., 1986. Distributed in the U.S. by the American Library Association.

United States Office of Management and Budget. *Standard Industrial Classification Manual*. Springfield, Virginia: National Technical Information Service (NTIS), U.S. Department of Commerce, 1987. A manual for the application of Standard Industrial Classification (SIC) codes for occupations and indutries.

University of Illinois at Urbana-Champaign, Graduate School of Library and Information Science. *Questions and Answers: Strategies for Using the Electronic Reference Collection. Proceedings of the 24th Annual Clinic on Library Applications of Data Processing, 1990*. Champaign, Illinois: University of Illinois at Urbana-Champaign, 1990. Covers the impact of automation in areas such as reference services, library organization, online searching, and the sharing of resources.

University of Washington Libraries. *Manual for Accessioning, Arrangement, and Description of Manuscripts and Archives*. Seattle, Washington: University of Washington Libraries, 1979.

Urbanski, Verna, Bao Chu Chang, and Bernard Karon. *Cataloging Unpublished Non-Print Materials: A Manual of Suggestions, Comments and Examples*. Jackson, Florida: Online Audio-Visual Catalogers (OLAC), projected publication Fall 1989.

Visual Resources: An International Journal of Documentation. New York, New York: Gordon and Breach, Science Publishers.

Vogt-O'Connor, Diane and Richard Pearce-Moses. *A Thesaurus of Photographic Terms*. Vogt-O'Connor is Audio-Visual Archivist at the Smithsonian Institution. A descriptive thesaurus covering historical and contemporary terms relating to the physical aspects of photography, including processes, trade names, techniques, formats, genres, and styles. The thesaurus includes extensive descriptions of the various processes that a cataloger might encounter, and guidelines for identifying technique and dating a photograph by physical characteristics, such as notches on a negative.

Volunteer National Center/The Taft Group. *Basic Computer Knowledge for Nonprofits: Everything You Need to Know Made Easy*. Washington, DC: American Association of Museums, 1985. A basic guide to computers for museum professionals.

Young, Heartsill, editor. *The American Library Association Glossary of Library and Information Science*. Chicago, Illinois: American Library Association, 1983.

Walker, Stephen and Richard Jones. *Improving Subject Retrieval in Online Catalogues: 1. Stemming, Automatic Spelling Correction, and Cross-Reference Tables*. London, England: British Research and Development Publications, 1987. Distributed in the U.S. by the American Library Association.

Ward, Alan. *A Manual of Sound Archive Administration*. Brookfield, Vermont: Gower Publishing Company, 1990.

Warwick, Robert and Jensen, Patricia E. *Using OCLC: A How-To-Do-It Manual for Libraries*. New York, New York: Neal Schuman Publishers, Inc., 1990. A training manual for using the national OCLC (Online Computer Library Center) database, both for searching and cataloging.

Webb, T. D. *The In-house Option: Professional Issues of Library Automation*. New York, New York: Haworth Press, 1987. Examines the impact of computers on the practice of librarianship.

Weber, Lisa B. "Educating Archivists for Automation". *Library Trends*, Volume 36, Number 3 (Winter 1988), pages 501–518. Weber looks forward to future automated systems that can import and export MARC records, control archival and manuscript material throughout their entire life cycle, maintain more detailed levels of description, keep track of data on donors, scheduling, patron use, reference requests, and other information, and support linked Authority Files. (page 515) To take advantage of the opportunities of the future, rather than letting the future pass them by, archivists must educate themselves thoroughly on the subject of automation. (page 516)

Weber, Lisa B. "The Implications of Format Integration for Archivists." Society of American Archivists Annual Meeting. September 30, 1988. A discussion of the possible impact on the cataloging of archival materials with the MARC-AMC format (MARC for Archives and Manuscripts Control) of the integration of the seven different MARC formats into a single format. The author advocates that archivists participate actively in the decision-making process regarding format integration.

Weihs, Jean and Shirley Lewis. *Non-Book Materials: The Organization of Integrated Collections*. Canadian Library Association, 1989. Distributed in the U.S. by the American Library Association.

Weinberg, Bella and James A. Benson. *Downloading/Uploading Online Databases and Catalogs*. Ann Arbor, Michigan: Pierian Press, 1985. Hardware, software, applications, and copyrights.

Weinberg, Nathan and Marshall, Robert G. *Archival Research Techniques for College Undergraduates: A Booklet for Researching and Writing Papers Using Secondary and Primary Source Materials*. Northridge, California: Urban Archives Center, California State University, Northridge, 1986. A very useful, short booklet with basic information for the beginning researcher on how to start work on an historical project that will use both primary and secondary sources.

Weiskel, Timothy C. "University Libraries, Integrated Scholarly Information Systems (ISIS), and the Changing Character of Academic Research." *Library High Tech*, Volume 6, Number 4 (Issue 24, 1988), pages 7–27. This article argues that libraries, in order to remain relevant and useful in an age of the rapid electronic exchange of information, must be prepared to deliver information to researchers in a useful form. Scholars will increasingly expect that they should be able to download information directly into their own databases, rather than sitting in the library and copying information with pencil and paper, for later typing into home or office computers. Weiskel warns that, "Over time computer literate scholars will discover that their own university libraries may be among the last resources that they consult in an electronic age." (page 23) As a consequence, "The future viability of the university library as a research institution is at stake." (page 8) "If scholars collectively get accustomed to by-passing the university library for access to needed information, the library's long-term viability as a research institution is in jeopardy." (page 22) If libraries do not participate in the development of Integrated Scholarly Information Systems, then libraries will become museums. He provides examples of before and after conversions of information from several Dialog on-line databases, including Books in Print, Magazine Index, and Dissertation Abstracts. Curiously, Weiskel does not mention the standardization of formats through the development of MARC, or the standardization of descriptive practices.

Wheeler, Helen Rippler. *The Bibliographic Instruction Course Handbook: A Skills and Concepts Approach*. Metuchen, New Jersey: Scarecrow Press, 1988.

White-Hensen, Wendy. *Archival Moving Image Materials: A Cataloging Manual*. Washington, D.C.: Library of Congress, 1984. Known as AMIM, this is the first guide to attempt to develop and provide instruction for cataloging film and video materials using the MARC-VM (Visual Materials) format.

Williams, David W. *A Guide to Museum Computing*. Nashville, Tennessee: American Association for State and Local History, 1987. An introductory guide to the use of computers in museums, this book is however not sufficiently detailed and specific in its examples to be useful to the type of reader who needs such a guide.

Wilson Library Bulletin. Bronx, New York: H. W. Wilson Co. Published monthly, September–June.

Wilsted, Thomas, and William Nolte. *Managing Archives and Manuscript Repositories*. Chicago, Illinois: Society of American Archivists, to be published as part of the new Archival Fundamentals Series.

Wynar, Bohdan S. Seventh edition by Arlene G. Taylor. *Introduction to Cataloging and Classification*. Englewood, Colorado: Libraries Unlimited, 1985. A guide to cataloging practices. Includes a detailed explanation of AACR2 rules, with examples, and matched with the appropriate MARC fields. Also contains chapters on Library of Congress Subject Headings, the Sears List of Subject Headings, and a glossary.

Yakel, Elizabeth. *Starting an Archives Manual*. Chicago, Illinois: Society of American Archivists, to be published as part of the new Archival Fundamentals Series.

Yee, Martha, compiler. *Moving Image Materials: Genre Terms*. Washington, DC: Library of Congress, 1988. Produced by the National Moving Image Database Standards Committee, National Center for Film and Video Preservation of the American Film Institute.

Zinkham, Helena and Parker, Elisabeth Betz. *Descriptive Terms for Graphic Materials: Genre and Physical Characteristic Headings*. Washington, D.C.: Library of Congress, 1986. Terms to use in MARC field 655 (Genre/Form Heading) and field 755 (Physical Characteristics). The terms are useful for planning exhibits. The thesaurus is known by the acronym DTGM.

Aids to research and style

Allen, Barbara and Lynwood Montell. *From Memory to History: Using Oral Sources in Local Historical Research*. Nashville, Tennessee: American Association for State and Local History, 1981.

"America: History and Life." A bibliographic database available through Dialog.

American Historical Review. Journal of the American Historical Association.

American Quarterly. Journal of the American Studies Association.

Arlen, Shelley. "Photographs: Interpretive and Instructional Strategies." Special Libraries. Volume 81, Number 4 (Fall 1990), pages 351–359. A good introduction to reading a photograph for issues of historical significance.

Barzun, Jacques, and Graff, Henry F. *The Modern Researcher*. Fourth edition. New York, New York and San Diego, California: Harcourt Brace Jovanovich, 1985. Since publication of the first edition in 1957, this book has been the standard guide for conducting research and for turning the data collected into a well-organized, written form. It is an absolutely essential reference for every researcher.

Baum, Willa K. *Oral History for the Local Historical Society*. Third edition, revised. Nashville, Tennessee: American Association for State and Local History, 1987. Since publication of the first edition in 1969 by the Conference of California Historical Societies, this sixty-page work has been considered a classic example of a useful guide. It is strongly recommended for anyone planning to conduct oral history interviews.

Baum, Willa K. *Transcribing and Editing Oral History*. Nashville, Tennessee: American Association for State and Local History, 1977.

Blumenson, John. *Identifying American Architecture: A Pictorial Guide to Styles and Terms, 1600–1945*. Nashville, Tennessee: American Association for State and Local History, 1987.

Brecher, Jeremy. *History from Below: How to Uncover and Tell the Story of Your Community, Association, or Union*. Nashville, Tennessee: American Association for State and Local History, 1985. A pamphlet not intended for the professional historian.

Brooks, Philip C. *Research in Archives: The Use of Unpublished Primary Sources*. Chicago, Illinois: University of Chicago Press, 1969. Written by an archivist for researchers.

Chandler, Alfred D., Jr. *The Visible Hand: The Managerial Revolution in American Business*. Cambridge, Massachusetts: Harvard University Press, 1977. Provides valuable insights into the types of documents found in business archives.

Chicago Manual of Style. Thirteenth edition. Chicago, Illinois: University of Chicago Press, 1982. The required style manual for publication in scholarly journals. An absolutely essential reference for every writer. The thirteenth edition is much easier to read and more helpful than previous editions, therefore purchase of the latest version is recommended even when earlier editions are available. Note that the Anglo-American Cataloguing Rules are generally in accordance with the Chicago manual, and mandate its use for those points of style that the rules do not cover. (See pages 1 and 3 of AACR2.) For the individual researcher, since the Chicago Manual is much easier to use than the Anglo-American Cataloguing Rules, if you are not going to use AACR2, at least use the Chicago Manual.

Collier, John, Jr. and Malcolm Collier. *Visual Anthropology: Photography as a Research Method*. Revised and expanded edition. Albuquerque, New Mexico: University of New Mexico Press, 1986.

Denley, Peter, Stefan Fogelvik and Charles Harvey, editors. *History and Computing 2*. Manchester, England: Manchester University Press, 1988. Distributed in the United States by St. Martin's Press. Thirty papers presented at the second annual conference of the British organization, the Association for History and Computing.

"Dissertation Abstracts." A bibliographic database produced by the University of Michigan and made available through Dialog.

Dunaway, David K. and Willa K. Baum. *Oral History: An Interdisciplinary Anthology*. Nashville, Tennessee: American Association for State and Local History, 1984. A collection of scholarly essays on oral history, each followed by a bibliography.

"English Short Title Catalog." Available online through RLIN (Research Libraries Information Network). A machine-readable cataloging of works printed in English in the Eighteenth Century.

Erskind, Andrew, editor. *An Index to American Photographic Collections*. Boston, Massachusetts: G.K. Hall and Company, 1989. Prepared by the International Museum of Photography at George Eastman House in Rochester, New York. An expansion of the 1982 guide compiled by James McQuaid.

Falk, Joyce Duncan. "OCLC and RLIN: Research Libraries at the Scholar's Fingertips." *Perspectives*. Washington, DC: American Historical Association. Volume 27, Number 5 (May/June 1989), pages 1, 11–13, 17. An excellent, succinct description of the OCLC and RLIN online databases, published in the newsletter of the American Historical Association.

Felt, Thomas E. *Researching, Writing, and Publishing Local History*. Second edition. Nashville, Tennessee: American Association for State and Local History, 1976.

Filby, P. William, editor. *Directory of American Libraries with Genealogy or Local History Collections*. Wilmington, Delaware: Scholarly Resources, Inc., 1988. A guide to 1,600 U.S. and Canadian libraries with notable genealogical or local history collections. The guide is organized by geographical area.

Gardner, James B. and George Rollie Adams. *Ordinary People and Everyday Life: Perspectives on the New Social History*. Nashville, Tennessee: American Association for State and Local History, 1983.

Geahigan, Priscilla C. *U.S. and Canadian Businesses, 1957 to 1987: A Bibliography*. Metuchen, New Jersey: Scarecrow Press, 1988. Includes over 4,000 corporate histories arranged by industry, the Standard Industrial Classification Code, with indexes for authors, company names, and personal names.

"George Eastman House Photographers Biography File." Rochester, New York: George Eastman House, International Museum of Photography. Available online or on microfiche through Light Impressions.

Grele, Ronald J. "On Using Oral History Collections: An Introduction." *Journal of American History*. Volume 74 (September 1987), pages 570–578.

Havlice, Patricia Pate. *Oral History: A Reference Guide and Annotated Bibliography*. Jefferson, North Carolina: McFarland and Co., 1985. A bibliography of oral history manuals, articles about oral history, guides to collections, and books based on oral history.

"Historical Abstracts." A bibliographic database for European history produced by ABC-CLIO and made available through Dialog.

History and Computing. Journal of the Association of History and Computing, beginning regular publication in 1989. Published by the Oxford University Press.

Investigative Reporters and Editors, Inc. *The Reporter's Handbook: An Investigator's Guide to Documents and Techniques*. Edited by John Ullman and Steve Honeyman. New York, New York: St. Martin's Press, 1983. A guide to research with public records, including use of the Freedom of Information Act.

Journal of American History. Journal of the Organization of American Historians.

Kammen, Carol. *A Guide for Local Historians*. Nashville, Tennessee: American Association for State and Local History, 1986.

Kammen, Carol. *On Doing Local History: Reflections on What Local Historians Do, Why, and What It Means*. Nashville, Tennessee: American Association for State and Local History, 1986.

Kerr, K. Austin, Amos J. Loveday, and Mansel G. Blackford. *Local Businesses: Exploring Their History*. Nashville, Tennessee: American Association for State and Local History, 1990. Part of the Nearby History series.

Kyvig, David E. and Myron A. Marty. *Exploring the Past Around You*. Nashville, Tennessee: American Association for State and Local History, 1982. Includes a section on interpreting historical photographs: "Visual Documents."

Lancashire, Ian and Willard McCarty. *The Humanities Computing Yearbook: 1988*. New York, New York: Oxford University Press, 1989. An annual reference guide to computer applications and databases for the humanities.

Makower, Joel, editor. *The American History Sourcebook*. New York, New York: Prentice Hall, 1988. A collection of information on the holdings of national archival repositories, state and local historical socities, museums, historic sites, and libraries. An index provides subject access to the listings.

Mauch, James E. and Jack W. Birch. *Guide to the Successful Thesis and Dissertation. Conception to Publication: A Handbook for Students and Faculty*. Second Edition. New York, New York and Basel, Switzerland: Marcel Dekker, Inc., 1988.

"Medieval and Early Modern Data Bank." New Brunswick, New Jersey: Rutgers University, Department of History. A database of information for the years 500-1800, with information such as currency exchange rates. An IBM PC-AT prototype version running on Advanced Revelation is available for $250. The online version is available on RLIN.

Naeve, Milo M. *Identifying American Furniture: A Pictorial Guide to Styles and Terms, Colonial to Contemporary.* Second edition. Nashville, Tennessee: American Association for State and Local History, 1984.

National Archives. *Guide to Genealogical Research in the National Archives.* Washington, DC: National Archives, 1985 revised edition.

National Archives. *Guide to the National Archives of the United States.* Second edition. Introduction by Frank B. Evans. Washington, DC: National Archives, 1987.

National Archives. *Select Lists of National Archives Microfilm Publications.* A separate edition is available by region for: New England, Chesapeake/Mid-Atlantic, the South and Southwest, Central States, and the West. Washington, DC: National Archives, 1986.

National Historical Publications and Records Commission. *Directory of Archives and Manuscript Repositories in the United States.* Second Edition. Phoenix, Arizona: Oryx Press, 1988. Contains descriptions of nearly 4,500 collections in the United States. Includes a subject index.

National Inventory of Documentary Sources in the United States. Part 1: Federal Records. Part 2: Manuscript Division, Library of Congress. Part 3: State Archives, Libraries and Historical Societies. Part 4: Academic Libraries and Other Repositories. Teaneck, New Jersey, and Cambridge, England: Chadwyck-Healey, 1984, 1985, 1986. Contains finding aids from the various repositories, reproduced on microfiche. Includes indexes for names of repositories and collections, and for subjects, including personal, corporate, and geographical names, and topical subject headings based on Library of Congress Subject Headings.

National Technical Information Service. *A Directory of Computerized Data Files.* Washington, DC: U.S. Department of Commerce, National Technical Information Service, Federal Computer Products Center, 1988.

Nevins, Allen. *The Gateway to History.* Revised edition. Chicago, Illinois: Quadrangle Books, 1963. A discussion of issues in historical thinking.

Nineteenth Century Short Title Catalog. Newcastle-upon-Tyne, England: Avero Publications Limited, a series of volumes have been published since 1983. Distributed by Chadwyck-Healey. A mammoth bibliographical project to make bibliographical information available for works in English printed in the period 1801–1918.

Online Computer Library Center (OCLC). *Guide to the OCLC Database and the Special Collections Therein.* Dublin, Ohio: OCLC, 1984.

Parker, Donald D. *Local History: How to Gather It, Write It, and Publish It.* Westport, Connecticut: Greenwood Press, 1979.

Perspectives: American Historical Association Newsletter. The newsletter has carried valuable articles on the use of computers by historians.

Previts, Gary John and Barbara Merino. *A History of Accounting in America: A Historical Interpretation of the Cultural Significance of Accounting.* New York, New York: John Wiley and Sons, 1979. Provides an excellent background for drawing historical interpretations from business accounting records.

Ray, Don. *A Public Records Primer and Investigator's Handbook.* Burbank, California: Don Ray, 1989. An excellent guide to the use of public records for research.

Rosner, Lisa. "Teaching Quantitative History with a Database." *Perspectives: American*

Historical Association Newsletter, Volume 28, Number 7 (October 1990), pages 18–20. A short but excellent article on the problems of convincing students in a history seminar of the need to use standardized procedures and vocabulary in order to create a useful database. I wish that more historians could be similarly persuaded.

Rudisill, Richard. "On Reading Photographs." *Journal of American Culture.* Volume 5, Number 1 (Fall 1982), pages 1–14.

Rundell, Walter, Jr. "Photographs as Historical Evidence: Early Texas Oil." *American Archivist.* Volume 41, Number 4 (October 1978), pages 373–398.

Szucs, Loretto Dennis and Sandra Hargreaves Luebking. *The Archives: A Guide to the National Archives Field Branches.* Washington, DC: National Archives, 1988. A guide to the holdings of the National Archives' eleven Regional Archives.

Smith, Betty Pease, editor and compiler. *Directory of Historical Agencies in North America.* Thirteenth edition. Nashville, Tennessee: American Association for State and Local History, 1986.

Society of American Archivists. *Directory of Business Archives in the United States and Canada.* Chicago, Illinois: Society of American Archivists, 1990.

Strunk, William, Jr., and White, E. B. *The Elements of Style.* New York, New York: Macmillan, 1959. An excellent, pithy guide to writing style.

Thompson, Paul. *The Voice of the Past: Oral History.* New York, New York: Oxford University Press, 1978. A guide to oral history by Britain's most prominent practitioner.

Trachtenberg, Alan. *Reading American Photographs: Images as History, Mathew Brady to Walker Evans.* New York, New York: Hill and Wang, 1989.

Tuchman, Barbara W. *Practicing History: Selected Essays.* New York, New York: Alfred A. Knopf, 1981.

Wagner, John, editor. *Images of Information: Still Photography in the Social Sciences.* Beverly Hills, California: Sage Publications, 1979.

Walch, Timothy, compiler. *Our Family, Our Town: Essays on Family and Local History Sources in the National Archives.* Washington, DC: National Archives, 1987.

Washington Researchers. *How to Find Financial Information About Companies.* Washington, DC: Washington Researchers, 1990. A guide to sources of financial information about public and private companies.

Wink, Robin W., editor. *The Historian as Detective: Essays on Evidence.* New York, New York: Harper and Row, 1970. Fascinating case studies of historical research which illustrate rules of evidence.

Wise, Gene. *American Historical Explanations: A Strategy for Grounded Inquiry.* Second edition. Minneapolis, Minnesota: University of Minnesota Press, 1980. Wise urges historians to see events from a variety of perspectives, rather than looking for one eternal truth.

Computer database management

ACM Guide to Computing Literature. New York, New York: ACM Press. An annual guide to publications on computing from the Association for Computing Machinery.

ACM Transactions on Database Systems. New York, New York: ACM Press. A quarterly journal on database management from the Association for Computing Machinery . The journal is very technical in nature.

Alberico, Ralph and Mary Micco. *Expert Systems for Reference and Information Retrieval.* Westport, Connecticut: Meckler Publishing Co., 1989.

Buckley, Jo Ann. *Database Management Systems.* Volume 7 in the series *Essential Guide to the Library IBM PC.* Westport, Connecticut: Meckler Publishing Co., 1986.

Codd, E. F. "A Relational Model of Data for Large Shared Data Banks." *Communications of the ACM.* Volume 13, Number 6 (June 1970). E. F. Codd's original definition of the relational database model.

Computing Reviews. New York, New York: ACM Press. A monthly journal from the Association for Computing Machinery, with reviews of recent computer publications.

Database: The Magazine of Database Reference and Review. Weston, Connecticut: Online, Inc. A journal on the subject of database management, particularly the use of online databases. The Online corporation also produces the Micro Software Directory on Dialog. The directory gives special emphasis to library software.

Data Based Advisor. San Diego, California: Data Based Solutions. A journal devoted to DOS database programs, including Pick-based Revelation.

Database Programming and Design. San Francisco, California: Miller Freeman Publications. A journal for database professionals.

Date, C. J. *An Introduction to Database Systems.* Reading, Massachusetts: Addison-Wesley. Volume 1, third edition, 1981. Volume 2, first edition, 1983. A detailed treatise on the underlying concepts of relational database management for the database professional.

Date, C. J. *Database: A Primer.* Reading, Massachusetts: Addison-Wesley, 1983. An introduction to database management for the user.

Date, C. J. *Relational Database: Selected Writings.* Reading, Massachusetts: Addison-Wesley, 1986. Date defines the relational data model as consisting of three distinct parts: the data, the operators used to manipulate the data, and the means for maintaining the integrity of the data.

Emerson, Sanda L. and Darnovsky, Marcy. *Database for the IBM PC.* Reading, Massachusetts: Addison-Wesley Publishing Co. 1984. The simplest general introduction to the subject of computer database management.

Fidel, Raya. *Database Design For Information Retrieval: A Conceptual Approach.* New York, New York: John Wiley and Sons, Inc., 1987.

Gillenson, Mark L. *Database: Step-by-Step.* New York, New York: John Wiley and Sons, Inc., 1985.

Grotophorst, Clyde W. "Keyless Entry: Building a Text Database Using OCR Technology." *Library Hi Tech,* Volume 7, Number 1 (1989), pages 7–15. Includes clear, concise explanations of digital image scanning, data compression, and Optical Character Recognition. The article reports on the creation of a full-text database of the dissertations at George Mason University. This is achieved through the use of scanning and Optical Character Recognition.

Humphrey, Susanne M. and John Melloni Biagio. *Databases: A Primer for Retrieving Information by Computer.* Englewood Cliffs, New Jersey: Prentice-Hall, 1986.

Martin, James. *Managing the Database Environment.* Englewood Cliffs, New Jersey: Prentice-Hall, Inc. 1983. The Bible on the subject of database management, from the foremost authority on the topic. The book is addressed to the administrator, rather than computer professional. Before choosing a Free Text or File Manager program rather than a true Database program, be sure to read the section on "Problems with File

Systems," starting at page 13. Martin demonstrates that a Free Text or File Management program will cost far more in time, money, effort and aggravation because of its inability to perform standard database maintenance tasks.

Palmer, Richard Phillips and Harvey Varnet. *How to Manage Information: A Systems Approach*. Phoenix, Arizona: Oryx Press, 1990. Provides a step-by-step analysis of the tasks to undertake in an information management project.

Rumsey, Eric T. "Choosing a Database Management System: Variable or Fixed Field?". *Small Computers in Libraries* (September 1988), pages 23–24.

Salton, Gerard and McGill, Michael J. *Introduction to Modern Information Retrieval*. New York, New York: McGraw-Hill, 1983.

Soergel, Dagobert. *Organizing Information: Principles of Data Base and Retrieval Systems*. Orlando, Florida: Academic Press (Harcourt Brace Jovanovich), 1985.

Sowa, J. F. *Conceptual Structures: Information Processing in Mind and Machine*. Reading, Massachusetts: Addison-Wesley, 1984.

Taylor, Robert S. *Value-Added Processes in Information Systems*. Norwood, New Jersey: Ablex Publishing, 1986.

Tenopir, Carol and Gerald Lundeen. *Managing Your Information: How to Create a Textual Database on Your Microcomputer*. New York, New York: Neal-Schuman Publishers, 1988. Principally, a guide to the use of free-text and indexing programs. I strongly recommend that, for the purpose of cataloging, you employ a powerful, relational database program rather than a free-text program.

Veith, Richard H. *Visual Information Systems: The Power of Graphics and Video*. Boston, Massachusetts: G. K. Hall, 1988.

Weinberg, Gerald M. *The Secrets of Consulting*. New York, New York: Dorset House, 1985. How to manage change in an organization using computers. His sequel, *Becoming a Technical Leader*, carries the same subject further. Weinberg also wrote *The Psychology of Computer Programming* and *An Introduction to General Systems Thinking*.

Pick operating system

The various basic introductions and guides to the Pick system listed below are each useful from the standpoint of providing different examples of database usage. The list also includes more advanced books for the programmer and system developer.

Access Magazine. See below under: *Unix/business*.

Alcyona Pick Catalog. Hollywood, California: Alcyona Computer Consultants, Inc. A free quarterly catalog and newsletter published by the largest Pick dealer in the United States. The publication includes technical suggestions and sound advice on products.

ALLM's Pick Resources Guide International. Bushey, Herts, England: ALLM Systems and Marketing. Product listings and directories of Pick vendors in Europe and Australia. Updated annually.

Bate, Joseph St. John and Wyatt, Mike. *The Pick Operating System*. London, England: Collins Professional and Technical Books, 1986. Published in the U.S. by Van Nostrand Reinhold Co., Inc., 1987. (Also distributed in England by ALLM and in the U.S. by Alcyona and Gardner.) An introduction to the principal features of the Pick system, with thorough coverage of Access and data dictionaries.

Behan, Kate and Ruscoe, David. *Understanding Pick*. East Hanover, New Jersey: Ultimate Corp., 1986. A basic introduction to the Pick operating system.

Benica, Bruno. *Advanced Pick & Unix: La Nouvelle Norme Informatique*. Aulnay sous Bois, France: Relais Informatique International, 1990. The first book available on Advanced Pick, the new version of the Pick operating system. In French.

Binney, James and Mark Newman. *Pick for Humans: A Powerful Business System Made Plain*. London, England: McGraw-Hill, 1990. Also distributed in the United States by TAB Professional and Reference Books.

Bourdon, R. J. *The Pick Operating System: A Practical Guide*. Reading, Massachusetts and London, England: Addison-Wesley, 1987. (Also distributed in England by ALLM and in the U.S. by Alcyona and Gardner.) The most comprehensive guide available for the Pick system, and a well-written book.

Bull, Malcolm. *A Guide to Databases*. London, England: Heinemann, projected publication 1990. A text on the principles of database management systems, intended for classroom use.

Bull, Malcolm. *The Pick Operating System*. London, England, and New York, New York: Chapman and Hall Computing, 1987. (Also distributed in England by ALLM.) As complete as Bourdon's book, but oriented more to the McDonnell Douglas (Microdata Reality) implementation of Pick.

Bull, Malcolm. *Systems Development using Structured Techniques*. Andover, Hampshire, England, and New York, New York: Routledge, Chapman and Hall, 1990.

Business Software Catalog. San Diego, California: IDBMA, Inc. An annual directory of products and services for computers using the Pick operating system.

Chapel, Hal J. and Clark, Richard G. *Revelation Revealed*. San Francisco, California: Paradigm Publishing, 1986. Revelation is a version of Pick which runs under the DOS operating system.

Clark, David L. *Programming with IBM PC Basic and the Pick Database System*. Blue Ridge Summit Pennsylvania: TAB Professional and Reference Books, 1989. (Also distributed by Alcyona and JES.) A programming language guide with parallel references and examples for Microsoft Basic and Pick Basic. The book demonstrates how to integrate the use of a Pick database with popular IBM PC DOS word processors and other applications.

Cook, Rick and Brandon, John. "The Pick Operating System." *BYTE Magazine* (October and November, 1985).

Dict & Data. Laguna Beach, California: Pick Software Developers Association. A technical journal devoted to the Pick system.

Dougherty, Dale. *A Guide to the Pick System*. Sebastopol, California: O'Reilly and Associates, Inc., 1990. A guide to the Pick system and database architecture, with useful information on file management and the use of the editor, printers, and backup tape or floppy disk units.

Gallant, Walter. *Pick Access: A Guide to the SMA/Retrieval Language*. Sebastopol, California: O'Reilly and Associates, Inc., 1990. A guide to Pick's data-searching facility, known as Access.

Gallant, Walter. *Pick Master Dictionary: A Reference Guide to User Accounts*. Sebastopol, California: O'Reilly and Associates, Inc., 1990. A detailed reference guide with examples for the commands used at the operating system level in a user database account. The book does not provide step-by-step lessons. It is a reference guide only, useful as a supplement to the Pick manual.

Guide to Products, Services, and Software for Pick-based Computer Systems. Laguna Hills, California: Thurman Marketing Services, Inc. An annual directory of products and services for computers using the Pick operating system.

Infocus Magazine. Philadelphia, Pennsylvania: Infocus, Inc. A bimonthly journal for users of the Prime implementation of Pick.

International Pick Users Association Journal. Los Gatos, California: International Pick Users Association. A bimonthly journal with technical articles and news from user groups.

Kitt, Nicola. *Pick—Your System.* Cheshire, England: Sigma Press, 1986. Published in the United States by Halsted Press, a division of John Wiley and Sons, Inc., 1986. (Also distributed in England by ALLM and in the U.S. by Alcyona and Gardner.) A basic introduction to the Pick system. The book unfortunately contains so many proof-reading errors that it would prove confusing rather than helpful to a novice Pick user.

Lallement, Michel. *Le Système Pick.* Aulnay sous Bois, France: Relais informatique international, 1987. Also distributed by IDBMA France S.A. A basic guide to the Pick system. In French.

Martin, Daniel and Benoît Michel. *Le Livre du Pick.* Banneux, Belgium: B.C.M. série professionnelle, 1988. A fascinating guide to the inner workings of the Pick operating system. In French.

MICRU Data. Boulder, Colorado: MICRU International. A bimonthly journal for users of the McDonnell Douglas (Microdata Reality) implementation of Pick.

Mui, Linda. *Pick Basic: A Reference Guide.* Sebastopol, California: O'Reilly and Associates, Inc., 1990. A reference guide, useful as a supplement to the Pick manual, rather than a step-by-step book of instruction to learn Pick Basic.

News and Review. Laguna Hills, California: Thurman Marketing Services, Inc. A free monthly newspaper for Pick users. Includes technical articles and advice for new users.

O'Reilly and Associates, Inc. Projected titles for 1990–1991 from O'Reilly and Associates include: *System Administration: A Guide to Managing the Pick/SMA Operating System, SYSPROG Reference Guide: SYSPROG Account Verbs,* and *PROC: A Guide to the PROC Processor.*

Pick Hits: Application Software and Resource Guide for the Pick System. Irvine, California: Pick Systems. An annual directory of products and services for computers using the Pick operating system.

Pick User Digest. Laguna Hills, California: Thurman Marketing Services, Inc. A technical journal on the Pick operating system, published eight times per year.

PickWorld. Irvine, California: Pick Systems. A quarterly journal dedicated to the Pick operating system. Includes technical articles and advice for new users. Each issue contains international listings of Pick dealers, educational centers, and user groups. Purchasers of the Pick operating system receive a free one-year subscription.

Puccini, R. *Pick par Coeur.* Banneux, Belgium: B.C.M. série professionelle, 1988. An excellent treatise on how to use the Pick system. In French.

The Register. Escondido, California: National Association of Pick. The newsletter of the association. Includes technical articles and advice.

Relais Informatique International. *Une Encyclopédie Pick: Pick de A à Z.* Aulnay sous Bois,

France: Relais Informatique International, projected publication in 1991. An encyclopedia on the use of Pick. In French.

Relational Database Management Computing. Fountain Valley, California: RDBM Computing. Formerly *PickWorld*. (*PickWorld* is now published directly by Pick Systems.) A quarterly journal dedicated to the Pick operating system. Includes technical articles and advice for new users. Each issue contains international listings of Pick dealers, educational centers, user groups, and the machines on which Pick has been implemented. Annually, the magazine lists all the books and journals available concerning the Pick system.

Repton Data of Swarthmore, Pennsylvania is currently producing and publishing a series of technical pamphlets on Pick. Each pamphlet is from twenty to fifty pages in length, and each deals with a specific feature of the Pick operating system. Already available are: *Performing File-Saves*, 1989, which explains how to back up a Pick database, and *Spooler Awareness*, 1989, which demonstrates how to control a shared printer in a multi-user Pick system. Coming soon are: *User Logon*, which provides basic information on a user's interaction with a terminal, and *Techniques for Efficiency*, a guide to increasing system performance for the experienced programmer. (Also distributed in the U.S. by Alcyona.)

Richardson, Wendy and Aldis, Margaret. *A Pick Handbook: Every Manager's Guide to the Pick Operating System*. Truro, England: Syntagma Systems Literature, 1985. (Also distributed in England by ALLM and in the U.S. by Alcyona and Gardner.) An explanation of the Pick system from the standpoint of a manager rather than a user or computer professional.

Rodstein, Harvey Eric. *Pick for Professionals: Advanced Methods and Techniques*. Blue Ridge Summit Pennsylvania: TAB Professional and Reference Books, 1990. An outstanding guide to little-known aspects of the system for experienced programmers and data processing managers.

Rodstein, Harvey. *How to Workbooks: Access*. San Diego, California: IDBMA, Inc., 1989. A workbook with exercises to teach novices how to use Pick's Access facility for database search and retrieval.

Rodstein, Harvey Eric. *How To Workbooks: The Editor*. San Diego, California: IDBMA, Inc., 1988. Exercises for novices on how to use the Pick Editor.

Sandler, Ian. *The Pick Perspective*. Blue Ridge Summit Pennsylvania: TAB Professional and Reference Books, 1989. (Also distributed by Alcyona, Gardner, and JES.) A detailed treatise on the inner workings of the Pick system and the future directions that Pick is likely to take.

Sisk, Jonathan E. and Steve Van Arsdale. *Exploring the Pick Operating System*. Berkeley, California and Hasbrouck Heights, New Jersey: Hayden Book Co., revised edition 1988. A(lso distributed by Alcyona, Gardner, and JES.) The simplest and best general introduction to Pick.

Sisk, Jonathan E. *Pick Basic: A Programmer's Guide*. Blue Ridge Summit Pennsylvania: TAB Professional and Reference Books, 1987. (Also distributed by Alcyona, Gardner, and JES.) A thorough reference to the Pick Basic programming language.

Sisk, Jonathan E. *Pick Pocket Guide. Version IV*. Irvine, California: JES and Associates, Inc., 1988. A handy quick reference to all of the Pick commands. The guide is updated frequently as new enhancements are added to Pick. The pocket version is spiral bound. The desktop version is standard book size. An online version called the "Help Processor" will display the information on the computer screen. Sisk has produced variations on the pocket guide specifically directed to the C. Itoh, McDonnell Douglas (Microdata Reality), Sanyo/Icon, and Ultimate implementations of Pick.

Spectrum. San Diego, California: IDBMA, Inc. A bimonthly journal that carries news and a few technical articles on the Pick operating system.

Spectrum France. Paris, France: IDBMA France S.A. A French version of the English-language publication.

Spectrum Tech. San Diego, California: IDBMA, Inc. A monthly technical journal dedicated to the Pick operating system. Harvey Rodstein shares his outstanding technical knowledge in a monthly column of replies to pleas for help.

SSelect Magazine. Philadelphia, Pennsylvania: Infocus, Inc. A bimonthly technical journal dedicated to the Pick operating system.

Stagner, Walter C. *Working with Pick*. Cleveland, Ohio: Weber Systems, Inc., 1986. (Also distributed by Alcyona and Gardner.) A practical guide to the Pick system, specifically directed to its use on the IBM PC-XT.

Stern, Matthew H. and Betsy Pollack. *Pick: The Easy Way. Volume I. Database and Word Processing for the New User*. Huntington, New York: Comprehensive Information Sciences, Inc., 1987. (Also distributed by Alcyona and Gardner.) An introduction to Pick and to the Pick-based Jet word processing program.

Stern, Matthew H. *Pick: The Easy Way. Volume II. Expanded Theory and Operation*. Huntington, New York: Comprehensive Information Sciences, Inc., second edition 1989. (Also distributed by Alcyona and Gardner.) An explanation of the concepts behind Pick and of the major categories of operations that you would perform with a Pick system.

Taylor, Martin. *Pick for Users*. Oxford, England: Blackwell Scientific Publications, 1985. (Also distributed in England by ALLM and in the U.S. by Alcyona, Computer Science Press, and Gardner.) An introduction to the Pick Basic programming language and to the principal features of the Pick operating system.

Unix/business. Tyne & Wear, United Kingdom: 4GL Publications Company Ltd. A monthly journal. The Pick journal *Access*, formerly a separate publication, was merged into *Unix/business* in 1990.

Watkins, Robert N. *The Craft of Information: Using Prime Information and Programming in Info/Basic*. Blue Ridge Summit Pennsylvania: TAB Professional and Reference Books, projected publication 1991. (Also to be distributed by Alcyona and JES.) A guide to the Prime implementation of Pick.

Winters, John W. and Winters, Dale E. *Pick for the IBM PC and Compatibles*. Blue Ridge Summit Pennsylvania: TAB Professional and Reference Books, 1989. (Also distributed by Alcyona and JES.) A beginner's guide to Pick fundamentals.

Publishers, distributors, and organizations

4GL Publications Company, Limited. 4 Carlton Court, Fifth Avenue, Team Valley, Gateshead, Tyne and Wear. United Kingdom NE11 OAZ. Telephone: 091 482 0220, International: +44 91 482 0220.

Ablex Publishing Corp. 355 Chestnut Street Norwood, New Jersey 07648. Telephone: (201) 767-8450.

ABC-CLIO. 130 Cremona Drive. Santa Barbara, CA 93117-2360. P.O. Box P.O. Box 1911. Santa Barbara, CA 93116-1911. Telephone: (800) 422-2546, (805) 968-1911. Producer of the online historical bibliographic databases Historical Abstracts and America: History and Life.

Academic Press. 465 South Lincoln Drive. Troy, Missouri 63379. Telephone: (800) 321-5068, (314) 528-8110. Remittances to: Book Marketing Department, 1250 Sixth Avenue. San Diego, California 92101-4311. A subsidiary of Harcourt Brace Jovanovich International, Orlando, Florida 32887.

ACM Press. 11 West 42nd Street. New York, New York 10036. Telephone: (212) 869-7440. The publications department of the Association for Computing Machinery.

ADAPSO. 1300 North 17th Street, Suite 300. Arlington, Virginia 22209.

Addison-Wesley Publishing Co. Microcomputer Books and Consumer Software: Jacob Way. Reading, Massachusetts 01867. Telephone: (800) 447-2226, (617) 944-3700. Distribution Center: 5851 Guion Road. Indianapolis, Indiana 46254. Telephone: (317) 293-3660. In England: Addison-Wesley Publishers, Ltd. Finchampstead Road. Wokingham, Berkshire. England RG11 2NZ. Telephone: 0734 794000.

Advanced Libraries and Information, Inc. 2570 S. Berentania St., Suite 207. Honolulu, Hawaii. Telephone: (808) 973-1111. Producer of the ALOHA and ADVANCE integrated library systems utilizing Pick and Pick-with-Unix operating environments.

Advanced Library Systems, Inc. 93 Main Street. Andover, Massachusetts 01810.

Alcyona Computer Consultants, Inc. 7080 Hollywood Blvd., Suite 718. Hollywood, California 90028-6933. Telephone: (213) 462-1549. In Asia: 875 Bukit Timah Road. Singapore 1027. Telephone: (65) 467-2080. A source of books, software, and hardware for the Pick operating system. The president, Brian Stone, is the author of many articles on the use of Pick in the journals listed above. Brian is one of the most knowledgeable and helpful individuals to be found in the Pick environment.

ALLM Systems and Marketing. 21 Beechcroft Road. Bushey, Herts. England WD2 2JU. Telephone: (0923) 30150. A distributors of books and journals on the Pick operating system in England.

AMACOM (American Management Association). 135 West 50th Street. New York, New York 10020. Telephone: (212) 586-8100.

American Association for Museum Volunteers. Care of Administrative Office, American Association of Museums.

American Association for State and Local History (known as AASLH). 172 Second Avenue North, Suite 102. Nashville, Tennessee 37201. Telephone: (615) 255-2971.

American Association of Museums. 1225 Eye Street NW. Washington, DC 20005. Telephone: (202) 289-1818.

American Council of Learned Societies. 1717 Massachusetts Avenue NW, Suite 401. Washington, DC 20036.

American Historical Association. 400 A Street SE. Washington, DC 20003. Telephone: (202) 544-2422.

American Library Association (known as ALA). 50 East Huron Street. Chicago, Illinois 60611-2795. Telephone: Publishing services: (312) 944-6780.

American National Standards Institute (known as ANSI). 1430 Broadway. New York, New York 10018. (212) 354-3300.

American Psychology Association. 1200 17th Street, NW. Washington, DC 20036.

American Society for Information Science. 8720 Georgia Avenue, Suite 501. Silver Spring, Maryland 20910-3602. (301) 495-0900.

American Studies Association. University of Maryland. 2140 Taliaferro Hall. College Park, Maryland 20742. Telephone: (301) 454-2533.

Applied Computer Research, Inc. Box 9280. Phoenix, Arizona 85068-9280. Telephone: (602) 995-5929.

Archives and Museum Informatics. 5501 Walnut St., Suite 203. Pittsburgh, Pennsylvania 15232-2311. Telephone: (412) 683-9775.

Archives Library Information Center. National Archives Library (NNIL), National Archives and Records Administration. Washington, DC 20408. Telephone: (202) 501-5423. Provides information for archivists and records managers. Note that "(NNIL)" is part of the mailing address, not an aside to the reader. The center is generally referred to as the ALIC.

ARLIS (Art Libraries Society). Nursey Road. Southgate, London. England N14 5QH.

ARLIS/NA (Art Libraries Society of North America). 3900 East Timrod Street. Tucson, Arizona 87511.

Art and Architecture Thesaurus (known as the AAT). Getty Art History Information Program, 62 Stratton Road. Williamstown, Massachusetts 01267. Telephone: (413) 458-2151.

Aslib. Association for Information Management. Information House. 26-27 Boswell Street. London, England WC1N 3JZ.

Association de l'Ecole Normale Superieure des Bibliothéquaires. 17-21 Boulevard du 11 Novembre. Villeurbanne, France 69100.

Association des archivistes du Quebec. Care of: Archives nationales du Quebec. C.P. 10450, Sainte-Foy, Quebec. Canada G1V 4N1

Association for Information and Image Management (known as AIIM). 1100 Wayne Avenue, Suite 1100. Silver Spring, Maryland 20910. Telephone: (301) 587-8202.

Association for Northern California Records and Research. P.O. Box 3024. Chico, California 95927. Telephone: (916) 895-6342.

Association for Recorded Sound Collections (known as ARSC). P.O. Box 10162. Silver Spring, Maryland 20904.

Association for the Bibliography of History. Executive Director: Gerald H. Davis. History Department. Georgia State University. Atlanta, Georgia 30303-3083. Editor of journal *Primary Sources and Original* Works: Dean Lawrence J. McCrank. Library and Instructional Services. Ferris State University. Big Rapids, Michigan 49307. Telephone: (616) 592-3729, 592-3611.

Association for Volunteer Administration. P.O. Box 4584. Boulder, Colorado 80306. Telephone: (303) 497-0238.

Association Française des Documentalistes et des Bibliothécaires Specialisés. 5 Avenue France Russe. Paris, France 75007.

Association Française des Utilisateurs de Pick. 12 rue Jacquemont. Paris, France 75017.

Association of Canadian Archivists (known as ACA). P.O. Box 2596, Station D. Ottawa, Ontario. Canada KIP 5W6. Telephone: (613) 232-3643.

Association of History and Computing. The association's journal, *History and Computing,* is published by the Oxford University Press. Membership secretary: Veronica Lawrence, 3 Crown Terrace, Stadhampton, Oxon, OX9 7TY. Editor: R. J. Morris, Dept. of Economic and Social History, William Robertson Building, George Square, Edinburgh, United Kingdom EH8 9JY.

Association of Records Managers and Administrators (known as ARMA). 4200 Somerset Drive, Suite 215. Prairie Village, Kansas 66208. Telephone: (913) 341-3808.

Association of Systematics Collections. University of Kansas. Lawrence, Kansas 66044.

Association pour l'Avancement des Sciences et des Techniques de la Documentation. 3839 rue St. Denis. Montreal, Quebec. Canada H2W 2M4. Telephone: 514-849-1889.

Avero Publications Limited. 20 Great North Road. Newcastle-upon-Tyne, England NE2 4PS. Telephone: (091) 2615790

Avery Video Index to Architectural Drawings on RLIN (known as AVIADOR). Avery Architectural and Fine Arts Library. Columbia University. New York, New York 10027.

Bantam Books/Doubleday Publishing Company. 666 5th Avenue. New York, New York 10103. Telephone: (212) 765-6500.

Basic Books. 10 East 53rd Street. New York, New York 10022. Telephone: (212) 207-7057.

B.C.M. *série professionnelle. 24 route de la sapinière. Banneux, Belgique* B-4960.

Bentley Historical Library. University of Michigan. 1150 Beale Avenue. Ann Arbor, Michigan 48109-2113. Telephone: (313) 764-3482. Directors: Francis X. Blouin and William K. Wallach. The library conducts a summer Research Fellowship Program for the Study of

Modern Archives, with funding from the Andrew K. Mellon Foundation and the National Endowment for the Humanities. The program has produced many thought-provoking papers on the role of archives.

Bibliothèque Nationale. 58 rue de Richelieu. Paris, France 75084. The national library of France.

Blackwell North America. 1001 Fries Mill Road. Blackwood, New Jersey 08012. Telephone: (800) 257-7341, (609) 629-0700. Also: 6024 S.W. Jean Road, Building G. Lake Oswega, Oregon 97035. Telephone: (800) 547-6426, (503) 684-1140. The most experienced provider of authority control services in the U.S.

Blackwell Scientific Publications, Ltd. Osney Mead, Oxford. England OX2 0EL. Telephone: 44 865 240201.

Bowker Magazine Group, Cahners Magazine Division. 249 West 17th Street. New York, New York 1011. Telephone: (800) 431-1713.

Brady Books (Simon & Schuster). 15 Columbus Circle, 14th floor. New York, New York 10023. Telephone: (212) 373-8093.

British Library. 2 Sheraton Street. London, England W1V 4BH.

BRS Information Technologies. 1200 Route 7. Latham, New York 12110. Telephone: (800) 468-0908; (518) 783-1161. An online database service.

Bureau of Canadian Archivists. Care of: National Archives of Canada. 344 Wellington Street, Room 4101. Ottawa, Ontario. Canada K1A 0N3.

California Association of Museums. 900 Exposition Boulevard. Los Angeles, CA 90007. Telephone: (213) 744-3343.

California Committee for the Promotion of History. California History Center. 21250 Stevens Creek Boulevard. Cupertino, California 95014. Telephone: (408) 996-4712. An advocacy organization for historians.

California Office of Historic Preservation. P.O. Box 2390. Sacramento, California 95811. Telephone: (916) 445-8006. Coordinates preservation activities under the National Historic Preservation Act, conducts historic sites surveys, nominates properties to the National Register of Historic Places, distributes federal and state grants-in-aid funds.

California Preservation Foundation. 1615 Broadway #705. Oakland, California 94612. Telephone: (415) 763-0972.

California State Genealogical Alliance. Coordinating agency for the state's genealogical societies. Regional Director Nancy Huebotter. 2634 Associated Road, #A110. Fullerton, California 92635. Telephone: (714) 990-5946.

Canadian Centre for Information and Documentation on Archives (CCIDA). National Archives of Canada. 395 Wellington Street, Room 182. Ottawa, Ontario, Canada K1A 0N3. Telephone: (613) 996-7686.

Canadian Conference on the Arts. 126 York Street, Suite 400. Ottawa, Ontario. Canada K1N 5T5.

Canadian Council of Archives. Care of: National Archives of Canada. 395 Wellington Street. Ottawa, Ontario. Canada K1A 0N3.

Canadian Library Association. 151 Sparks Street. Ottawa, Ontario. Canada K1P 5E3.

Canadian Pick Users. P.O. Box 876, Postal Station B. Willowdale, Ontario. Canada M2K 2R1.

Center for California Studies. California State University, Sacramento. 6000 J Street. Sacramento, California 95819. Telephone: (916) 278-6906.

Center for the History of Computing. 103 Walter Library, 117 Pleasant Street, SE. Minnesota 55455.

Chadwyck-Healey Limited. Cambridge Place. Cambridge, England CB2 1NR. Telephone: (0223) 311479. In the U.S.: 1101 King Street. Alexandria, Virginia 22314. Telephone: (703) 683-4890. In France: *3 rue de Marivaux. Paris, France* 75002. Telephone: (1) 42-86-80-20.

Chapman and Hall Computing. See: Routledge, Chapman and Hall, Inc.

Chicago Historical Society. Clark Street at North Avenue, Chicago, Illinois 60614. Telephone: (312) 642-4600.

Chilton Trade Book Publishers. 201 King of Prussia Road. Radnor, Pennsylvania 19089-0230. Telephone: (215) 964-4709.

Clive Bingley, Ltd. An imprint of the Library Association, England.

Cobb Group, Inc. 9420 Bunsen Parkway, Suite 300. Louisville, Kentucky 40220. Telephone: (800) 223-8720.

Collins Professional and Technical Books. 8 Grafton Street. London. England W1X 3LA.

Columbia University Center for Computing Activities. See: Kermit Distribution.

Comité International d'Histoire de l'Art. Palais Universitaire. Strasbourg, France F-67084.

Comprehensive Information Sciences, Inc. Department PW-101. P.O. Box 622. Huntington, New York 11743. Telephone: (516) 581-7919. An educational center, offering books and courses on the Pick system.

CompuServe, Inc. P.O. Box 20212. 5000 Arlington Centre Blvd. Columbus, Ohio 43220. Telephone: (800) 848-8199, (614) 457-8600. An online database and users' forum service.

Computer Science Press, Inc. 11 Taft Court. P.O. Box 6030. Rockville, Maryland 20850. Telephone: (301) 251-9050.

Computers and the History of Art. 43 Gordon Square. London, England WC1.

Computers in Libraries, Annual Conference. Nancy Melin Nelson, Chair. 42 Grandview Drive. Mount Kisco, New York 10549. Telephone: (914) 666-3394

Conference of California Historical Societies. University of the Pacific. Stockton, California 95211. Telephone: (209) 946-2169. Coordinating body for the states historical organizations.

Conservation Information Network (known as CIN). Getty Conservation Information Institute. 4503 Glencoe Avenue. Marina del Rey, California 90292-6537. The Conservation Information Network maintains online databases for bibliographic items dealing with conservation, conservation materials, and suppliers of conservation products. The journal Art and Archaeology Technical Abstracts is produced from the bibliographic database.

Council on Library Resources. 1785 Massachusetts Avenue NW. Washington, DC 20036.

Crown Publishers. 225 Park Avenue, South. New York, New York 10003. Telephone: (212) 254-1600.

D.A.C. Publications. 3354 30th Street. San Diego, California 92104.

Dalhousie University Occasional Papers Series. Director, SLIS, Dalhousie University. Halifax, Nova Scotia, Canada. B3H 4H8.

Data Based Solutions. 4010 Morena Boulevard, Suite 200. San Diego, CA 92117. Telephone: (619) 483-6400.

Datastorm Technologies, Inc. 1621 Towne Drive. Columbia, Maryland 65202. Telephone:

(314) 474-8461. Producer of the program ProComm, for communications and terminal emulation.

Delphi. General Videotex Corp. 3 Blackstone Street. Cambridge, Massachusetts 02139. Telephone: (800) 544-4005, (617) 491-3393.

Dialog Information Services, Inc. 3460 Hillview Ave. Palo Alto, CA 94304. Telephone: (800) 334-2564, (415) 858-3785. An online database service.

Don Ray. 1314 West Verdugo Avenue. Burbank, California 91506. Telephone: (818) 843-6397, THE-NEWS.

Dorset House Publishing Company. 353 West 12th Street. New York, New York 10014. Telephone: (800) DHBOOKS, (212) 620-4053.

Dow Jones News Retrieval. P.O. Box 300. Princeton, New Jersey 08543-0300. Telephone: (800) 522-3567.

EasyNet. Telebase Library Center. A division of Telebase Systems, Inc. 763 West Lancaster Avenue. Bryn Mawr, Pennsylvania 19010. Telephone: (800) 841-9553, (215) 526-2800. A telecommunications service providing access to a variety of online databases.

Eighteenth Century Short Title Catalogue (known as ESTC). Henry Snyder, Director. College of Humanities and Social Sciences. University of California, Riverside. Riverside, California 92521.

Elsevier Advanced Technology Publications. Mayfield House. 256 Banbury Road. Oxford, England OX2 7DH.

Forest Press. A division of OCLC. 85 Watervliet Avenue. Albany, New York 12206-2082. Telephone: (518) 489-8549.

Gale Research Co. Book Tower. Detroit, Michigan 48226. Telephone: (313) 961-2242.

Gardner, Levsen & Associates. The Bookstore. 1670 South Amphlett Boulevard, Suite 317. San Mateo, California 94402. Telephone: (415) 341-PICK. A source for books on the Pick operating system.

Genealogical Publishing Co., Inc. 1001 North Alvert Street. Baltimore, Maryland 21202. Telephone: (301) 837-8271. Publishes general reference books as well as manuals for genealogists.

GENIE. General Electric Information Services. 401 North Washington Street. Rockville, Maryland 20850. Telephone: (800) 638-9636.

Getty Art History Information Program (known as AHIP). 62 Stratton Road. Williamstown, MA 01267. Telephone: (413) 458-2151. Also: 401 Wilshire Blvd. Santa Monica, CA 90401-1455.

Getty Conservation Information Institute. 4503 Glencoe Avenue. Marina del Rey, California 90292-6537.

G.K. Hall. 70 Lincoln Street. Boston, Massachusetts 02111-2685. Telephone: (800) 343-2806, (617) 423-3990.

Gordon and Breach, Science Publishers. Marketing Department. P.O. Box 786 Cooper Station. New York, New York 10276. In England: P.O. Box 197. London WC2E 9PX England.

Gower Publishing Company. Old Post Road. Brookfield, Vermont 05036. Telephone: (802) 276-3162.

Gower Publishing Group. Gower House. Croft Road. Aldershot, Hampshire. England GU11 3HR.

G.P.O. (Government Printing Office). See: "United States Government Printing Office."

Graphics Press. P.O. Box 430. Cheshire, Connecticut 06410. Telephone: (203) 272-9187.

Greenwood Press. 88 Post Road West, P.O. Box 5007. Westport, Connecticut 06881. Telephone: (203) 226-3571.

Haworth Press, Inc. 12 West 32nd Street. New York, New York 10001-3813. Telephone: (800) 3-HAWORTH, (800) 342-9678, (212) 279-1200. Customer service: 75 Griswold Street. Binghamton, New York 13904. Telephone: (607) 722-2493. Editorial: 28 East 22nd Street. New York, New York 10010. Telephone: (212) 2800. Production: 53 Main Street. Binghamton, New York 13905. Telephone: (607) 722-5857. England: 3 Henrietta Street. London, England WC2E 8LU.

History Database, 24851 Piuma Road. Malibu, California 90265. Telephone: (818) 888-9371. Supplier of the History Database program.

Howard W. Sams & Co. (MacMillan) 4300 West 62nd Street. Indianapolis, Indiana 46268. Telephone: (800) 428-7267, (317) 298-5400.

H. W. Wilson Co. 950 University Avenue. Bronx, New York 10452-9978. Telephone: (800) 367-6770, (212) 588-8400.

IASSIST (International Association for Social Science Information Services and Technology or: Association Internationale pour les Services et Techniques d'Information en Sciences Sociales). Care of Judith Rowe. U.S. Secretariat. Princeton University, Computer Center. 87 Prospect Avenue. Princeton, New Jersey 08544. Telephone: (609) 452-6052. Also: Jackie McGee, IASSIST Treasurer. Rand Corporation. P.O. Box 2138. Santa Monica, CA 90406-2138. Telephone: (213) 393-0411.

IDBMA, Inc. (International Data Base Management Association). 10675 Treena Street, Suite 103. San Diego, California 92131. Telephone: (619) 578-3152. The association organizes conferences around the world on the subject of the Pick system, as well as publishing books and journals on Pick.

IDBMA France S.A. *90 rue de la Victoire*. Paris, France 75009.

IDG Communications/Peterborough, Inc. 80 Elm Street. Peterborough, New Hampshire 03458. Telephone: ((603) 924-9471.

Infocus, Inc. SSelect Magazine. P.O. Box 28397. Philadelphia, Pennsylvania 19149-9986. Telephone: (215) 743-2985.

Information Intelligence, Inc. Box 31098. Phoenix, Arizona 85046. Telephone (800) 228-9982.

Information Resources Press. 1700 North Moore Street, Suite 700. Arlington, Virginia 22209. Telephone: Orders: (800) 451-7363. Information: (703) 558-8270.

Information Transform, Inc. 502 Leonard St. Madison, Wisconsin 53711. Producer of the MITINET for cataloging records in MARC format on an IBM PC or Apple II.

Institute of Information Scientists. 44-45 Museum Street. London, England WC1A 1LY. Telephone: (020) 5803 747.

Institute of Museum Services (known as IMS). 1100 Pennsylvania Avenue, NW. Washington, DC 20506. Telephone: (202) 786-0536

International Council on Archives. P.O. Box 3162, Station D. Ottawa, Canada K1P 6H7

International Council on Museums (known as ICOM). *Maison de l'UNESCO. 1 rue Miollis.* Paris, France 75721. CEDEX 15.

International Federation for Information Processing (known as IFIP). 16 Place Longemalle. Geneva, Switzerland CH-1204.

International Information Management Congress. 345 Woodcliff Drive. Fairport, New York 14450. (716) 383-8330.

International Museum of Photography, at the George Eastman House. Rochester, New York. Produces the Photographers Biography File, which is distributed by Light Impressions.

International Pick Users Association. 23386 Deerfield Road. Los Gatos, California 95030. Telephone: (408) 353-2231.

Inter-University Consortium for Political and Social Research (known as ICPSR). P.O. Box 1248. University of Michigan. Ann Arbor, Michigan 48106.

JERA. James E. Rush Associates, Inc. 2223 Carriage Road. Powell, Ohio 43065-9703. (614) 881-5949. A publisher of books on library automation.

JES and Associates, Inc. P.O. Box 19274. Irvine, California 92713. Telephone: (714) 553-8200. The largest educational firm for the Pick operating system. JES conducts courses throughout the United States, Canada, and Australia. President Jonathan E. Sisk is the editor of a series of works on Pick for TAB Professional and Reference Books.

Johns Hopkins University Press, Journals Publishing Division. 701 West 40th Street, Suite 275. Baltimore, Maryland 21211-2190.

John Wiley & Sons, Inc. 605 Third Avenue. New York, New York 10158-0012. Telephone: (212) 850-6418, 850-6000, 850-6311.

J.W. Edwards, Inc. 2500 South State Street. Ann Arbor, Michigan 48104. Publisher of library and information science materials.

Kermit Distribution. Columbia University Center for Computing Activities. 612 West 115th St. New York, New York 10025. Telephone: (212) 854-3703. Distributes the terminal emulation program Kermit free of charge.

Knowledge Industry Publications, Inc. 701 Westchester Avenue. White Plains, NY 10604. In England: 3 Henrietta Street. London, England WC2 8LU.

Krieger Publishing Company. P.O. Box 9542. Melbourne, Florida 32902-9542. Telephone: (305) 724-9542, 727-7270.

LaGuardia Community College. Archives and Museum. 31-10 Thomson Avenue. Long Island City, New York 11101. Telephone: (718) 626-5078. Director Richard K. Lieberman has developed a computerized information retrieval system for small photographic collections.

Learned Information. 143 Old Marlton Pike. Medford, New Jersey 08055-8707. Telephone: (609) 654-6266. Organizer of the annual conference: National Online Meeting.

Lexis/Nexis. Mead Data Central. P.O. Box 933. Dayton, Ohio 45401. Telephone: (800) 227-4908, (513) 865-6800.

Libraries Unlimited. P.O. Box 3988. Englewood, Colorado 80155-3988. Telephone: (303) 770-1220.

Library and Information Technology Association (known as LITA). A division of the American Library Association. Within LITA there is an Interest Group for Microcomputer Support of Cataloging.

Library and Information Technology Center, Polytechnic of Central London. 235 High Holborn. London, England WC1V 7DN. Telephone: 01-430 1561.

The Library Association. 7 Ridgmount Street. London, England WC1E 7AE. Telephone: 01 636 7543, Publishing: Extension 360.

Library Association of Australia. 376 Jones Street. Ultimo, New South Wales. Australia 2007.

Library Automated Systems Information Exchange. P.O. Box 602. Lane Cove, New South Wales. Australia 2006.

Library of Congress, Catalog Management and Publications Division, Symbols of American Libraries. Washington, DC 20540. Telephone: (202) 707-5000. The division will assign on request a National Union Catalog Symbol to identify the cataloging agency that contributed records to a shared database.

Library of Congress, Cataloging Distribution Service, Customer Services. Washington, DC 20541. Telephone: (202) 707-6100. To order copies of *Library of Congress Subject Headings* and other cataloging publications.

Library of Congress, Cataloging in Publication Service. Washington, DC 20540. Telephone: (202) 707-9797, 707-9792. The Cataloging in Publication service will provide a catalog card for a book prior to publication, so that the Library of Congress Classification number, Dewey Decimal number, and cataloging information can be printed on the verso of the title page for use by librarians.

Library of Congress, Gifts Section, Exchange and Gifts Division. Washington, DC 20540. Telephone: (202) 707-5000. Send a copy of a book to the Gifts Section for cataloging after publication.

Library Professional Publications. A subsidiary of Shoe String Press, Inc. 925 Sherman Ave. Hamden, Connecticut 06514. Telephone: (203) 288-8707.

Library Technologies, Inc. 1142E Bradfield Road. Abington, Pennsylvania 19001. Telephone: (215) 576-6983. A private company that will convert MARC records from DOS diskettes to 1/2 inch tape, or from tape to diskette. The company offers a variety of technical services related to the production and use of MARC records, including the printing of barcode labels.

Light Impressions. 439 Monroe Avenue. Rochester, New York 14607-3717. Telephone: (800) 828-6216. In New York state: (800) 828-9629.

Livia Press. 967 Neilson Street. Albany, California 94706.

Lomond Publications, Inc. Box 88. Mount Airy, Maryland 21771. Telephone: (301) 829-1496.

Los Angeles City Historical Society. P.O. Box 41046. Los Angeles, California 90041. For the society's History Computerization Project (pronounced "hiccup"): 24851 Piuma Road, Malibu, California 90265. Telephone: (818) 888-9371.

Los Angeles Conservancy. 433 South Spring Street, Suite 1024. Los Angeles, California 90013. Telephone: (213) 623-2489. Assists in preservation efforts and conducts local tours.

Los Angeles County Historical Records and Landmarks Commission. Hall of Administration, Room 383. 500 West Temple Street. Los Angeles, California 90012. Telephone: (213) 974-1431. Recommends applications to the National Register of Historic Places and for the Points of Historical Interest designation.

Los Angeles Pick Users Group (LAPUG, pronounced "La Pug"). P.O. Box 7987. Van Nuys, California 91409. May also be contacted through its president, Brian Stone, at Alcyona Computer Consultants (213) 462-1549.

Macmillan Publishing Company. 866 3rd Avenue. New York, New York 10022. Telephone: (212) 702-2000.

Marcel Dekker, Inc. 270 Madison Avenue. New York, New York 10016. Telephone (212) 696-9000. Also: Hutgasse 4, Postfach 812. CH-4001 Basel, Switzerland. Telephone: 061/25 84 82

McGraw Hill. Princeton Road. Hightstown, New Jersey 08520. Telephone: (212) 512-2000.

McGraw-Hill, TAB Professional and Reference Books Division. P.O. Box 40, Blue Ridge

Summit, Pennsylvania 17294-0850. Telephone: (800) 233-1128, in Pennsylvania and Arkansas: (717) 794-2191.

Meckler Publishing Corporation. 11 Ferry Lane West. Westport, Connecticut 06880. Telephone: (203) 226-6967. Europe: Meckler Publishing. 3 Henrietta Street. London WC2E 8LU. United Kingdom.

Medieval and Early Modern Data Bank. Department of History, CN 5059. Rutgers, The State University of New Jersey. New Brunswick, New Jersey 08903. Telephone: (201) 932-8316, 932-8335.

Metropolitan Museum of Art. 5th Avenue at 82nd Street. New York, New York 10028. (212) 570-3935. The museum is a leader in art computerization projects, such as the Clearinghouse Project on Art Documentation and Computerization.

Microsoft Corporation. 10700 Northup Way, P.O. Box 97200. Bellevue, Washington 98009. Telephone, Information center: (800) 426-9400; Customer service: (206) 882-8088; Technical product support: (206) 454-2030.

Microsoft Press. 16011 NE 36th Way, P.O. Box 97017. Redmond, WA 98073-9717. Telephone (800) 638-3030, (206) 882-8088.

MICRU International. 1732 Montane Drive East. Golden, Colorado 79491. Telephone: (303) 526-9862. The international users organization for the Microdata/McDonnell Douglas implementation of the Pick operating system.

Mid-Atlantic Regional Archives Conference. Department of Special Collections and Archives. Rutgers University Library. New Brunswick, New Jersey 08903. Telephone: (201) 932-7006.

Midwest Archives Conference. Membership: Dennis Meissner. Minnesota Historical Society. 1500 Mississippi Street. St. Paul, Minnesota 55101. Telephone: (612) 296-6980. Editor, *Midwestern Archivist:* Nancy Lankford. Western Historical Manuscripts Collections. 23 Ellis Library. University of Missouri. Columbia, Missouri 65201. Telephone: (314) 882-6028.

Miller Freeman Publications. 500 Howard Street. San Francisco, California 94105. Telephone: (415) 397-1881.

Minnesota Historical Society. 1500 Mississippi Street. St. Paul, Minnesota 55101. Telephone: (612) 296-6980, Library: (612) 296-2143.

Minnesota Scholarly Press. P.O. Box 611. DeKalb, Illinois 60115. Telephone: (815) 895-6842. The press is owned and run privately by Michael Gabriel.

MIS Press. P.P. Box 6277. Portland, Oregon 97208. Telephone: (800) 626-8257, (503) 222-2399.

MIT Press. (Massachusetts Institute of Technology.) 55 Hayward Street. Cambridge, Massachusetts 02142. Telephone: (617) 253-5643.

Modern Language Association. 10 Astor Place. New York, New York 10003. Telephone: (212) 614-6375.

Modular Information Systems. 436 Ashbury Street. San Francisco, California 94117. Telephone: (415) 552-8648.

Mountainside Publishing, Inc. 321 South Main Street, Box 8330. Ann Arbor, Michigan 48107. Telephone: (313) 662-3925.

Museum Computer Network. 5001 Baum Road, Pittsburgh, Pennsylvania 15213-1809. Telephone: (412) 681-1818.

Museum Documentation Association. Building O, 347 Cherry Hinton Road. Cambridge CB1 4DH. United Kingdom. Telephone: (0223) 242848, International: +44 223 242848.

Music Library Association. P.O. 487. Canton, Massachusetts 02021.

National Agricultural Library. Beltsville, Maryland 20705. Telephone: (301) 344-3834.

National Archives. 8th and Constitution Avenue. Washington, DC 20408. General information: (202) 501-5500. Library: (203) 501-5423. Publications Services Branch: (202) 501-5240. Archives Library Information Center (ALIC): (202) 501-5423.

National Archives, Pacific Southwest Regional Archives. 24000 Avila Road. P.O. Box 6719. Laguna Niguel, California 92677-6719. Telephone: (714) 643-4220.

National Archives of Canada. 395 Wellington Street. Ottawa, Ontario. Canada K1A 0N3.

National Association of Government Archives and Records Administrators (known as NAGARA). New York State Archives, Room 10A75, Cultural Education Center. Albany, New York 122301. Telephone: (518) 473-8037.

National Association of Pick. 1147 Jackson Place. Escondido, California 92026. Telephone: (619) 594-7500. A national Pick users group.

National Council on Public History. 403 Richards Hall. Northeastern University. Boston, Massachusetts 02115. (617) 437-2762.

National Endowment for the Arts (known as NEA). 1100 Pennsylvania Avenue, NW. Washington, DC 20506. Telephone: (202) 682-2000.

National Endowment for the Humanities (known as NEH). 1100 Pennsylvania Avenue, NW. Washington, DC 20506. Telephone: (202) 786-0438.

National Federation of Abstracting and Information Services (known as NFAIS). 1429 Walnut Street. Philadelphia, Pennsylvania 19102. Telephone: (215) 563-2406.

National Historical Publications and Records Commission. (NPR) National Archives Building. Washington, DC 20408. Telephone: (202) 501-5610. Note that "(NPR)" is part of the mailing address, not an aside to the reader. The commission is generally referred to as the NHPRC.

National Information Center for Local Government Records (known as NICLOG). 172 Second Avenue, North, Suite 102. Nashville, Tennessee 37201. Telephone: (800) 284-5456. A service of the American Association for State and Local History, providing help for local government officials with records management problems.

National Information Standards Organization. National Institute of Standards and Technology. Administration 101, RIC E-106. Gaithersburg, Maryland 20899. Telephone: (301) 975-2814. Mailing address: P.O. Box 1056. Bethesda, Maryland 20827. Known as NISO.

National Library of Australia. Parkes Place. Canberra, A.C.T., 2600. Australia 062 621111

National Library of Medicine. Bethesda, Maryland 20894.

National Register of Historic Places. 1100 L Street, Suite 6209. Washington, DC 20005. (202) 343-9536.

National Research Council. 2101 Constitution Avenue. Washington, DC 20418.

National Science Foundation (known as NSF). Public Information Office. 1800 G Street, NW. Washington, DC 20550. Telephone: (202) 357-9498.

National Technical Information Service (known as NTIS). U.S. Department of Commerce. 5285 Port Royal Road. Springfield, Virginia 22161. Telephone: (703) 487-4650, 487-4630.

National Trust for Historic Preservation. 1785 Massachusetts Avenue NW. Washington, DC 20036. (202) 673-4000.

NC Press. 260 Richmond Street, West, Suite 401. Toronto, Canada M5V 1W5. Telephone: (416) 593-6284.

Neal-Schuman Publishers. 23 Leonard Street. New York, New York 10013. Telephone: (212) 925-8650.

New American Library. P.O. Box 999. Bergenfield, New Jersey 07621. Telephone: (800) 526-0275, (201) 387-0600.

NewsNet, Inc. 945 Haverford Road. Bryn Mawr, Pennsylvania 19010. Telephone: (800) 345-1301, (215) 527-8030.

Northern California Pick Users. P.O. Box 884474. San Francisco, California 94188-4474. President M. Dennis Hill: (415) 237-1424.

OCLC Pacific Network. 250 West 1st Street, Suite 330. Claremont, California 91711-4731. Telephone: (800) 854-5753, (714) 621-9998, in California: (800) 472-1787.

Office of Humanities Communication. University of Leicester, Leicester, England LE1 7RH.

OLAC (Online Audiovisual Catalogers, Inc). Care of Grace Agnew, Editor of the OLAC Newsletter, 1903 Edinburgh Terrace. Atlanta, Georgia 30307.

Online, Inc. 11 Tannery Lane. Weston, Connecticut 06883. Telephone: (203) 227-8466, (800) 248-8466.

OPL Resources, Ltd. Murray Hill Station. P.O. Box 948. New York, New York 10156-0614. FAX: (212) 683-6285. Publisher of the newletter *The One-Person Library*.

Oral History Association. 1093 Broxton Avenue, #720. Los Angeles, California 90024. Telephone: (213) 825-0597.

Online Computer Library Center, (known as OCLC). 6565 Frantz Road. Dublin, Ohio 43017-0702. Telephone: (800) 848-5878, (614) 764-6000, in Ohio: (800) 848-8286. Book orders for nonmembers: OCLC, Department 630, Box ONB, Columbus, Ohio 43265.

Online Computer Library Center (OCLC) Europe. 7th Floor, Tricorn House. 51-53 Hagley Road. Five Ways, Edgbaston, Birmingham B16 8TP. United Kingdom. Telephone: 011-44-21-456-4656.

Orbit Search Service. Maxwell Online. 8000 Westpark Drive. McLean, Virginia 22102. Telephone: (800) 45-ORBIT, (703) 442-0900.

O'Reilly and Associates, Inc. 632 Petaluma Avenue. Sebastopol, California 95472. Telephone: (800) 338-6887, in California: (800) 533-6887. Local: (707) 829-0515. Publishers of books on the Pick and Unix operating systems.

Organization of American Historians. 112 North Bryan Street. Bloomington, Indiana 47408-4199. Telephone: (812) 855-7311.

Oryx Press. 2214 North Central at Encanto. Phoenix, Arizona 85004-1483. Telephone: (800) 457-ORYX, (602) 254-6156.

Osborne Publishing. 2600 Tenth Street. Berkeley, California 94710. Telephone: (800) 262-4729, (415) 548-2805.

Oxford English Dictionary. TriStar Publishing. 475 Virginia Drive. Fort Washington, Pennsylvania 19034. Telephone: (800) 872-2828, (215) 641-6200. An online database service.

Oxford Text Archive. Oxford University Computing Service. 13 Banbury Road. Oxford, United Kingdom OX2 6NN.

Oxford University Press. In the United States: 200 Madison Avenue. New York, New York 10016. In the United Kingdom: Pinkhill House. Southfield Road. Eynsham. Oxford, United Kingdom OX8 1JJ.

Pacific Information. 979 Eaton Drive. Fenton, California 95018.

Pantheon Books. A division of Random House. 201 East 50th Street. New York, New York 10011.

Paradigm Publishing. 111 Pine Street, Suite 1405. San Francisco, California 94111. Telephone: (415) 391-3976.

Penguin Press. 40 West 23rd Street. New York, New York 10010. Telephone: (212) 337-5200.

Pergamon Press. Maxwell House, Fairview Park. Elmsford, New York 10523. Telephone: (914) 592-7700.

Philadelphia Name Authority File, Philadelphia Area Consortium of Special Collections Libraries. David Weinberg, Urban Archives Center, Temple University Central Library. Philadelphia, Pennsylvania 19122. A grass-roots effort to create a shared authority file for local personal and corporate names.

Pick Software Developers Association. P.O. Box 1672. Laguna Beach, California 92652-1672. *Dict & Data* journal: 1152 Stratford Drive. Encinitas, California 92024.

Pick Systems. 1691 Browning Avenue. Irvine, California 92714. Telephone: (714) 261-7425. Producer of the Pick operating system and publisher of *PickWorld.*

Pierian Press. P.O. Box 1808. 5000 Washtenaw Avenue. Ann Arbor, Michigan 48106. Telephone: (800) 678-2435, (313) 434-5530.

Pocket Books. 1230 Avenue of the Americas. New York, New York 10020. Telephone: (212) 698-7000.

Popular Culture Association. Popular Culture Center. Bowling Green University. Bowling Green, Ohio 43403. Telephone: (419) 372-2981.

Prentice-Hall, Inc., a division of Simon and Schuster, Inc. Englewood Cliffs, New Jersey 07632. Telephone: (201) 592-2000.

PresNet. John T. Fawcett. Assistant Archivist for Presidential Libraries. National Archives. Washington, DC 20408. Telephone: (202) 523-3212.

Que Corporation. P.O. Box 90. 11711 North College Avenue. Carmel, Indiana 46032. Telephone: (800) 428-5331, (317) 573-2510.

Random House. 400 Hahn Road. Westminister, Maryland 21157. Telephone: (800) 638-6460, in Maryland: (800) 492-0782.

RDBM Computing. P.O. Box 9539. Fountain Valley, California 92728-9539. Telephone: (714) 839-6708. Publisher of the journal *Relational Data Base Management Computing.*

Relais informatique international. 7bis, rue Charles Dordain. Aulnay sous bois, France 93600. Telephone: (1) 48.79.07.03

Relational Institute. 6489 Camden Avenue #106. San Jose, California 95120. The institute of Edgar F. Codd, who first formally proposed the relational model for database design in 1970.

Repton Data. P.O. Box 120. Swarthmore, Pennsylvania 19081. Telephone: (215) 544-6304. Produces pamphlets on Pick.

Research Libraries Group, Inc. (Known as RLG. Producer of the RLIN online bibliographic utility.) 1200 Villa St. Mountain View, CA 94041-1100. Telephone: (415) 962-9951. For information on obtaining an individual account to search the RLIN databases, contact: RLIN Information Center, telephone: (800) 537-RLIN.

Rothman Press. Littleton, Colorado.

Routledge, Chapman and Hall, Inc. 29 West 35th Street, New York, New York 10001-2291. Telephone: (212) 244-3336. In England: North Way. Andover, Hampshire. England SP10 5BE. Telephone: 011 442 646 2141.

Rowman and Littlefield, Inc. 81 Adams Drive. Totowa, New Jersey 07512.

R.R. Bowker Company. P.O. Box 766. New York, New York 10011. Also: 245 West 17th Street. New York, New York 10011. Telephone: (800) 521-8110, (212) 645-9700. Order Department: P.O. Box 762.

Scarecrow Press. P.O. Box 4167. Metuchen, New Jersey 08840. Telephone: (800) 537-7107, (201) 548-8600.

Scholarly Resources, Inc. 104 Greenhill Avenue. Wilmington, Delaware 19805-1897. Telephone: (800) 772-8937, (302) 654-7713.

Semaphore Corporation. 207 Granada Drive. Aptos, California 95003. Telephone: (408) 688-9200.

Shoe String Press, Inc. P.O. Box 4327. 925 Sherman Avenue. Hamden, Connecticut 06514. Telephone: (203) 248-6307, 288-8707.

Sigma Press. 98a Water Lane. Wilmslow. Cheshire, England.

Simon and Schuster. 1230 Avenue of the Americas. New York, New York 10020. Telephone: (212) 698-7000.

SJA, Inc. P.O. Box 5118. Lighthouse Point, Florida 33074. A distributor of Pick shareware programs.

Small Library Computing, Inc. 48 Lawrence Avenue. Halbrook, New York 11741. Telephone: (516) 588-1387. Offers a service converting information between MARC tapes and floppy disk.

Smithsonian Institution Bibliographic Information System (known as SIBIS). Natural History Building, Room 4. 10th and Constitution, NW. Washington, DC 20560.

Smithsonian Institution. Museum Reference Center. Office of Museum Programs. Arts and Industries Building, Room 2235. Washington, DC 20560. Telephone: (202) 357-3101

Smithsonian Institution Traveling Exhibition Services (known as SITES). 1100 Jefferson Drive SW, Room 3146. Washington, DC 20560. Telephone: (202) 357-3168.

Society of American Archivists, 600 South Federal, Suite 504. Chicago, Illinois 60605. Telephone: (312) 922-0140.

Society of Archivists. Care of Dr. J. B. Post, editor. Public Record Office. Kew, Richmond, England. TW9 4DU.

Society of Georgia Archivists. Georgia State University. University Plaza. Atlanta, Georgia 30303. Telephone: (404) 651-2476.

Soldier Creek Press. The press is owned and run privately by Nancy Olson, an audio-visual cataloger at Mankato State University.

Nancy B. Olson. Postal Drawer "U", Lake Crystal, Minnesota 56055. Telephone: (507) 726-2985, evenings.

Sharon Olson, Post Office Box 134, Belle Plaine, Minnesota 56011. Telephone: (612) 873-6620.

Special Libraries Association. 1700 18th Street NW. Washington, DC 20009. Telephone: (202) 234-4700.

St. Martin's Press. 175 5th Avenue. New York, New York 10010. Telephone: (800) 221-7945, (212) 674-5151.

Stanford University Libraries. Publication Sales Office. Stanford, California 94305-2393.

Stuart F. Cooper Company. 1565 East 23rd Street. Los Angeles, California 90011. Telephone: (800) 821-2920. Manufactures envelopes specially designed for laser printers.

Sybex Computer Books. 2021 Challenger Drive. Alameda, California 94501. (415) 523-8233.

Syntagma Systems Literature. Chestnut Farm, Ponsanooth, Truro, England TR3 7JB. Telephone: 0872 864651.

Technical Book Company. 2056 Westwood Boulevard. Los Angeles, California 90024. Telephone: (213) 475-5711. A good source for books on computer science and other technical subjects.

Technical Data Publishing Co. 91 No. Betrand Road. P.O. Box 458. Mount Arlington, New Jersey 07856.

Telebase Library Center. Provides the EasyNet telecommunications service. See: "EasyNet".

Thurman Marketing Services, Inc. 23181 Verdugo, #104A. Laguna Hills, California 92653. Telephone: (714) 855-4442. Organizes conferences around the world, as well as publishing a product guide and a journal, on the subject of the Pick system.

Transaction Publishers. Rutgers University. New Brunswick, New Jersey 08903. Telephone: (201) 932-2280.

United Nations Educational, Scientific and Cultural Organization. Division of the General Information Programme. 7 Place de Fontenoy. Paris, France 75700. Distribution in the U.S. by Unipub. 4611-F Assembly Drive. Lanham, Maryland 20706-4391.

United Nations Educational, Scientific and Cultural Organization. International Council on Museums (UNESCO ICOM). Documentation Centre. Maison de l'UNESCO. 1 rue Miollis. Paris, France 75721. CEDEX 15.

United Kingdom Pick Users' Association. See: ALLM Systems and Marketing.

United States Government Printing Office. Department SSMC. Washington, DC 20402.

United States Newspaper Program. Office of Preservation. National Endowment for the Humanities. 1100 Pennsylvania Avenue, N.W. Washington, DC 20506. Telephone: (202) 786-0438. A program for locating, cataloging, and preserving U.S. newspapers.

United States Newspaper Project. Robert B. Harriman, Jr. Serial Records Division. LM 515. Library of Congress. Washington, DC 20540.

University Microfilms International. Order Fulfillment. 300 North Zeeb Road. Ann Arbor, Michigan 48106.

University of California Press. 2120 Berkeley Way, Berkeley, CA 94720. Telephone: (800) 822-6657, (415) 642-6683.

University of California, Los Angeles. Graduate School of Library and Information Science. 405 Hilgard Avenue. Los Angeles, California 90024. Telephone: (213) 825-1379.

University of Chicago Press. 5801 Ellis Avenue. Chicago, Illinois 60637. Telephone: (800) 621-2736, (312) 962-7693.

University of Illinois at Urbana-Champaign, Graduate School of Library and Information Science. 249 Armory Building, 505 East Armory Street. Champaign, Illinois 61820. Telephone: (217) 333-1359.

University of Illinois Press. 54 East Gregory Drive. Champaign, Illinois 61820. Telephone: (217) 333-0950.

Urban Archives Center, California State University, Northridge. 205 South Library. 1811 Nordhoff Street. Northridge, California 91330. Telephone: (818) 885-2487.

Van Nostrand Reinhold. 115 Fifth Avenue. New York, New York 1003. Telephone: (212) 254-3232.

Vintage Books/Random House. 400 Hahn Road. Westminister, Maryland 21157. Telephone: (800) 638-6460, in Maryland: (800) 492-0782.

Visual Resources Association. For membership, publications: Christina Updike, VRA Treasurer. Art Department James Madison University. Harrisonburg, Virginia 22807. News items and articles: Joy Alexander, Bulletin editor. Slide and Photograph Collection. Department of the History of Art. Tappan Hall. University of Michigan. Ann Arbor, Michigan 48109-1357. Annual conference: Lise Hawkos. School of Art. Arizona State University. Tempe, Arizona 85287. Telephone: (602) 965-6163.

VNU Publications. Ten Holland Drive. Hasbrouck Heights, New Jersey 07604.

Washington Researchers. Telephone: (202) 333-3533.

Weber Systems, Inc. 8437 Mayfield Road. Chesterland, Ohio 44026. Telephone: (800) 851-6018.

Weingarten Publications, Inc. 38 Chauncy Street. Boston, Massachusetts 02111. Telephone: (617) 542-0146.

Glossary

This Glossary is provided as a ready reference to computer and cataloging concepts. The list is also intended as a tool for survival when you delve into the sources cited in the bibliography for further information on computer database management or archival cataloging methods. The list will help you overcome the predilection of computer professionals for technical terms and the affection of archivists for acronyms.

000-999 Numbers in 3 digits (001, 600, etc.) are Tags that refer to MARC fields. Thus Tag 001 refers to the field in which the Control Number or Record-ID is stored, and field 600 is for Subject Added Entry—Personal Name, meaning the name of a person who is the subject of the material. RLIN in some cases uses a letter rather than a number as the third character of a MARC Tag.

0xx-9xx A number followed by "xx" refers to all the numbers that begin with the leading digit, thus 6xx refers to all MARC Tag fields beginning with 6, all of which are types of "Subject Added Entry".

8088 The CPU (Central Processing Unit) of the IBM PC and PC-XT. The chip processes data internally in groups of 16 bits, and inputs and outputs data in groups of 8 bits. Memory access is limited to 640K.

80286 The CPU (Central Processing Unit) of the IBM PC-AT, and PS/2 Model 50. The chip processes data internally, and also inputs and outputs the data, in groups of 16 bits. Although the 80286 was intended to address memory beyond the 8088's limit of 640K, the chip cannot do this easily, so the 640K limit remained.

80386 The CPU (Central Processing Unit) of the IBM PS/2 70 and 80. The chip processes data internally, and also inputs and outputs the data, in groups of 32 bits. The 80386 chip does the job that the 80286 was intended for, addressing memory beyond the 640K limit.

80836SX The CPU (Central Processing Unit) of the IBM PS/2 55. The chip processes data internally in groups of 32 bits, but inputs and outputs the data in groups of 16 bits, in order to make use of lower-cost 16 bit facilities.

80486 The newest CPU (Central Processing Unit) for IBM PC-compatible computers. The chip processes data internally, and also inputs and outputs the data, in groups of 32 bits. The chip also incorporates a built-in math coprocessor, data cache, and elements of RISC (Reduced Instruction Set Computing) technology, to process data approximately three times as fast as the 80386.

AACR2 *Anglo-American Cataloguing Rules.* Second edition, 1988 Revision. The standard set of rules for cataloging materials in a library. Available from the American Library Association.

AAM American Association of Museums.

AAT Art and Architecture Thesaurus. A list of subject terms for art and architecture begun in 1981 by the Getty Art History Information Program. The list includes a hierarchical structure and attempts to provide access via all known synonyms and variants. The 30,000 terms cover the following categories: Design Concepts, Design Elements and Attributes, Styles and Periods, People and Organizations, Processes and Techniques, Disciplines and Occupations, Materials, Architectural Components, Single Built Works, Complexes, Settlements and Landscape, Tools and Tool Components, Drawings, Documents Types and Visual Genre.

aboutness The subject content of an item to be cataloged. See: "Subject analysis".

ABS In the Pick operating system, the portion of memory reserved for the operating system and for Assembly Language routines. The name ABS stands for "Absolute" because the software routines reside at absolute or permanent addresses.

ACA Association of Canadian Archivists

access To grant access is to grant permission to a researcher to examine a body of materials. Note that right of access is different from right of use. The researcher might be given the right of access to examine a photograph, but not be given permission to obtain a copy of the photo or to use a reproduction of the photograph in a publication. Physical access would most often be limited by factors such as the hours of operation of a facility, while the right to publish a photograph, to play a musical score, or to quote a document might be limited by the terms of the original gift. Restrictions on access should be placed in MARC-AMC field 506 (Restrictions on Access), while restrictions on use belong in field 540 (Terms Governing Use and Reproduction). Information on the copyright holder should be included with the restrictions on use.

access In the Pick operating system, search statements can be entered directly at the operating system level, without the use of a program. Such statements are known in Pick as "Access" statements. In the McDonnell Douglas version of Pick, Access is known as "English".

access point The individual field of information used to search for a record. For example, you might look up a record for a photograph by the name of the photographer, the name of a person in the photo, a topical subject, or the time period in which the photo was taken, presuming that this information has been included in the record. It is important to think in advance of the access points to information that are likely to be the most valuable, and to record that information in a standardized manner that will facilitate computer database searching. To have only a Record-ID or Accession number as an access point is to defeat much of the purpose of computerization.

access time In a computer database system, the amount of time that it takes the system to retrieve the information requested.

accession When an archival center accessions a body of materials, the center takes custody of the materials and establishes some basic method of control over them, generally in advance of complete cataloging. Materials taken at the same time from the same source will be referred to as a single accession.

Accession Number A unique number given to all or part of an accession. After a photo collection has been accepted from a donor, an Accession Number should be given to each photograph, or to logical groupings of photographs. If the photos are later computer-cataloged, each cataloging record must be given a unique Record-ID. The Accession Number identifies the physical object, the Record-ID identifies the location of the information about the object. The Record-ID and Accession Number may not be the same, but it will be more convenient if they are. If you wish to make them the same, keep in mind that it will be much easier to change computer database Record-IDs, thousands of which can be changed with a single command, than to change Accession Numbers that have been written onto photo sleeves. A flexible database management system will allow you to adopt Record-IDs that will match the format of your Accession Number. The Record-ID should be placed in MARC-AMC field 001 (Control number), and only one Record-ID should be assigned per record. If the Accession number is separate, it should be placed in MARC-AMC field 035 (System control number). Although the MARC format permits multiple Accession Numbers per record, it is strongly recommended that only a single Accession Number be included, in order to allow the use of the Accession Number (or perhaps a future combined Accession Number and Record-ID) as a unique access point to the record. If you have an Accession Number in hand, that number should give you immediate access to the computer database record in which the photo is described.

accompanying material Part of a work that is complementary to the predominant part but physically separate from it. For example: A map inside the pocket of a guidebook, a written commentary meant for use with a group of transparencies in a presentation. In each case, the textual materials and the graphic materials are complementary.

accretion Adding to a collection.

ACM Association for Computing Machinery.

ACRL Association of College and Research Libraries, part of the American Library Association.

action Any action taken, or that needs to be taken, with regard to the materials, such as sending a photo negative to a lab to have a print made.

active records Materials that are required for the day-to-day functioning of an agency.

ADA A computer programming language developed for the U.S. Department of Defense.

added entry A secondary entry, of secondary importance in identifying the work in comparison with the Main Entry. For example, the Main Entry might be the name of an author, photographer, or other creator of the work. Added entries would include headings for subjects, persons other than the creator, organizations, and geographic places. Compare with: "Main Entry".

address For computers, the location of a piece of data in the computer's storage.

administrative history The history of an organization, including its structure, the functions of the various divisions, and its relationship to other organizations. Historical background of this type is often necessary for an understanding of the archival materials generated by that organization.

administrative value For archival records, or potential archival records, the value of the records for the conduct of current administrative business. Compare with: "Evidential value" and "Informational value".

agency As used in archival literature, any organizational entity that creates documents as part of its normal administrative activities.

agency-assigned data element For the MARC format, the entry has been created, not by the cataloger who wrote the record, but by an agency. For example, the control number appearing in MARC field 010 Library of Congress Control Number would be assigned by the Library of Congress.

AHA American Historical Association.

AHC Association for History in Computing.

AHR *American Historical Review.* Journal of the American Historical Association.

AI Artificial Intelligence.

AIIM Association for Information and Image Management.

ALA American Library Association.

ALGOL A computer program language, ALGorithm Oriented Language.

algorithm A prescribed series of steps for accomplishing a task. Computers require that all of the necessary steps, and responses to all possible contingencies, be prescribed in advance. That is why a computer can store a database with millions of records, but cannot walk two blocks to mail a letter.

ALIC Archives Library Information Center, of the National Archives Library and the National Archives and Records Administration. The center provides information for archivists and records managers.

alphabetic code A code that uses only the letters of the alphabet. If a code is designated as Alphabetic, you cannot use numbers or special characters such as a dash or asterisk. Compare with: "Alphanumeric code", "Numeric code".

alphabetical catalog: See: "Dictionary catalog".

alphabetico-classed catalog See: "Classed catalog".

alphabetize To sort a list in alphabetical order. The two principal methods employed are letter-by-letter and word-by-word. For more information, look under: "Sort".

alphanumeric code Alphabetic-Numeric code: A code that uses both letters and numbers, and perhaps also special characters such as the asterisk. Compare with: "Alphabetic code", "Numeric code".

alternative title Look for title variations under "Title".

AMC Archival and Manuscripts Control. MARC-AMC is the MARC Format for archives and manuscripts. Also abbreviated "AM". See "MARC".

AMIM *Archival Moving Image Materials.* A cataloging manual for motion pictures by Wendy White-Hensen.

analog data Information represented in a continuous and physically variable form. For example, when a photo image is stored on an optical disk in analog form, the disk contains a miniature version of the image. Compare with: "Digital data".

analytical entry Information that applies to only part of a larger item. An Analytical Record describes only one photo in a collection or only one article in a journal, or analytical information in a description note distinguishes between different photos in a series. Also referred to as "analytics".

annotation A note in a bibliography or catalog that provides information in addition to the main headings such as author, title, publisher, etc. The note serves to describe or to evaluate the item listed.

ANSEL American National Standard for Extended Latin alphabet coded character set for bibliographic use. An extension of the ASCII standard to cover diacritical accent marks required by foreign language characters. See "ASCII".

ANSI American National Standards Institute. ANSI is the accrediting agency for standards organizations in the United States. Thus it was ANSI that accredited the National Information Standards Organization (NISO) as the official technical standards agency for libraries in the United States. See also: "ISO" and "NISO".

APL A Programming Language for computers.

APPC Application Program-to-Program Communications. A computer industry definition for exchanging data between application programs.

application A computer program or group of programs used for a specific purpose, such as word processing or database management. Microsoft Word, for example, is a word-processing application, while DOS (Microsoft Disk Operating System) is a general-purpose operating system, not built for any particular type of application. In contrast to DOS, the Pick operating system bridges the separation between operating system and application, because Pick is an operating system built specifically to facilitate applications in the area of database management.

APPM *Archives, Personal Papers and Manuscripts: A Cataloging Manual for Archival Repositories, Historical Societies and Manuscript Libraries.* Written by Steven L. Hensen and published by the Library of Congress in 1983. APPM supplements AACR2 as a standard source of descriptive practice for archival and manuscript materials. See "AACR2".

appraisal The process of deciding which items will be kept and which will be discarded. Also, the determination of the monetary value of donated materials, usually for tax purposes.

archival The distinction usually made between archival materials and library materials is that library holdings are published works, of which many identical copies can be found, while archival materials are unpublished and unique. It is generally assumed that the materials held in a library were deliberately created for the purpose of publication, while most archival materials, such as the records of a business or a military campaign, are the written remains of daily activities. The distribution of materials in electronic form through on-line reference services now tends to erode the distinction between published and unpublished work.

archival management The fundamental assumption of the archival method of managing records is that context is the key to understanding. As distinguished from books and most other published materials, the documents were not created for a deliberate purpose of instruction in a given topic. Instead, archival documents were created as a by-product of day-to-day activities, most often the administrative functions of an agency. The documents are therefore best understood within the context of the other documents created by that same agency or other creator. For these reasons it is important to record information about the creating agency and its position within an administrative hierarchy, and possibly its relationships with other organizations. For further discussion, see "Provenance" and "Respect des fonds".

archival value Archival materials, or potential archival materials, that have value for administrative, evidential, or informational purposes. For more information, see: "Administrative value," "Evidential value", and "Informational value".

archives The materials, the place where they are put, and the organization that puts them there and cares for them. Archival materials are materials that are no longer in active use and have been selected for permanent retention because of their historical value. The archives or repository is the place where the materials are kept. The organization that acts as custodian of the materials, that selects materials for preservation or discard, and that makes the materials available to researchers, is also referred to as an archives. Note that the use of "archives" as a singular noun is proper but awkward.

ARIC Archives and Records Information Coalition. Established in 1988 following recommendations by NAGARA. For the archival profession, the National Archives Library is putting together a central database of printed literature, research reports, and descriptions of innovative programs.

ARLIS/NA Art Library Association of North America.

ARMA Association of Records Managers and Administrators.

arrangement The placing of documentary materials into an order that corresponds to the archival principles of provenance (history of the custody of the materials) and original order (the order in which the materials were originally created or kept).

array A list of values on a common level. In a computer database, a file consists of an array of records, and each record in turn consists of an array of fields. A database thus constitutes a two-dimensional array. You could refer to the information in a given field as held in, for example, record number 3, field number 5, or Data-file(3,5). Note that the Pick database system provides a four-dimensional array, because each field can contain discrete sub-fields, and each sub-field can contain separate sub-sub-fields. It is normal practice to treat each Pick record as a separate three-dimensional array of fields, sub-fields, and sub-sub-fields.

artefact An object made or modified by humans. Also spelled "Artifact".

ASCII American Standard Code for Information Interchange. Pronounced "as-key". A standard designation for each character on the computer. This standard allows computers from different manufacturers to exchange information, thus computers that are not "compatible" in the sense of using the same type of equipment can still be "information compatible". Note that the computer does not actually store characters, such as the letter "a". Instead, it stores numbers that the ASCII standard defines as representing certain characters. The numbers 65-90 inside the computer are interpreted as upper case letters A-Z and the numbers 97-122 are interpreted as lower case letters a-z. Because all letters are really numbers to the computer, the difference between lower and upper case letters is crucial. Because all of the upper case letters represent numbers that come before any of the lower case letters, the computer, when sorting a list, will place an upper case "Z" before a lower case "a". Conclusion: when entering information, the distinction between upper and lower case should always be observed, particularly in the case of subject terms that will be searched and that might be sorted for a printed index. Note that while there is wide agreement on the designations for the standard letters and numbers, there are many differing versions for special graphic and foreign language characters. See also "Byte".

ASIS American Society for Information Science. Formerly the American Documentation Association.

assembly language A computer language very close to the machine language of the computer. Assembly language is difficult and time-consuming for humans to write or modify, and is usually wedded to a particular machine. Also called "Assembler" or "Assembler language".

asynchronous port A Serial Port that sends or receives data one bit at a time, with no requirements that the transmission of bits in a group be synchronized together. For further explanation, see: "Serial Port".

audiovisual materials Materials that are audio and/or visual in format, rather than textual. For example: photographs, maps, charts, models, motion pictures, and oral history tapes.

authentication In archives, the determination that a document actually is what it is represented to be.

author The individual chiefly responsible for the intellectual or artistic content of a work. For example, the writer of a book, the composer of a symphony, the photographer who took the photograph, the compiler of a bibliography, the cartographer who created the map, painter who created the painting. Performers can also be considered the authors of sound recordings, films, or video recordings.

authoritative agency data element For the MARC format, the data element has been defined in relation to an agency that maintains the list of possible terms or the rules that must be applied. For example, the National Union Catalog symbol for the organization performing the cataloging must be taken from Symbols of American Libraries.

Authority File Terms for a prime field for searching, such as SUBJECTS, PERSONAL NAMES, and CORPORATE NAMES. These should be taken only from a predetermined list of terms. Such a list is referred to as a Controlled Vocabulary or an Authority File. The cataloger cannot invent and use new terms without first adding them to the list, perhaps with the approval of others and a verification that the new term does not duplicate or conflict in style with existing terms. The use of an Authority File is essential for efficient searching. The searcher must know what terms the cataloger would have entered to describe a given activity. Even if the searcher and cataloger are the same person, the individual cannot rely on memory alone to know if harbor activities have been placed under the subject heading "Harbors", "Port", "Ports", "Port activities", etc. Note that although a "contains" search utilizing the word "Port" would also pick up "Ports" and "Port activities", because "Port" is contained in those terms, the "contains" approach would in addition retrieve "Port wine", "Portable computers", "Portages", "Porters", "Portfolio management", "Portraits", "Portugal", and perhaps also "Airports". It is more reliable to stay with the Library of Congress Subject Heading "Harbors".

Authority Record A record in an Authority File will contain the following information: 1. The approved form of a heading such as a personal name or subject term. 2. References to and from the heading. Such references will include variant or synonymous forms for which the preferred form is to be substituted. For a subject term, references can also include terms that are more broad, more narrow, or otherwise related. 3. Documentation for the decision made to prefer a certain form. For personal and corporate names, the cataloger would cite the reference from which the preferred form was taken. For an individual, the full name and the birth and death dates might have been taken from an obituary notice. For an organization, reference might be made to the minutes of the board of directors.

autograph A person's signature, or a manuscript in the author's own handwriting.

automatic Done by the computer, rather than manually.

background process A computer process or operation taking place in the background, while the user continues with another task. For example, the user might continue entering or editing data, while the computer sorts a long list from a database. A background process can also be called a phantom process.

base In the Pick operating system, the beginning of the space that a particular file occupies. Since Pick divides all memory and disk space into Frames, the Base of a file is expressed numerically as the Frame ID of the file's first Frame.

BASIC A computer programming language. The name is an acronym for Beginner's All-purpose Symbolic Instruction Code. Basic is the most widely-known computer language. IBM PC and compatible computers include some form of Microsoft Basic. The Radio Shack portable Model 100 has Microsoft Basic installed. The programming language of the Pick system is Pick Basic. Pick Basic, and newer DOS Basic versions such as QuickBasic and TurboBasic, include the structured programming tools made popular by Pascal.

basic weight The weight in pounds of a ream of paper, usually consisting of 500 sheets.

batch files A Batch file in the DOS operating system is a command file containing a series of computer commands. A batch file might take a user to a subdirectory that contains only his own files, or automatically begin a word-processing application. In the Pick operating system, a much more powerful form of Batch file is known as a Proc, for Stored Procedure.

batch processing system In contrast to an interactive or real time system. Operations are written out and then executed later in batches, rather than activated immediately by an operator at a terminal.

baud A rate of data transmission, measured in bits per second. Common rates used for communication between computers over telephone lines are 300, 1200, and 2400 baud. A terminal generally communicates with a host computer at a rate of 9600 baud.

biannual A serial publication issued twice each year. Compare with: "Biennial".

bibliographical ghost A work that does not exist but is cited in reference.

bibliographic item A document or set of documents treated as a single entity, and cataloged with a single bibliographic record.

bibliographic network A network for sharing bibliographical information.

bibliographic utility An organization that maintains a database of bibliographic information, which may be accessed online via computer. The principal bibliographic utilities are: RLIN, OCLC, UTLAS, and WLN.

bibliography A list of works and documents, not restricted to the holdings of a single institution.

biennial A serial publication issued every two years. Compare with: "Biannual."

bimonthly A serial publication issued every two months. Compare with: "Semimonthly".

binary A number system based on 2. The only two numbers in the binary system are 0 and 1. The decimal system is based on 10, using numbers 0 through 9.

binary search A method of computer searching that continues to divide by half a sorted list of items to be searched, excluding at each stage the half that could not include the searched-for item, until the requested information is found. For example, if from a list of names the computer were searching for "Smith", the first step would be to divide the list in half, and to exclude the half for the first part of the alphabet from further searching. The computer would continue to divide the list in half in this way until it found "Smith".

bit The smallest unit of information on a computer, consisting of one of the binary numbers, 0 or 1. The word is a contraction of "Binary digIT".

biweekly A serial publication issued every two weeks. Also referred to as semimonthly.

BK Book. MARC-BK is the MARC Format for books. See "MARC".

blind reference In an index, a reference to a heading that does not appear in the catalog.

block For computer data transmission, a group of bytes transmitted as a unit. When using a terminal in block mode, the user can perform all of the operations for entering or editing a record before sending the record to the host computer.

BN Bibliothéque Nationale. The National Library of France.

BNB British National Bibliography.

book catalog A catalog in the form of a book, rather than in the form of cards, as in a card catalog. The book can be loose-leaf or bound. Libraries replaced book catalogs with card catalogs because the latter were much easier to update. Computer databases and printers have partially revived the book catalog.

boolean logic A system of algebraic logic formulated by George Boole, and used in computer database searching. The various conditions applied to a search will be connected with "AND" or with "OR" or modified by "NOT".

boot To "boot" the computer is to start it up. The "bootstrap loader" is a small routine built into the computer hardware that begins the process of loading in the operating system, usually from the hard disk or floppy diskette.

BPI Bits Per Inch. A measure of the density of information on a tape. To exchange tapes, the sender and receiver must use the same BPI setting. The most widely supported standard for 1/2 inch tape is 1600 BPI. Another common speed is 6250 BPI. If an average record held 800 bytes, then about 20,000 records could be stored on a 1/2 inch, 2400 foot tape at 1600 BPI.

BPS Bits Per Second, for computer data transmission. The number of bits transmitted per second.

broad classification A system which classifies only according to broad classes, without detailed subdivision.

BT Broader Term. Indicates more general terms one level up in a hierarchy from the defined term. Used in a thesaurus such as Library of Congress Subject Headings. For example: Crime and criminals; BT Deviant behavior; Sociology.

buffer For computers, a temporary storage area for data. Buffers are used most often in the course of transmitting data from a relatively fast device to a slow one, such as from a computer to a printer. Rather than sending the data all at once, the data will be held in a buffer and "spooled out" to the printer, in the manner of a fisherman spooling out a fishing line. The process used for this purpose is generally called a Spooler. The advántage of the spooling is that the computer can be performing other tasks at the same time, rather than operating at the slower speed of the printer. For the Pick operating system, all printing jobs are handled automatically by the spooler while the user continues to perform other work. The Pick spooler will also handle printing jobs coming at the same time from various users, by placing the jobs in a queue, to be taken in order.

bug A malfunction in a computer program, named for the insects that jammed up the early vacuum-tube computers.

bulk dates The time period when the bulk of the materials described were created. As distinguished from inclusive dates, which would include the entire time period when all of the materials were created.

bus On computers, a circuit for transmitting data.

byte A series of 8 Bits. Since 8 bits are used to represent a single character, such as the letter "A", the word "character" is often used instead of byte when speaking of the length of a file. Note, however, that bytes also include unseen characters, such as blank spaces between words, "Delimiters" that tell the computer how to separate records and fields within a database, and "Control Characters" that tell the printer to underline a word or skip to the top of the next page.

C A computer programming language known for its terse commands. The UNIX operating system is written in the C language.

cadastral map A property map, of land boundaries.

CAI Computer Assisted Instruction.

CAIE Committee on Archival Information Exchange. The committee of the Society of American Archivists charged with maintaining the consistency of the MARC-AMC format.

calendar A chronological list of documents.

call number A designation, which may include both numbers and letters, that gives the location of an item within a repository.

canonical model In database theory, a model of data that represents the inherent structure of the data, rather than the requirements of a particular application or the limitations of specific computer hardware or software. The canonical model will not contain redundant items.

canonical synthesis In computer database management, the process of creating the clearest and simplest overall data structure possible, by applying the rules of Normalization. The process of combining separate data structures into a canonical model.

caption A brief description employed with an illustration.

CAR Computer Assisted Retrieval. The use of a computer to retrieve information from microfilm or microfiche.

card catalog A catalog with records on separate cards, usually one record per card. The requirements for punctuation, indentation, etc. for typed catalog cards may be found in Chan, Cataloging and Classification, pages 48-52 or Wynar, *Introduction to Cataloging and Classification,* pages 27-38.

Carriage Return The ENTER key on a computer keyboard. It performs a function of moving back to the left margin, similar to the Carriage Return key on a typewriter. On a typewriter, the carriage moves. On a computer, the cursor moves. The action of Carriage Return is usually combined with that of Line Feed, of moving down to the next line rather than staying at the current line, thus the whole operation is referred to as Carriage Return—Line Feed. On a word processor, a Carriage Return—Line Feed marks the end of a paragraph. When entering data with a data entry form or answering a prompt, pressing the ENTER or Carriage Return key tells the computer that you have finished typing the field or response and that you wish for the computer to process what you have typed. If you have a data file in the DOS operating system with each field stored in a separate paragraph, the Pick operating system can accept that file, placing each paragraph into a separate Pick data field. The key may be designated as ENTER, RETURN, CR, or CRLF, or marked by an arrow pointing down and to the left.

Carriage Return—Line Feed Marks the end of a paragraph. See: "Carriage Return".

cartographic materials Maps.

case In printing, a drawer for holding type. The expressions "upper case" and "lower case" derive from storing the capital letters in a case above that used for the small letters.

case file A folder or other unit of archival materials relating to a specific action, event, person, place, project, or other subject.

catalog A file of bibliographic records. Generally used for the purpose of describing the materials held in a particular collection.

cataloging in publication Cataloging at the time of publication. Many publishers provide galley proofs for the Library of Congress or other central cataloging agencies. The agency prepares a cataloging record, which the publisher prints on the back side of the title page.

centralized cataloging The cataloging of books and other bibliographic items by a central agency, such as the Library of Congress, which distributes its cataloging records to other libraries. The advantage of centralized cataloging is that every library does not have to create its own cataloging record for *David Copperfield.* Instead, the library can simply use a card from the Library of Congress.

central processing unit See: "CPU".

CF Computer Files. MARC-CF is the MARC format for files, such as computer software or census data, which exist in their original form on a computer.

CGAP Committee on Goals and Priorities of the Society of American Archivists.

channel A path for sending data.

character A letter, number, or symbol stored by a computer as a single byte of data consisting of an ASCII (American Standard Code for Information Interchange) number. Note that on a computer, a space is not simply nothing, it is as much a character as the letter "A".

character set The characters corresponding to the ASCII codes stored by a computer. Most computers use the same character set for ASCII 32-127, which represent letters, numbers, and standard punctuation. ASCII 0-31 is used for computer control codes. Above ASCII 127, different computers will use different foreign language characters, math symbols, and graphics characters for drawing lines and boxes. The most widely-used character set above ASCII 127 is the Extended ASCII set employed by the IBM PC. Radio Shack uses a different set, on the portable Model 100. The American Library Association has also established an extended character set for foreign language characters. Beware of differences in character sets when using foreign language characters, if the data might later be transferred to another computer.

charge units See: "CPU cycles, time, or charge units".

chief source of information The source given first preference in identifying the title, author, description, etc. of a work. Generally the preferred source is text appearing on the item itself, such as the title page of a book, or supplied by the creator, such as notes from a photographer.

CHIN Canadian Heritage Information Network. The Canadian government's organization for museum information management.

chip An integrated circuit in a computer, placed on a tiny flake of silicon. The term is employed loosely for the CPU (Central Processing Unit), which is the brains of a computer. Thus the IBM PC-XT uses the 8088 chip, the IBM PC-AT uses the 80286 chip.

chronological order To arrange documents in a collection according to time. The time chosen might be date of creation, date of publication or copyright, or the period of time covered.

chronological subdivision The division of a Library of Congress Subject Heading by time period. For example: "California—History—1850-1950." Most of the time period subdivisions offered by LCSH are so broad as not to be useful. When cataloging with computer database management methods, it is better to specify the time period in a separate field provided for that purpose. Also called Period Subdivision.

CIDOC International Committee for Documentation of the International Council of Museums, created to oversee global computerization projects. The committee is currently conducting surveys of the terminology and databases used by museums, to find common elements.

circuit An arrangement of electrical elements through which a current flows in order to transmit a signal.

citation A note referring to a work used as a source.

citation order A prescribed order for a series of elements. For Library of Congress Subject Headings, the prescribed order for the different types of subdivisions.

CJK Chinese, Japanese and Korean. An RLIN project to allow cataloguing in those languages.

class In classification, a group of items sharing a common characteristic.

classed catalog A catalog in which entries are arranged in a hierarchy according to a system of classification. Broad entries are followed by series of subdivisions. In contrast, a Dictionary catalog arranges entries in alphabetic order. An Alphabetico-classed catalog will first list broad topics in alphabetical order, and then present the subdivisions under those topics.

classification A system for shelving together materials that share a common characteristic, such as subject, form, or provenance. The process of classification combines two opposite procedures: 1. To distinguish an object from others to which it might appear similar, on the basis of characteristics judged to be significant. 2. To group objects together, on the basis of shared characteristics, despite differences. Thus, lemons are distinguished from oranges, but both are grouped together as citrus fruits. Attempts to provide hierarchical classifications for thematic subjects have not been as successful as the scientific classifications on which the subject hierarchies are modeled.

close classification A classification system that specifies detailed subdivisions. In contrast, a system of broad classification assigns only broad classes.

closed catalog A catalog into which new bibliographic records are not entered, or entry is limited to certain categories. Old records can be deleted, perhaps as the information is entered into a computer database that will replace the old system. In contrast, a frozen catalog is left completely unchanged.

COBOL A computer programming language. The name is an acronym for COmmon Business Oriented Language.

CODASYL COmmittee on DAta SYstems Languages of the American National Standards Institute. The committee's proposed model was implemented in the form of network databases on minicomputers. The hierarchical and network database models have largely been superseded by the more flexible relational model.

code 1. A set of symbols used to represent something. 2. A set of rules. 3. A set of computer instructions, contained in a computer program.

CODEN A code assigned to publications by the Chemical Abstracts Service.

coextensive heading A subject heading that represents exactly the subject content of a work, no more and no less. The concept is taken from the cataloging of books that usually have a definable subject, but coextensive heading does not apply well to photographs, manuscripts, and other materials that were not created to explain one given topic.

collate 1. To compare two documents to see if they are identical. 2. To merge two sets of data in some specified order.

collection 1. A body of documents having a common source, such as the administrative records of an agency or the papers of a family or individual. 2. An accumulation of documents around a common theme. 3. The total holdings of a repository.

collective title Look for title variations under "Title."

collocation Bringing together in the same location in a list of those headings that concern the same or similar subjects. The most common reason for the use of inverted headings is collocation. For example, in order to make it easier for the cataloger to find the correct term for an architectural style, the Library of Congress Subject Headings list uses "Architecture, French", "Architecture, Gallo-Roman", and "Architecture, Norman" rather than "French architecture", "Gallo-Roman architecture", and "Norman architecture".

colophon Used by a printer at the back of a book, an identifying symbol or a statement with information on the author and publisher.

COM Computer-Output Microform. The equivalent of a card catalog, but generated by computer and printed on microfilm or microfiche.

COM Communications Port, also known as a Serial Port, on a computer. A computer device for sending and receiving information. On an IBM PC-XT, the two Serial Ports are identified as COM1 and COM2. For further explanation, see: "Serial Port".

communications format A format used to exchange data. The individual repository might not use this same format for local use. When data is to be sent or received, a computer database program will convert the data between the local and the communications format.

compatibility The ability of a computer device or system to accept data, physical components, or programs from another computer device or system. A loosely-used and much-abused term. 1. Data compatibility exists if records can be taken from one database and incorporated into another database. For example, a repository may create cataloging records using the MARC format. Those records may then be uploaded to a master database, from which the same records can later be downloaded into the databases of other participating repositories. The data records are compatible because all of the participants use the same MARC format. It does not matter that those participants might use completely different computer systems. They are not exchanging pieces of hardware or computer programs, they are only exchanging data. 2. Hardware compatibility exists if two devices can exchange components. Disk drives for 3 1/2 inch diskettes and 5 1/4 inch diskettes are not compatible because they will not accept the same diskettes. 3. Software compatibility exists if the same program can run on different computers.

Software compatibility generally requires some degree of hardware compatibility. The Pick operating system extends considerably the idea of compatibility, because Pick will allow the same program to run on a wide variety of different machines, extending from an IBM desktop computer to a mainframe. After Pick is implemented on a particular machine, a program will talk only to the Pick operating system. The operating system will interpret the program's instructions for that particular computer. The user can move back and forth between the different machines, with no need for an awareness of the differences, other than for external matters such as keyboard layout.

compiler 1. A person who brings together materials from different sources into a single collection or work. 2. A computer program that translates other programs from the source code written by a programmer in a symbolic language such as Basic, which a human can understand, into object code in the machine language, which the computer understands. A compiler will translate an entire program at one time. The resulting object code is then stored for use. For example, in Pick Basic the instruction to read a record from a file, and store the information in a variable named "Data.Record", would resemble the following:

```
READ Data.Record FROM Data.File, Item.ID
```

The compiler will translate this instruction into machine language, and store it as object code. In contrast to a compiler, an interpreter will translate only one instruction at a time. The interpreter must be used every time the program is run, slowing down the program's speed considerably.

component part Part of a larger entity, which is the Host Item. For example, a single photograph is part of a collection.

compound subject heading A subject heading with two or more words, such as "Outdoor cookery" or "Cookery, Oriental" or "Cookery for the sick".

compound surname A surname made up of more than one proper name. For example: "Pierre Mendés-France".

computer program A written set of instructions for a computer.

concatenate To join together two or more pieces of data into a single piece. For example, if a cataloging record has been written for a collection designated as number "1", series number "3", item number "200", these elements may be concatenated together to form a Record-ID, with hyphens included to mark off the separate elements. The resulting Record-ID would be: "1-3-200".

conceptual model The logical structure of a database, independent of the actual methods of physical storage. Also called the logical model.

connect time The amount of time that a user has been logged onto a computer system.

CONSER CONversion of SERials. An OCLC retrospective conversion project for serial publications, such as journals.

content designator In a MARC format record or other computer record, a character or code that identifies some portion of the record content. For example: MARC tag "650", which identifies a field as 650 (Subject Added Entry—Topics), an indicator that signifies that a personal names field contains a compound surname; a sub-field code that identifies a particular sub-field within a field, or a delimiter that separates fields within a computer record.

contents note In a bibliographic record, a list of the parts of the item cataloged, similar to a Table of Contents for a book.

Controlled Vocabulary A limited list of terms that can be used when entering data into a particular field. For more information, see: "Authority File".

CONTU Committee on New Technological Uses of Copyright.

conventional name A name, other than the legal or official name, by which an organization or place is known.

cooperative cataloging An arrangement whereby different agencies create cataloging records and share them with each other, usually by means of uploading copies of the records to a master database from which the other repositories can download records.

copy cataloging Cataloging an item by using and editing an already-existing bibliographic record.

corporate name The name of an organization or group, including not only business corporations but also government agencies, clubs, universities, churches, etc.

cover date The date of publication as it appears on the cover of a work.

cover title The title as it appears on the cover.

CPI Characters per Inch, for magnetic tape.

CPS Characters Per Second, for data transmission or printing.

CPU Central Processing Unit. The brain of the computer. An integrated circuit that performs the computer's functions, with the aid of other devices such as memory, disk drives, and ports. The speed and capabilities of the CPU determines much of the power of the computer. IBM desktop computers utilize a series of CPU chips created by the Intel corporation. The CPU of the IBM PC and PC-XT is the 8088. The CPU for the IBM PC-AT and the members of the PS/2 line below 70 is the 80286. The IBM PS/2 70 and 80 are powered by the 80386.

CPU cycles, time, or charge units The amount of time or the number of cycles expended by the CPU. A user on a computer system might be charged for Connect Time, for CPU cycles, for pages printed, or for some combination of these factors. The Pick operating system maintains an Accounting history file of this information for each Account, including the date and time of usage.

CR Carriage Return

credit A statement giving credit to the photographer or repository that supplied a photograph, or to the creator or holder of a work or portion of a work that is reproduced. Most libraries and archives require the use of a specified credit line, naming the institution and perhaps also the donor of a major collection.

CRLF Carriage Return—Line Feed

cross reference To allow reference to an item by more than one access point. In a card catalog system, you would create a Main Entry card, usually under the name of the author, and then perhaps additional cards for the title and principal subjects. In a computer database system, there is no need to create duplicate records. You can search for a record according to any piece of information contained in the record.

CRT Cathode Ray Tube. The computer screen, also referred to as the Monitor or Terminal.

CSV Comma-Separated Values. A standardized format for storing information that is divided into separate fields, as in a database, or separate Cells, as in a spread-sheet. Each field is separated from the next with a comma. If the field is composed of text, the field is also surrounded by quote marks. The end of a record is generally marked by a Carriage Return—Line Feed. The Basic programming language stores data in this format. Many DOS database programs such as dBase and R:base and will import and export data in comma-separated format.

CULDAT Canadian Union List of Machine Readable Data Files. A computerized inventory of machine-readable data in Canada, using the MARC format for machine-readable files.

cursor On a computer screen, an indicator of the user's current position while typing. A small flashing rectangle or underline character is generally used as the cursor. For example, when filling in data on a data entry form, the cursor will appear at the beginning of each field to be filled in. In the following case, the field name "ENTRY-DATE" provides a prompt message to indicate the type of information requested. The field name is followed by a colon. After the colon the underline character in boldface indicates the cursor, which shows the position where the first character typed will appear:

ENTRY-DATE: __

cutter number, cutter table, cutter-sanborn table A code for author names. The code is added to a classification number from Library of Congress classification or Dewey Decimal classification to provide a call number for the item.

cylinder A single track on a computer disk. A series of disks can be combined to perform a disk pack. The same track number on each disk collectively constitutes one cylinder.

dash A punctuation symbol that in printing is represented by a line about the length of two characters. (In printing, known as the em dash. An em is a piece of type as wide as it is tall.) When typing, a dash is represented by two hyphens, to distinguish the dash from a single hyphen used with a compound term. When typing Library of Congress Subject headings, type two hyphens to indicate a subdivision. For example:

Automobiles—Equipment and supplies

Note the distinction between two hyphens representing a dash, and a single hyphen used with a compound term. The distinction is made more obvious by capitalization:

Water—Distribution
Water—Pollution
Water—Purification
Water-power
Water-supply
Water-towers

database An organized body of data. Within a given data entry field, such as "ENTRY-DATE" or "PHOTOGRAPHER", you can always expect to find the same sort of information in the same format in each record. Note, however, that the same information can be presented differently to different groups of users. Thus, within a business, the accounting, sales, and engineering departments can all use the same database of information about the company's products, but the database management program used might present the information in different forms, and using different terminology, according to the needs of each department. (The words "data" and "base" were first merged into "database" in the 1979 *Annual Review of Information Science and Technology.)*

database administrator The individual charged with the administration of a database of information. The person is responsible for designing, and obtaining agreement on and understanding of, the data model and the data dictionary.

database program A program for managing a database. A true database program is "Relational" in that it allows you to establish relationships between different files or different levels within a collection. For example, when producing an invoice, the program will combine a name, address and other information from the Customer File with up-to-date pricing and sales tax information from the Price List file. The program will use the Price List data to compute the total price. If a distinction is made in the Customer File between categories of customers, such as between non-profit organizations and commercial accounts, the program will apply any indicated discounts to the final price. A database containing descriptions of individual items, such as photos, is most efficiently organized with all of the information that applies to an entire collection, such as the name of the donor and the required credit line, stored in one collection record. The records for the individual photos (or perhaps series of photos) will contain only the information unique to that photo or series, such as the date when it was taken and the subjects that it includes. Rather than repeating the collection level information over and over again for each photo, the record for the photo will simply refer to the collection record. A database program will combine the information from different records for printing or display. Thus, the printed page given to the patron who purchases a photo will contain both the collection information taken from the single collection record and the description of the individual photo. A database program will also allow you to change and re-structure the information after it has been entered, without having to edit each record manually. This database ability is extremely important, considering the changes continuing to take place in the MARC format. Thus, old fields can be combined or split apart into new fields. See also "Search and Replace".

data compression The reduction of the amount of space required to store computer data, generally by coding information about redundant elements, rather than repeating each of those elements individually. Because images require large amounts of space to store in digital form, data compression is an important component of an image database capability.

data dictionary Definitions of the fields in a database record. The definitions will include the field name and the type of data to be stored, such as data that consists of numbers, of dollar amounts, of dates, or of text. The dictionary will also show relationships and rules for usage. For example, an entry in a field for two-letter state codes will not be accepted unless it matches one of the codes in a state codes list. In the Pick operating system, a dictionary file holds the definitions for the fields in a data file. For more information, see: "File".

data model The logical structure of the data, designed to match the inherent properties of the data independently of specific hardware, software, or usage.

data set A collection of logically-related data items.

DBMS Database Management System. A program for managing a database.

DDC Dewey Decimal Classification system.

deaccession To remove materials from an archives.

debug To correct the errors in a computer program.

decollate To separate the parts of a multipart form.

dedicated word processor A computer designed to be used only for word processing. In contrast, the IBM PC is a general use computer, which can be used also for database management, accounting, and other purposes.

deduping Reconciling duplicate records. For example, in a computer database, two cataloging records have been entered for the same photograph, perhaps because different copies of the photo came into the collection at different times.

delete To remove a piece of information. For example, when entering or editing data, the DELETE key on the computer keyboard will be used to delete unwanted letters and words. A database program will also provide commands for deleting an entire record from a database, or for deleting an entire database file from the computer disk.

delimiter A boundary marker. A special character used to separate elements within a database, so that the computer will know where one record, field, sub-field, or sub-sub-field ends and the next begins. A user of the History Database program would use the following delimiters, which the program will convert to the appropriate system codes. The user can choose other delimiting characters instead of those shown here. Since each record and each field will appear separately, it is not necessary to enter record or field delimiters.

Sub-Field Semicolon (or semicolon and space): ";"
Sub-Sub-Field Backslash (or backslash and space): "\"

MARC uses the following delimiters:

Record ASCII 29 at the end of each record
Field ASCII 30 at the end of each Field and Directory
Sub-Field ASCII 31 before the Sub-Field Code

Pick employs the following delimiters internally:

Record ASCII 255 at the end of each record
Field ASCII 254 at the end of each field
Sub-Field ASCII 253 at the end of each sub-field
Sub-Sub-Field ASCII 252 at the end of each sub-sub-field

dependence A piece of information is dependent on a controlling piece of information, if the dependent information can only have a single value for each value of the controlling information. For example, the street address, phone number, and required credit line of the repository holding a particular photograph. Address, phone number, and credit line are each dependent on repository. It would be redundant to store any of this dependent information in cataloging records for the photographs. You would have to repeat the same information for every photograph. Such information would instead be kept in a separate repositories file. When printing out a cataloging record for a patron, a relational database program would reach across from the photos file to the repositories file, according to the name of the repository, in order to include the required credit line.

dependent work In cataloging, a related work. For example, a dramatization of a novel, or an abridged edition of a dictionary.

deposit To place documents in a repository without transferring ownership.

derived cataloging See: "Copy cataloging".

description The process of establishing intellectual control over holdings.

descriptive cataloging The process of describing items and providing access points for their retrieval. In library practice, the process of subject analysis, which is the providing of access points by subject, is considered a separate process from describing bibliographic elements such as author and title.

descriptive standards Standards that guide the process of bibliographic description, in order to provide consistency. Descriptive standards govern the values that are placed in the various fields. A format standard, such as the MARC format, governs the structure of fields provided.

descriptor A term used to indicate the subject of a work.

Dewey decimal classification Since its initial formulation by Melvil Dewey in 1872, the Dewey Decimal system has become the most widely-used book classification system in the world. It is used by more than 85 percent of the libraries in the U.S. and Canada. Responsibility for modifications to the system lie with the Processing Department of the Library of Congress. Both the Dewey Decimal and the Library of Congress Classification system organize subjects into hierarchies, preceding from the general to the specific, according to academic disciplines of study. Under both systems a number is derived that will be used to determine the shelf location of the book classified.

DF machine readable data files See "MRDF".

dictionary catalog A catalog in which entries appear in alphabetical order, in the manner of a dictionary. Library of Congress Subject Headings is a Dictionary catalog. Also called an Alphabetical catalog. In contrast, a Classed catalog lists entries according to a hierarchical scheme of classification.

DIF Data Interchange Format. A standardized format for transferring spread-sheet or database information from one program to another.

digit A single element used to form a number, such as the decimal Arabic numerals 0-9. Thus, the zip code "90265" is five digits long. If you intended to store a full nine-digit zip code instead, you would have to leave room for the extra four digits on your data entry form.

digital data Data represented in the form of discrete bits. For example, when a photo image is stored on an optical disk in digital form, the image is broken up into separate pieces of information, called Pixels for Picture Elements. Each Pixel is equivalent to one small dot or piece of the image. For each Pixel the computer will record information about its color and its lightness or darkness. Thus, the image has been stored in the form of pure information. Compare with: "Analog data".

diode A semiconductor that converts alternating current to direct current.

direct and specific entry See: "Specific and Direct Entry".

direct access The ability to access a computer data item by its address. Also called random access, because the data item can be stored anywhere on the device. In contrast, in a system of sequential access, data items are stored in order as they are received; to find an item, you must read through the file until the requested item is encountered. Direct or random access is much faster than sequential access.

direct subdivision For Library of Congress Subject Headings, the subdivision of a subject heading by locality such as a city, without first subdividing by a larger geographical unit such as state or country. If indirect subdivision were employed, the larger unit would precede the smaller.

directory (MARC record) Defines the contents of each MARC record. Each Directory entry is 12 characters long and defines a single field in the following format. Characters

0-2: MARC Tag for the field; 3-6: Length of the field; 7-11: Starting Character Position of the field.

directory (DOS operating system) A hard disk will usually be divided into several directories. Each directory holds files. The normal practice is to place the files used by particular programs, or by individuals if more than one person is using the computer, into separate directories. Directories are sometimes referred to as subdirectories. In the Pick operating system, the approximate equivalent to a directory is an Account.

discipline An organized field of study. Classification systems such as Dewey Decimal Classification and Library of Congress Classification divide knowledge according to academic discipline.

disk A magnetic storage medium for computer information, somewhat resembling a phonograph disk. Computer disks are generally described either as "hard disks", which store large amounts of information and are installed permanently in the computer, or as "floppy disks" or "diskettes", which do not store as much information as a hard disk, but which can be removed. In this guide, all disks are referred to either as hard disks or as diskettes.

disk, hard A disk that stores large amounts of information, and which is usually installed permanently in the computer. The original IBM PC-XT introduced in 1983 included a hard disk with a capacity of 10 megabytes (about 10 million characters of information). Most people wondered what they would ever do with that much storage space. Five years later, most desktop computers contained hard disks holding 30 megabytes or more, and still it was not enough.

diskette A small disk. A removeable disk with less storage capacity than a "hard disk", which is usually installed permanently. Removeable disks were generally referred to as "floppy disks" until the advent of the 3.5 inch format, in which the disk is protected inside a hard case. Note that compatibility of physical size does not guarantee that a particular computer can read a particular diskette. The computer must also use the same operating system that was used to write the diskette, unless a special conversion facility has been supplied. Thus, the Pick operating system will not read a DOS diskette, and DOS will not read a Pick diskette, without the use of a conversion utility such as Main-Link or PK Harmony.

diskette, 3.5 inch As used in the IBM PS/2 computers, a double-sided 3.5 inch diskette will hold 1.4 megabytes of information. The single-sided version employed by the low end of the PS/2 line will hold only 720 kilobytes. A double-sided drive can read a single-sided diskette, but a single-sided drive cannot read a double-sided diskette. To tell if a 3.5 inch diskette is double-sided or single sided, look for the square holes on the bottom of the diskette, away from the metal apparatus that slides back to give the computer access to the diskette. A double-sided diskette has two square holes, a single-sided diskette only one. To format a double-sided diskette for use in a single-sided drive, in order to transfer data between computers, add the parameters shown below to the FORMAT command. The diskette to format is in the A: drive.

```
FORMAT A: /N:9 /T:80
```

Other types of computers might use the same size of diskette, but the diskettes will not be interchangeable. For example, the portable disk drive available with the Radio Shack Model 100 portable computer uses a 3.5 inch diskette, on which is stored either 100k or

200k of information, depending on whether the drive and the diskette are single or double-sided. A diskette written to by the Model 100 could not be placed inside an IBM diskette drive and read by it.

diskette, 5.25 inch As used by the IBM PC computer, a double-sided 5.25 inch diskette will hold 360 kilobytes of information. The 360K diskette is referred to as a "double density" diskette. Note carefully that the same size is used by the IBM PC-AT, but that the AT diskette is different. The PC-AT version, referred to as a "high density" or "quad density" diskette, holds 1.2 megabytes of information. The physical difference between the two is that the 360K diskette is a very dark brown, while the 1.2M diskette is black. In addition, the 360K diskette has a reinforcing strip at its hub, which the 1.2M version lacks. When purchasing diskettes, look for the terms "high density" or "quad density" as indicating the AT diskettes, and "double density" for the PC diskette. A 360K diskette drive will not read a 1.2M diskette. A 1.2M diskette drive can read a 360K diskette. Although manufacturers claim that the 1.2M drive can also write to a 360K diskette, many problems have been reported in trying to read a diskette with a 360K drive after the diskette has been written to by a 1.2M drive. If you are going to use 360K diskettes to transfer information between a PC with a 360K drive and an AT with a 1.2M drive, make sure than each diskette is written to only by one kind of drive. Reserve some of the diskettes for writing by the 360K drive, and other diskettes for writing by the 1.2M drive. To format a 360K diskette using a 1.2M drive, add the parameters shown below to the FORMAT command. Do not try to format a 1.2M diskette as a 360K diskette. The diskette to format is in the A: drive.

```
FORMAT A: /4
```

Disposition Actions taken in regard to archival records. The records might be kept for permanent storage, stored, reproduced in a more convenient form such as microfilm, or destroyed.

distributed database A database that appears to the user as a single logical unit, although it is physically spread across different locations.

divided catalog A catalog divided into separate sections, generally for subject headings and for author-title headings.

document A single item. A photograph is a document. A letter sent from one person to another is a document.

documentation Information necessary to make effective use of a computer program or to access a computer database. Any person or institution maintaining a computer database should also maintain documentation on all of the decisions made as to how the database is to be used. For example, if only Library of Congress Subject Headings are to be used in the Subjects field, that decision should be written down, so that it will be applied consistently, and any future searcher of the database will know what to expect. The need for documentation applies even to an individual researcher, who is not likely to remember all of the choices made years previously.

DOS Disk Operating System. A shorthand reference to the standard, single-user operating system for the IBM PC, supplied by the Microsoft corporation. Also known as PC-DOS or MS–DOS.

DOT *Dictionary of Occupational Titles.* Prepared by the U.S. Dept. of Labor.

dot matrix printer For varieties of printers, look under: "Printer".

double indexing To enter a subject heading twice in different forms. Also referred to a duplicate entry. Double indexing usually takes the form of reversing elements in a sequence, when the elements have a reciprocal relationship. For example:

SUBJECTS[650]:France—Foreign relations—United States;
United States—Foreign relations—France

If Geographical Subdivisions are employed, double indexing might become extensive. For example:

SUBJECTS[650]:Los Angeles (Calif.)—Factories;
Factories—Los Angeles (Calif.)

down time The time that the computer is not working. The traditional excuse of "The dog ate my homework" has been replaced by "My computer is down."

downward reference For subject headings, a reference from a broad term down to a narrow one.

dumb terminal A low-cost computer terminal with no processing capabilities of its own, which is connected by cable to a host computer.

dummy value A value used temporarily, to hold a place in a database record.

dump To copy the contents of a computer file onto disk or tape, for backup storage.

duplex transmission The transmission of data simultaneously in both directions. Also referred to as full-duplex transmission.

dynamic array An array that is not limited in the number of elements that it can hold. In contrast, in the case of a fixed array, the maximum number of elements is specified when the array is created. In the Pick operating system, a record in a database file is a dynamic array, which can hold any number of fields.

EBCDIC Extended Binary Coded Decimal Interchange Code. An alternative to the ASCII standard (American Standard Code for Information Interchange) for representing characters on a computer. EBCDIC is used by most IBM mainframe computers, ASCII is employed by microcomputers and minicomputers. The Pick operating system makes it easy to convert data between the two standards with an ASCII command that converts from EBCDIC to ASCII and an EBCDIC command that translates from ASCII to EBCDIC.

editor A computer program for editing text.

EDP Electronic Data Processing.

empty digit In a notational system, a digit used to separate other digits, to maintain the positions of the various elements.

English The searching language used at the operating system level by the McDonnell Douglas version of Pick. On most other Pick systems the language is known as "Access".

enlargement ratio The ratio of the enlarged image to the original.

enter To enter information into a computer, generally by typing the information and then pressing the ENTER key. For example, the prompt appears:

Enter the Date:

You type the date and then press the ENTER key.

ENTER key A key on a computer keyboard, equivalent to the Carriage Return key on a typewriter. When entering data or responding to a prompt, pressing the ENTER key

signifies that you want what you have written to be entered into the computer. You have finished typing and you want the computer to take action on the command or to move on to the next field on the form. The key can be designated as ENTER, RETURN, CR, or CRLF, or marked by an arrow pointing down and to the left, as shown in FIG. G-1.
For additional information, see: "Carriage Return".

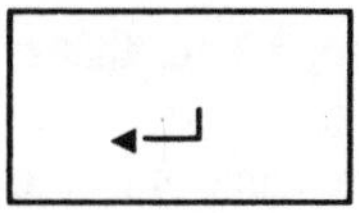

Fig. G-1. The ENTER key on the computer keyboard

entity Something for which data is to be stored. Concrete objects or concepts of interest to the repository or researcher. Note the distinction between an entity and the characteristics or attributes of that entity. A photograph is an entity. So is the photographer and the camera. The dates when the photo was taken, the photographer was born, and the camera was manufactured are characteristics of their respective entities.

entry A record that has been entered into a computer database. Thus, you can say that an entry has been made for a particular document or collection of documents.

entry word The first word for searching or sorting. For more information, see: "Filing word".

ERICD Educational Resources Information Center Descriptors. A list of special subject terms for education.

ESCAPE A key on a computer keyboard. The key is generally marked "ESC". The key is most often used to quit or to escape from a process. For example, when entering new records into a database, you might press the ENTER key as you finished with each field, and the ESCAPE key when you were finished with an entire record.

escape code A code that a computer program sends to a printer or screen to perform certain functions, such as showing characters in boldface.

estray A record or document that is held by someone other than its legitimate custodian.

evidential value For archival records, the value of materials as documentation of the operations and activities of an organization or individual. Such materials might serve to protect property or other legal rights. For example, diaries or photographs might document the creation of an invention. Photographs might show whether a particular piece of property had customarily been used as a public right-of-way. Compare with: "Administrative value" and "Informational value".

exchange format A format for data exchange and communication, which may or may not also be employed for local usage.

execute a command The computer carries out a command entered by the user.

exhaustive indexing Assigning headings to all the significant subject concepts contained in a work.

existence In a database, a test for existence determines whether or not any data exists in a field, rather than checking for some particular value. For example, a bibliographic database might have an ACTIONS field to indicate any actions that should be taken with the materials, such as actions to preserve a photograph or a manuscript. On a weekly basis, you might check this field to see if there are any actions that you should be taking. Use the search statement:

```
SELECT ITEMS IF ACTIONS
```

existence dependency A record cannot be created in one file unless a corresponding record already exists in another file. For example, a bibliographic database contains a COLLECTIONS file and an ITEMS file. You cannot create an item-level record without identifying the collection of which the item is a part. For that collection a record must already exist in the COLLECTIONS file. For more information, see: "Identifier dependency".

explanatory reference A reference, such as a scope note, that explains how a heading should be used.

extension, for a DOS filename The portion of the name after the period. For example, a word-processing document might be named "Story.doc". The portion of the name called "Story" would commonly be referred to as the filename, while the ending "doc" would be referred to as the extension. Many DOS programs use standard extensions to indicate the nature or purpose of a file. Microsoft Word and many other word processors automatically use the Extension "doc" to end all text files written by the user.

extensions, for MARC Additions to MARC of extra fields, sub-fields, etc.

external view The user's view of the database. Different users might see the same database in different ways, each according to his or her own requirements and frames of reference. The manner in which the data is actually stored physically on the computer can be quite different than the way the user perceives the data.

facet An aspect of a subject. For example, a subject can be said to have a geographical facet or a literary form facet.

faceted classification A classification system in which subjects are analyzed according to specified facets.

fair use Usage that is not considered to infringe upon a copyright. For example, the use of short quotations from a novel in a literary review of that novel.

false combination In computer database searching, a danger that arises from the use of short, simple subject headings that are later combined in a search statement (postcoordination), rather than longer and more complicated headings that are combined at the time of data entry (precoordination). The short terms might be combined in ways that were not intended. For example, imagine a Subjects field containing the following three terms:

SUBJECTS:Mistresses; Sculptors; Painters

The field does not specify which of the four possibilities hold true for the information contained in the document:

- Mistresses of sculptors only
- Mistresses of painters only
- Mistresses of both sculptors and painters
- Mistresses connected with neither sculptors nor painters

A search statement intended for only one of these possibilities will also retrieve the other three. Thus a searcher looking only for mistresses of painters will retrieve some documents relating to mistresses who are not connected to painters, but instead to sculptors. In this case, the subject terms "Mistresses" and "Painters", appearing separately in the Subjects field, have been brought together in a false combination. An alternative would be to use subdivisions at the time of data entry. Rather than entering the terms for mistresses and painters separately, you would enter "Painters—Mistresses". Such a subdivision is in fact specified for the subject headings "Presidents" and "Kings and rulers". However, creating a system to apply subdivisions consistently brings a host of different problems.

favored category A category of document featured prominently in the classification system of a repository because of the particular strengths of that institution's holdings, or due to local needs or interests.

fax Facsimile transmission.

field A subdivision within a record for a specific piece of information, such as "ENTRY-DATE" for the date when the record was entered.

field delimiter The delimiter that marks off separate fields within a record.

pick field delimiter ASCII 254. When data is imported from DOS, Pick will automatically convert each Carriage Return Line Feed to a Field Delimiter. When exporting data to DOS, Pick will automatically convert each Field Delimiter to a Carriage Return Line Feed. If the DUMP command is used to display a Pick Frame, the Field Delimiter will appear as a caret: " ". The delimiter appears at the end of each field. No delimiter is necessary for the final field within a record. Within the Pick Editor, each field will appear as a separate paragraph. The Field Delimiter can be entered directly within the Editor by typing CTRL-[], but this procedure should be discouraged for any but the most experienced Pick users.

MARC field delimiter ASCII 30. MARC cataloging manuals generally show each field in a separate paragraph, rather than using a symbol to represent the Field Delimiter. The delimiter occurs at the end of each field and at the end of the Directory.

field length The physical length of a computer database field. The database system used can employ fixed-length or variable-length fields.

FID *Federation International de Documentation.*

FID In the Pick operating system, Frame ID. The sequential number of the Frame.

file For a word-processing program, a file generally consists of a textual document, such as a business letter or a chapter written for a book. In contrast, for a database program a file is a collection of records. A record in turn is composed of fields. Each record within a given file has the same structure. In other words, each record is composed of the same fields, in the same order. A Pick database file has two levels, A Dictionary level and a Data level. The Dictionary holds the definitions for the fields in which information is stored at the Data level. For example, for a database of names and addresses, in the Dictionary you might define the following structure of fields for the Data records:

Field Number	Field Name
1	NAME
2	ADDRESS
3	PHONE-NUMBER

filing indicator A sub-field used in a MARC record to indicate how a title should be handled for sorting. For example, when the title "The Fall of the House of Usher" is to be included in a sorted list of titles, you would want this title to appear under "Fall" rather than under "The". In the Filing Indicator Sub-Field, you would specify that the first four characters of the title are to be treated as Non-filing Characters. Note that the space after "The" should be included in the character count.

filing order The order in which items are sorted in a list. The order will differ according to the method used. For more information, see: "Sort".

filing word The first word in a value by which that value will be searched or sorted in a database. Articles such as "The" and "A" are omitted, therefore the filing word for the title "The Fall of the House of Usher" will be "Fall". Also referred to as entry word.

finding aids Guides to the documents held in an archives. These guides might include shelf lists, inventories, and indexes.

fixed length In some database systems, the lengths of records and fields are fixed. A record or field can be no longer than the fixed length, and the entire space for the fixed length is taken up on disk even when not required. In contrast, the Pick operating system utilizes variable-length records and fields.

fixed location A method for classifying and arranging items in a repository so that each item has a permanent, absolute location. For example, a photograph is designated as residing in file cabinet 2, drawer 3. An alternative classifying method is Relative Location.

flag In a computer system, a single character used to indicate whether or not a condition exists. A flag will have one of two possible values: True or False. False is indicated by zero. True is indicated by a number other than zero, most often by 1.

flat file A non relational collection of information. Because relationships cannot be drawn between files, a computer program cannot check an Authority File for subjects, for example, to make sure that a subject term entered was already in use.

floppy disk A disk that is flexible, as compared with a hard disk, which is enclosed in an inflexible case. Also called a "diskette". A floppy disk or a diskette can be removed from the computer, whereas most hard disks are installed permanently. A floppy disk or diskette will have less storage capacity than a hard disk.

foliation The numbering of only the recto (right-hand side) of the pages of a document.

fonds A French archival term for a body of materials that constitute the records of a single individual or organization. The equivalent term in English is record group. The archival principle of *respect des fonds* means that such a body of materials should be kept as a whole, rather than broken up and mixed with materials from other sources. The fact that the materials were accumulated by a certain agency, and kept in a certain order by that agency, might convey information that individual records in isolation would not convey.

font A set of type of a certain style and size. For example, on a laser printer, a widely-used font is Times-Roman, 10 point. The style is Times-Roman, similar to newspaper print, and the height of the characters is about 10/72, with about six lines fitting into an inch.

foreword Introductory remarks to a book written by someone other than the author. When written by the author, referred to as a preface.

form An outline, on paper or on a computer screen, indicating the information to be entered, and providing space for that information. Also referred to as a data entry form. The same form can be used for entry and for editing.

format integration The process of consolidating the seven separate MARC formats for Books, Serials, Visual Materials, Archival and Manuscripts Control, Maps, Music, and Computer files into a single format that will allow all of the data elements to be used with all of the different types of material and control.

form subdivision A division of a Library of Congress Subject Heading that indicates the genre or form of a work. For example, the heading "California—Gold discoveries—Juvenile literature" would indicate works about the Gold Rush that are intended for children. When cataloging into a computer database with the MARC format, rather than using a form subdivision, information about the form of a work should be placed in MARC field 655, "Genre/Form Heading". Information about the physical form of the materials should be placed in MARC field 755, "Physical Form".

format A defined, standardized pattern for entering information. The purpose of following a format is to make it possible for others to retrieve and to understand the data. Even the person who originally entered the information will find it very difficult to use the information later if the data was not written into a standard format designating records, fields, subject terms and punctuation.

format The physical form or genre type of a document.

Fortran A computer programming language. The name is a contraction for Formula Translator.

frame In the Pick operating system, all of the physical memory and disk space is divided into units called Frames. Depending on the version of Pick used, a Frame is composed of 512, 1024, or 2048 bytes.

frame fault In the Pick operating system, the need to read data from disk to memory. This is not an error, but operations will be faster if the required data is already in memory. For more information, see: "Memory".

free-floating subdivision A subdivision for Library of Congress Subjects Headings that can be used under any appropriate heading, even though the subdivision is not specified in the list of subdivisions shown under a particular heading. For example, the subdivision "Study and teaching" can be applied to any subject that can be studied and taught. The use of free-floating subdivisions is governed by Pattern Headings. For example, to find a list of the subdivisions applicable to any chemical, the cataloger would look under the heading "Copper", and use the subdivisions appearing there.

free-text system A system for information storage and retrieval that does not use a consistent database structure of uniform records and fields. Free-text systems are generally used for taking in a large body of existing data, such as news stories, and then searching for words or combinations of words in the text.

front end For computer systems, a procedure that handles communication with the user, particularly when the user first starts a given program.

frozen catalog A catalog that is not changed. New bibliographic records are not entered into it, and old records are not removed or edited. For example, a card catalog might be frozen because all new cataloging, as well as the editing of old records, will take place on a computer database. In contrast to a catalog that is completely frozen, a closed catalog might incorporate new records in limited categories, and old records can be deleted, as those records are typed into the new computer system.

function For archival description, when recording information about an organization that created or maintained archival records, a function is an area of responsibility in which an organization conducts activities in order to accomplish a purpose.

garbage in, garbage out If information is entered into a computer database in a careless and non-standardized manner, the information will probably be worthless. The computer cannot do your thinking for you. Not yet, anyway.

gazetteer A dictionary of geographical place names.

generalia class For classification systems, a fancy name for a miscellaneous category. For types of materials that bridge the principal subdivisions.

general reference For Library of Congress Subject Headings, a broad reference to a group of headings, in the place of explicit references to individual headings. For example, under the heading "Architecture", the note appears, "See also headings beginning with the word Architectural". The general reference takes the place of an explicit listing of every architectural term.

generation The number of reproductive processes between the original document and the document in hand. A copy of a copy is a third generation document.

genre A class of documents distinguished by a certain style or technique. For example, diaries, hymns, detective stories. MARC field 655 should be used for headings indicating genre.

genus In classification, a class that is divided into subgroups, each of which constitutes a species.

geographic filing method Arrangement of materials by geographic place. Commonly used for photo collections, with photos of the same area kept together in a file folder.

geographic subdivision The division of a Library of Congress Subject Heading by the name of a geographic place. For example, "Factories—Los Angeles, Calif." When cataloging with the MARC format and a computer database, it would be better to indicate the geographical subject separately in MARC field 651, "Subject Added Entry—Geographic Name".

GFE Group Format Error. In the Pick operating system, a Group Format Error occurs when the delimiters and links between pieces of data have not been placed properly. The most common cause of a Group Format Error is a sudden power loss that interrupts the operating system while the system is in the middle of writing data out to the disk.

gigabyte One billion bytes.

global search and replace See: "Search and Replace".

GMD General Material Designation. The broad class of materials to which an item belongs, such a photographs, manuscripts, or sound recordings.

GMGPC The Library of Congress Graphic Materials Genre and Physical Characteristics heading list.

go list In an automatic indexing system, a list of words deliberately selected for indexing. The opposite of a stop list, which consists of words such as "the" and "and" which are not to be indexed.

GPO Government Printing Office

graphic A two-dimensional visual image.

group In the Pick operating system, a file is divided physically into Groups. Each Group is composed of one or more Frames. The file's records (items) are stored in the Groups. Pick assigns a record to a Group by applying a mathematical formula (hashing algorithm) to the Record-ID (Item-ID). To provide an even distribution of records among the Groups of a file, the Record-IDs should not use the same numbers of letters repetitively, particularly at the end of the ID. Thus, you would not assign Record-IDs for a photo collection ending with the photo sizes, such as 4 x 5, 5 x 7, 8 x 10, etc. Many Record-IDs would end with the same numbers and the records would not be distributed evenly.

handshaking In data communications, a series of procedures by which two devices coordinate the transmission protocols to be employed.

hanging indentation The first line of text extends further to the left than the lines which follow, thus the first line hangs out over the rest.

hard copy A print out of information stored in a computer.

hard disk For varieties of computer disks, look under: "Disk".

hardware The physical aspects of a computer system, such as the keyboard and screen.

hashing A method of computer direct access. In the Pick operating system, the Frame into which a data record is to be stored is determined by applying a formula to the Record-ID. When a user subsequently asks for that record, Pick knows where to look for it.

heading A term applied to a bibliographic record as an access point. In a card catalog, a heading such as title, author, or subject will appear at the head or top of the card.

hertz A unit of frequency equal to one cycle per second. Named for Heinrich R. Hertz. The central processing unit (CPU) of an IBM PC operates at a speed of 4.77 megahertz. Abbreviated as Hz.

heuristic Learning by trial and error.

hexadecimal A numbering system based on 16. The decimal system is based on 10. The hexadecimal numbers are 0, 1, 2, 3, 4, 5, 6, 7, 8, 9, A, B, C, D, E, F.

hierarchical classification A system of classifying subjects according to a natural order, proceeding from broad topics or disciplines of study down to specific subjects. This method is modeled on scientific classifications of animals, plants, etc. As is often the case however, borrowing the language and methods of science does not guarantee precision when the methods and vocabulary are applied outside of their intended realm. The difficulty with applying subject hierarchies is that historical subjects really do not possess any natural order.

hierarchical database A database system in which information is stored in a defined hierarchy. This method is not as flexible as a relational database system.

hit In a database, to find the information desired. If the user is searching for records containing the subject heading "Architectural models", and fifteen records are retrieved, the user had fifteen hits.

hit rate The number of records retrieved in comparison to the number of records searched.

holdings All of the materials held by a repository.

holdings format A tentative MARC Format for recording the actual holdings of a library, such as the issues of a magazine that the library has on hand.

Hollerith card A punch card, originally developed by Herman Hollerith to tabulate the results of the 1890 United States census.

holograph A document in the handwriting of the person who signs it. The term is employed to indicate that the entire document, rather than only the signature, is hand-written by the signer. In contrast, a manuscript can be type-written.

host computer The primary computer in a multi-user or network system.

host item An Item that contains a component part, such as a photo collection contains individual photos.

hypertext Non-sequential access by cross-references under the user's control.

Hz Abbreviation for Hertz.

IASSIST International Association for Social Science Information Service and Technology. An association of data archivists, data librarians, and computer database professionals.

ICA International Council on Archives

id Item-ID, Record-ID. The information that uniquely identifies a data record within a database file. In the Pick database system, no more than one record can have the same Record-ID. For more information, see: "Record-ID".

identifier dependency The Record-ID of one record in a database must include the Record-ID of another record. For example, a bibliographic database contains a COLLECTIONS file and an ITEMS file. An "existence dependency" would mean that you cannot create an item-level record without identifying the collection of which the item is a part. For that collection a record must already exist in the COLLECTIONS file. A further "identifier dependency" would require that you include the Record-ID of the collection-level record in the Record-ID of any record for an item contained in that collection. Thus, if item number 2000 is contained in collection number 6, the Record-ID for the item would include both values, in a form such as "6-2000".

IFLA International Federation of Library Associations

ILL Inter-Library Loan

illegal character A character that is unacceptable for entry under specific circumstances for a particular computer program. For example, you would presumably not want to allow the entry of graphics characters as data into a database. If you were to enter characters as data that the computer system regarded as delimiters between fields, a system crash would probably occur. A data entry program should prevent the accidental entry of illegal characters.

imprint date For cataloging, the year of publication, distribution, or manufacture, depending upon the type of material.

inclusive dates The time period during which all of the materials described were created. As distinguished from bulk dates, which indicate when the bulk of the materials were created.

indentation The space from the margin to the text.

in-depth indexing Assigning subject headings to individual parts of a work, rather than to only the work as a whole.

index For a computer database, a table, similar to an index at the back of a book, that gives the Record-IDs of the records containing a given entry in a particular field. Thus, a subjects index will contain the Record-IDs of each record containing a particular subject term. Under the subject heading "Freight and freightage", the database program can immediately find the IDs of all the records containing this term. The advantage of an index is speed. The program need only look in the index, rather than having to search through the entire database. The disadvantage is space, because indexes take up space. Under the Pick database system, it is standard practice to create a separate index for each of the fields that are most frequently searched, and to interrogate the less-used fields by searching through the database.

index librorum prohibitorum The Index of Prohibited Books issued by the Catholic Church until 1966.

indicator A 2-character code at the beginning of each MARC field used for interpretation of the data in the field. For example, an Indicator of "10" before a field containing Personal Names tells a program that the field contains a single surname, followed by a comma, space, and the given names, and that the name corresponds to Library of Congress usage. If the field contained only a first name, or only a last name, or the name was drawn from the National Library of Medicine or the National Agricultural Library, different

Indicators would be applied, and the computer would interpret the information differently.

indirect subdivision For Library of Congress Subject Headings, when subdividing a subject term by geographical location, the name of a larger unit such as a country or state will appear before the specific smaller unit such as city or county. In contrast, with direct subdivision, the city or country name would follow directly after the subject heading.

informatics The study of the structure of information and the application of technology to its organization.

informational value For archival records, the value of the information in the materials for research. Researchers will often find information to be of value in ways not originally intended. For example, records of oil-drilling operations would provide information not only about the particular company manning the rigs, but also about the petroleum industry in that locality and the history of its technology. A price list for groceries in 1900 would have informational value for a study of the living standards of the time. Compare with: "Administrative value" and "Evidential value".

ink jet printer For varieties of printers, look under: "Printer".

in press A work in the process of being printed.

in process Materials that have been received by a repository, but for which physical processing and cataloging has not been completed.

input To enter information into a computer. Also, the information entered, as distinguished from output, which is the data sent to a printer, screen, or other output device.

input device Most often a keyboard is used to input information, but a mouse or scanner can also be used to convey information to a computer.

insert mode When typing on a computer, while entering data or using a word processor, each new character typed is inserted into the line at the position of the cursor, pushing all the characters after it over to the right. In contrast, if over-type mode were in effect, the new character would replace the character already at the cursor position.

integer A whole number, including both positive and negative numbers and zero. The following are integers: 1, -124, 0. The following are not integers: 10.36, 1/4. Integers are generally faster to use in arithmetic operations and require less computer memory than fractional numbers. If your database will include a numeric field on which arithmetic will be performed, consider whether the use of integers only might be practical.

integrated catalog A catalog in which the attempt is made to reconcile older forms of headings with newer forms. A difficult and time-consuming task, which is virtually impossible to accomplish without computer database management facilities. Most collections, in the words of Katherine Morton of the Yale Library, contain various "strata" of data from past bibliographical ages.

integrated circuit A computer electronic circuit in which all of the component's needs have been placed together on a single chip of silicon.

integrated shelving The shelving together of all materials according to classification, regardless of format. Thus, books would appear beside photographs and oral history transcripts.

integrity The consistency of a computer database.

intellectual control The assignment of appropriate subject headings and bibliographic descriptions to a body of materials, as distinguished from the physical arrangement and care of the materials. This guide is concerned only with matters of intellectual control.

intelligent database A database that contains its own logic, rather than having logic applied to it by a program. The data dictionary of the database will contain the controls and constraints to be applied to each field as well as the links between fields and files.

interactive system A computer system in which the user enters and edits data interactively, at a terminal, in contrast to a batch processing system, in which additions and changes are submitted for later batch processing. Also called a real time system.

interest profile A list of subject terms that reflect a user's interests. The list is used by a Selective Dissemination of Information (SDI) system to provide a user with items related to his or her interests. Also called a user profile.

interface The point of connection between two components that must work together in order to accomplish a given task. In a computer system, the user interface refers to communication between the human operator and the machine.

interfiling Filing variations of a heading as if they were same, generally in response to a change in cataloging rules or heading lists. In contrast, split files will incorporate a new heading without changing records filed under the old heading.

internal structure The physical storage structure of the data, which can be quite different from the user's external perception.

interpolate To make an estimate between two values that are certain. For example, when cataloging a photo, the cataloger recognizes an automobile manufactured in 1910 and a building that was torn down in 1920. To date the photo, the cataloger might indicate the range 1910–1920 or interpolate a single year between the two known dates.

interpreter A computer program that translates other programs from symbolic language to machine language, one instruction at a time. Compare with: "Compiler".

inventory An archival finding aid that generally includes a history and description of the agency from whom the records came, a description of each record series and its relationship to other series, and a highlighting of important subject content.

inverted file An index file.

inverted heading A heading with normal word order reversed, in order to group like headings together in an alphabetical catalog under the second word. For example, in the Library of Congress Subject Headings list, styles of architecture appear in the form of inverted headings, such as "Architecture, Spanish colonial" and "Architecture, Victorian", in order to facilitate making a choice among related terms.

inverted title A title with word order changed so that when a list of titles is sorted, the title will be listed under the first significant word, rather than under an article such as "the" or "a". For example, James Fenimore Cooper's novel would be listed as "Deerslayer, The" rather than as "The Deerslayer".

I/O Input/Output, in regard to a computer system.

ISAM Indexed Sequential Access Method.

ISBD International Standard Bibliographic Description. The ISBD rules for punctuation have been used in the MARC Format since 1974.

ISBN International Standard Book Number. The number is given to a book before publication. The four parts of the number consist of identifiers for the geographic region or language, publisher, title, and a check digit. Used in Britain since 1967, in the U.S. since 1968.

ISO International Standards Organization. The international organization for voluntary standards.

ISO-8211 A standard promulgated by the International Standards Organization for the exchange of database files between different computer systems. The packet of data sent from one system to another contains information about how the data is to be mapped into various database structures. The standard is supported by the American National Standards Institute.

ISO-OSI International Standards Organization Open Systems Interconnection. An open system is one that can exchange communications among different computer programs and hardware. The OSI standard identifies seven levels of system interfaces, beginning at the lowest physical level of data bits up to an applications level to specify programming commands. The need for such standardization arises from the growth of large, integrated computing environments with hardware and software from many different manufacturers. The earliest example of OSI is MAP—the Manufacturers Automation Protocols, a family of standards created to support plant automation. Presently developing is TOPS—The Office Protocols.

ISSN International Standard Serial Number. Placed in MARC field 022.

issue Copies of an edition that form a distinct group because of some defined difference that sets them apart from other copies produced under the same edition. For example, the title page might be altered.

ITAL *Information Technology and Libraries.* Official journal of the Library and Information Technology Association of the American Library Association. Formerly the *Journal of Library Automation.*

item 1. In an archival collection, the smallest unit of material. For example, an individual document. 2. In a database system, a record can be referred to as an Item, particularly in the Pick database system. For more information, see: "Record".

item-id Also called a Record-ID or Control Number, it is a unique identifying number for that Item or record. The Item-ID is placed in the first MARC field, MARC Tag 001.

item-level cataloging To catalog separately each item in a collection, such as each photograph in a photo collection. In most cases, rather than actually creating a separate cataloging record for each item, like items would be grouped together. For example, photos of an aircraft assembly line, all taken of the same plant, on the same day, by the same photographer, would probably be cataloged into a single item-level record. Within the record, the cataloger would indicate how many photos were actually included, and would also perhaps, in a narrative description field, draw attention to particular features of individual photos.

item size The total size or length in bytes of a database item or record. For more information, see: "Record size".

JAH *Journal of American History.* The journal of the Organization of American Historians.

JCL Job Control Language, used to give a computer instructions for batch processing.

joint author A coauthor, who collaborates on a work, with each collaborator performing a similar function. Coauthorship falls under the bibliographic category of shared responsibility. In contrast, in a case of mixed responsibility, the collaborators perform different functions.

journal A periodical, generally of a more scholarly nature than a magazine.

jurisdictional name heading The name of a political or ecclesiastical jurisdiction.

jurisdictional qualifier A term for the type of jurisdiction, added in parentheses, to distinguish between places having the same name. For example: "New York (State)", "Los Angeles (County)". Also referred to as a political qualifier.

K Kilobyte.

KB Kilobyte.

key Identifying information used to locate a data record. For more information, see: "Record-ID".

keyword A word selected from the title or abstract of a work and placed in an index, to be used later to locate the bibliographic record.

kilobyte A thousand bytes or characters (actually 1,024 bytes), equivalent to about half of a typed, double-spaced page. The storage capacity of a floppy disk on the IBM PC is 360K or 360,000 characters.

kit A multimedia item in which no one form of material is considered predominant. For example, a museum exhibit might contain a combination of photos, artefacts, and text. In contrast, in the case of a slide show, the photo transparencies might be considered dominant, while a printed outline of the presentation would be subordinate.

KWIC Key Word In Context. The listing of keywords will include material before and after each keyword, to show the context in which the word appeared.

KWOC Key Word Out of Context. The listing of keywords will not include the context. Each keyword will instead be followed by the title of the work.

label A name used to identify a computer instruction or a data element.

lacuna A gap in a repository's collections.

LAN Local Area Network.

language material Textual material, whether printed, in manuscript, or microform.

laser printer For varieties of printers, look under: "Printer".

LC Library of Congress

LCCN Library of Congress Card Number, stored in MARC field 010.

LCD Liquid Crystal Display. A computer display that employs reflected light. Because of its low power consumption, it is used in portable computers.

LCGM *Graphic Materials: Rules for Describing Original Items and Historical Collections.* By Elisabeth Betz (now Elisabeth Betz Parker). For more information, look in the Bibliography.

LCNAF Library of Congress Name Authority File. The source for the standard version of personal and corporate names used by libraries. Names entered into a database should be checked against the authority files whenever possible. The files are available for on-line reference through the Bibliographic Services, and in microfiche form from the Library of Congress. Note that a good database program will include a Global Search and Replace utility that will allow an incorrectly-entered name to be replaced easily. If a name has been entered incorrectly hundreds of times, all of the entries can be corrected with a single command. Note also that AACR2 specifies the use of the most common form of a name. Names of local rather than national significance, and the names of persons who are not the authors or subjects of books, will probably not appear in the LCNAF. See also "Controlled Vocabulary".

LCRI Library of Congress Rule Interpretations. Interpretations of the rules contained in AACR2 (Anglo-American Cataloguing Rules, Second edition), as applied by the catalogers at the Library of Congress.

LCSH Library of Congress Subject Headings. The most complete list of general subject headings available. The use of LCSH for entering and searching subjects is strongly recommended. The list is maintained and updated by the Subject Cataloging Division of the Library of Congress.

LCTGM *Library of Congress Thesaurus for Graphic Materials:* Topical Terms for Subject Access. A special subjects list for graphic materials compiled by Elisabeth Betz Parker of the Prints and Photographs Division of the Library of Congress. For more information, look in the Bibliography.

leader The first 25 characters of each MARC record contains information that will allow a computer receiving the record to process it properly.

lead-in key A keystroke on a computer keyboard that causes no action by itself, but does affect the result of the next keystroke. For example, you can type foreign characters with lead in keys using the Pick operating system running on an IBM PC-XT or PC-AT. In order to type "a" with an umlaut, you might first press CONTROL-:, by holding down the CONTROL key while pressing the key for a colon, and then typing "a".

least significant digit In a numbering system, the digit with the least weight. Thus, for the number 127, 1 is the most significant digit, and 7 is the least significant digit.

legal custody Ownership of title to documentary materials. If materials are deposited in an archival center without a deed of gift, then the center has physical custody but not legal custody.

letter See "ASCII" and "Byte".

letter-by-letter For varieties of sorting and alphabetizing, look under: "Sort".

level of description The degree of bibliographic detail supplied for an item.

library For computers, a collection of utility programs and routines that can be accessed by the operating system.

Library of Congress The Mother Church for rules of cataloging and classification in the United States.

Library of Congress Classification The favorite classification system for academic and very large libraries, approximately two-thirds of whom utilize this classification scheme. Development of the system began in 1897. Revisions are the responsibility of the Subject Cataloging Division of the Library of Congress. Like the Dewey Decimal system favored by most public libraries, the Library of Congress Classification system seeks to organize all human knowledge into a hierarchical structure according to the academic disciplines involved. Each system provides a number that a library will use to determine the appropriate shelf location for a book. The Library of Congress Subject Headings list includes Library of Congress Classification numbers after many of the headings. Thus, after the LCSH term "Labor and laboring classes" the notation in brackets "[HD4801-HD8942]" appears, indicating the range of Library of Congress Classification Numbers under which aspects of the topics of labor and workers would appear. The letter "H" indicates social sciences, the letters "HD" indicate the subject of economic history, considered as a class within the social sciences, and the numbers represent divisions within that class.

linear feet The length of drawers for vertically-stored files, or the thickness of horizontally-stored materials.

line editor A very crude type of computer editing facility that does not allow the user to move the cursor freely about the screen. In contrast, a full screen editor would allow the user to move the cursor from the middle of one line to the middle of the next line.

line printer A computer printer that prints an entire line at one time.

link A relationship between two database records, perhaps in two different databases. One record might contain bibliographic information for an entire collection, while another describes an individual photo within the collection without repeating the bibliographic data. See also "Database". In the MARC format, position 19 in the Leader contains an "r" if the additional record is required in order to process this record completely. For example, the bibliographic or collection-level record might be necessary to provide the name of the collection in which the individual photo is contained. MARC field 773 will contain the Control Number of the collection-level record.

linking entry field In a database record, a field that contains the information necessary to link one record to another. For example, in an item-level record, the linking entry field would contain the Record-ID of the collection-level record for the collection that contains the item.

LITA Library and Information Technology Association, a division of ALA.

literary warrant The creation of a list of subject headings or a classification system based on materials actually cataloged, rather than on the basis of an overall theoretical framework. Thus, the Library of Congress Subject Headings have accumulated as headings have been needed for works to be cataloged. As a result, the parallel headings that you might expect often do not exist. For example, there is a heading for "Afro-American evangelists", but none for Asian-American evangelists, presumably because no books have been written about the latter.

load To transfer a computer program or data from disk or tape into memory.

Local Area Network A system for linking together users who are employing computers and an operating system intended originally for stand-alone use. Networking is much more difficult and expensive than the employment of a multi-user system, such as the Pick operating system, which has been designed from the ground up specifically to provide many users with access to the same database. For a local area network, each user must have a stand-alone computer, such as an IBM PC, plus additional hardware and software to operate the network. For a multi-user system, each user requires only a terminal, which costs approximately $400, and a cable connection to the serial port of a host computer.

local subdivision See: "Geographic subdivision".

location index A finding aid listing items and their physical locations within the repository.

lock To maintain a database record for the exclusive use of a single operator, while that operator is editing the record. Other users trying to edit the same record at the same time will be locked out until the first user has finished. Locking is a vital part of a multiuser database management system. On older systems, when several records are stored in a single Group, an entire Group might be locked, rather than only the individual record. Newer systems use record-level locking. When editing data in a multiuser environment, an operator should not leave his or her terminal in the middle of editing a record, because other users will be locked out of that record until the first operator returns.

logbook A written record of events as they occur. A primitive type of archival control consists of making logbook entries for items as they are accessioned, with the accession number and perhaps a brief description.

logical As distinct from physical. Used to describe a system as it is perceived by those who use it. This perception might be very different from the underlying physical reality.

logical database The database as it is perceived by those who use it, independently from the actual physical storage arrangements. An external view of the database. Many different logical databases can exist for one physical database. The logical database should conform to the model that those who employ it will find most useful. In contrast, the underlying physical storage arrangements will depend upon the technical details of computer software and hardware. Insofar as is possible, the users should not be bothered by these technical details, nor expected to change the procedures for data entry and searching when hardware and software are changed. Furthermore, each group of users should be presented with the data in the form that is most useful for that group's tasks. Thus, for historical collections held by a repository, data records meant for the staff might include detailed information on preservation actions to be taken or additional research to be conducted. Information printed from the same database for a patron might exclude the action fields, and include other fields such as any required credit line, as well as information drawn from other files that will help to explain the data. From the patron's logical or external point of view, the credit line information is included with every record. Physically, the credit line is probably stored only once, as applicable to an entire collection.

log off To end a session on a multiuser computer system. Before turning off the terminal, the operator will give a specific log off command. On a virtual memory system, the log off command is necessary to ensure that all of the new data stored in the computer's active memory will be written onto the disk for permanent storage. If someone should simply turn off the power, without performing the log off procedure, data might be lost or, even worse, written to disk in an incomplete form, causing the database to become corrupted.

log on To begin a session on a multiuser computer system. The operator will first turn on an individual terminal, and then log on to the system to which the terminal is attached. Before the operator is allowed access to the system, the operator might be required to specify the Account that is to be used, and perhaps also to give a password.

loop A repeating set of computer instructions.

lowercase letters The small letters of a type face.

LSP Linked Systems Project. Since 1985 OCLC, RLIN, WLN, and the Library of Congress have been creating communications protocols to exchange information. As a result, a user of OCLC can access the Library of Congress Name Authority File.

M Megabyte

machine-independent A computer program or operating system organized in terms of the type of task to be accomplished, rather than according to a specific kind of hardware. The Pick operating system, for example, was created for the purpose of database management, rather than written in order to provide capabilities for a particular machine. Of course, to run, Pick must actually be implemented on specific machines, but this is done in such a manner that the system appears the same to the user, despite the underlying hardware differences. The rapid changes taking place in computers make machine independence highly desirable for databases that are meant to be used for many years. The MARC format is machine-independent and software-independent.

machine language Instructions in the language of the machine that is to execute them.

machine-readable Data stored so that it can be read by a machine. For example, a letter written with a word processor and stored on disk, or cataloging records stored in a computer database.

macroinstruction A single instruction to a computer, which will cause it to carry out a series of commands. Word processors such as Microsoft Word and Wordperfect offer "macro" capabilities that allow a user to type a single character or command in order to carry out a series of instructions. For example, you might create a macroinstruction so that typing Control-F caused a block of identifying bibliographic information to be taken out of the text of a document and stored in a footnote, and the footnote numbered automatically.

magnetic media Media such as tapes or disks that are coated or impregnated with magnetic particles. A computer stores information on a disk or tape by causing magnetic variations that remain in place after electrical power has been shut off. Thus, storage on the magnetic media is permanent, while storage in the computer's electronic memory is volatile, ending as soon as the power supply ends.

main entry The person, family or organization chiefly responsible for the creation of the cataloged item. Examples: the author of the book, the photographer who took the picture, the board of directors of a corporation whose deliberations are recorded in the board minutes. In some cases a donor or collector is used as the Main Entry when the collection is generally known under that name, the sources of creation are scattered and unclear, or the library was required under the conditions of the donation to give credit to the donor as the source of the materials. For example: C. C. Pierce, as the collector of the C. C. Pierce Collection, or Security Pacific National Bank, as the donor of the Security Pacific National Bank Collection. Only one Main Entry can be placed in a record. The Main Entry concept is a carry-over from card catalog files, in which the card could be placed physically in only one location. That location was determined by the Main Entry.

manuscript A handwritten or typed document.

mapping Definitions of record linkages.

MARBI Machine-Readable Bibliographic Information. The committee of librarians and representatives of the bibliographic networks that advises the Library of Congress on proposed changes to the USMARC format.

MARC Machine-Readable Cataloging. A standard format for entering bibliographical data. MARC is composed of a "family" of somewhat different formats: MARC-BK (Books), MARC-SE (Serials), MARC-MP (Maps), MARC-MU (Music), MARC-AMC or MARC-AM (Archival and Manuscripts Control), MARC-VM (Visual Materials) and MARC-CF (Computer Files, referred to formerly as MRDF or DF for Machine-Readable Data Files) in which the original file, such as a computer program or census data, exists in computer form. There is also a format for Authorities (records of standard definitions for personal and corporate names, subject terms, etc., including the source of the definition) and a tentative format for Holdings (information on the actual holdings contained within a collection, such as issues of a journal). The MARC formats are continuing to change. The current direction of change is to combine the different varieties into a single MARC format.

USMARC refers to the U.S. version of MARC, CANMARC is the Canadian variety, UKMARC is the British version, and INTERMARC is an international type. The Library of Congress publishes and has final authority over the USMARC formats. Proposals for changes are discussed with librarians and archivists through MARBI (Machine-REadable Bibliographic Information), and with the bibliographic services and other parties. The proposals are channeled through the MARC Development and Network Standards Office in the Library of Congress.

MARC-compatible A system that can send and receive MARC records with other systems.

materials Physical objects that contain information. For example: photographs, manuscripts, books, computer data files from the Census Bureau, and oral history tapes.

mathematical data area The part of a bibliographic description for maps that carries information about scale and projection.

matrix A two-dimensional array or table of information stored in rows and columns.

MB Megabyte

MDA Museum Documentation Association. The British national information management organization for museums.

media Materials that carry information.

medium The physical material on which information is recorded.

megabyte One million bytes or characters (actually 1,048,576), equivalent to about 500 typed, double-spaced pages. The original configuration of the IBM PC-XT included a hard disk drive with 10 megabytes of storage. Abbreviated as M or MB.

MEMDB Medieval and Early Modern Data Bank. A program at Rutgers University, affiliated with the Research Libraries Group (RLG), to make available information such as currency exchange rates for the years 500 to 1800.

memory A computer's facilities for storing information to be used by a computer program. The term "memory" is generally used in the sense of main memory or RAM (Random Access Memory) as the temporary storage of information for immediate program access. In contrast, the term "storage" is generally used to refer to permanent storage devices, such as a disk drive. Under the DOS operating system, a desktop computer can have 640 kilobytes of memory, and 32 megabytes of storage space available on a hard disk. A DOS program might run out of memory, and so be unable to perform a function, even though ample space is available on the disk. This might occur, for example, with a word processing program when compiling an index, performing a global search and replace, or using a spelling checker. The Pick operating system, in contrast, uses a process called "virtual memory". The operating system will make available to a program all of the computer's storage space, including disk drives, as one continuous memory. The operating system will transfer information from disk to main memory as required, without any action required of the program. The transfer operation is referred to as "paging", because data is read from disk to memory, or written back from memory to disk, one page or Frame at a time. When a program needs data not available in memory, and the data therefore must be read from disk, a Frame Fault is said to occur. This is not an error, but it does slow down an operation because of the delay required to read the data from disk. The operating system will retain data in memory for later use, until the space is required for other data. Thus, the more memory a system has, the faster the system will tend to be, after taking into account the number of users and the amount of data being processed. When using the Pick system, you might notice that a particular operation takes two or three seconds the first time it is performed, and then occurs almost instantly the next time. The difference occurs because on the first occasion, the system had to read the data from disk to memory. On the next occasion, the data was already in memory, and so was instantly accessible.

menu A list of choices displayed on a computer screen. For an example, see: "Prompt".

metadata Data about data. Data dictionaries or data models. Information in a MARC record meant to tell a computer how the data is to be interpreted.

MFBD *MARC Formats for Bibliographic Data.* A very large, loose leaf publication of the Library of Congress that serves as the authoritative reference and definition of the USMARC format. It is updated quarterly.

MHz Megahertz. One million hertz.

microcomputer A desktop or portable computer.

microform Materials such as microfilm and microfiche used to store images in a reduced size format.

micron One-millionth of a meter. Individual transistors on a computer chip are measured in microns.

microprocessor The CPU (Central Processing Unit) of a microcomputer.

microsecond One-millionth of a second.

microsoft corporation Producer of the DOS operating system, the Microsoft Word word processing program, the QuickBasic computer language, and many other computer software products.

microsoft word Computer word processing program produced by the Microsoft corporation.

millimeter One-thousandth of a meter. Abbreviated as "mm.".

millisecond One-thousandth of a second.

minicomputer Bigger than a microcomputer, smaller than a mainframe.

MIS Management Information System.

mixed notation Refers to a coding or classification system which, rather than using only numbers or only letters, uses both.

mixed responsibility A case in which the collaborators on a work perform different functions. For example, to produce a military history, one person might write the text while another supplies maps and illustrations. In contrast, in a case of shared responsibility, collaborators such as co-authors would perform the same type of function.

mnemonic Codes used for classification or for computer instructions that are designed to add memory. Thus, the Assembly Language instruction JMP causes a jump from one place in a program to another.

mode For computers, a particular method or condition of operation. For example, when editing data, if insert mode is in effect, a new character typed will be inserted into a line, pushing the other characters over to the right. In over-type mode, the new character will over-type or replace the character currently at the cursor position. For an example, see: "Insert mode".

model heading See: "Pattern heading".

modem A device used for transmitting computer data over telephone lines. The term is a contraction for MOdulator-DEModulator. The data is converted from digital to analog form and then back to digital.

MODES Museum Object Data Entry System of the Museum Documentation Association of England. A hierarchical system of cataloging created by the Museum Documentation Association of Britain and used by approximately 150 museums.

modula-2 A computer programming language developed by Niklaus Wirth, the creator of the Pascal language.

modular programming The creation of computer programs in the form of self-contained modules. For example, the portion of a database program that handles the printing of reports might constitute a separate module. If changes were needed in the reporting function, that module alone could be changed, without having to change the entire program. Modular programming makes long and complex programs easier to maintain by breaking them up into smaller units.

module A component of a computer program or application that can be replaced separately.

modulo In the Pick operating system, the number of Groups in a file. When a file is created, a Modulo (number of Groups) is assigned. Each Group usually starts out as a single Frame. This space is set aside as the Primary Allocation Space for the file. If a file were assigned a Modulo of 19, then 19 contiguous Frames of space would be set aside for the file. If more space is needed, the Pick system will attach extra Frames to the various Groups. The Modulo should be altered periodically as a file grows in size. Even though Pick will automatically attach extra Frames to the various Groups as needed, searching will not operate as efficiently with many such overflow Frames attached.

monitor The computer screen. In the Pick operating system, the term "Monitor" also refers to the underlying system supplied by Pick that communicates directly with the hardware, interpreting the user's commands in the manner required to operate a particular computer or peripheral device. The user can therefore give the same commands on many different types of computers, leaving to Pick the work of translating those commands for each computer.

monograph A work that is complete in itself, rather than part of a series. For example, a book in contrast to an issue of a journal.

morgue A reference collection maintained by a newspaper. The original meaning of the term expanded from the practice of storing biographical information about prominent individuals in preparation for writing their obituaries.

most significant digit In a numbering system, the digit with the greatest weight. Thus for the number 127, 1 is the most significant digit, and 7 is the least significant digit.

MP Maps. MARC-MP is the MARC format for maps. See "MARC".

MRDF Formerly Machine-Readable Data Files. Now CF for Computer Files. MARC-CF is the MARC Format for files, such as computer software or census data, which exist in their original form on a computer. See "MARC".

MS-DOS Microsoft Disk Operating System. The standard operating system for the IBM PC, supplied by Microsoft corporation. Usually referred to just as DOS.

MU Music. MARC-MU is the MARC format for music. See "MARC".

multimedia item A group of related materials, intended to be used together, in which no one form of material is dominant. Also known as a kit.

multipart item A monograph that is intended to be complete in a limited number of separate parts.

multiplexor A device that allows several computer communication lines to share a single channel.

multi-tasking The computer performs more than one task at a time. For example, you might ask to have a long report printed, and while the computer is printing the report, you also use the computer to enter and edit data. Technically, the computer might not be performing true multi-tasking, which is carrying out the two tasks simultaneously, but rather switching back and forth rapidly between the tasks.

multi-user system An operating system, such as Pick or UNIX, designed to be used by more than one operator at the same time. A single computer acts as the host. Users work at terminals connected to the host computer. Pick is designed specifically as a multi-user database management system. Any repository, even a small one, will require access to its bibliographic database by more than one person at a time. It is much easier and cheaper to share database information with a system designed for that purpose than to try to create a network among machines that were designed to operate independently. Compare with: "Network". Note that a terminal emulation program will allow a stand-alone computer, such as the IBM PC, to act as a terminal in a multi-user system.

multi-values Individual values within a field, in a computer database record. In the Pick database system, individual values in a field, such as the names of different persons in a field for SUBJECTS-PERSONS, can be searched and handled as separate data elements.

MUMPS A computer programming language designed for handling medical records, and possessing many database management facilities. The name is an acronym for Massachusetts General Hospital Utility Multi-Programming System.

NACO Name Authority Cooperative. Member institutions contribute records to the Library of Congress Name Authority File.

NAGARA National Association of Government Archives and Records Administrators.

NAL National Agricultural Library.

name authority file An Authority File of personal, organizational, or geographical names. An individual record in the file will contain the approved form of name to be used in cataloging, as well as cross-references to variant forms and documentation for the decision of which form to employ. A corporate name authority record for an organization will include a history of the name changes of that organization, and perhaps also linking references to superior, subordinate, and related organizational units. A name authority record for a person will include brief biographical information. For example, it will be valuable for the cataloger trying to date a photograph to have a ready reference to the years when the photographer was plying his trade.

name-title entry An access point for a bibliographic record, consisting of a combination of the name of the creator of a work and the title of the work. Most searches for books are conducted on the basis of author's name and book title.

NAMID National Moving Image Database.

nanometer One-billionth of a meter.

nanosecond One-billionth of a second. Abbreviated as "ns".

NAPA National Academy of Public Administration.

NARA National Archives and Records Administration. Generally referred to by non-archivists simply as the National Archives.

national-level bibliographic record A record that meets national standards in regard to format and descriptive practices, and which therefore can be exchanged with other institutions who follow those same standards.

national union catalog symbol The code that uniquely identifies each library sending records for inclusion in the National Union Catalog. The NUC symbol appears in MARC field 040 and elsewhere to identify the agency that created the record. To obtain a symbol, write to: Library of Congress, Catalog Management and Publications Division, Symbols of American Libraries. Washington, DC 20540.

natural language interface A computer facility for allowing humans to search a database by entering search requests in normal, everyday language, rather than requiring the searcher to adopt a more limited and structured grammar and vocabulary. Complete natural language searching is difficult to achieve in practice, because of the many ambiguities of normal language. The Pick database system uses a syntax that is fairly close to natural language. The system also allows you to create as many synonyms as you want for any of the terms used in a search request, and to employ empty terms that are not necessary for the request, but help to put the request in the form of a complete sentence. For example, you could ask for database records pertaining to ships with either of the following statements:

```
SELECT ITEMS WITH SUBJECTS = "Ships"
```

or:

```
GET FROM THE ITEMS FILE THE RECORDS FOR THE SUBJECT OF "Ships"
```

An alternative to entering search statements is to present the user with a menu of options.

NCPH National Council on Public History.

network A system for sharing information among independent organizations or computers. A group of libraries and archives may participate in a bibliographic network to share information about their holdings.

network A local area network refers to the sharing of information among desktop machines like the IBM PC, which were designed to operate independently. For more information, see: "Local Area Network". Compare with: "Multi-user system".

newsprint A low cost paper made of pulp and used for newspapers. Newsprint discolors and deteriorates very quickly.

NFAIS National Federation of Abstracting and Information Services.

NHPRC National Historical Publications and Records Commission.

NIDS National Inventory of Documentary Sources. A compilation of finding aids, printed on microfiche. Refer to the bibliography.

NISO National Information Standards Organization. NISO is accredited by the American National Standards Institute (ANSI) as the standards agency for libraries, information science and publishing. NISO is thus the library technical standards agency for the United States. Most of the technical standards embodied in the MARC (Machine-Readable Cataloging) format derive from NISO. Technical standards that carry a designation "Z39" originated with NISO, which was previously known as ANSI Committee Z39. ANSI Z39.2-1985 is the American National Standard for Bibliographic Information Interchange. Released in 1971, it provides the basic structure for a MARC record.

NIST National Institute of Standards and Technology. Formerly the National Bureau of Standards.

NISTF National Information Systems Task Force. A group that represented the Society of American Archivists in the creation of the MARC-AMC (Archives and Manuscript Control) format. David Bearman, now editor of the *Archival Informatics Newsletter,* was director of the task force. The reports produced have been published by the SAA as the *NISTF Papers,* and are listed in the Bibliography under Bearman.

nitrate film Photographic film made from a base of cellulose nitrate. It is much more flammable and subject to deterioration than the safety film that began to replace it in the 1930s.

NLA National Library of Australia.

NLC National Library of Canada.

NLM National Library of Medicine.

node A communications junction.

nomenclature *The Revised Nomenclature for Museum Cataloging,* published by the American Association for State and Local History. For more information, look in the Bibliography.

nonbook materials Audiovisual materials.

noncurrent records Inactive records. Records not required for the contact of current business, which may therefore be transferred from the primary place of business to an archival repository.

nonfiling characters Characters at the beginning of a title, to be ignored when sorting a list of titles in alphabetical order. The character count should be placed in the Filing Indicator Sub-Field provided by the MARC format. For more information, see: "Filing Indicator".)

nonfiling element An element in a name or title, such as the article "the", which will be ignored when sorting a list of titles into alphabetical order.

nonprint materials Audiovisual materials.

normal form, third Every field in the database record is dependent on the Record-ID, on the whole ID, and only on the ID. As a simple example, a cataloging record for a book would not include any information about the publisher other than the name. Information that is logically dependent on the publisher, such as the address, telephone number, etc., would be stored in a separate PUBLISHERS file, rather than repeated for every book the company published. It would be inefficient to repeat the same information for every title, especially considering that if the publisher changed location, the information would have to be changed in every record where it appeared.

normalization The process of taking a complex body of information and placing it in a series of simple, stable structures organized according to third normal form. Also, the process of taking a piece of data from the user and converting it into a stable and predictable form. For example, a computer database system might be able to accept date information from users in a variety of formats, but store the information in a single format that will allow reliable searching and sorting on date fields. Without such normalization, if a cataloger described a document as having been created on "07/04/1776", a searcher would not be able to find the document by asking for "July 4, 1776".

note Explanatory information for a bibliographical entry, such as a description of the contents of a work or the circumstances of its creation. Such information will not fit into the more specific and structured fields such as Author, Title, etc. Because a note field is less specific and structured, it will be more difficult to conduct searches on it. Avoid the temptation to throw into note fields information that should instead be stored in a more standardized format.

NOTIS Northwestern On-line Technical Information System. A library automation system created by Northwestern University.

NT Narrower term. Indicates more specific terms one level down in a hierarchy from the defined term. Used in a thesaurus such as Library of Congress Subject Headings. For example:

Domestic animals
  NT Dogs
    Horses

NTIS National Technical Information Service.

NUC National Union Catalog.

NUC code See: "National Union Catalog Symbol".

NUCMC National Union Catalog of Manuscript Collections. The version of the NUC for archives, produced by the Manuscripts Section of the Special Materials Cataloging Division in the Library of Congress.

NUC symbol See: "National Union Catalog Symbol".

null A field in a database record might be left empty or null either because the appropriate value is unknown, such as in the case of a photograph when the name of the photographer is not known, or because no value would be applicable in the particular case.

numeric code A code that uses only numbers. If a code is designated as Numeric, you cannot use letters or special characters such as a dash or asterisk. The code might or might not permit the use of a period or decimal point. Compare with: "Alphabetic code", "Alphanumeric code".

OAH Organization of American Historians.

object code A computer program after compilation, in the machine language of the computer. For more information, see: "Compiler".

OCLC Online Computer Library Center, formerly the Ohio College Library Center. The largest of the on-line bibliographic services. Dial-access users can connect with OCLC via CompuServe. See "Bibliographic Services".

OCR Optical Character Recognition. The reading of printed or typed characters by a computer.

OEM Original Equipment Manufacturer

office of origin The organization that originally created the archival records.

official name The legal name of an organization.

offline Equipment not in direct communication with the computer. Compare with: "On-line".

offset Relative position, established from a starting point. Position 0 (zero) in a string is by definition the first position, because it has a zero offset from the beginning. Position 1 has an offset of 1 from the beginning, thus position 1 is actually the second character. When calculating position, you must always know if the count is to begin at 0 or 1. This difference is a frequent source of confusion.

omni catalog A single catalog maintained for different types of materials, such as manuscripts, photographs, and books, rather than creating a separate catalog for each format.

online An interactive system in which the user enters or receives data in direct communication with the computer storing the data, rather than writing the data or request offline for later batch processing.

online catalog A bibliographic catalog accessed via computer terminals.

online cataloging The cataloger is in direct communication with the computer database into which he or she is entering new information. The advantage of online cataloging is that the information already in the database can be checked for consistency with the new information that is being entered. Such checking might take the form of looking up records that deal with the same subjects, or the automatic use of Authority Files to maintain a Controlled Vocabulary in the fields that are crucial for searching.

OPAC Online Public Access Catalog. A bibliographic catalog presented to users of a library or other repository via computer terminals.

open catalog A catalog with no restriction on the entry of new records, as compared to a closed catalog or a frozen catalog into which new records are not entered, most often because the old manual catalog is being replaced with a new computerized system.

open entry A bibliographic entry for which the information is incomplete, with additional information to be entered later. Also, the item itself might not be complete, as in the case of an incomplete set of journals.

operand The computer data to be operated upon.

operating system The software that handles the overall management of the computer, including the running of individual programs. Thus on the IBM PC-XT computer, you might use the DOS operating system (Microsoft-Disk Operating System), and under that system you would run an individual program such as Word or R:base. Or you could use the Pick operating system, and under that system run individual programs such as the Jet word processor or the History Database program. An operating system provides various facilities that are used by the individual program to operate the printer, locate a file on the disk, accept input from the keyboard, etc. In effect, the program asks the system, "Please get this file for me" or "Please tell me which keys have been pressed on the keyboard". It would be much more difficult if a program had to perform every chore itself, down to the level of the bare machinery. The Pick system is intended specifically for database management, and provides extensive facilities for database management tasks. If an individual program does not handle a given task, the user can probably accomplish it directly at the operating system level. Pick allows the use of variable length fields without sacrificing any of the database program facilities for changing a field or a database structure after information has been entered.

operation The carrying out of a single defined action. A complete task may include several operations.

optical disk A high-density storage device that uses laser beams to write and read the information.

oral history A tape or transcript of an interview that was conducted for the purpose of collecting historical information,

organization file A special library's collection of information about its host organization.

original cataloging A repository's creation of an original cataloging record. In contrast, in the case of copy cataloging, the repository uses an already-existing record, which the repository can then edit.

original order The order in which materials were originally created or kept. The order can provide information about the materials. For example, you can presume certain information about photos kept together in a family scrapbook. The photographs might have much less informational value for researchers if taken out of the scrapbook and stored individually. If it is necessary to remove the photos, perhaps for preservation purposes, information about their original order should be entered into the cataloging record. Thus, it will be possible to reproduce the original order of the family scrapbook from the computer database. Much of the value of the element of original order depends on determining the organizing principle under which the materials were placed together, and whether the principle was applied consistently. It is easy to be lured into mistakes of identification by apparently similar photos appearing together in a folder, but which were actually taken at different times and places.

orphans (cataloging) In a database or catalog, orphans are references to items that do not exist, at least not under the name supplied in the reference. For example, a list of database records includes the Record-ID "Smith, Mary", but there is no record for Mary Smith in the database. Mary might have moved out of town, and so her record was deleted, or she may have changed her name. In either case, the reference is out of date. The "mother record" in the database is gone, and so the reference is an orphan. A database program should update automatically any references contained in indexes. Do not bury references to specific Record-IDs in long note fields, where the references cannot easily be updated automatically. The reference will be orphaned if the Record-ID is changed.

orphans (printing) In printing terminology, an orphan is created when the first line of a new paragraph is printed by itself at the bottom of a page, and thus separated from the remainder of the paragraph. See also: "Widows".

OS/2 Operating System 2. The operating system that IBM intends as the successor to DOS, to supply capabilities that the earlier system lacks.

other title information Look for title variations under "Title".

output Data sent from a computer out to devices such as the screen or printer.

overflow In the Pick operating system, overflow occurs when the data exceeds the capacity of the Group originally allocated to store it. No error occurs because Pick automatically takes a spare Frame from overflow space and attaches it to the Group.

oversize An item, such as a book or photograph, that is too big to fit into its normal shelving location. A real pain in the neck for all concerned.

over-type mode When typing on a computer, a new character typed will replace any character currently at the cursor position. Compare with: "Insert mode".

packet A block of data, sent from one communications device to another.

pagination The marking of each page of a document in order. In contrast, in the case of foliation, only the recto (right-hand side) of the pages are numbered.

paging The transfer of information between disk and memory in a computer operating system such as Pick, which employs a Virtual Memory process. For more information, look under: "Memory".

papers A natural accumulation of personal and family materials, in contrast to the administrative records of an agency.

parallel port A communications device that is most often used to send data from a computer to a printer. A Parallel Port sends bits of data grouped together and transmitted simultaneously, in parallel. Whereas a Serial Port would send eight bits of data one at a time, a Parallel Port will send all eight bits at once, synchronized in parallel with each other over eight separate lines.

parallel title Look for title variations under "Title".

parameter An operational limit or guide used when running a computer program. For example, for each field that is to be displayed for entry and editing on a data entry screen, the program will read in a series of stored parameters for the name of the field, the position of the field on the screen, the type of data to be stored, whether the entries should be checked against Authority Files, and other guides and constraints. Because of the use of parameters, which are stored separately from the computer program, the same database program can be used for many different kinds of data. To switch from storing bibliographic records to storing the names and addresses of volunteers, you do not have to change the program. You only need to give the program a new set of parameters.

parity checking Automatic error detection on a computer. If you are using an IBM PC and the "Parity check" message appears, it means that the computer has detected an error, perhaps because of the faulty operation of a memory chip. Write down the entire message, which will indicate which chip went bad, and call the dealer who sold you the equipment.

part A subordinate unit of a bibliographic item. In the case of books, generally a volume.

partition A hard disk can be divided into several separate partitions, with a different operating system in each partition. Thus, an IBM-compatible desktop computer's hard disk can easily hold separate partitions for the DOS and Pick operating systems. The user can jump back and forth between the two partitions and operating systems with a single command. Data can easily be transferred between partitions, such as from a Pick database to DOS word processor, or in the other direction.

pascal A computer programming language created in 1971 by Professor Niklaus Wirth at the Federal Institute of Technology in Zurich to foster the use of structured programming techniques.

PASCAL An acronym for *Programme Appliqué à la Selection et la Compilation Automatique de la Literature.* A classification system.

pass A complete cycle in processing data. For example, a sequential search makes a complete pass through the database.

password A password might be required in order to gain access to a multiuser system.

patron The user of a library or archival center.

pattern headings Headings given as examples for the use of subdivisions with Library of Congress Subject Headings. The editors of LCSH, rather than listing every applicable subdivision under each subject heading, have provided Pattern Headings. For example, to find the subdivisions applicable to "Petroleum industry and trade," first look under that term, and then look under the Pattern Headings assigned for industries, which are "Construction industry" and "Retail trade". If the petroleum industry activity concerned is the drilling of oil wells, construction headings will probably be more relevant. If the activity shown is the operation of a gas station, "Retail trade" will come closer to the mark.

PBX Private Branch Exchange.

PC Personal Computer. Generally refers to the IBM PC.

PC-DOS Personal Computer Disk Operating System. The standard operating system for the IBM PC, supplied by Microsoft corporation. Usually referred to just as DOS.

period subdivision See: "Chronological subdivision".

periodical A serial publication appearing at regular intervals and intended to continue indefinitely. Newspapers and conference proceedings are not classed as periodicals.

peripheral Equipment, such as a printer, used in conjunction with a computer system.

personal name reference The MARC format includes several fields in which personal names are entered. For example, MARC field 600 (Subject Added Entry—Personal Name) would be used for the names of individuals who in some sense are the subjects of the materials, such as people appearing in a photograph or described in a diary. Animals that have been given names might also appear in any of the MARC personal name fields. Thus, Rin Tin Tin and Lassie can have their own entries.

personal papers Private documents accumulated by an individual.

phantom process See: "Background process".

phoenix A mythological bird that arose from its own ashes. The term is used to refer to something that is entirely reborn. A Phoenix Schedule in the Dewey Decimal Classification system is a set of numbers that has been completely reassigned to carry new meanings.

photographers biography file A file of the names and dates of approximately 20,000 photographers, with cross references for different forms of the photographer's name. The file is produced by the International Museum of Photography at the George Eastman House, and is distributed by Light Impressions. The file can be purchased on microfiche or accessed on-line by modem.

physical As distinct from logical. The underlying physical reality of a computer database system and how it stores data. The physical reality can be very different from the logical perception of the system by its users.

physical description area The portion of a bibliographic entry devoted to describing the physical item. Includes information such as the dimensions, the number of units, and the specific material designation.

pica-size A type face size of 10-pitch, 12-point, which equals ten characters per inch on a line and six lines per inch down the page.

pick Pick Operating System. A computer operating system intended for database management. Created by Dick Pick and available from Pick Systems of Irvine, California. See: "Operating System".

picosecond One-trillionth of a second. Abbreviated as "ps".

pitch A horizontal measurement for type faces, equal to the number of characters that will fit side-by-side along one inch in line. The higher the pitch number, the smaller the characters. The most common type face size is 10-pitch, 12-point. Fixed-pitch type faces or fonts such as Pica and Courier always print the same number of characters per inch, regardless of whether the character is a fat one like "w" or a thin one like "i". Proportional-pitch type faces such as Times-Roman and Helvetica print a variable number of characters per inch.

PL/1 Programming Language One. A computer programming language developed by IBM.

plate A leaf containing one or more illustrations, such as photographs or drawings, and that is not numbered consecutively with the pages of the book.

point A vertical measurement for type faces, equal to 1/72 of an inch. The higher the point number, the larger the characters. The most common type face size is 10-pitch, 12-point. A 12-point type face will print six lines per inch down the page (12/72 = 1/6).

pointer For a computer database, an item that points to another item. For example, an index file for subjects contains pointers to the records that contain given subject terms. The pointer will probably take the form of a Record-ID, which will be used to retrieve a record. In this case the pointer is symbolic, because it does not contain the actual physical address of the record on the disk. The Pick operating system will use the Record-ID to determine the actual address of the record.

political qualifier See: "Jurisdictional qualifier".

port A computer communications channel used to send or receive information to or from another computer, a printer, a mouse, or another device. For more information, see: "Parallel Port" and "Serial Port". The term can also be used as a verb, referring to the adaptation of a software system to run on a different machine. Thus, the Pick operating system has been ported onto a great variety of different computers.

portable 1. A computer that can be carried by hand from one place to another. 2. Reference to a computer program that can be used on different machines.

portability The ease with which a computer program or operating system can be used on a different machine. If you are going to store information that is permanent in nature, such as historical or bibliographic data, the portability of the program and operating system that you intend to use is an important consideration. As computer technology continues to change, you will want to move your data from one machine to another. Although the data could be moved to a new program and operating system, it will be most convenient if the original program and operating system are portable to the new machine.

postcoordination To combine single-term headings in a search statement. For example, the searcher might ask for materials about factories in Dallas with a search statement such as:

```
SELECT ITEMS WITH SUBJECTS = "Factories" AND CITY = "Dallas"
```

See also: "Precoordination".

power loss Sudden power loss to a computer system should be avoided. Sudden power loss to a database program can cause the database to become corrupted. As explained above, a database consists of structured information, in which a file is divided into records and each record is divided into fields. If a database management system program is suddenly interrupted while the system is writing new or changed data out to the disk for permanent storage, the dividing lines between records, fields, or other elements of information might not be put in place properly. The data on disk will thereby become meaningless to the system. For the Pick operating system, this type of disaster is called a Group Format Error, and there are means available to fix the error or to limit the damage. On other systems the entire database might be worthless. If your electrical system is subject to power outages, avoid sudden power loss with an Uninterruptible Power Supply (UPS).

PRECIS PREserved Context Index System developed for the British National Bibliography. Under PRECIS, the various facets of the subject analysis are synthesized into a single long heading, with role operators used to indicate the relationships between the different terms in the heading. (For a detailed discussion of PRECIS, see: Chan, *Cataloging and Classification,* pages 187-206.)

precision When searching a database, the proportion of relevant documents among those retrieved by a search. A precision rating of 100 per cent would indicate that all of the materials retrieved were relevant. Note that search strategies most often involve a choice between high Precision and high Recall.

precoordination The attempt to represent complex subjects with single headings, by combining separate elements in the heading. For example, to find materials about factories in Dallas you would use a geographical subdivision under the Library of Congress Subject Heading. The search statement might be:

SELECT ITEMS WITH SUBJECTS = "Factories—Dallas (Texas)"

See also: "Postcoordination".

predominance The Rule of Predominance applied by the Library of Congress is 80 percent. Thus, for a particular variant of a personal name to be considered predominant, it must occur in 80 percent of the cases in which the name appears.

predominant name The form of a personal or organizational name that appears most frequently. The use of a name employed in the works of that individual or organization is preferred over a name used by other sources. If no name is judged to be predominant, then the most complete name available should be used. For example, if a person in his own writings never used his middle name, his name without the middle portion would be considered the predominant name. The form of name with the middle portion included would be the full name, which might also be recorded elsewhere in the cataloging record.

preface Remarks that explain the origin or purpose of a book, written by the author. When written by someone other than the author, referred to as a foreword.

PRIMA Program for Research Information MAnagement. An RLIN project to record and make available to researchers non-bibliographic data, such as statistical data in tabular form.

primary sources Original sources, created at the time of the event by the individual or organization. In contrast, secondary sources are interpretations. Thus a letter from Cardinal Richelieu to King Louis XIII is a primary source for a study of the period. A biography of the cardinal is a secondary source.

printer The device that takes output from the computer and prints the information on paper. Popular types of printers include dot matrix, ink jet, laser, and thermal.

dot matrix printer A printer whose characters are composed of a matrix of dots. A 5 x 7 dot matrix printer will form characters from a grid of five dots across times seven dots high. Dot matrix printers tends to be cheap, reliable, and noisy.

ink jet printer A very quiet printer, which squirts ink onto the page.

laser printer A high-quality, high-speed printer that uses the same type of technology found in copying machines. The amount of noise produced is the same as for a copying machine. Also like a copying machine, the printer uses a toner cartridge rather than an ink ribbon. Laser printers such as the Hewlett-Packard Laser Jet have speeds of eight pages per minute and offer many different type styles.

thermal printer A printer that uses heat, either to form an image on special thermal paper, or to transfer ink from a thermal ribbon onto regular paper. Portable, battery-operated printers most often use thermal technology. Thermal paper tends to produce a very poor image, not suitable for any purpose other than personal note-taking. Thermal ribbons with regular paper produce a better image, but one that is still inferior to other types of printers.

printout Computer output printed on paper.

private papers See: "Personal papers".

proc A Batch file in the Pick operating system. Proc is a Batch programming language that can be used to display a menu or start up a series of programs after a user has logged onto his Account. A user without programming experience might create a simple Proc to perform a repetitive series of operations.

procedural language A computer programming language that carries out tasks by means of a series of defined steps. The Pick operating system provides a procedural language, Pick Basic, for programming purposes. Pick also provides a non-procedural language or processor, called Access, to allow a user to make inquiries of a database without having to use a program.

processing The work of making library or archival materials available for use. Processing includes sorting, labeling, and shelving the materials.

processor A device or system that performs operations on data. The brains of a computer is the CPU (Central Processing Unit). The term processor can also refer to software. A compiler processes source code written by a programmer to produce object code which can be understood by a machine. An operating system can include processors for different purposes. Under the Pick operating system, the Access processor can be used to search for data and to present the data in various report formats.

procomm A classic shareware communications program, which has been greatly improved and released commercially for $75. ProComm can be used for terminal emulation, to hook an IBM PC into a Pick multi-user system. From Datastorm Technologies, Inc.

program A series of instructions on a computer.

program maintenance Making necessary changes and correcting errors ("bugs") in a computer program.

programming The writing of computer programs.

PROM Programmable Read-Only Memory. Computer memory that can be programmed or changed only by the use of a special device, as contrasted with the computer's active or working memory that can be changed by the computer's own CPU (Central Processing Unit).

prompt A message on the computer screen requesting information from the user. For example, a user might be prompted to make a selection from a menu of numbered choices by the prompt message "Pick a number", followed by a colon and the flashing cursor, indicated here by a boldface underline character:

```
1. Add new data
2. Edit old data
3. Quit

Pick a number:
```

On a data entry form, the field name for each field is most often used as the prompt message. For example, a data entry form might include a field for the name of the cataloger. The cataloger would be prompted for his or her name as follows:

```
CATALOGER: __
```

protocol A set of conventions for communication between devices.

provenance History of the custody of the materials. The development and recording of provenance information, including an administrative history of each organization that has created or maintained the records in a collection. Provenance is an integral part of archival description. Archival description differs in this manner from bibliographic descriptions of published works, which are normally limited to information about the item in hand.

Provenance is generally of no interest for books or magazines, but in the case of a collection of papers or photos, the various owners of the materials might have added to or subtracted from the collection and might have arranged it in various ways that indicate the owner's attitudes toward or usage of the materials. The grouping of items together by the original owner can also provide clues that will help a future cataloger identify some of the items, therefore the information that certain items were originally grouped together should be preserved in the cataloging records, even if it is necessary to separate the items for preservation or storage purposes. If the materials are ever to be used as legal evidence, a thorough tracing of their provenance will be required. See also: *"Respect des fonds"*.

pure notation A system of codes that uses either letters or numbers, but not both.

QBE Query By Example.

qualified heading A heading that includes a qualifying term. The qualifier is generally enclosed in parentheses. For example: "New York (State)", and "Bands (Music)". Among Library of Congress Subject Headings, qualifiers distinguish "Drill (Agricultural implement)" from "Drill (not military)", used for activities such as baton twirling and school marching bands, and finally from "Drill and minor tactics", which would include military parade ground drill.

query A search request made of a computer database.

query by example (QBE) To make a search request of a computer database by filling out a blank data entry form. Into the blank space for each field, you would enter the terms that you were looking for in that field. For example, to find all photos of dairy farming in a photo database, in the Subjects field you would enter the term "Dairy farming".

queue A waiting line. Several reports can be sent at the same time to the printer spooler of the Pick operating system. The first report will go directly to a printer. If only one printer is available, the other reports will be placed in a queue, to be acted upon in turn.

RAM Random Access Memory.

random access See: "Direct access".

RBGENR *Genre Terms: A Thesaurus for Use in Rare Book and Special Collections Cataloguing.* A list of terms used in MARC field 655: "Genre/Form Heading". Produced by the Association of College and Research Libraries.

read To retrieve information from a computer storage device. In a computer database system, the system will read database records from the disk as the records are needed.

read-only memory (ROM) Computer memory that is permanently programmed with frequently-used instructions required for the machine to operate. The contents of ROM cannot be changed, in contrast with Random Access Memory (RAM), also called Direct Access Memory, which can be used to enter and edit new data.

read-write head The device used to read data from and to write data to a tape or disk. The access time required to retrieve information from a computer will depend partly on the time required to position the read-write head to the correct position on the disk.

real time system An interactive system, in contrast to a batch processing system. For example, in an interactive system, to change a database record, you would edit the record directly on the computer screen, and the change would take effect almost immediately. In a batch processing system, you would write out a series of changes, which would take place at some later time.

realia Actual objects, whether human-created artefacts or natural specimens, as distinguished from replicas.

recall When searching a database, the proportion of relevant materials retrieved to the total number of relevant items contained in the database. A Recall rating of 100 percent would indicate that every relevant piece of information in the database had been found. Note that search strategies generally involve a choice between high Recall and high Precision.

RECON Retrospective Conversion, such as of manual records to a computer system.

record A record is the principal unit of information in a database. A record is divided into fields that contain information such as the Entry Date, Title, Subjects, etc. Within a given file, each record will have the same format with regard to the fields it contains.

record group A group of archival records that share a common origin and are maintained and described as a unit.

record delimiter The delimiter used internally by a system to mark off separate records within a database. The average user will have no reason to be aware of how Record Delimiters are used.

pick record delimiter ASCII 255. If the DUMP command is used to display a Pick Frame, the Record Delimiter will appear as the underline character: "__". The delimiter appears at the end of each record. A user should never be allowed to enter ASCII 255 as data. The data input program should filter out any such entry. Pick manuals generally refer to the Record Delimiter as the Segment Mark.

MARC record delimiter ASCII 29. The delimiter occurs at the end of each record.

record-ID The unique identifier of a particular cataloging Record. A Record will always have one, and only one, Record-ID, which will not be repeated elsewhere in the database. The Record-ID is also known as the Item-ID or Control number, and should be placed in MARC field 001 (Control number). For the distinction between Record-ID and Accession number see the definition for "Accession number".

record integrity The requirement that a bibliographic record must be self-explanatory and complete in itself, rather than relying upon links with other records to supply necessary information.

records Information maintained by an organization in the course of performing its functions. Administrative records are distinguished from "Papers" or "Personal Papers" accumulated by a family or an individual.

record series See: "Series".

record size The total size of all the fields and delimiters in a database record. Some computer database management systems will limit the maximum allowed size of a record. Under R:base 5000, a record could contain no more than 1530 characters. In older versions of Pick, a record was limited to 32,267 characters. Newer versions of Pick allow unlimited record size. Record size can also be limited by the rules of the format employed, or by the network to which the record will be sent. The maximum length of a MARC format record is 99,999 characters. The maximum length of a MARC format record on OCLC (Online Computer Library Center) is 4,000 characters.

record status A single character in position 5 of the USMARC Leader. A new record is indicated by "n", a changed record by "c" and a deleted record by "d".

record terminator See: "Record Delimiter".

records management Management of the process of creating, using, maintaining, retrieving, and disposing of administrative records. The volume of records created by business and governmental organizations, and the high cost of storing all of these records in the offices where they were created, has put a premium on the records management function of archives. Noncurrent records, which are not needed for the day-to-day transaction of business, can be stored much more efficiently and economically in a records center or archival center.

recto The right-hand page of a book. The side of a printed sheet that you would normally read first.

reduction ratio The ratio of the original size of an image to the size to which it has been reduced, generally for storage on microfilm or microfiche. A common ratio is 18X, indicating that if the original image was eighteen inches in length, the reduced image is one inch in length.

reference In a list of subject headings or authority records, a reference from one heading to another. Among Library of Congress Subject Headings, a "USE" reference would point from a term that is not to be used to the term that is to be used instead. Thus, under "Cantaloupe" you find the reference "USE Muskmelon".

referential integrity For every reference, the item referenced must actually exist under the name indicated. In the Library of Congress Subject Headings under "Cantaloupe", you will find the reference "USE Muskmelon". If there were no entry under "Muskmelon", the reference would be an orphan.

regional catalog A union catalog of the collections of repositories in a particular geographical area. Also called a regional union catalog.

register A list of events or documents kept in the order in which they occur or are received. For example, a hotel register lists the guests who stayed there in the order that they arrived, and might also include the date and time of arrival. An archival center might use a register of materials processed as a finding aid. For computers, a register refers to an area of memory in the CPU (Central Processing Unit) for handling data, usually in groups of one, two, or four bytes at a time.

registry principle Same as *respect des fonds*.

related body An organization that is related to another organization by some tie other than that of subordination within a hierarchy. For example, an alumni association is related to a university.

related materials Materials that are related to the materials in hand by subject content but not by provenance.

relation In a computer database, a file containing database records. A Relation is a two-dimensional table or array. The Relation contains records, each of which contain an identical number of fields.

relational database system A relational database system has the ability to relate together information from different Relations or tables (files). Relational capabilities are an essential part of database management. For example, collection-level and item-level records can be related to provide complete bibliographical information for an item, without the need to repeat the information for each item entered. The information from the Collections level will be called up automatically when information on the item is printed or displayed on the computer screen. Relational capabilities also aid in the consistency of description. For example, when entering personal names into a database record, the system will refer to an Authority File for personal names, and warn if any names are entered which do not already appear in the Authority File.

The first formal definition of the relational database model was set forth by Edgar F. Codd in "A Relational Model of Data for Large Shared Data Banks," in *Communications of the Association for Computing Machinery,* Volume 13, Number 6 (June 1970). Codd defined a relational database as a database that is perceived by the user as a collection of tables, with each table consisting of a set of rows. His Twelve Rules for Database Design defined the abilities that a relational database program should have. Each individual database program that describes itself as relational abides by those rules to a greater or lesser degree.

relative location A method for classifying and arranging items in a repository so that the location of each item is defined in terms of position relative to other items, rather than designating for each item a permanent, absolute location. For example, a photograph is designated as Item number 13, within Collection number 2. The collections, and the items within collections, are stored in numerical sequence. The Dewey Decimal Classification system and the Library of Congress Classification system are both systems of Relative Location. A system of Relative Location is much more easily adaptable to change than the alternative method of Fixed Location.

relator For cataloging, a term that specifies the relationship between a person or organization and the material cataloged. For example: author, collector, donor, editor, interviewee, interviewer, photographer, translator.

relator code A three-letter code specifying the relationship between the person or organization and the item cataloged. The codes are taken from the Library of Congress publication, *USMARC Codes for Relators, Sources, Description Conventions.* For example, the Relator Code for a photographer is "pht". There is no Relator Code for an author. The closest code is "org" for originator.

remote access Communication with a computer from a distance, perhaps over telephone lines via a modem.

replevin The recovery of property by an institution claiming ownership. For example, an official state archives might claim ownership of the records of state officials, if those records are placed in other repositories.

report Data from a computer database, printed or displayed in a report format, with identifying information such as explanatory field names that will help the user or patron to understand the meaning of the data. Data that is simply dumped onto the screen or paper will not be intelligible to anyone except the person who entered it.

repository A place where archives, records, or manuscripts are kept.

respect des fonds Respect for the source. Respect for the original order and arrangement of a body of materials, and for the unity and uniqueness of the materials deriving from a single source. In archival usage, the records originating from a particular office or other source will be kept together, and the original order of the materials will be preserved. In standard library practice, the materials would be combined with materials from other sources, and then arranged by subject or other classification scheme. Computer cataloging methods offer the potential for preserving information on the original order and source of the materials, while also offering access by subject and other criteria. [See also: "Provenance".]

repeatability The MARC Format for each field and sub-field includes the designation "R" if that field or sub-field can be repeated, and "NR" if repetition is not allowed. For example, a record can include only one Main Entry (fields 1xx), but it can contain many different Subject Added Entries (fields 6xx).

RI Rule Interpretations See: "LCRI".

RISC Reduced Instruction Set Chip computer. The CPU (Central Processing Unit) of the computer is designed with fewer different instructions. The reduced set of instructions is run more efficiently at a greater speed.

RLG Research Libraries Group. The RLG is based at Stanford University, and created RLIN.

RLIN Research Libraries Information Network. The on-line bibliographic service of the RLG. See "Bibliographic Services".

role operators Symbols that indicate relationships between terms.

ROM Read-Only Memory.

romanization Conversion of letters not written in the roman alphabet to a roman alphabet form.

root directory In the DOS operating system, the main directory on a disk, before any subdirectories (also called directories) have been created. The root directory will be referred to with a backslash and no following name. Thus the root directory of the disk in disk drive "C" would be "C:\". The subdirectory named "Word" on the same disk would be referred to as "C:\Word".

RPG Report Program Generator. A computer language used to create reports.

RS-232C A set of industry standard specifications for communication through a Serial Port.

RT Related term. Indicates terms that are closely related to the term defined, but that are not in a hierarchy above or below the defined term. Used in a thesaurus such as Library of Congress Subject Headings. For example:

Clothing and dress
RT Costume
Fashion

RT IBM RT computer. A RISC (Reduced Instruction Set Chip) computer that will support sixty-four users running the Pick operating system. The machine will also run Pick and UNIX concurrently, offering the advantages of both systems.

running head A repetition of the title of a work, placed at the top of each page. Other information such as chapter, date, author, and page number can also be included.

SAA Society of American Archivists.

SAA Systems Applications Architecture. IBM's attempt to standardize applications across many different hardware platforms. The Common User Access component of SAA sets standards for screen appearance and keyboard use. For example, the F1 key would always invoke Help information. The Common Programming Interface component defines programming tools such as languages and interfaces to databases. The Common Communications Support element defines the connections between applications, systems, networks, and terminals. Most of the communications component is taken from the already-existing Systems Network Architecture (SNA). Common Applications are those applications that conform to the user access, programming interface, and communications components of SAA.

safety film A photographic film, based on cellulose acetate, that is not as flammable as nitrate film.

scale For maps, the ratio of the distance between two points on a document with the distance between the corresponding two points on the ground.

scope and contents note In a MARC record, a summary of the scope and contents of the described materials.

scope note A note under a Library of Congress Subject Heading to indicate the intended use of the term. For example, the scope note under the heading "Dairy farming" indicates that this term applies to the care and milking of dairy cattle, while the term "Dairy processing" should be used for the processing of milk and milk products.

scores Musical notation, cataloged in the MARC Music Format.

screen The computer screen, where information is displayed. Also called a CRT (Cathode Ray Tube), a VDT (Video Display Tube), a display, or a monitor.

screening In an archives, to examine materials to determine if access to some must be restricted.

SDI Selective Dissemination of Information. A system for automatically providing each individual user with information that corresponds to his or her interest profile, which is a list of subject terms related to that person's interests. For example, a user of the Dialog online database system can place an SDI order, and Dialog will automatically provide printouts of items related to the user's area of interest.

SE Serials. MARC-SE is the MARC Format for Serial publications such as journals and numbered monographs published as part of a series. See "MARC".

search To examine records in a computer database, looking for those records that match the conditions specified by the user.

search and replace A standard database program feature that allows the user to change a term throughout a database, with a single command. For example, if the Library of Congress subject heading "Agricultural implements" were changed to "Farm tools", or if in place of the name "Kerckhoff, W. G." you decided to use, "Kerckhoff, William G.", the change could be accomplished with a single command, without having to edit each item manually. This is true even in a very large database. Note that this database function is not the same as "Search and Replace" in a word processing program. The word processor will not distinguish one field from another. Thus, a change intended only for the field containing Subject Added Entries—Topics would take place in other fields also, with unintended results. In addition, the word processor will not allow conditions. In a database, you might specify that the change should only take place if the record concerned a given time period, concerned a particular industry or included other conditions that would separate the records that you wanted to change from those that were to remain untouched.

search by example See: "Query by Example".

search statement A query directed to a computer database, entered in the form of a command. For example:

```
SELECT ITEMS WITH AGENCIES-OF-ORIGIN = "United States. Army"
```

A database program might instead present the searcher with a menu of options, and use the selected options to construct a search statement.

search strategy A plan for searching a computer database. When searching very large online remote systems, such as Dialog, search strategies can become quite elaborate.

Sears list of subject headings First published in 1923 as the List of Subject Headings for

Small Libraries, the Sears List is widely used by school libraries, small public libraries, and book indexers. The Sears list follows the general principles of the Library of Congress Subject Headings, but is not an abridgement of LCSH.

secondary sources Interpretive works that describe people and events. In contrast, primary source materials were created at the time by the people and organizations directly involved.

secondary value A subdivision within a value. A value is contained within a field. For more information, see: "sub-field" and "sub-sub-field".

section A separately published part of a serial publication.

selective cataloging To vary the completeness of the cataloging record according to the type or historical value of the material to be cataloged.

self-defining A piece of data that contains within itself all of the information necessary for understanding. For example, a pure MARC record contains a Directory that defines each field within the record. In practice, every piece of information always presumes other information.

semiconductor Material, such as silicon, that can control a flow of electricity.

semimonthly A serial publication issued every two weeks. Also referred to as bi-weekly. Compare with: "Bi-monthly".

separation In the Pick operating system, the initial assignment of the number of Frames per Group when a file is created. In most cases a Separation of 1 is used, for 1 Frame per Group. A file's physical space is divided into Groups.

sequential access The storage and retrieval of computer data items according to when they were received. Compare with: "Direct access".

sequential location For library and archival arrangement, a method for arranging items in a sequence that cannot be disrupted by interposing new items. For example, storing items by the sequential Accession Numbers that they were originally given.

sequential search A search through a computer database on a record-by-record basis. Records are examined in the order in which they are stored, which probably corresponds to the original order in which they were entered. Each record in the database is examined in order to determine if it meets the conditions specified by the operator. In contrast, a search using an index takes from the index file the Record-IDs of the records that meet the conditions. For example, if the operator asks for all the records in which the Subjects field contains the Library of Congress Subject Heading "Last meal before execution". In a sequential search, the system will read each record from the disk, and look in the Subjects fields for the term. If, however, an index was created for the Subjects field, the system would instead go to the Subjects index file. For each Subject term, the Subjects index file would contain the Record-IDs for the records in the Subjects field that contained that term. For example:

```
Last meal before execution: 23; 56; 115
```

The numbers indicate Record-IDs. The database system then retrieves the records for those IDs. For more information, see: "Index".

serial A publication issued in successive parts, with designations for number or date, and intended to be continued indefinitely. Serials include newspapers, periodicals, conference proceedings, annual reports, and monographic series.

serial port A computer device for sending and receiving information in serial fashion. A

Serial Port sends or receives one bit of data at a time. A Parallel Port sends or receives multiple bits of data at a time, with the requirement that the sending or receiving of the bits in each grouped be synchronized. A Parallel Port can therefore be referred to as a Synchronous Port, while a Serial Port is an Asynchronous Port. Parallel Ports are most often used to send information to a printer. Serial Ports are most often used for exchanging information with other computers, either directly through cables or over the telephone lines via a Modem. On a multi-user system, such as the Pick operating system, the main computer communicates with terminals through Serial Ports.

series Archival documents described and maintained as a unit in accordance with a filing system decided upon by the repository. The records are generally kept together because: 1. They were together in the original filing system of the agency of origin, 2. They resulted from the same activity or function, and they are of the same format, or 3. They share a common subject matter..

series statement The portion of a bibliographic record devoted to information about the series to which the item belongs.

set Two or more physical items that form the basis for a single bibliographic description.

SGML Standard Generalized Markup Language. An effort to define conventions to mark structural parts of a text, such as chapters and indirect quotation.

shared cataloging Cooperative cataloging. The participating repositories make their cataloging records, and perhaps also cataloging facilities such as Authority Files, available to each other.

shared responsibility A case in which the collaborators on a work perform a similar function, such as in the case of coauthorship. Because the function is similar, it may not be possible to separate the contributions of the collaborators. In contrast, in a case of mixed responsibility, the collaborators perform different functions.

shelf list A catalog containing one record for each title in a collection, arranged by call number or accession number.

SIBIS Smithsonian Institution Bibliographic Information System.

s.l. sine loco, without location. The place of publication or distribution is unknown.

slide A photo transparency.

smart terminal A computer terminal with some degree of independent processing capabilities, in contrast to a dumb terminal, which has none.

SMD Specific Material Designation.

s.n. sine nomine, without a name. The name of the publisher or distributor is unknown.

SNA Systems Network Architecture. IBM's network standard.

software The operating system and application programs that tell the computer hardware what to do.

sort To arrange a list in order. Results will differ according to whether the sort is alphabetical or numerical, and if alphabetical, whether the method is letter-by-letter or word-by-word. A computer will sort according to the ASCII code of each character, which may cause differences in capitalization to produce unexpected results. The 1980 filing rules of the American Library Association recommend the word-by-word method rather than letter-by-letter. Previous rules recommended the "as if" procedure. The name "McPherson" was treated as if it had been written "MacPherson", "Dr." was treated as "Doctor", and the number 2 was handled as if it had been written as "two". The 1980 rules use the "as is" procedure, filing the term exactly as it is written. Arabic numerals are filed before letters, and numbers written alphabetically are filed alphabetically. Roman numerals are treated as Arabic numerals.

alphabetical sort An alphabetical sort evaluates each character position from left to right, placing terms in order according to the value of the left-most character, rather than according to the number of characters in the term. Thus, the two codes "b, aa" will sort alphabetically as "aa, b". An alphabetical sort of a list of numbers will produce unexpected results. The sequence of numbers, "2, 11" will sort alphabetically as "11, 2", in a manner equivalent to the example of "aa, b" given above. When an alphabetical sorting method is the only one available, extra zeroes can be placed at the beginning of numbers, so that all numbers will have the same number of digits. Thus, the sequence of numbers "02, 11" will sort correctly. The disadvantages of this method are that you must predict in advance the longest number that you will ever have, and you must type and use storage space for many extra zeroes. The Pick operating system will allow you to define a field as alphabetical or numeric for storage and sorting.

letter-by-letter alphabetical sort An alphabetical letter-by-letter sort will ignore spaces and punctuation appearing between words. Dictionaries use the letter-by-letter sorting method. For example, from Webster's Collegiate Dictionary: Blue, Blue baby, Blueberry, Bluebird, Blue blood, Blue crab, Blue-collar, Bluegrass, Blue jay, Blue law, Bluenose, Blueprint, Blues, Blue-sky law, Bluestocking, Blue streak

word-by-word alphabetical sort An alphabetical word-by-word sort will treat whole words, rather than individual letters, as the filing element. All of the terms beginning with a given word will appear before any of the terms that begin with the same letters, but have other letters attached. The Library of Congress Subjects Headings list uses the word-by-word sorting method. For example, from Library of Congress Subject Headings, eleventh edition: Blue, Blue baby, Blue collar workers, Blue crab, Blue jay, Blue laws, Blue Streak rocket, Blueberries, Bluebirds, Bluegrass, Bluenose goby, Blueprints, Blues (Music).

ASCII sort A computer will sort according to the ASCII (American Standard Code for Information Interchange) value of each character. Each character is stored in the computer as an ASCII number from 1 to 255. The upper case letters of the alphabet A-Z are represented by the numbers 65-90. The lower case letters are stored as 97-122. If a sort is made without making some provision for differences in capitalization, all of the upper case letters will appear before any lower case letters. Thus, the sequence "aa, bb, ZZ" would be sorted as "ZZ, aa, bb". It might also be relevant to note that the digits "0-9" are stored as ASCII values 48-57, thus numbers will always sort before letters. For example, the sequence "First Street, 23rd Street" would sort as "23rd Street, First Street". Spaces and punctuation marks will also be treated by the computer as ASCII values for sorting. The space, comma, and hyphen have ASCII values that appear in that order, all of which are below the ASCII values for numbers and letters. Thus, in a computer-sorted list, headings consisting of words separated by a space would appear first, then words separated by a comma and space, then words joined by a hyphen, and finally words joined without a hyphen. For example: "data base; data, base; data-base; database". If headings include parentheses, brackets, colons, and other symbols, those symbols will affect sorting, according to their ASCII values.

numerical sort A numerical sort evaluates each character position from right to left, placing numbers in order according to the number of digits they contain, rather than merely the value of the first character. Thus the two numbers "11, 2" will sort numerically as "2, 11".

source code A computer program in a symbolic language such as Basic or Pascal, which a human can understand. For more information, see: "Compiler".

species A subclass into which a genus may be divided.

specific and direct entry The rule that only the most specific subject headings available should be used. For a photo of a cow, you would enter only the heading "Cows", without including "Cattle", "Livestock", "Animals", etc.

specific material designation (SMD) In cataloging, a term for the specific class of physical object to which the item being cataloged belongs. More specific than the GMD (General Materials Designation). The terms to apply for both the specific and the general material designations should be taken from standardized lists, such as *Descriptive Terms for Graphic Materials: Genre and Physical Characteristic Headings,* edited by Helena Zinkham and Elisabeth Betz Parker.

SPINDEX Selective Permutation Indexing. A mainframe computer system developed by the Library of Congress and the National Archives for keyword indexing.

split files When a change in cataloging rules or heading lists results in the change of an existing heading, records are cataloged under the new heading while those records previously cataloged under the old heading are left undisturbed. In contrast, the practice of interfiling would treat the new and old headings as if they were the same.

spooler A buffer for data transmission between devices, usually between a computer and a printer. For more information, see: "Buffer".

SPSS Statistical Package for the Social Sciences.

SQL Structured Query Language.

SSHRC Social Sciences and Humanities Research Council of Canada.

standard A set of rules that provide for consistency and compatibility. True standards are explicitly defined and formally agreed upon, and cannot be changed unilaterally. Informal standards do not have guaranteed stability. In the computer industry, standards have generally been defined by success in the marketplace. Thus, the conventions used by Hayes modems have become standard for communications only because that brand of modem has been the most popular. Every other modem manufacturer would like to topple the Hayes standard with a new one of his own making.

starting character position In the MARC Record Directory, the starting character position of each field is specified relative to the first character of the first field in the record. Thus, a different computer will know exactly where to look for each field. See also "Offset".

statement of responsibility An identification of the persons or corporate bodies responsible for the creation of a work.

stop list A list of common words, such as "the" and "and", that are not to be indexed by an automatic indexing program.

storage Computer hardware for storing data. The term is generally used for permanent storage, such as on a disk drive, in contrast with the term "memory", used to refer to temporary storage for active use by a program.

string A connected series of characters, such as the word "database". The term string is often used to designate groups of characters that are not numbers, and on which arithmetic will not be performed. Individual fields in a database record can be designated as either string or numeric in type. If a field is numeric, only numbers should be allowed for data entry. If strings are entered into the field, and an attempt is later made to perform arithmetic with the field, an error will result.

structured query language (SQL) A standard set of database management commands, which theoretically should provide the ability to access and manipulate data across totally different machines, programs, and operating systems. IBM's goal in promoting SQL is to connect desktop computers to already-existing corporate mainframe databases. In practice, SQL is more an idea than a reality. The implementation of complete SQL capability may involve costly trade-offs in performance and database features.

sub-field A subdivision of a field.

pick sub-fields The Pick operating system handles individual values within a field as separate entities. These values are stored in separate sub-fields, marked off by a Value Delimiter or Sub-Field Delimiter, which is ASCII 253. Within a value, Pick will also store separate sub-values. These sub-values are stored in separate sub-sub-fields, marked off by a Sub-Value Delimiter or Sub-Sub-Field Delimiter, which is ASCII 252. Pick thus provides, within a record, a three-dimensional data structure of fields, sub-fields, and sub-sub-fields.

MARC sub-fields MARC terminology does not follow standard database practice. For MARC, multiple headings in a field are not considered separate values within a single field. Instead, the entire field is repeated. Within that field, each different type of information is set off by a Sub-Field Delimiter and a Sub-Field Code. The code specifies the type of information that the sub-field contains. For example, in a personal names field, the sub-field marked by code "a" will contain the person's name, and sub-field "d" will hold the person's birth and death dates.

sub-field delimiter The delimiter that marks off separate sub-fields within a field.

pick sub-field delimiter ASCII 253. When viewing data in the Pick Editor, the Sub-Field Delimiter will appear as a right bracket: "]". The Sub-Field Delimiter can be entered directly within the Editor by typing CTRL-], but this procedure should be discouraged for any but the most experienced Pick users. The delimiter appears at the end of each sub-field. No Sub-Field Delimiter is necessary for the final sub-field within a field.

MARC sub-field delimiter ASCII 31. MARC cataloging manuals generally represent the sub-field with a dollar sign "$" or with the symbol "ǂ" (ASCII 197, in IBM Extended ASCII). The delimiter appears at the beginning of each sub-field, including the first sub-field within the field. The delimiter is followed by a Sub-Field Code that designates the type of information which the sub-field contains.

subheading The name of a subordinate body, added to the name of the organization. For example: "United States. Congress. Senate".

subject analysis To identify and make decisions on the relative significance of the subjects relevant to a body of materials. When cataloging photographs, manuscripts, or other types of documents or objects not intended for publication or to provide instruction, the cataloger must decide what the photo, personal letter, or artefact is really "about". When dealing with published materials, the book *Joy of Cooking* tells the cataloger very clearly that the book is "about" cooking. The subject of the book is made clear in the title, the table of contents, the introduction, and elsewhere. A photo of a cook at work, or a utensil used for cooking, does not state its subject content so clearly. In addition, many different subjects can be included in materials such as photographs or personal papers. Since the people who appear in photographs will most often be shown wearing clothes, when should you include the subject heading "Clothing and dress"? The cataloger must decide.

subject authority file A file of authorized subject headings. Each record will include the approved heading, cross-references to variant forms and broader and narrower terms, and documentation of the decision on which form to employ.

subject cataloging The assigning of subject headings.

subject heading A word or phrase that designates the subject content of a bibliographic item.

subject heading list A standard list of terms to be used as subject headings. The nationally standard list for subject terms designating general topics is the Library of Congress Subject Headings. Other lists, such as that of the National Agricultural Library, have been created for specific areas of information.

subject specialist A person with thorough knowledge of a particular subject. A subject specialist might be employed as a consultant in a library or archives to catalog materials related to that subject.

subject subdivision Library of Congress Subject Headings can be subdivided by form (form subdivision), place (geographic subdivision), time period (chronological subdivision, also called period subdivision), or by a narrower aspect of the topic (topical subdivision).

subordinate body A part of a larger body within an organizational hierarchy.

sub-sub-field A subdivision of a sub-field. See: "Sub-Field".

sub-sub-field delimiter The delimiter that marks off separate sub-sub-fields within a sub-field. The Pick Sub-Sub-Field Delimiter is ASCII 252. When viewing data in the Pick Editor, the Sub-Sub-Field Delimiter will appear as a backslash: "\". The Sub-Sub-Field Delimiter can be entered directly within the Editor by typing CTRL-"\" but this procedure should be discouraged for any but the most experienced Pick users. The delimiter appears at the end of each sub-sub-field. No Sub-Sub-Field Delimiter is necessary for the final sub-sub-field within a sub-field.

sub-title Look for title variations under "Title".

sub-value A subdivision within a value. A value is contained within a field. For more information, see: "Sub-Field" and "Sub-Sub-Field".

summary indexing Assigning broad subject headings to cover the overall content of a work or collection, rather than attempting to cover all relevant subjects or all parts of the collection.

supplied title Look for title variations under "Title".

symbolic language A computer programming language in which machine instructions are represented by symbolic terms that the human programmer can understand. For more information, see: "Compiler".

synchronous data transmission Data transmission of characters, which may be sent along separate parallel lines in a synchronized, fixed-rate flow. Parallel Ports use synchronous transmission. Serial Ports use asynchronous transmission.

syndetic structure The relationships between subject headings. The relationships among Library of Congress Subject Headings are indicated by the references Narrower Term, Broader Term, Related Term, Use, and Used For.

synthesis To combine separate terms into a single subject heading. See: "Precoordination".

tag Each MARC field is identified by a 3-character Tag, such as "001" or "245".
task A complete unit of work, which may consist of a number of individual operations.
TERM The built-in communications and terminal emulation program supplied with the Radio Shack Model 100 portable computer. The Model 100 is most often used as a stand-alone portable computer. Through the use of the TERM program, a Model 100 may also be employed as a Terminal connected to the Pick multi-user operating system.
terminal A computer screen is often referred to as a Terminal. In a multi-user system, such as the Pick operating system, the word "Terminal" refers to the point of interaction between the user and the system. Each Terminal will be connected to the main computer through a cable and a Serial Port. An individual Terminal generally consists of a screen, a keyboard, and a Serial Port. A stand-alone computer, such as an IBM PC, can also be used as a Terminal by means of a terminal emulation program.
terminal emulation program A program that allows a stand-alone computer, such as the IBM PC, to act as a terminal in a multi-user system.
thermal printer For varieties of printers, look under: "Printer".
thesaurus A compilation of terms showing relationships, and used to maintain a Controlled Vocabulary.
third normal form See: "Normal Form, Third".
title Name of a bibliographic item. Variations on a title include:

title proper The chief name of the item, including any Alternative Title introduced by "or" but excluding a Sub-title separated by a colon.

alternative title The second part of a title, generally introduced by "or". For example, Shakespeare's play, *The Tempest, or, the Enchanted Island.*

collective title A title that is applied collectively to several works, each of which might also have its own title. For example, a collection or anthology can be entitled the "Complete Works" or "Collected Works" of an author or composer.

other title information A Sub-title, preceded by a colon, which expands on the intent or content of the work. For example, Carey McWilliams' book *Southern California Country: An Island on the Land.* It has become common, for scholarly works, to employ a Title Proper that is very broad in scope, followed by a Sub-title that explains the actual limits of the research conducted. Thus the Title Proper might suggest a sweeping study of women in the early Industrial Revolution, while the Sub-title informs us that the author has only examined sources for women working at three textile mills in Toulouse between 1750 and 1760.

parallel title The Title Proper in another language. In a card catalog, a Parallel Title is introduced with an equals sign. For example, Thomas Mann's novel, *Der Zauberberg = The Magic Mountain.*

sub-title Referred to by catalogers as Other Title Information. See above.

supplied title A title supplied by the cataloger, when no title appears on a title page or other Chief Source of Information. For archives, a cataloger would in most cases have to supply titles for collections of papers or photographs.

uniform title The title by which a work is to be identified, for a work that has appeared under different titles. The cataloger would chose the title that has been used predominantly, or if predominance is not applicable, choose the title that is the most complete.

topical subdivision The division of a Library of Congress Subject Heading by further specification of the topical subject concerned. For example, the heading "Factories—Equipment and supplies" would be used to specify equipment and supplies used in factories.

tracing In a bibliographic catalog, a listing of the headings under which a record can be found in the catalog. For example, in a library card catalog, the bibliographic card for a book will in most cases be stored under the name of the author. At the bottom of the card will be listed secondary access points under which the card could be found, such as subject headings or the title.

track The portion of a computer disk or tape directly below a read-write head.

trade publisher A publisher of books sold through retail book stores.

transaction For a computer database, a single event applied to an established file. The result will be that a record will be added, changed, or deleted, and that records in related files, such as index files, might also be added, changed or deleted. The series of necessary changes constitutes a single transaction. If power is cut off before the transaction has been completed, the result is likely to be a corrupted database. For example, if the term "Harbors" has been deleted from the Subjects field of a record in the Photos file, but the Subjects Index has not been updated, the index for "Harbors" will continue to point to a record in which that term does not exist.

transactions file A file containing information on all of the transactions that have occurred in a given time period. The file might later be used to restore the database after a disk crash or to monitor usage of the system.

transfer To move or copy computer data from one place to another, such as from a portable computer to a desktop computer.

transistor A semiconductor device capable of rapid switching.

transitive dependency One field in a record is dependent upon another field. For example, a bibliographic record in BOOKS database includes fields for PUBLISHER-NAME and PUBLISHER-ADDRESS. The address field does not stand alone in relation to the book. It is dependent upon the identity of the particular publisher. This situation violates Third Normal Form and should be avoided. A separate PUBLISHERS file should be created with information on the different publishers.

transliteration A representation of the characters of one alphabet by those of another.

transparent An adjective applied to computer systems to indicate that certain underlying complexities of the system are hidden from the user. For example, the Pick operating system will run on a variety of different computers. The underlying differences between the machines will be transparent to the user, who may enter the same commands regardless of machine.

transparency A photo slide.

truncate 1. In computer database searching, to cut a search term at the beginning or end. For example, to look for information on both airports and airplanes, you might search for just "air". 2. When loading information into a database, to truncate or cut off the information at some point. For example, when loading information from a word processor into a database, if the database program allows only fixed-length fields, and the data to be entered exceeds the designated length, the information will be truncated.

tuple In a computer database, a group of related fields.

turn-key system A complete computer system assembled by a vendor. The purchaser need only turn the key to begin using the system. If you really believe that such a thing is possible, why are you reading this book?

typescript A work in typewritten form, as distinguished from handwritten.

UF Used For. Indicates terms for which the defined term should be used instead. Used in a thesaurus such as Library of Congress Subject Headings. For example:

Clothing and dress
  UF Apparel
    Garments

uniform title Look for title variations under "Title".

union catalog A catalog with entries for the holdings of more than one repository. For example, the National Union Catalog of Manuscript Collections.

UNIX A computer operating system developed at Bell Laboratories. It is a powerful, multiuser system designed for scientific and mathematical applications.

unprecedented heading A heading that has not been used before for a bibliographic record in a particular database. A computer database program can provide a link from the data record to an Authority File, in order to warn if a heading is unprecedented.

update To change information in a computer database.

upgrade A new version of a computer program.

uppercase letters The capital letters of a type face.

UPS Uninterruptible Power Supply. A heavy-duty battery that will maintain electrical power to a computer when a power blackout occurs. The battery will supply about fifteen minutes of power, during which the computer log-off procedure can be accomplished, thereby avoiding corruption of the database. For more information, see: "GFE (Group Format Error)", "Log-off", and "Power supply".

upward reference For subject headings, a reference from a narrow term up to a broader one.

use To grant the right of use is to grant to a researcher a type of permission that goes beyond access to reproducing the materials in some manner. Examples would include using a photo in a publication, quoting from correspondence, or recording a musical score for distribution. Information about the copyright holder and the details of restrictions of use should be placed in MARC-AMC field 540 (Terms Governing Use and Reproduction). For the distinction between use and access, see the definition for "Access".

USE Indicates preferred terms that should be used instead of the defined term in a thesaurus such as Library of Congress Subject Headings. For example:

Cloud seeding
  USE Rain-making
    Snowpack augmentation

user profile See: "Interest profile".

USMARC USMARC Format for Bibliographic Data is the master reference for the USMARC formats and serves as the data dictionary for Library of Congress MARC Distribution Services. For more information, see: "MARC".

utilities Small programs or parts of a program that perform housekeeping chores, such as formatting a new disk. Database program utilities will include methods to modify the structure of a database, without having to re-type the data previously entered. The

Bibliographic Services (RLIN, OCLC, etc.) are sometimes loosely referred to as "utilities".

UTLAS University of Toronto Library Automation Systems. A primarily Canadian on-line bibliographic service. See "Bibliographic Services".

value The information placed in a field. The Pick operating system will handle individual values within a field as separate entities, storing each in a separate sub-field marked off by the Sub-Field Delimiter ASCII 253. For more information, see: "Sub-Field".

value delimiter In Pick, ASCII 253. For more information, see: "Sub-Field Delimiter".

variable-length field A field can vary in length according to the amount of data it contains. The Pick database system provides variable-length fields. In contrast, fixed-length fields will not allow more data than will fit into the designated length, and that length will be taken up on the disk no matter how little data the field actually contains.

VDT Video Display Tube. The computer screen, also referred to as the CRT (Cathode Ray Tube), monitor, or terminal.

verso of the title page The back side of the title page of a book, usually containing information such as the year of copyright and the name of the copyright holder.

virtual Appearance rather than reality. Data or features are supplied by the computer system at the time of a request, rather than stored physically.

virtual field A field in a computer database that is computed or derived from other data, rather than input directly. For example, a library that sells copies of its photographs keeps track of the sales in an INVOICES file. Print-outs and screen displays for records in that file show a field named TOTAL-PRICE. A library manager can enter search statements based on the TOTAL-PRICE field, such as:

```
SELECT INVOICES WITH TOTAL-PRICE > "$10"
```

However, no TOTAL-PRICE field appears on the data entry screen. No such field is input. Instead, the field is calculated from other data for unit price, number of units, purchaser discount, and sales tax. TOTAL-PRICE is a Virtual Field. In the Pick operating system, this field will be defined in the data dictionary with calculations specified on the data in other fields, and also defined as a dollar amount.

virtual memory A process, such as used by the Pick operating system, for making all of the computer's storage space available to a program as active and accessible memory. The system will treat disk space as memory, reading information from the disk into active memory as the information is required. The virtual memory process avoids the "Out of Memory" error condition that you may encounter when trying to perform an operation on a large file with an DOS word processor. When using a virtual memory system, the system will perform faster when the information required is already in active memory, and the system does not need to read the information from the disk. Thus, you may notice that the same operation will take different amounts of time on different occasions.

VM Visual Materials. MARC-VM is the MARC format for Visual Materials. MARC-VM is very close to MARC-AMC, the MARC format for Archives and Manuscripts Control. Note, however, a subtle difference: The term "archival" does not describe a type of materials, but a method of organizing materials, based on concepts such as provenance and respect for original order. The term "visual materials" describes a type of material, rather than a principle of organization. In 1987 the MARC-VM format was extended from two-dimensional objects, such as photographs and paintings, to three-dimensional objects, such as museum artefacts. For more information, see: "Archival management" and "MARC".

volatile file A computer database file subject to frequent change.

volatile storage Active memory, the contents of which disappear when electric power is turned off. In contrast, information stored on a disk does not disappear when no power is supplied. However, using information from a disk is much slower than using information from active memory.

widows In printing terminology, a widow is created when the final line of a paragraph is stranded by itself at the top of a new page. See also: "Orphans (Printing)".

WLN Washington Library Network. An on-line bibliographic service used primarily in the Pacific Northwest. See "Bibliographic Services".

word Computer word processing program Microsoft Word, produced by the Microsoft corporation.

word-by-word For varieties of sorting and alphabetizing, look under: "Sort".

WordPerfect Computer word processing program produced by the WordPerfect corporation.

word wrap A feature of computer word processing programs that moves a word to the next line if there is not sufficient remaining space on the current line. For example, the words on this printed page are not cut in the middle at the page margin, instead the line is "broken" at the space or hyphen nearest to the right margin, and the next word is moved down to the following line.

work-space Space in active memory set aside by a computer system for performing the operations requested by a particular user.

workstation An individual personal computer or terminal connected to a larger system.

WORM Write Once, Read Many times. An optical disk that can be written to only once, because there is no means of erasing previous information and rewriting over it. The disk, however, can be read many times. This type of storage will be most useful for information that does not change rapidly, or that the user does not want to change accidentally.

WP Word processing.

write To store information on a computer storage device. In a computer database system, the system will read database records from the disk and write new or changed records to the disk.

x Indicates a "See" reference from Library of Congress Subject Headings before the Eleventh edition. Published in 1988, the 11th edition replaced "x" with "UF" for "Used For".

xx Indicates a "See Also" reference Library of Congress Subject Headings before the Eleventh edition, published in 1988, replaced "xx" with "BT" for "Broader Term".

Index